D1714950

Slave Cultures

and the

Cultures of Slavery

Slave Cultures and the Cultures of Slavery

Edited by Stephan Palmié

The University of Tennessee Press • Knoxville

Copyright © 1995 by The University of Tennessee Press / Knoxville.
All Rights Reserved. Manufactured in the United States of America.
First Edition.

The paper in this book meets the minimum requirements of the
American National Standard for Permanence of Paper for Printed Library Materials.

∞

The binding materials have been chosen for strength and durability.

Library of Congress Cataloging-in-Publication Data

Slave cultures and the cultures of slavery / edited by Stephan Palmié.—1st ed.
    p. cm.
  Includes index.
  ISBN 0-87049-903-3 (cloth: alk. paper)
  1. Slavery—History I. Palmié, Stephan.
HT861.S35 1995
306.3'62'09—dc20   95-4374
                                    CIP

Contents

Acknowledgments   vii

Introduction   ix
    Stephan Palmié

1.   "Analyze the Sounds": Frederick Douglass's Invitation
to Modern Historians of Slavery   1
    David W. Blight

2.   Slave Life on Caribbean Sugar Plantations:
Some Unanswered Questions   12
    Sidney W. Mintz

3.   African Cultural Principles in Caribbean Slave Societies:
A View From the Danish West Indies   23
    Karen Fog Olwig

4.   A Taste for Human Commodities: Experiencing
the Atlantic System   40
    Stephan Palmié

5.   The Gold Coast, the Closing of the Atlantic Slave Trade,
and Africans of the Diaspora   55
    Richard Rathbone

6.   Preliminary Remarks on the Oldendorp Manuscripts
and Their History   67
    Gudrun Meier

7. Slavery and Slave Cultures in a Hydraulic Society:
    Suriname   78
    Gert Oostindie and Alex Van Stipriaan

8. Female Slave-Owners on the Gold Coast:
    Just a Matter of Money?   100
    Adam Jones

9. Dangerous Ancestors: Ambivalent Visions of Eighteenth-
    and Nineteenth-Century Leaders of the Eastern Maroons
    of Suriname   112
    H. U. E. Thoden van Velzen

10. Indian-Black Relations in Colonial and
    Antebellum Louisiana   145
    Daniel H. Usner, Jr.

11. Native American Tribes and Their African Slaves   162
    Renate Bartl

12. Theft, Moral Economy, and the Transition from
    Slavery to Freedom in the American South   176
    Alex Lichtenstein

13. The Creolization of African-American Slave Kinship
    in Jamaican Free Village and Maroon Communities   187
    Jean Besson

14. The Transformation of Slave Experience: Self and
    Danger in the Rituals of Creole Migrant Women
    in the Netherlands   210
    Ineke van Wetering

    Bibliography   239

    Contributors   275

    Index   279

Acknowledgments

The essays in this volume originated as presentations at a conference held at the Amerika-Institut of the University of Munich, Germany, in February 1993. The participants included six historians, nine anthropologists, two scholars of literature, and one linguist. The participants had regional expertise in such widely divergent areas as colonial Louisiana, the antebellum and Reconstruction South of the United States, Jamaica, Puerto Rico, Haiti, Cuba, the Danish West Indies, Suriname, and the Gold Coast. Not all the papers given at the conference could be included in this volume. I would like, however, to thank Geneviève Fabre, Klaus Benesch, and Peter Stein for their valuable participation in the conference.

Conference organizers and volume editors incur diverse debts. Here I would like to acknowledge the German Association of American Studies and the German Marshall Fund for financial support for this conference. My particular thanks go to Berndt Ostendorf for his invaluable help in securing these subventions. I am grateful to Meredith Morris-Babb of the University of Tennessee Press for her faith in the project. As always, my wife Doris was the single most important source of moral support.

Introduction

Stephan Palmié

Today, the term *slavery* evokes a historical reality as unsettling as it is variegated and complex. From our vantage point at the end of the twentieth century, a little over a hundred years after the last nation in the Americas—Brazil—abolished slavery, we look back on a recorded history of at least four millennia of institutionalized human unfreedom. "The earliest known legal documents," anthropologist Jack Goody (1980: 18) tells us, "concern not the sale of land, houses, animals, boats, and such like, but the sale of slaves." Yet it is not only that the written history of humanity commences with records of slavetrading. These ancient documentary vestiges have a peculiarly timeless ring. For, as Goody continues, the first legal code of which we have any knowledge, the Mesopotamian Ur-Nammu tablet, refers to a problem that was to vex slaveholders from Sumerian times down to the eve of the American Civil War: the slaves' perennial attempts to escape from bondage. No less disturbing is the geographical ubiquity of slavery. Indeed, as Orlando Patterson (1982: vii) asserts, there may be nothing peculiar about the peculiar institution. We have evidence for its existence, at one time or other, in virtually every part of the globe.

Even more puzzling to the modern mind is what appears to be a strangely close—and seemingly transhistorical—linkage between slavery and freedom. With hindsight, we can appreciate the tragic historical ironies Edmund S. Morgan (1972) alludes to when he speaks of slavery and freedom as the "American Paradox." Morgan argues that the rise of egalitarian ideologies among white Americans was predicated upon the proportionate denial of equality and liberty to the blacks in their midst. That the high-spirited language of the American Declaration of Independence flowed from the pen of a large-scale slaveholder was, in Morgan's view, a logical outcome of a larger historical process encompassing economic, political, and cultural-ideological developments. Large as it looms in our historical memory, however, the "American Paradox" may not be so American after all. For, as the classical scholar Moses I. Finley (1968: 308) points out, terms referring to, and concepts about, personal freedom *only* emerged in classical antiquity "when slaves became the main dependent labor force" of Greek city states. Indeed, slavery and freedom, Patterson (1982: ix) reminds us, may be more "intimately connected" than we are wont readily to acknowledge.

Nor could we easily single out peculiarly "modern" or even only "Western" forms of bondage as historical and cultural exceptions. To be sure, in terms of scale and perhaps also brutality, slavery may have reached unprecedented levels in the plantation societies of the post-Columbian Americas. But, while it lasted, American slavery was but one variant (or set of variants) of far more general modes of institutionalized unfreedom. As Finley (1968: 308) observes, from a political-economic point of view, slavery "is a species of dependent labor and not the genus." Whether accompanied by force or defined by socially recognized rights and obligations,[1] the extraction of labor from subordinated individuals is by no means unique to slavery. Despite their fundamental dissimilarity in many other respects, serfdom in medieval Europe and pre-Manchu China, early modern English villeinage, African forms of lineage dependency or pawnship, Latin American peonage, sharecropping in the post-Reconstruction U.S. South, and modern conscript labor, all exemplify this basic pattern. Neither has involuntary labor ended with the abolition of slavery (cf. Kloosterboer 1960). Indeed, it may have been no accident that the metaphor of "wage slavery" arose at precisely the time when slavery as such was waning in Europe's colonial periphery. As David Eltis (1993: 207) argues, it may be more useful, perhaps, to see both slave and nonslave (whether free or coerced) labor "as part of a continuum than as polar opposites."

Similarly, the two other major definitional criteria for "slavery" encountered again and again in the vast literature on the topic—institutionalized property rights in human beings, and the slave's socially anomalous status as a perpetual outsider—fail analytically to distinguish American slavery from a wide variety of social arrangements existing, often simultaneously, in Europe, Africa, and Asia. On the one hand, one thinks of configurations of corporate kinship or brideprice institutions, which, in many societies, hinge upon concepts of legal ownership over human individuals. More significantly, perhaps, some such conceptions entail ideas about the alienability of property rights in people validated by monetary transactions. On the other hand, the slave's fundamental alienation resembles to some degree the institutionalized "stranger" status of Athenian metics and medieval European Jews. More generally, the position of members of what Philip Curtin (1984) has called trading diasporas vis-à-vis their host societies, at times exhibits features resembling the slaves' characteristic deracination and exclusion.

Yet our difficulties in disentangling slavery from other forms of bondage, exploitation, and marginality are only part of the problem. For even within a single geographical locale and societal context, slavery was never a stable institution. Rarely was it a monolithic one. And quite often it coexisted with, or shaded into, other social arrangements involving substantial measures of domination and servility. In Virginia's first half-century of settlement, for example, there is evidence for the employment of varied forms of dependent labor. We know that no hard and fast distinction had yet been drawn between temporary servitude and permanent enslavement. African bondage remained economically and socially insignificant as long as bound European laborers could be procured at lower cost. And the primary criterion for defining social marginality was not skin color or geographic origin, but landlessness (cf. Breen 1973, Edmund S. Morgan 1975, Breen and Innes 1980, Kulikoff 1986).[2] Moreover, together with the crystallization of the legal institution of racial slavery within the framework of Virginia's budding plantation agriculture, a process of internal differentiation took place. As Edgar Thompson pointed out long ago (1932), plantation economies are characterized by an extensive division of labor, as well as by complex structures of authority and command. The successful operation of a seventeenth-century Virginian tobacco plantation, an eighteenth-century Surinamese coffee plantation, or a nineteenth-century Cuban sugar mill hinged not only on the sheer manpower of varying numbers of field hands, but on the skills of slaves trained for specific agricultural and processing tasks, unfree artisans, and managerial personnel—including the ominous as well as ubiquitous enslaved slave-driver.[3] Likewise, wherever slaveholders did not choose absenteeism over direct involvement in the management of their human and inanimate possessions, we must reckon with the growth of a division between slaves engaged in productive activities, and those catering to the needs—both physical and psychological—of their masters.[4] What further complicates the picture is the employment of slave labor in urban situations. Here, the spectrum ranges from domestic services to artisanal production under the master's supervision and finally to a wide variety of economic activities performed "on hire," or by the slave's own choice.[5]

We could cite many cases not only in which types of servility that are sometimes subsumed under the problematical categories of "domestic slavery" and "chattel slavery" coexisted side by side, but also in which single enslaved individuals, in the course of their lives, stood a chance of making the transition from field hand to house slave, from menial labor to skilled work, and, indeed, from slave to kinsman or kinswoman. Moreover, excepting those cases in which human bondage played only the most marginal of social and economic roles, slavery was part and parcel of a total social arrangement. In other words, it affected not only the lives of masters and bondsmen, but even of those individuals and groups who had no direct involvement in it. We know today that only a minor proportion of white southerners ever held slaves. Many may have aspired to the status of slaveholders, and most came to subscribe to the ideals of what Pierre van den Berghe (1967) and George Frederickson (1981) have called a "Herrenvolk democracy." But even those who never dreamed of owning slaves themselves eventually were swept up in a brutal war ostensibly fought for the preservation of slavery on North American soil.[6] Even more obvious is the case of free African Americans, whose social position within New World slaveholding societies, while always precarious, was closely linked to the local historical evolution of racially-defined structures of inequality, which, in turn, were related to the developmental stages of slave-based agricultural labor regimes.[7]

Nor can we discount the fact that systems of slaveholding often did not evolve in isolation. In legal terms, for example, there are obvious continuities from Roman slave law to the slave codes of medieval Castile. This legal apparatus, in turn, was harnessed—with but minor modifications—to the task of regulating slavery in Spain's and Portugal's American possessions (cf. William D. Phillips 1985, 1991). Since the publication of Frank Tannenbaum's influential *Slave and Citizen* in 1946, much has been made of this transfer of "relatively humane" Spanish slave laws as an explanation for the allegedly more benign forms slavery assumed in Iberoamerica, in contrast to those areas colonized by the British or Dutch. As Stanley Elkins (1959) opined, the relative autonomy Britain granted its colonies in legislative matters gave free reign to the "dynamics of unopposed capitalism," whereas in Iberoamerica premodern metropolitan slave laws limited the extent of exploitation. Obviously, the argument championed by Tannenbaum and his followers rests on an unexamined—and in fact fundamentally naïve—assumption: that the letter of the law equaled its social enactment. Interestingly, however, some of Tannenbaum's and Elkins's harshest critics pointed toward another continuity, this one on a political-economic level. Particularly in the case of sugar cultivation, it can be shown how the historical spread of this particular cultigen—from Asia to the Near East, North Africa, Sicily, southern Spain, the Canary Islands, Madeira and São Tome, and finally the Antilles—was accompanied not only by advances in productive technology, but also by the evolution of a slave-based labor regime that reached its final and fullest stage of elaboration in the huge steam-driven sugar mills of nineteenth-century Cuba.[8] Viewed from this angle, the developmental stage of local plantation economies, their labor supply, and their linkages with a world market for tropical staples seem to provide far more powerful explanations for the extent and relative brutality of slavery in particular localities, than any kind of cultural or legal precedent (Mintz 1969 [1961]).[9]

Such controversies about continuities and contrasts in the evolution and differentiation of servile institutions are not mere academic quibbles among modern scholars. The conflicting interpretations and arguments on which they are based manifest both historical tenacity and continuing political import. In more than a few cases, students of comparative slavery find themselves heirs to debates initiated centuries ago by supporters and opponents of the "peculiar institution." Moreover, some such debates relate directly to current attempts to explain the origins of present-day global political-economic divisions between the so-called "First World" and "Third World."

Take the controversy about the indigenous origin or Atlantic causation of African slavery. Except for a few dissident voices, until the second half of the eighteenth century, the prevailing European view was that slavery represented a "natural" form of social existence in Africa, part and parcel of the African's alleged "savage" state. Buttressed by reports from European travelers to Africa (many of whom were themselves agents of the slave trade), such notions helped to defend slavetrading and slavery.[10] By the end of the eighteenth century, however, abolitionists began to argue that reports about the allegedly endemic nature of slavery in Africa mirrored a state of depravity and degradation induced by (rather than antedating or merely being incidental to) the ravages of the European slave trade.[11] This interpretation in turn was to dovetail with later rationalizations of European imperialist ventures in Africa—framed, as they often were, in terms of redressing past wrongs or "uplifting the benighted African." Yet it did introduce a theme into the historiography of slavery which—in various permutations—has continued to engage scholars to the very present. Today we

wonder how the American historian U. B. Phillips could get away with
stating (even if only figuratively), in 1929, that racial slavery was introduced into the Americas as the result of a conspiracy between "civilized
European sailors," and "barbaric African slaveholders" (Phillips 1963
[1929]: 188). However, writing Phillips off as a blatant racist (which he
undoubtedly was) does not advance our understanding of the problem
his bizarre formulation points to: how did the various and changing
slave regimes coexisting in the post-Columbian Atlantic world[12] influence, reinforce, or challenge each other's viability?

As one of the most distinguished heirs to the "abolitionist" tradition, the Guyanese historian Walter Rodney put forward the thesis that,
prior to Africa's involvement in the Atlantic slave trade, servile institutions had played but a minor social and economic role in Upper Guinea
coastal societies. A genuine "slave class," Rodney argued, emerged only
when the economic incentives provided by the European demand for
slaves, led to the rise of African slavetrading elites. These not only took
to raiding and conquest as modes of procuring slaves for export purposes, but gradually integrated forms of chattel slavery into their domestic economies (Rodney 1966). Rodney's thesis immediately sparked
considerable debate,[13] especially since its author elaborated it within the
framework of then-current dependency theories (Rodney 1972). Initially the controversy revolved around methodological questions, such
as Rodney's tendency toward unwarranted generalizations and his use
of inadequate data to establish temporal sequence.[14] However, as scholars including Claude Meillassoux (1982, 1986) and Emmanuel Terray
(1974, 1983) seem to have realized, criticizing Rodney on such grounds
did not solve the fundamental theoretical problems he raised. For them,
the question was how to weigh the respective roles of "domestic" and
"export" slavery in the history of West African societies and, particularly, in the formation of indigenous states. Though much of this debate revolved around issues of Marxist theory,[15] it was, in essence, also
about African agency in world history. Since many of the most powerful precolonial West African states were based—economically as well as
politically—not only on productive activities performed *by* slaves but on
the production *of* slaves for export, was the rise of such polities an autonomous development, or was it merely a byproduct of European
slavetrading?[16]

While no easy solution to this question is in sight, a rather different recent attempt to tackle it seems to lead us back to fundamental
questions about the nature of slavery. In an essay much acclaimed and
much criticized, Kopytoff and Miers (1977) maintain that studies of

slavery in Africa suffered from a general misunderstanding of the institution as such. Partly skirting the issue of Atlantic slave exports, they argue that "internal African slavery" cannot fruitfully be separated from other institutionalized social bonds. Instead, it was one institution among others (such as exogamous marriage, adoption, pawnship, or clientage) by which African kin groups assimilated personnel to augment their social and economic leverage. Hence the status of an African slave was one sliding (both temporally and conceptually) into others—such as the status of a member of a corporate lineage which held collective rights in the persons of its constituent individuals. The failure to appreciate this, Kopytoff and Miers maintain, derives largely from an undue application of modern ideas about freedom and autonomy to the realities of precolonial African societies. Within African societies and cultures, they argue, "the antithesis of 'slavery' was not 'freedom' qua autonomy but rather belonging" (Igor Kopytoff and Miers 1977: 17). Freedom from social obligation spelled rightlessness. Belonging, on the other hand, was both belonging *in* as well as belonging *to* social units defined by what they call a "slavery-to-kinship continuum."

Here, it would seem, we return to a view of African slavery as ancient and often only marginally affected by the slave trade as such. Yet these authors insist that what we call "slavery" in Africa, and slavery in the New World are fundamentally different institutions. Perhaps one can imagine Rodney's ghost haunting Kopytoff and Miers's interpretations with questions such as these: If general African conceptions about corporate "rights-in-persons" lead to the formation of a "slavery-to-kinship continuum," how could the trans-Sahara and Atlantic trade have triggered such massive (and internally probably unprecedented) transfer of rights-in-persons by way of sale?[17] Still, the salutary effect of Kopytoff and Miers's intervention is to return us to the basic question about the comparability of historical instances of human bondage.[18] Indeed, as David Brion Davis (1984: 8) states, it may well be that the "more we learn about slavery, the more difficulty we have defining it."

The present volume makes no attempt to supply yet another formulation aimed at capturing the not-so-peculiar institution's essence, or defining its place in the history of humanity. Instead, the authors take their cues from a statement one of them wrote some thirty years ago. Harking back to E. B. Tylor's characterization of slavery and freedom as the "greatest of all divisions" known to mankind, Sidney Mintz argued in 1969 [1961] that this "'greatest of all divisions' involves in every instance a way of life, a conception of the human condition, an ideology of society, and a set of economic arrangements, in short, a cultural apparatus by which slaves and masters are related" (27–28). As Mintz implies, such slave cultures, and indeed cultures of slavery and slaveholding, emerging within the post-Columbian Atlantic world, did not spring ready-made from either economic or ideological molds. Since at least the sixteenth century, systems of slavery, in both Old World and New, were shaped by a wide and shifting variety of factors— some antedating their "Atlantic" conjunction, some arising out of local options and exigencies, some relating to their mutual articulation.[19] Mintz's statement points to another important dimension of slavery: for both master and slave, slavery was not merely a legal or economic arrangement. To them it defined a tangible everyday reality: a world which they shared and in which they lived and struggled with each other—in sometimes violently antagonistic, sometimes tensely controlled, sometimes ostensibly amiable, but always contradiction-ridden encounters and relationships. In every instance, this was a complex and changing world. Master and slave alike tried to make sense of that world, albeit under very different circumstances and often in radically different ways. Within this world both sought to realize their hopes and aspirations, make choices, and pursue courses of action under varying and highly unequal constraints.

Those recorded instances of behavior which make up the historical balance of the multiple and complex relationships between slaves and masters present us with formidable problems of interpretation. Surely, visions of morality, personal gain, human destiny, or social and natural orders informed the behavior of slave and slaveholder alike. Yet, quite apart from the question of the rationality of the behavioral choices they made, need we not also consider the very real possibility of their acting on impulses of fear, hate, desire, or sheer physical necessity?[20] At such motives we, in the aftermath, can only guess. Whether a master's violent behavior bespeaks a sadistic disposition, rational economic calculation, a socially expected way of acting toward slaves or other subalterns, or a dire fear that only demonstrations of brute force will guarantee his dominance or even his personal survival, is a question more easily asked than answered. So are—as Mintz argues in his contribution to this volume—similar questions about the slaves' responses to slavery.

Today, our historical sensibilities are attuned to a fairly unambiguous view of the slaves' resistance to slavery. This, however, is a relatively recent development. Since the massive revisionist turn in the historiography of slavery that occurred during the 1960s and 1970s, our perception of the slaves' agency and experience has changed significantly.

While "progressive" historians from Phillips onward had emphasized a benign view of slavery, in the 1950s historians such as Kenneth Stampp and Stanley Elkins foregrounded the dehumanizing aspects of North American slavery. Yet, by denouncing the system's overpowering brutality, they also relegated the slaves to the role of abject victims. As Elkins (1975: 40) later conceded, the historiographical dilemma they had faced was how to "emphasize vitality and achievement while you are also emphasizing decline and degradation." His generation, it seems, opted for the latter.

Concurrent with the massive social and cultural changes in the wake of the American Civil Rights movement, slave agency surfaced as a major research issue. As early as 1944, Ralph Ellison (1964: 315) posed the question of how a people can be presumed to "live and develop for over three hundred years simply by *reacting*? Are American Negroes simply the creation of white men, or have they at least helped to create themselves out of what they found around them?" By the mid-1970s, a flood of publications on the resilience and vitality of cultures developed *in spite of* slavery was providing the answer. The scholarly discourse on the enslaved finally switched from the passive into the active voice (cf. Davis 1974).

Numerous studies since have emphasized the slaves' will to resist and capacity for resistance.[21] If slave rebellions once had been treated as sporadic, desperate, and often politically irrational outbreaks,[22] they have come to be seen as part and parcel of the history of social arrangements geared towards reducing people to things.[23] Individual acts of insubordination, sabotage, theft, slowing down work rhythms, malingering, or feigned stupidity no longer are interpreted as symptoms of a psychology shaped by persistent degradation, but as evidence of willful defiance. Some authors, indeed, have gone so far as interpreting slave suicide as a last and desperate act of resistance—whether in the sense of hurting the master's economic interest, or as a final assertion of personhood and control over one's destiny.

Still, as Mintz has argued again and again, and as Eugene Genovese (1974) has shown most eloquently, the very idea of domination and resistance as a kind of zero-sum game—the commonsense view of the relationship between slave and master—may be too simplistic. To be sure, slaves resented slavery and at times tried forcefully to free themselves from its degrading stranglehold—just as masters, at times, used naked force to guarantee slaves' subjugation. But to construe the matter in terms of polar opposites masks the fact that much of what we should consider the slaves' most remarkable achievement—the creation of complex and meaningful ways of life in the face of overwhelming odds—was based not on resistance pure and simple, but on some measure of accommodation as well. In forming stable personal relationships, founding families, planting gardens, acquiring property, burying the dead, or enacting ritual relationships with the divine, slaves did not break the bonds of slavery. Rather, they bent them in ways that allowed them to carve out a meaningful existence in the face of a regime often geared—at least theoretically—towards denying them just that.

Recognition of this multidimensionality of slave behavior has led several authors, including some contributors to this volume, to abandon a rigid dichotomy between resistance and accommodation. Instead, they speak of patterns of "resistant accommodation" or "resistant response" to slavery. Though perhaps cumbersome and seemingly paradoxical, this terminology conveys a much broader spectrum of historical possibilities—both with regard to how slaves might have conceived of the means and ends of their actions, and in terms of the unintended consequences of their behavior.[24] Moreover, it allows us to approximate more closely the complexity and the sometimes contradictory nature of their experience.[25] As David Barry Gaspar (1991: 130) suggests, such a view of slavery "is not meant to downplay its wrongs, but rather to approach them from a different direction, from the vantage point of the slave. How slaves coped with slavery, survived it, and built from it and within it, is a remarkable achievement worth recognizing and celebrating as a triumph of the human spirit." Gaspar's point bears emphasizing. To a large extent, the study of the history of African-American cultures revolves around the question of how to conceptualize adequately those small but exceedingly significant increments by which enslaved Africans and their descendants built rich and vibrant cultures under starkly oppressive circumstances. Indeed, to paraphrase Blight's contribution to this volume, the fact that we *can* talk of slave cultures—and not just cultures of slavery!—bespeaks the crucial importance of this task. Yet how are we to approach the intricacies of the processes by which New World slave cultures emerged? Where should we look for their sources? How to describe the manifold ways in which enslaved Africans and their descendants built memories of past ways of life, fragments of alien cultures, and new modes of adaptation into coherent strategies for dealing with their American predicament? How, finally, are we to assess the conditions under which certain cultural forms—regardless of their provenience—stabilized into genuinely *African-American* traditions?

These questions hark back to another famous and still active debate. Ever since the publication of Melville J. Herskovits's *Myth of the Negro*

Past (1941), in which he presented a massive body of evidence for the carryover of African cultural forms to the New World, students of African-American cultures have faced an uneasy analytical choice. Should the history of African-American cultures be discussed primarily in terms of Old World origins or New World destiny? Though naïve in its theoretical suppositions about cultural dynamics, Herskovits's work pointed to a clear research agenda: by comparing cultural elements on both sides of the Atlantic and identifying formal similarities, transatlantic cultural continuities presumably could be ascertained. His critics, on the other hand, maintained that the dynamics of cultural transfer from Africa to the Americas could not realistically be studied apart from the social conditions of slavery, and its aftermath of persistent racist marginalization and oppression. Indeed, Herskovits's leading American opponent, the black sociologist E. Franklin Frazier, went so far as to posit a complete destruction of whatever cultural elements may have carried over from Africa to the New World.[26] More cautious, the Jamaican anthropologist Michael G. Smith did not deny the significance of an African background to African-American cultures. Yet he took Herskovits to task for the methodological flaws in his approach—particularly for the tendency to divorce culture from the historical context of its enactment. Among other things, Smith argued that, since the end of the slave trade stopped the influx of African "culture bearers" to the Americas, the probability that twentieth-century evidence for cultural similarities reflected transatlantic continuities was not necessarily greater than the likelihood that such formal semblances were the results of independent adaptations to local social circumstances (cf. Smith 1965: 24–37). The problem thus boiled down to the question of where to look for explanations. Were African-American cultures primarily shaped by African cultural precedents? Or did the answer lie in the social contingencies of specific New World contexts?

Here, an important breakthrough was achieved by Mintz and Price in their 1976 essay *An Anthropological Approach to the Afro–American Past,* recently republished as *The Birth of African-American Culture* (Mintz and Price 1992). Cautioning against Herskovits's tendency to reify cultural "traits" and resort to mechanistic theories of culture change, Mintz and Price argue for the investigation of *both* the cultural resources available to African Americans at particular moments in history *and* the constraints presented by the respective "social arenas" in which such cultural resources were put to use. According to their view, African-American cultures emerged from the processes by which enslaved Africans initially transformed themselves from mere collectivities of deracinated individuals—"socially dead" human commodities, from the trader's point of view—into viable communities. The study of slave cultures, therefore, is inseparable from the study of those social institutions within which certain behavioral patterns and cultural forms could stabilize and turn into incipient traditions.[27]

As far as research on slavery in the Americas is concerned, it is well nigh impossible to overrate the seminal importance of Mintz and Price's contribution.[28] One of its most salutary effects, perhaps, was that it led a growing number of scholars to discard, as inadequate, commonsense views of culture as "the traditional ways of life of a people." Just as, initially, little "society"—in the sense of culturally ordered human relationships—existed among newly enslaved Africans wrenched from all previously salient ties and relationships, so there existed little "culture"—in the sense of a collective body of knowledge and interaction patterns—among the men and women haphazardly thrown into the holds of slave ships and unloaded on the docks of New World slavetrading entrepots. As Mintz and Price (1992: 18) state the matter: "What the slaves undeniably shared at the outset was their enslavement; all—or nearly all—else had to be *created by them*" (emphasis in the original). Whatever knowledge of their cultures of origin they brought with them in the form of individual memories, that knowledge would only survive the Atlantic passage if it could be translated into collective practice within the framework of American slavery.

Obviously, this notion directs our attention to the precise historical circumstances under which enslaved Africans forged new social relationships. Yet we cannot regard the conditions set by New World slaveholding societies and cultures as a set of stable parameters. American regimes of slaveholding and labor extraction went through various and regionally distinct stages of evolution and decline that are strongly linked to the developmental patterns of local Euro-American societies and cultures (cf. Berlin 1980; Usner, this volume). In fact, one of the most powerful lessons to be drawn from the study of the emergence of an Atlantic World since the fifteenth century is that none of the cultures involved in this process can be viewed as stable or clearly bounded entities. As Timothy Breen (1984: 197) puts it for colonial America, we rather should think of the cultures developing in the post-Columbian Atlantic World as "continuing series of reciprocal relationships [between human individuals and groups], involving borrowing and resistance, conflict and cooperation, modification and invention." Discarding much of an older analytical vocabulary involving concepts such as "culture contact" or "acculturation," Breen opts for the term "cultural

conversations" and urges us to investigate the local historical constraints—ecological, demographic, economic, social, and political—
under which actors of various cultural backgrounds, and in various positions of power or dependence, engaged each other in forging distinctly
different but nonetheless interdependent New World cultures.

Some of the most impressive recent attempts to unlock the history
of particular—often regional—African-American cultures have adhered
to such models. Part of this research has focused on the external conditions under which African-American culture-building must be presumed to have taken place. Thus, at least in some areas (most prominently the Chesapeake, the British Caribbean, and northeastern Brazil),
we have a fairly good idea of the wide array of variables affecting the
development of regional African-American societies and cultures.
These range from local peculiarities of ecology, climate, and topogra-
phy, through epidemiological conditions and changing demographic
constellations (such as ratios of male to female slaves, Africans to
creoles, blacks to whites, slaves to free people), to the timing, volume,
and African origins of slave imports; mortality rates and demographic
behavior of slave populations; nature and developmental stage of agricultural production; regional nutritional self-sufficiency or import-de-
pendence; crop-specific labor regimes; degree of consolidation of European rule; maturational stage of white colonial society and culture;
regional patterns of urbanization; the proximity of unsettled or politically contested frontier areas; and a host of other factors.[29] Indeed, quite
apart from the question of agency, assessing the range of options and
constraints faced by the enslaved in particular historical situations now
presents a major challenge.

Building on such research, another line of inquiry has focused on
the institutional frameworks within which African-American culture-
building took place. Here, particularly significant advances have been
made in the study of African-American social organization. Since
Herbert Gutman's pioneering work on North American slave families
(Gutman 1976), a number of important studies have greatly expanded
our knowledge of the history and structural features of local African-
American kinship systems. As Gutman was first to demonstrate, far
from being crushed by the southern plantation regime, the North
American slave family served as a crucial institution facilitating the generational transmission of evolving African-American cultural forms.
More recently, Alan Kulikoff's research on the colonial Chesapeake
(1986) has clarified how slave cultural patterns emerging on single plantations spread along interlocking networks of kinship among slaves on

different plantations, thus gradually giving rise to fairly uniform regional cultural complexes. At the same time, Caribbeanists have shown that the structural type of the slave family common in the American South was but one of several forms of kin-based association (albeit apparently one of regionally overriding importance)[30] which historically served both as a venue for the integration of, and as a conduit of transmission for, evolving African-American cultures. Case material on the transition from slavery to freedom in the Caribbean, for instance, demonstrates that the transition from what Mintz (1989 [1974]) called the stage of "proto-peasantries" to the (usually precarious) stage of freeholding on the "plantation-peasantry interface" occasioned momentous cultural transformations related to new opportunities for definition of collective identities. Here, the social and economic arrangements known as "family land" in the Caribbeanist literature[31] are particularly pertinent. Though ostensibly emerging in the post-emancipation period, such systems of customary land tenure often can be linked to earlier forms of agricultural production and/or marketing of surplus that took shape wherever slaves were allotted provision plots on plantation fringe-areas.[32] Formed and maintained in resistant adaptation to plantation regimes, such landholding institutions must be viewed not only as venues for the transgenerational management of scarce economic resources, but also as serving symbolic functions. This is particularly well documented in the Haitian case, where Larose (1977) and Lowenthal (1987: 183–283) have shown how the transmission of rights of ritual access to, and obligations toward, the *lwa* (deities) relate to patterns of landholding and inheritance within corporate bilateral descent groups.[33]

Several other significant "growth areas" in the study of slave cultures could be mentioned.[34] Important new research has been done on the slaves' independent productive and marketing behavior, as well as on ways in which they created unique and symbolically charged consumption patterns.[35] We have also learned much about the extent to which slaves bent and transformed the labor regimes forced upon them.[36] We have a wealth of fresh data on how they defended practices grown into customary rights—e.g., rights to clothing and food rations, property-holding, allotments of spare time, or the celebration of funerals and Christian holidays—as part of a total "moral economy."[37] Likewise, a spate of new publications on rebellion, flight, and day-to-day resistance has broadened considerably our understanding of the scope and variety of such phenomena, as well as the problems of adequate conceptualization.[38] Maroon scholarship too has expanded greatly in recent years, producing some of the most sophisticated work, methodologically and theoretically, on the borders between anthropology and history.[39]

Perhaps somewhat less significant advances have occurred in the study of slave religion. Especially with regard to North America, little genuine progress has been made over Herskovits's programmatic search for "Africanisms," on the one hand, and Genovese's magisterial treatment of the dialectic of resistance and control in early African-American Christianity, on the other.[40] This is somewhat surprising, since one would expect some cross-fertilization with the burgeoning Africanist research on conversion processes. It is thus strikingly ironic that one of the most theoretically sophisticated studies of an *African-American* conversion process does not deal with the New World at all; its setting is nineteenth-century Nigeria, and it concerns the Yoruba-Brazilian *babalawo* Philip José Meffre—an ex-slave returnee, whose protracted and psychologically painful adoption of Protestant Christianity has been discussed by Peel (1990).[41]

Several studies of the role of women in (and the female experience of) slavery have begun to chart the long-neglected dimension of gender in the making of New World slave societies and cultures.[42] A few authors have broached the issue of slave ethnicity and its bearing upon stages or processes of plural cultural development within single regional African-American slave populations.[43] Finally, one of the most prolific fields—too prolific, in fact, to mention even the more important works—has been the study of abolition and post-emancipation processes.[44]

Given this state of affairs, one might well wonder whether the future of slave studies lies in ever-increasing specialization, so that synthesis will become impossible for all but the most superficial purposes. Commenting on sweeping statements about the Slave Community endemic in the 1970s, Ira Berlin (1980) rightfully demanded that time and space be put back into the picture. Some fifteen years later, we seem to face the question of whether talking about slavery, slave culture, or slave experience in the singular makes sense at all. Of course, the most significant recent advances have accrued from the study of local historical incidents of slavery. But does not this increasing attention to particularities entail the danger of sacrificing our view of the forest for that of the trees? For anthropologists and historians, this is a question not of essence, but of the relationship between regularity and variation. And it is also a question of analytical scale and the salience of comparative methodology.

To be sure, in recent years we have begun to appreciate the manifold ways in which the development of local slave cultures and cultures of slavery is linked to much larger historical processes operating, at times, on a genuinely Atlantic scale. We may disagree on how, precisely, to conceptualize such linkages or weigh their importance.[45] But there is little question that the growth of the cultures central to this volume is intimately connnected with the evolution of a geohistorical sphere defined by the interaction—economic as well as social and cultural—among Africans, Europeans, indigenous Americans, and New World "creole" populations of diverse Old World origins.

If, for example, a boom in production of cotton for the world market underwrote the manner in which southern planters forged a paternalistic ideology of slavery, the "new" Old South culture of slaveholding that emerged towards the end of the eighteenth century also set the historical limits within which—and against which—distinctly "southern" slave cultures took shape (cf. Genovese 1971 [1969]: 95–102). Since global market forces had set the southern states on a course of agricultural expansion, the inability to reproduce their enslaved labor force through replacement with new African imports after 1808 effectively imposed an economic brake upon planter abuse of their slaves. It also provided an incentive to the improvement of their living conditions and eventually *may* have contributed to changing previously dominant perceptions of slaves as "mere chattel" into paternalistic views of them as individualized (though "childlike") dependents. For the slaves, these "systemically triggered" modifications in southern slaveholding seem to have resulted in improved material conditions, greater chances of maintaining stable families, and, not least, some bargaining power accruing from their masters' dependence on their labor power. On the other hand, as Genovese has argued, these very changes in southern slavery stifled slave rebelliousness—not necessarily because southern slaves were any more content with their lot than their Caribbean counterparts, but because their partial (and often strategic) adoption of the social idiom of paternalism bound them in what Eric Wolf (1971 [1959]) has called "personalistic" relationships with their oppressors. Also, as planters knew well, the development of ties of family and kinship bound slaves to a plantation grown into a slave community more effectively than laborious policing measures ever could. Finally, the uniquely high natural reproduction rates of North American slave populations in the republican era meant that a rapid process of creolization—both demographically and culturally—increasingly distanced American blacks from their African origins.

If this looks like a fairly "localized" scenario (which it certainly is not), there are more obviously "global" examples. In a virtual reversal of the transformation of the U.S. South into the Cotton Kingdom, Cuba's emergence in the early nineteenth century as the world's largest sugar producer obliterated whatever "paternalistic" modes of slaveholding had developed during Cuba's long period of economic dormancy. In contrast to the U.S. trend, Cuban slavery entered its harshest and most degrading stage only in the nineteenth century, when slave-based sugar production began to overwhelm all other economic sectors on the island. This process resulted partly from changes in Spain's commercial policy, which facilitated the accumulation of capital necessary for setting up a plantation infrastructure and allowed Cubans access to the global sugar market. At the same time, Cuba assumed another new role as large-scale purchaser in a global market for human commodities. Its "sugar revolution" was fueled by massive illegal slavetrading operations in the Bights of Benin and Biafra. These in turn relate to the rapid decline of the paramount Yoruba state of Oyo and to the previous rise of slavetrading city-states in the Niger Delta—processes accompanied by significant changes in patterns of enslavement and slaveholding in the respective African regions.[46] Even according to Curtin's (1970) conservative estimates, in the five decades following the end of the slave trade to the United States, Cuba imported more African slaves than ever reached North America. Moreover, there are good grounds for arguing that this late influx of large numbers of slaves from narrowly confined areas of West Africa relates (in complex ways) to the prominence of Yoruba and Efik/Ejagham elements in contemporary Afro-Cuban religious culture (Sosa Rodríguez 1982; Palmié 1991, 1993). Thus, at the same time that slave cultures in the American South may have been becoming increasingly homogeneous and "creole" in character, Afro-Cuban slave cultures must be presumed to have been undergoing an obverse process of differentiation and "Africanization."

Nor were these exceptional cases. Indeed, as Sidney Mintz (1978) has argued for Caribbean slaves and European laborers, and as, e.g., Trouillot (1982), Joseph Miller (1988), and Tomich (1990) have exemplified in case studies drawing all three continents into a single field of analysis, attempts to draw too rigid boundaries around any one social unit affected by the "Atlantic economy" are more likely to produce artifacts than insights. Fascinating though such issues are, they present us with enormous methodological difficulties. Whether in anthropology or history, the danger inherent in broadly systemic perspectives is sacrificing much of the specificity and analytical acumen characteristic of the best endeavors in both fields. Surely, as far as the New World is concerned, the coming together of European master and African slave in the Americas may well be viewed as "systemically determined." So, in a sense, were the manifold and temporally mutable cultural ways in which actors maneuvering within the perimeters of different local slavehold-

ing societies of both the Old and New worlds related to each other. Yet
the content of their interaction—the ways in which they thought about,
and dealt with, each other—cannot be adequately assessed within frameworks sensitive to large-scale structural developments alone. How men and
women of different Old World origins, skin colors, statuses, and cultural
backgrounds forged, maintained, and remodeled distinct but nonetheless historically interrelated cultures largely evades such calculations.

How, then, are we to perform the crucial feat of shuttling back and
forth, in both theory and method, between the undulating conjunctures of
an "Atlantic" (or even only local) *longue durée*, and the erratic—though by
no means unpatterned—momentary deflections we register on scales attuned to the behavior of concrete historical actors? More problematical
even: how may we calibrate the results of their manifold mutual interference? At the conference on which this volume is based, Mintz probably came closest to an operationally valid answer. In what he called an
"intermittent episode of undisciplined imagination," he suggested that
we start by suspending received classificatory distinctions and try to "see
everything in everything else, only then to sort out the like and the unlike, with different—possibly even with better—criteria." Since a book
can, at best, recapture fragments of the interchanges that take place at
conferences geared towards generating debate rather than summing up
the "state of the art," the reader will be the ultimate judge whether the
present collection tends more to the undisciplined or to the imaginative
end of the scale. Nonetheless, I believe, that—despite obvious shortcom-
ings, such as the lack of a balance between Americanist and Africanist contributions—we succeeded in achieving three interrelated goals.

First of all, the case studies presented in this volume expose the full
range and stunning diversity of problems encapsulated in the phrase
"slave cultures and the cultures of slavery." Thus the contributions by
Bartl and Usner take up the much-neglected issue of Native American
slaveholding and African–Native American interaction. While Bartl
discusses some of the special historiographical problems this complex
and politically sensitive subject presents, Usner explores a regional the-
ater of interaction in long-range perspective. Surveying the evolution of
various patterns of social and economic relations among Lower Mississippi Valley white settlers, servants, and colonial officials, and among
Native Americans, black slaves, and maroons, Usner shows how the
changing parameters set by European colonial development, and the
later political history of the encompassing Euro-American state(s) im-
pacted on the emergence and transformation of—at first surprisingly
volatile—racial and ethnic identities. Rathbone likewise breaks new

ground in problematizing the cultural modalities of the insertion of ex-
slave returnees from the Americas into nineteenth-century Gold Coast
society. If there was nothing "automatic" and predictable about this process, the reverse—i.e., the initial incorporation into American slavery of
newly enslaved Africans—may, as Fog Olwig and I argue (albeit in rather
different ways), have been marked by much greater continuities on the level
of behaviorally significant cultural conceptions than usually has been acknowledged. Meier's essay highlights another aspect of the role of ideological factors in shaping the modalities of encounter among Old World actors in the Americas. Though largely concerned with demonstrating the
unique significance of Moravian materials for the study of Danish West
Indian slave and slaveholding cultures, her essay—especially if read in
conjunction with Fog Olwig's—exposes some of the peculiar contradictions of the Moravian missionary ideology in a culture where Africans
had to be transformed into "things" before their individual humanity
could be "re-discovered" in the course of Christianization.

Oostindie and Van Stipriaan present us with an experiment in
thinking through the implications of different ecological adaptations of
the plantation model. Their essay reminds us of the necessity to heed
regional variations in the manner in which local means of production
(including the transfer of Dutch *polder* technology to Suriname) affected
not only the structuring of productive relations, but the ways in which
such relations were experienced and culturally elaborated. Jones's contribution in some ways provides a counterpoint to this kind of argument. For in questioning strictly "economistic" interpretations of female
slaveholding on the Gold Coast in a long-range perspective, he highlights the variety of cultural uses—such as the "production" of prestige—to which slave labor might be harnessed locally.

Second, a number of essays address larger theoretical and concep-
tual problems which, though of fundamental importance, are rarely ex-
plicated in current slavery scholarship. Blight, for one, tackles the sensitive issue of a potential "post-revisionist turn" in the historiography of
slavery, highlighting once more the harshness, inhumanity, and debili-
tating impact of the system. Yet, taking his lead from Frederick
Douglass, Blight also shows how the experiential contradictions of life
under the "peculiar institution" *always* have been mirrored in conflicting modes of historical narrative, ultimately (and perhaps inevitably)
vacillating between the poles of systematic victimization and resilient
agency. In focusing on what arguably can be called the key concepts of
recent slave studies, Mintz goes even further in exposing the analytical
muddles surrounding such increasingly popular, and seemingly matter-

of-fact, constructs as "everyday" or "cultural" resistance. Unless our data allow us unambiguously to pinpoint individual volition, Mintz argues, categorizing instances of slave behavior as "resistant" is risky business—as risky, in fact, as assuming that intentional acts of resistance must, of necessity (and in order to meet taxonomic requirements), have a deleterious impact on their object (i.e., the individual, group, or system against which resistance is directed). The danger inherent in such reasoning, Mintz implies, ultimately amounts to putting the cart before the horse; once "resistance" becomes a transhistorical "essence" rather than a problem demanding empirical attention, we are left at best with a stale typological contrast between heroes and villains, and at worst with a pseudohistorical farce.

In this sense, Thoden van Velzen's chapter on the "natives' point of view" concerning the use and abuse of power in Suriname's maroon societies represents a unique attempt to explore the experiential contradictions of "resistance" on the frontiers between the maroons and the Dutch colonial state. If—as Bartl argues—the study of Native American slaveholding has been hampered by the politically inopportune character of the subject, the exploitation (and sometimes *de facto* enslavement) of dependent latecomer fugitives by post-treaty maroons may be one of the best-guarded skeletons in the closet of African-American historiography (cf. Mavis Campbell 1988: 13). But Thoden van Velzen is not intent on exploding myths about (as well as current among) these paragons of resistance. Rather, his aim is to unravel the complex moral dilemmas of indigenous maroon historiographical praxis in relation to power itself. For Ndyuka historians face the fundamental contradiction of having—for reasons pertaining to communally-held "egalitarian" ideologies—to depict powerful leaders of their struggle for freedom as heroes and villains at one and the same time.

A final group of chapters is concerned with conceptualizing continuities of cultural process across the historical threshold between slavery and freedom. Except for Lichtenstein, who highlights the cultural implications of structural shifts in the transitional period itself, the authors do not aim to document the adaptation of social and ideological complexes forged under slavery to post-emancipation social contexts. Rather they seek to elucidate the significance of such processes of creative adaptation for an understanding of the cultural dynamics of contemporary African-American societies. Due to its closeup focus, Lichtenstein's chapter, perhaps, best illustrates exactly what differences the "great transformation" wrought upon the moral relations between ex-slaves turned sharecroppers or wage laborers, and ex-slaveholders turned landlords and employers. Focusing on the criminalization of the appropriation and autonomous disposal of agricultural products in the post-Reconstruction South in the United States, he shows how a "moral economy" developed under slavery (and comprising economically crucial customary obligations on the part of the slaveholders to provide subsistence goods or to tolerate their production by the slaves) had to be broken down by legal reformulations of property rights in order to ensure the freedmen's effective proletarianization.

If Lichtenstein presents a sobering perspective on emancipation within the context of larger economic shifts, Besson's case study of the formation and dynamics of Afro-Jamaican kinship and landholding systems demonstrates the remarkable resilience of peasant cultural adaptations under external political and economic pressures. Besson takes a long-range perspective on the evolution of notions and practices relating to conjugality, kinship, descent, and customary land tenure in the free villages of Jamaica's Trelawny Parish and among the Accompong maroons. This stance allows the author to expose brilliantly the continuity of differently elaborated adaptive strategies geared towards maximizing human and productive resources in peasant societies endangered by both pre- and post-emancipation economic regimes.

Van Wetering, finally, brings us up to the very present in her discussion of how female creole migrants from Suriname harness symbolic resources, developed under slavery or in its early aftermath, to the problems presented by their host environment in the contemporary Netherlands. Her focus on the immediate present both extends and provides a stimulating counterpart to the other two papers in this section. Although the historical trajectory of the cultural forms these Surinamese women employ in coping with their daily tribulations still constitutes a much-neglected research problem, van Wetering amply demonstrates how such forms are both refracted in and transformed by the very process of their continued enactment.

In the end, then, we come full circle: from the initial formation of culturally preconditioned but historically determined experiences of (and reactions to) the process of human commodification, through the manifold contradictions of life within the changing parameters of various historical manifestations of the "peculiar institution," and finally to its lasting heritage among people who—consciously or not—continue to reproduce, and thereby transform, the social and cultural arrangements that emerged from the interactions among Africa, Europe, and the Americas in the formation of an Atlantic economy based partially on slavery. Hence the development of slave cultures, cultures of slavery, and—if such terminological extravagance be permitted—cultures of en-slavement, slaveholding, and slavetrading, in the Atlantic rimlands, is by no means a process easily divorced from the course of what we tend to call the cultural history of the "modern" period. On the contrary: rather than representing a collection of scholarly disquisitions on a ghastly but happily terminated phase of global history, the volume at hand, perhaps speaks to a fundamental need to balance our understanding of the present against ever more sophisticated (re-)constructions of the past.

Notes

1. Watson (1980) is certainly right when he argues that, even in the case of slavery, the moment of physical violence does not exhaust the meaning of the term *coercion*. As many slaveholders well knew, and as Genovese (1974) has argued most persuasively, brutality alone rarely advanced the interests (economic, social, and psychological) of the master class beyond achieving certain short-term goals.
2. A similar case could be made for the introduction of Asian contract labor in the Caribbean after the end of the (legal) slave trade, or for the increasing debasement of the landless free population of Puerto Rico under the regime of the workbook (on the latter, see Mintz 1989 [1974]: 82–94). As Walton Look Lai (1993: 267) puts it: "Contract labor was not always as easily distinguishable from other coercive labor systems after arrival in the New World as the formal laws would have it seem, whether in the seventeenth century or the nineteenth."
3. Peter Wood's *Black Majority* (1974) remains one of the best illustrations of the internal differentiation of a single colonial labor regime. For the division of labor in different types of plantation economies, see, e.g., Moreno Fraginals (1976) and Joyner (1984), as well as the classic studies by Guerra y Sánchez (1964 [1927]) and Ortiz (1947 [1940]). On the complex, myth-shrouded role of the slave driver or "black agricultural labor supervisor," see Van Deburg (1979).
4. See Freyre (1947 [1934]) for a classic account of "domestic" slavery in Brazil, and Genovese (1974) for his much-discussed thesis concerning the role of ideologies of "paternalism" in situations where close relations between masters and slaves obtained. Fox-Genovese (1988) provides fascinating glimpses of the female world of the antebellum plantation household. For particularly interesting attempts to situate Islamic East African slavery within this broader discussion, see Cooper (1977, 1981).
5. Monographic studies of urban slavery in the Americas are few. For North America, see Wade (1964), Blassingame (1973), Philip D. Morgan (1984), Gary B. Nash (1988), and White (1991). Though urban slave labor seems to have played a more significant role in certain regions of the Hispanic Caribbean and Latin America, the subject remains similarly understudied there, except in the case of Brazil. See, e.g., Deschamps Chapeaux (1971) and Ortiz (1975 [1916]) on Havana; Bowser (1974) on Lima; Palmer (1976) on Mexico; Andrews (1980) on Buenos Aires; Reis (1982) and Nishida (1993) on Salvador

de Bahia; and Karasch (1987) on Rio de Janeiro. A useful overview of what little we know about comparable situations in the British Caribbean is presented in Higman's magisterial *Slave Populations of the British Caribbean* (1984: 226–59).

6. Compare Genovese (1974) and Oakes (1982) for different views on this issue. Campbell (1987) and Faust (1987) provide convenient overviews of recent research trends. For an interesting, though not unproblematic, attempt at comparative analysis of the functional integration of slavery with other institutional spheres in two very different societies—Jamaica and the Hausa Emirate Zaria— see Michael G. Smith (1965: 116–61).

7. An obvious and well-documented example is the fate of the comparatively large and economically important free black population of Cuba. As a result of liberal Spanish self-purchase and manumission laws, this population emerged during Cuba's long period of economic stagnation. In the nineteenth century, this group became one of the first casualties of the "sugar revolution." As Knight (1970) persuasively argues, free African Cubans increasingly came to be seen as dangerous anomalies in a society that strove toward the ideal of an unambiguous linkage between skin color and legal and economic disability. For other examples, see the contributions in Cohen and Greene (1972).

8. Compare Ratekin (1954), Mintz (1985, 1989 [1974]), Greenfield (1977), Craton (1984), and William D. Phillips, Jr. (1985).

9. Compare Nieboer (1900) and Edgar T. Thompson (1932) for particularly cogent early formulations of such approaches. A similar argument could be made in weighing the relative importance of Islamic slave law and local political-economic contingencies in shaping slavery in Muslim Africa. As Cooper (1977, 1981) has demonstrated for the case of slavery on Zanzibar's spice plantations, one of the most extensive and brutal systems of slaveholding on the African continent emerged from the transfer of liberal Ibadi-Islamic Arabian slave law from Oman to the East African Coast. He writes: "Among Islamic political philosophies, Ibadism tilted towards the side of egalitarianism and asceticism, yet [in nineteenth-century Zanzibar] Ibadis had built a profitable plantation system based on the subordination of slave labor. In parts of the coast, working conditions resembled Alabama more than Oman" (Cooper 1981: 281).

10. In a classic late-eighteenth-century statement of this view, the Jamaican planter-historian Bryan Edwards quotes the following opinion of an African traveler about whose "veracity and candour" Edwards seems to harbor no doubts: "In all parts of the [African] coast, and I apprehend it to be the same inland, the body of the people are in a state of absolute and unlimited slavery: their children are born to no other inheritance, and are liable to be sold by their owners as they think proper" (Edwards 1972 [1793]: vol. 4, p. 94). Given this state of affairs, Edwards's colleague Edward Long (1970 [1774]: vol. 2, p. 403) proclaimed, enslaved Africans could only profit from being transported to the Americas.

11. "The Slave Trade," wrote the British abolitionist Thomas F. Buxton (1840: 227), "is the great cause of the depopulation and degradation of Africa, not merely from its keeping the people in a state of disorganization, but from its poisoning the whole policy of the country." Its most deleterious effects upon Africa, Buxton argued (227), were that it "suppresses all other trade, creates endless insecurity, kindles perpetual war, banishes commerce, knowledge, social improvement, and, above all, Christianity, from one quarter of the globe, and from a hundred millions of mankind."

12. The concept of an "Atlantic world" is, of course, a problematical one. For our present purposes, it may be sufficient to define it as a historically mutable sphere of human interaction integrated by the operation of what Philip Curtin calls the "South Atlantic System"; Curtin defines the latter as "a complex economic organism centered on the production in the Americas of tropical staples for consumption in Europe, and grown by the labor of Africans" (Curtin 1970: 3). Thornton (1992) provides a useful introduction to the problems involved in dealing with the Atlantic as a geohistorical unit. For an innovative alternative conception of this historical space, see Linebaugh and Redicker (1990).

13. Compare Fage (1969) for the original counterposition. See Klein and Lovejoy (1979), Inikori (1982), Eltis and Jennings (1988), Manning (1990), and Thornton (1992) for more recent assessments.

14. Ryder's findings concerning an early indigenous demand for slaves on the Gold Coast may have played a key role in this. As Ryder (1969) pointed out, in the fifteenth century, the Portuguese seem to have established slave-trading operations in the Bight of Benin, not in order to satisfy a European (not to speak of an American) demand, but *because* slaves provided the only commodity acceptable on what, for the Portuguese, was then the target market: the gold-producing societies of the region of present-day Ghana.

15. Such as the question of whether the available evidence supported conclusions about the existence of a "slave mode of production" in Africa.

16. Compare Cooper (1979) for a most thoughtful comparative review of these problems. The debate sparked by Rodney certainly is not the only one of these seemingly endless controversies. A not unrelated intellectual tug-of-war surrounds the so-called "Williams thesis," which posits that the exploitation of slave labor in the Caribbean generated the wealth that was to finance the British industrial revolution. Though developed in 1944 by the Trinidadian scholar Eric Williams, it harks back to older debates about the profitability of slavery. This controversy has a North American equivalent in the fierce debates sparked by the publication of Fogel and Engerman's *Time on the Cross* (1974). In this massive econometric reinterpretation of historical data, Fogel and Engerman tried to "prove"—contrary to prevailing views—not only that southern slavery was at least as profitable as free agricultural labor, but also that both masters *and* slaves had profited from the institution. For recent assessments of the "Williams thesis" from a variety of perspectives, see the contributions to Solow and Engerman (1987) and Inikori and Engerman (1992). For the response to Fogel and Engerman's *Time on the Cross,* see Gutman (1975), David et al. (1976), and Fogel (1989). Prior arguments about the profitability of North American slavery are conveniently sampled in Aitken (1971), and the linkages of such debates to similar ones about ancient slavery are discussed in Finley (1980).

17. Indeed, in Jack Goody's view, the problem boils down to the question of how to maintain a slave population (and we know that many African societies were reluctant to release relatively large contingents of slaves when the colonial powers eventually forced them to), when constant depletion is occurring by way of both sale and assimilation. As Goody trenchantly writes:

> Where there is no mobility for slaves out of the slave class, the original population can be maintained without acquisition from the outside. But the more liberal their treatment and the more numerous their [institutionalized]

escape routes, the more devastating the results. I mean devastating here in the literal sense of the word. Economists and others have rightly argued that there is no slavery without the slave trade. But the social consequences begin further aback, because in order to supply the trade, violence has to be applied by someone, in many cases far removed from the eventual slave owner. So that the consequence of the sliding status of the slave is the continual violence required to replenish the ever-emptying pool of forced labor. (1980: 41)

For criticism of the Kopytoff-Miers thesis, see Cooper (1979) and the contributions to Watson, ed. (1980), and Lovejoy (1981).

18. Though coming from a rather different theoretical position and addressing the Latin American situation, Lombardi (1974) likewise argues for decomposing the analytical category of "slavery" into less sweeping units of interregional comparison.

19. See Mintz (1959), Lombardi (1974), Berlin (1980), Schwartz (1982), Breen (1984), and Menard and Schwartz (1993) for different statements of the problem of conceptualizing diversity and mutual articulation of slave systems in space and time.

20. Mullin (1992: 131ff.), e.g., convincingly argues that variations in seasonal food supply significantly influenced both slaves' *and* masters' behavior and their interaction patterns. See also Dirks (1987) and—on a somewhat different note—Van Lier (1971).

21. See Wood (1978) and Dew (1987) for comprehensive reviews of major research trends in the past decades. Though not unproblematical in terms of their theoretical orientations, Genovese (1979) and Craton (1982) together give a good impression of the incidence and extent of slave rebellions in the Western Hemisphere.

22. Aptheker's monumental but somewhat idiosyncratic *American Negro Slave Revolts* (1969 [1943]) represents a notable exception.

23. The current tendency to investigate the *non-occurrence* of rebellion is indicative of this change of perspective. Philip D. Morgan (1984), e.g., opens his excellent study of eighteenth-century black Charleston with the question of why no major insurrection was mounted by the slaves during the second half of that century, a time when so many major rebellions erupted in other locations. Geggus (1987) poses similar questions in regard to the absence of slave rebellions in Jamaica during the 1790s.

24. The latter point is well addressed in the introduction and several contributions to a recent volume on slaves' independent economic activities—behaviors which, arguably, benefited both slaves and slaveholders, albeit in very different ways (Berlin and Morgan 1991).

25. Compare Schwartz (1977) for the stunning example of a group of Brazilian maroons bargaining with their former owner about the conditions—such as increased control over the allocation and structuring of their own labor—under which they would return to his plantation.

26. See Szwed (1974) and Jackson (1986) for overviews of the major theoretical issues in the so-called Frazier-Herskovits debate, as well as for comments on its social and political context. Neither view has been completely superseded. See, e.g., Robert Faris Thompson (1983) or Stuckey (1987) for latter-day Herskovitsian "formalistic" approaches, or Moreno Fraginals (1984) for a "neo-Frazerian" approach with a Marxist bent.

27. Problematizing the historical conditions of social re-aggregation among enslaved Africans, Mintz and Price directed attention not only to possible
discontinuities in cultural transmission, but also to the necessity of assuming
that cultural creativity and large-scale syntheses precipitated the institutionalization of such cultural forms as are observable in contemporary African-American
societies. What came into view, then, were processes of "creolization" informed
both by Old World cultural resources *and* by New World social options and
exigencies. For an earlier and somewhat different usage of the "creolization"
metaphor, see Brathwaite (1971), whose usage resembles Breen's (1984) broad
use of the term. In many ways, Fernando Ortiz's (1947 [1940]) concept of
transculturación stands as a distinguished precursor of such views.

28. In view of the massive evidence for African-American cultural creativity under
slavery—and the considerable theoretical debate concerning it—it is somewhat
surprising that Africanists, so far, rarely have raised such issues. This lack of
attention is particularly striking in light of the fact that even staunch advocates
of "African exceptionalism," such as Kopytoff and Miers, emphasize that African slavery is functionally geared to the absorption of *ethnically as well as culturally alien* individuals into new social contexts. Nor is historical evidence for cultural divisions between African slaveholders and their slaves entirely absent.
Cooper's work (1977, 1979, 1981), though highly suggestive in this regard, remains focused on questions of political economy. One of the few Africanists
who explicitly raises the issue (Rathbone 1985) points to the (equally
underresearched) possibility that some of the forms of slave resistance we have
come to think of as peculiarly American—such as *grand marronage*—may have
African antecedents. For a suggestive case study of an East African "maroon
society," see Casanelli (1987).

29. See, e.g., Dunn (1977), Craton (1979), Berlin (1980), Philip D. Morgan (1982),
Breen (1984), Higman (1984), Kiple (1984), Schwartz (1985), Kulikoff (1986),
Bailyn (1986), the essays in Berlin and Morgan (1991), and the contributions by
Besson, Oostindie and van Stipriaan, and Usner in this volume.

30. Compare Mullin (1992: chap. 7).

31. Compare Besson (1979, 1984, 1992, this volume), as well as Mintz (1989: 225–50).

32. See Mintz (1989 [1974]: chap. 7) and Mullin (1992: chaps. 6 and 7).

33. For a case study suggestive of how conceptions of kinship and domestic relations
continue to mediate both secular and sacred exchanges among Surinamese migrants in the Netherlands, see van Wetering (this volume).

34. The following—highly eclectic—survey is restricted to the period after 1980.

35. For the former, see, e.g., the contributions to Berlin and Morgan (1991). The
latter aspect (particularly foodways, clothing, and personal adornment) is dealt
with in Genovese (1974: 524–61), Philip D. Morgan (1984), Joyner (1984: 90–
106), White (1991: 185–206), Prude (1991), and Mintz (1993). It is worth noting that Mintz had broached these issues as early as the mid-1950s in his pioneering studies of Caribbean peasant economic adaptation and resistance (some
of this important early work is conveniently reprinted in Mintz 1989 [1974],
chaps. 7–9). Though ostensibly a biography of a freedman, Silva (1993) provides
a fascinating glimpse into the world of black Cariocans during the last years of
slavery. The republication of Fernando Ortiz's writings on Havana's *negros curros*
(Ortiz 1986) should provide an incentive further to study this particularly flam-
boyant early-nineteenth-century urban black subculture.

36. See, e.g., Joyner (1984), Philip D. Morgan (1982, 1988), Sobel (1987), and Turner (1991).

37. See, e.g., Philip D. Morgan (1983), Joyner (1984), Gaspar (1985, 1988), Kay and Cary (1985), Dirks (1987), Hall (1992), Lichtenstein (1988, this volume).

38. See, e.g., the contributions in Heuman (1985) and Okihiro (1986), as well as thoughtful comments by Paquette (1991) and Mintz (this volume).

39. In addition to Richard Price's highly acclaimed studies of the Saramaka of Suriname (1983, 1990), see Thoden van Velzen and van Wetering (1988); Thoden van Velzen (this volume) on the neighboring Ndyuka; and Bilby (1984a, 1984b), Sheridan (1986), and Barbara K. Kopytoff (1987) on the Jamaican maroons. For examples of recent maroon scholarship more strictly historiographical in orientation, see Mavis C. Campbell (1988), Deive (1989), and Hoogbergen (1990, 1993).

40. This state of affairs is reflected in the very different general tenors of two recent collections (Boles 1988, Holloway 1990). Creel (1988) attempts to strike a balance between these two approaches. In the case of Jamaica, Turner (1982) provides useful new data on pre-emancipation missionary endeavors, while Schuler (1980) offers a reinterpretation of "myalism" in light of Africanist models. However, since Schuler's main body of evidence relates to a group of post-emancipation African immigrants, it is questionable whether her hypotheses would hold up when projected backward into the period of slavery. The same caveat would seem to apply to Maureen Warner-Lewis's (1991) work on the descendants of indentured Yoruba in Trinidad. As regards slave religion in Haiti, the most significant research in the past few years has aimed at debunking historiographical myths, rather than at presenting novel data or theory (compare Hoffmann 1990, Geggus 1991). In Latin America, the situation appears to be roughly similar. Little has been published in recent years that is comparable to Bastide's (1978 [1960]) broad—though certainly not unproblematic—long-range historical treatment of African-American religion in Brazil. But see the novel approaches by Costa Lima (1976) and Gois Dantas (1988). Though concerned mainly with the history of Suriname maroon religion since the late nineteenth century, Thoden van Velzen and van Wetering's (1988) encyclopedic study of religious movements among the Ndyuka likewise breaks new ground.

41. The speculative "Africanist" readings of Equiano's writings by Edwards and Shaw (1989) and Paul Edwards (1990) are limited in usefulness by a paucity of evidence. Sobel's (1979) thoughtful discussion of Baptist conversion experiences in the U.S. South is marred by the heterogeneity of her sources. To use, as she does, data from the Fisk and Works Progress Administration (WPA) slave narrative collections to complement the documentary record on the first late-eighteenth-century Baptist communities is by no means an unproblematic maneuver.

42. See, e.g., Mintz (1981), Mullin (1985), White (1985), Fox-Genovese (1988), Morrissey (1989), Beckles (1989), and Bush (1990). For recent research on female slavery and slaveholding in Africa, see Robertson and Klein (1983), Meillassoux (1986), and Jones (this volume).

43. See Barbara K. Kopytoff (1976), Higman (1979), Littlefield (1981), Nishida (1993), and Palmié (1993).

44. Indispensable are the monographs by Foner (1983), Scott (1985), and Holt (1992), as well as the collections by Moreno Fraginals, Moya Pons, and

Engerman (1985); Scott, Drescher, Mattos de Castro, Andrews, and Levine (1988); Miers and Roberts (1988); and McGlynn and Drescher (1992).

45. Though of major importance in this respect, the debate about Immanuel Wallerstein's "world systems theory" cannot be dealt with here. See Wallerstein (1974–89) for the original formulation, as well as Mintz (1977), June Nash (1981), Wolf (1982), Asad (1987), and Stern (1988) for particularly cogent criticism.

46. See Law (1977) and Agiri (1981) on the Yoruba, and Latham (1973) and Northup (1978) for the Niger Delta states.

References

Agiri, Babatunde
1981   Slavery in Yoruba Society in the Nineteenth Century. In *The Ideology of Slavery in Africa*, ed. Paul E. Lovejoy, 123–48. Beverly Hills, Calif.: Sage.

Aitken, Hugh G. J., ed.
1971   *Did Slavery Pay? Readings in the Economics of Black Slavery in the United States.* Boston: Houghton Mifflin.

Andrews, George R.
1980   *The Afro-Argentines of Buenos Aires, 1800–1900.* Madison: Univ. of Wisconsin Press.

Aptheker, Herbert
1969 [1943]   *American Negro Slave Revolts.* New York: International Publishers [New York: Columbia Univ. Press].

Asad, Talal
1987   Are There Histories of Peoples Without Europe? A Review Article. *Comparative Studies in Society and History* 29: 594–607.

Bailyn, Bernard
1986   *The Peopling of British North America.* New York: Vintage Books.

Bastide, Roger
1978 [1960]   *The African Religions of Brazil: Toward a Sociology of the Interpenetration of Civilizations.* Baltimore, Md.: Johns Hopkins Univ. Press.

Beckles, Hilary M.
1989   *Natural Rebels: A Social History of Enslaved Women in Barbados.* London: Zed Books.

Berlin, Ira D.
1980   Time, Space, and the Evolution of Afro-American Society on British Mainland North America. *American Historical Review* 85: 44–78.

Berlin, Ira D., and Philip D. Morgan, eds.
1991   *The Slaves' Economy: Independent Production by Slaves in the Americas.* London: Frank Cass. Special issue of *Slavery and Abolition* 12 (1).

Besson, Jean
1979   Symbolic Aspects of Land in the Caribbean: The Tenure and Transmission of Land Rights among Caribbean Peasantries. In *Peasants, Plantations and Rural Communities in the Caribbean*, ed. Malcolm Cross and Arnaud Marks, 86–116. Guildford, England: Univ. of Surrey.

1984   Land Tenure in the Free Villages of Trelawny, Jamaica: A Case Study in the Caribbean Peasant Response to Emancipation. *Slavery and Abolition* 5: 3–23.

1992   Freedom and Community: The British West Indies. In *The Meaning of Freedom*, ed. Frank McGlynn and Seymour Drescher, 183–219. Pittsburgh, Pa.: Univ. of Pittsburgh Press.

Bilby, Kenneth M.

1984a The Treacherous Feast: A Jamaican Maroon Historical Myth. *Bijdragen tot de Taal-Land-en Volkenkunde* 140: 1–31.

1984b "Two Sister Pikni": A Historical Tradition of Dual Ethnogenesis in Eastern Jamaica. *Caribbean Quarterly* 30: 10–25.

Blassingame, John W.

1973   *Black New Orleans, 1860–1880*. Chicago: Univ. of Chicago Press.

Boles, John B., ed.

1988   *Masters and Slaves in the House of the Lord: Race and Religion in the American South, 1740–1870*. Lexington: Univ. of Kentucky Press.

Bowser, Frederick P.

1974   *The African Slave in Colonial Peru, 1524–1650*. Stanford, Calif.: Stanford Univ. Press.

Brathwaite, Edward

1971   *The Development of Creole Society in Jamaica, 1770–1820*. New York: Oxford Univ. Press.

Breen, Timothy H.

1973   A Changing Labor Force and Race Relations in Virginia, 1660–1710. *Journal of Social History* 7: 3–25

1984   Creative Adaptations: Peoples and Cultures. In *Colonial British America*, ed. Jack P. Greene and J. R. Pole, 195–232. Baltimore, Md.: Johns Hopkins Univ. Press.

Breen, Timothy H., and Steven Innes

1980   *Myne Owne Ground: Race and Freedom on Virginia's Eastern Shore, 1640–1675*. New York: Oxford Univ. Press.

Bush, Barbara

1990   *Slave Women in Caribbean Society, 1650–1838*. Bloomington: Indiana Univ. Press.

Buxton, Thomas F.

1840   *The African Slave Trade and its Remedy*. London: John Murray.

Campbell, Mavis C.

1988   *The Maroons of Jamaica, 1655–1796*. Granby, Conn.: Bergin and Garvey.

Campbell, Randolph B.

1987   Planters and Plain Folks: The Social Structure of the Antebellum South. In *Interpreting Southern History*, ed. John B. Boles and Evelyn Thomas Nolen, 48–77. Baton Rouge: Louisiana State Univ. Press.

Casanelli, Lee V.

1987   Social Construction on the Somali Frontier: Bantu Former Slave Communities in the Nineteenth Century. In *The African Frontier*, ed. Igor Kopytoff, 216–38. Bloomington: Indiana Univ. Press.

Cohen, David W., and Jack P. Greene, eds.

1972   *Neither Slave nor Free: The Freedmen of African Descent in the Slave Societies of the New World*. Baltimore, Md.: Johns Hopkins Univ. Press.

Cooper, Frederick
1977   *Plantation Slavery on the East African Coast.* New Haven, Conn.: Yale Univ. Press.
1979   The Problem of Slavery in African Studies. *Journal of African History* 20: 103–25.
1981   Islam and Cultural Hegemony: The Ideology of Slaveowners on the East African Coast. In *The Ideology of Slavery in Africa,* ed. Paul E. Lovejoy, 271–307. Beverly Hills: Sage.
Costa Lima, Vivaldo da
1976   O conceito de "naçao" nos Candomblés da Bahia. *Afro–Asia* 12: 65–91.
Craton, Michael
1979   Changing Patterns of Slave Families in the British West Indies. *Journal of Interdisciplinary History* 10: 1–35.
1982   *Testing the Chains: Resistance to Slavery in the British West Indies.* Ithaca, N.Y.: Cornell Univ. Press.
1984   The Historical Roots of the Plantation Model. *Slavery and Abolition* 5: 189–221
Creel, Margaret W.
1988   *"A Peculiar People": Slave Religion and Community-Culture Among the Gullahs.* New York: New York Univ. Press.
Curtin, Philip D.
1970   *The Atlantic Slave Trade: A Census.* Madison: Univ. of Wisconsin Press.
1984   *Cross-Cultural Trade in World History.* New York: Cambridge Univ. Press.
David, Paul A.; Herbert G. Gutman; Richard Sutch; Peter Temin; and Gavin Wright
1976   *Reckoning with Slavery.* New York: Oxford Univ. Press.
Davis, David Brion
1974   Slavery and the Post–World War II Historians. *Daedalus* 103: 1–16.
1984   *Slavery and Human Progress.* New York: Oxford Univ. Press.
Deive, Carlos Esteban
1989   *Los guerrilleros negros: Esclavos fugitivos y cimarrones en Santo Domingo.* Santo Domingo, Dominican Republic: Fundación Cultural Dominicana.
Deschamps Chapeaux, Pedro
1971   *El negro en la economía habanera del siglo XIX.* Havana, Cuba: UNEAC.
Dew, Charles B.
1987   The Slavery Experience. In *Interpreting Southern History,* ed. John B. Boles and Evelyn Thomas Nolen, 120–61. Baton Rouge: Louisiana State Univ. Press.
Dirks, Robert
1987   *The Black Saturnalia: Conflict and Its Ritual Expression on British West Indian Slave Plantations.* Gainesville: Univ. of Florida Press.
Dunn, Richard S.
1977   A Tale of Two Plantations: Slave Life at Mesopotamia in Jamaica and Mount Airy in Virginia, 1799 to 1828. *William and Mary Quarterly* 34: 32–65.
Edwards, Bryan
1972 [1793]   *The History Civil and Commercial of the British Colonies in the West Indies.* New York: Arno Press.
Edwards, Paul
1990   "Master" and "Father" in Equiano's *Interesting Narrative. Slavery and Abolition* 11: 216–26.
Edwards, Paul, and Rosalind Shaw
1989   Equiano's Invisible *Chi:* Igbo Belief and Tradition in the *Interesting Narrative. Journal of Religion in Africa* 19: 146–56.

Elkins, Stanley M.
1959   *Slavery: A Problem in American Institutional and Intellectual Life*. Chicago: Univ. of Chicago Press.
1975   The Slavery Debate. *Commentary* 60 (6): 40–55.
Ellison, Ralph
1964   *Shadow and Act*. New York: Random House.
Eltis, David
1993   Labour and Coercion in the English Atlantic World from the Seventeenth to the Early Twentieth Century. In *The Wages of Slavery. From Chattel Slavery to Wage Labour in Africa, the Caribbean and England*, ed. Michael Twaddle, 207–26. London: Frank Cass.
Eltis, David, and Lawrence C. Jennings
1988   Trade Between Western Africa and the Atlantic World in the Pre-Colonial Era. *American Historical Review* 93: 936–59.
Fage, John D.
1969   Slavery and the Slave Trade in the Context of West African History. *Journal of African History* 10: 393–404.
Faust, Drew Gilpin
1987   The Peculiar South Revisited: White Society, Culture, and Politics in the Antebellum Period, 1800–1860. In *Interpreting Southern History*, ed. John B. Boles and Evelyn Thomas Nolen, 78–119. Baton Rouge: Louisiana State Univ. Press.
Finley, Moses I.
1968   Slavery. In *International Encyclopedia of the Social Sciences*, ed. David Sills, 14: 307–13. New York: Macmillan.
1980   *Ancient Slavery and Modern Ideology*. New York: Viking Press.
Fogel, Robert W.
1989   *Without Consent or Contract*. New York: Norton.
Fogel, Robert W., and Stanley L. Engerman
1974   *Time on the Cross: The Economics of American Negro Slavery*. New York: Little, Brown.
Foner, Eric
1983   *Nothing but Freedom: Emancipation and Its Legacy*. Baton Rouge: Louisiana State Univ. Press.
Fox-Genovese, Elizabeth
1988   *Within the Plantation Household: Black and White Women of the Old South*. Chapel Hill: Univ. of North Carolina Press.
Frederickson, George M.
1981   *White Supremacy: A Comparative Study in American and South African History*. New York: Oxford Univ. Press.
Freyre, Gilberto
1947 [1934]   *The Masters and the Slaves*. New York: Knopf.
Gaspar, David Barry
1985   *Bondmen and Rebels: A Study of Master-Slave Relationships in Antigua*. Baltimore, Md.: Johns Hopkins Univ. Press.
1988   Slavery, Amelioration and Sunday Markets in Antigua, 1823–1831. *Slavery and Abolition* 9: 1–28.
1991   Antigua Slaves and Their Struggle to Survive. In *Seeds of Change*, ed. Herman J. Viola and Carolyn Margolis, 130–37. Washington, D.C.: Smithsonian Institution.

Geggus, David
1987   The Enigma of Jamaica in the 1790s: New Light on the Causes of Slave Rebellions. *William and Mary Quarterly* 49: 274–99.
1991   Haitian Voodoo in the Eighteenth Century: Language, Culture, Resistance. *Jahrbuch für Geschichte von Staat, Wirtschaft und Gesellschaft Lateinamerikas* 28: 21–51.

Genovese, Eugene D.
1971 [1969]   *The World the Slaveholders Made*. New York: Vintage Books.
1974   *Roll, Jordan, Roll: The World the Slaves Made*. New York: Pantheon.
1979   *From Rebellion to Revolution: Afro-American Slave Revolts in the Making of the Modern World*. Baton Rouge: Louisiana State Univ. Press.

Gois Dantas, Beatriz
1988   *Vovó Nago e Papai Branco: Usos e abusos da África no Brasil*. Rio de Janeiro, Brazil: Graal.

Goody, Jack
1980   Slavery in Space and Time. In *African and Asian Systems of Slavery*, ed. James L. Watson, 16–42. Berkeley: Univ. of California Press.

Greenfield, Sidney M.
1977   Madeira and the Beginnings of New World Sugar Cane Cultivation and Plantation Slavery: A Study in Institution Building. In *Comparative Perspectives on Slavery in New World Plantation Societies*, ed. Vera Rubin and Arthur Tuden, 536–52. New York: New York Academy of Sciences.

Guerra y Sánchez, Ramiro
1964 [1927]   *Sugar and Society in the Caribbean*. New Haven, Conn.: Yale Univ. Press.

Gutman, Herbert G.
1975   *Slavery and the Numbers Game*. Urbana: Univ. of Illinois Press.
1976   *The Black Family in Slavery and Freedom, 1750–1925*. New York: Random House.

Hall, Neville T.
1992   *Slave Society in the Danish West Indies*. Mona: Univ. of the West Indies Press.

Herskovits, Melville J. *The Myth of the Negro Past*. New York: Harper and Bros.

Heuman, Gad, ed.
1985   *Out of the House of Bondage*. London: Frank Cass. Special issue of *Slavery and Abolition* 5 (3).

Higman, Barry
1979   African and Creole Slave Family Patterns in Trinidad. In *Africa and the Caribbean*, ed. Margaret E. Crahan and Franklin W. Knight, 41–64. Baltimore, Md.: Johns Hopkins Univ. Press.
1984   *Slave Populations of the British Caribbean, 1807–1834*. Baltimore, Md.: Johns Hopkins Univ. Press.

Hoffmann, Léon-François
1990   Histoire, mythe et idéologie: La cérémonie du Bois-Caiman. *Études Créoles* 13: 9–34.

Holloway, Joseph E.
1990   *Africanisms in American Culture*. Bloomington: Indiana Univ. Press.

Holt, Thomas C.
1992   *The Problem of Freedom: Race, Labor, and Politics in Jamaica and Britain, 1832–1838*. Baltimore, Md.: Johns Hopkins Univ. Press.

Hoogbergen, Wim
1990 *The Boni Maroon Wars in Suriname.* Leiden, Netherlands: E. J. Brill.
1993 Marronage and Slave Rebellions in Suriname. In *Slavery in the Americas,* ed. Wolfgang Binder, 165–95. Würzburg, Germany: Königshausen and Neumann.
Inikori, Joseph E.
1982 Introduction. In *Forced Migration,* ed. Joseph E. Inikori, 13–60. New York: Africana Publishing Company.
Inikori, Joseph E., and Stanley L. Engerman, eds.
1992 *The Atlantic Slave Trade.* Durham, N.C.: Duke Univ. Press.
Jackson, Walter
1986 Melville Herskovits and the Search for Afro-American Culture. In *Malinowski, Rivers, Benedict, and Others: Essays on Culture and Personality,* ed. George W. Stocking, 95–126. Madison: Univ. of Wisconsin Press.
Joyner, Charles
1984 *Down by the Riverside: A South Carolina Slave Community.* Urbana: Univ. of Illinois Press.
Karasch, Mary
1987 *Slave Life and Culture in Rio de Janeiro, 1808–1850.* Princeton, N.J.: Princeton Univ. Press.
Kay, Marvin L. Michael, and Lorin Lee Cary
1985 "They Are Indeed the Constant Plague of Their Tyrants": Slave Defense of a Moral Economy in Colonial North Carolina, 1748–1772. In *Out of the House of Bondage,* ed. Gad Heuman, 37–56. London: Frank Cass.
Kiple, Kenneth F.
1984 *The Caribbean Slave: A Biological History.* Cambridge: Cambridge Univ. Press.
Klein, Martin, and Paul E. Lovejoy
1979 Slavery in West Africa. In *The Uncommon Market,* ed. Henry A. Gemery and Jan S. Hogendorn, 181–212. New York: Academic Press.
Kloosterboer, W.
1960 *Involuntary Labour Since the Abolition of Slavery.* Leiden, Netherlands: E. J. Brill.
Knight, Franklin W.
1970 *Slave Society in Cuba during the Nineteenth Century.* Madison: Univ. of Wisconsin Press.
Kopytoff, Barbara K.
1976 The Development of Jamaican Maroon Ethnicity. *Caribbean Quarterly* 22: 33–50.
1987 Religious Change among the Jamaican Maroons: The Ascendance of the Christian God within a Traditional Cosmology. *Journal of Social History* 20: 463–84.
Kopytoff, Igor, and Suzanne Miers
1977 Introduction: African "Slavery" as an Institution of Marginality. In *Slavery in Africa: Historical and Anthropological Perspectives,* ed. Suzanne Miers and Igor Kopytoff, 3–81. Madison: Univ. of Wisconsin Press.
Kulikoff, Alan
1986 *Tobacco and Slaves: The Development of Southern Cultures in the Chesapeake, 1600–1800.* Chapel Hill: Univ. of North Carolina Press.
Larose, Serge
1977 The Meaning of Africa in Haitian Vodu. In *Symbols and Sentiments,* ed. Ioan M. Lewis, 85–116. London: Tavistock.

Latham, A. J. H.
1973   *Old Calabar, 1600–1800.* Oxford: Clarendon Press.
Law, Robin
1977   *The Oyo Empire, c. 1600–c. 1800.* Oxford, England: Clarendon Press.
Lichtenstein, Alex
1988   "That Disposition to Theft with which They Have Been Branded": Moral
        Economy, Slave Management, and the Law. *Journal of Social History* 21: 413–40
Linebaugh, Peter, and Marcus Rediker
1990   The Many-Headed Hydra: Sailors, Slaves, and the Atlantic Working Class in
        the Eighteenth Century. *Journal of Historical Sociology* 3: 225–52.
Littlefield, Daniel C.
1981   *Rice and Slaves: Ethnicity and the Slave Trade in Colonial South Carolina.* Baton
        Rouge: Louisiana State Univ. Press.
Lombardi, John V.
1974   Comparative Slave Systems in the Americas: A Critical Review. In *New Ap-
        proaches to Latin American History,* ed. Richard Graham and Peter H. Smith,
        156–74. Austin: Univ. of Texas Press.
Long, Edward
1970 [1774]   *The History of Jamaica.* London: Frank Cass.
Look Lai, Walton
1993   *Indentured Labor, Caribbean Sugar.* Baltimore, Md.: Johns Hopkins Univ.
        Press.
Lovejoy, Paul E., ed.
1981   *The Ideology of Slavery in Africa.* Beverly Hills, Calif.: Sage.
Lowenthal, Ira P.
1987   "Marriage Is 20, Children Are 21:" The Cultural Construction of Conjugality
        and the Family in Rural Haiti. Ph.D. diss., Johns Hopkins Univ.
Manning, Patrick
1990   *Slavery and African Life: Occidental, Oriental and African Slave Trades.* Cam-
        bridge: Cambridge Univ. Press.
McGlynn, Frank, and Seymour Drescher, eds.
1992   *The Meaning of Freedom: Economics, Politics and Culture after Slavery.* Pitts-
        burgh, Pa.: Univ. of Pittsburgh Press.
Meillassoux, Claude
1982   The Role of Slavery in the Economic and Social History of Sahelo-Sudanic
        Africa. In *Forced Migration,* ed. Joseph E. Inikori, 74–99. New York: Africana
        Publishing Company.
1986   *Anthropologie de l'esclavage.* Paris: Presses Universitaires de France.
Menard, Russell, and Stuart B. Schwartz
1993   Why African Slavery? Labor Force Transitions in Brazil, Mexico, and the
        Carolina Lowcountry. In *Slavery in the Americas,* ed. Wolfgang Binder, 89–
        114. Würzburg, Germany: Königshausen and Neumann.
Miers, Suzanne, and Richard Roberts, eds.
1988   *The End of Slavery in Africa.* Madison: Univ. of Wisconsin Press.
Miller, Joseph E.
1988   *Way of Death: Merchant Capitalism and the Angolan Slave Trade, 1730–1830.*
        Madison: Univ. of Wisconsin Press.
Mintz, Sidney W.
1959   Labor and Sugar in Puerto Rico and in Jamaica, 1800–1850. *Comparative
        Studies in Society and History* 1: 273–83.

1969 [1961]   Slavery and Emergent Capitalism. In *Slavery in the New World*, ed. Laura
Foner and Eugene D. Genovese, 27–37. Englewood Cliffs, N.J.: Prentice-Hall.
1977   The So-Called World System: Local Initiative and Local Response. *Dialectical Anthropology* 2: 253–70.
1978   Was the Plantation Slave a Proletarian? *Review* 2: 81–98.
1981   Economic Role and Cultural Tradition. In *The Black Woman Cross-Culturally*,
ed. Filomena Chioma Steady, 515–34. Cambridge, Mass.: Schenkman.
1985   *Sweetness and Power: The Place of Sugar in Modern History.* New York: Penguin.
1989 [1974]   *Caribbean Transformations.* New York: Columbia Univ. Press.
1993   Tasting Food, Tasting Freedom. In *Slavery in the Americas*, ed. Wolfgang
Binder, 257–75. Würzburg, Germany: Königshausen und Neumann.
Mintz, Sidney W., and Richard Price
1992 [1976]   *The Birth of African-American Culture: An Anthropological Perspective.*
Boston: Beacon Press. [Originally published as *An Anthropological Approach to
the Afro-American Past: A Caribbean Perspective.* ISHI Occasional Papers 2.
Philadelphia: Institute for the Study of Human Issues.]
Moreno Fraginals, Manuel
1976   *The Sugarmill: The Socioeconomic Complex of Sugar in Cuba.* New York:
Monthly Review Press.
1984   Cultural Contributions and Deculturation. In *African in Latin America*, ed.
Manuel Moreno Fraginals, 5–22. Paris: UNESCO.
Moreno Fraginals, Manuel; Frank Moya Pons; and Stanley L. Engerman, eds.
1985   *Between Slavery and Freedom: The Spanish-Speaking Caribbean in the Nineteenth
Century.* Baltimore, Md.: Johns Hopkins Univ. Press.
Morgan, Edmund S.
1972   Slavery and Freedom: The American Paradox. *Journal of American History* 59:
5–29.
1975   *American Slavery—American Freedom: The Ordeal of Colonial Virginia.* New
York: Norton.
Morgan, Philip D.
1982   Work and Culture: The Task System and the World of Lowcountry Blacks,
1700–1880. *William and Mary Quarterly* 39: 563–99.
1983   The Ownership of Property by Slaves in the Mid-Nineteenth-Century Low
Country. *Journal of Southern Studies* 49: 399–420.
1984   Black Life in Eighteenth-Century Charleston. *Perspectives in American History*
1: 187–232.
1988   Task and Gang Systems: The Organization of Labor on New World Plantations. In *Work and Labor in Early America*, ed. Stephen Innes, 189–220.
Chapel Hill: Univ. of North Carolina Press.
Morrissey, Marietta
1989   *Slave Women in the New World: Gender Stratification in the Caribbean.*
Lawrence: Univ. of Kansas Press.
Mullin, Michael
1985   Women and the Comparative Study of American Negro Slavery. *Slavery and
Abolition* 6: 25–40.
1992   *Africa in America: Slave Acculturation and Resistance in the American South and
the British Caribbean, 1736–1831.* Urbana: Univ. of Illinois Press.
Nash, Gary B.
1988   *Forging Freedom: The Formation of Philadelphia's Black Community, 1720–1840.*
Cambridge, Mass.: Harvard Univ. Press.

Nash, June
1981   Ethnographic Aspects of the World Capitalist System. *Annual Review of Anthropology* 10: 393–423.
Nieboer, Herman J.
1900   *Slavery as an Industrial System.* The Hague, Netherlands: Martinus Nijhoff.
Nishida, Mieko
1993   Manumission and Ethnicity in Urban Slavery: Salvador, Bahia, 1808–1888. *Hispanic American Historical Review* 73: 361–91.
Northup, David
1978   *Trade Without Rulers: Pre-Colonial Economic Development in South-Eastern Nigeria.* Oxford, England: Clarendon Press.
Oakes, James
1982   *The Ruling Race: A History of American Slaveholders.* New York: Knopf.
Okihiro, Gary, ed.
1986   *In Resistance: Studies in African, Caribbean, and Afro-American History.* Amherst: Univ. of Massachusetts Press.
Ortiz, Fernando
1947 [1940]   *Cuban Counterpoint.* Trans. Harriet de Orís. New York: Knopf.
1975 [1916]   *Los negros esclavos.* Havana, Cuba: Editorial Ciencias Sociales.
1986   *Los negros curros,* ed. Diana Iznaga. Havana, Cuba: Editorial Ciencias Sociales.
Palmer, Colin A.
1976   *Slaves of the White God: Blacks in Mexico, 1570–1650.* Cambridge: Cambridge Univ. Press.
Palmié, Stephan
1991   *Das Exil der Götter: Geschichte und Vorstellungswelt einer afrokubanischen Religion.* Frankfurt, Germany: Peter Lang.
1993   Ethnogenetic Processes and Cultural Transfer in Afro-American Slave Populations. In *Slavery in the Americas,* ed. Wolfgang Binder, 337–63. Würzburg, Germany: Königshausen and Neumann.
Paquette, Robert L.
1991   Social History Update: Slave Resistance and Social History. *Journal of Social History* 24: 681–85.
Patterson, Orlando
1982   *Slavery and Social Death.* Cambridge, Mass.: Harvard Univ. Press.
Peel, John D. Y.
1990   The Pastor and the Babalawo: The Interaction of Religions in Nineteenth Century Yorubaland. *Africa* 60: 338–69.
Philips, Ulrich B.
1963 [1929]   *Life and Labor in the Old South.* New York: Little, Brown.
Phillips, William D., Jr.
1985   *Slavery from Roman Times to the Early Transatlantic Trade.* Minneapolis: Univ. of Minnesota Press.
1991   The Old World Background of Slavery in the Americas. In *Slavery and the Rise of the Atlantic System,* ed. Barbara L. Solow, 43–61. Cambridge: Cambridge Univ. Press.
Price, Richard
1983   *First Time: The Historical Vision of an Afro-American People.* Baltimore, Md.: Johns Hopkins Univ. Press.
1990   *Alabi's World.* Baltimore, Md.: Johns Hopkins Univ. Press.

Prude, Jonathan
1991   To Look upon the "Lower Sort": Runaway Ads and the Appearance of Unfree
       Laborers in America, 1750–1800. *Journal of American History* 78: 124–59.
Ratekin, Mervyn
1954   The Early Sugar Industry in Española. *Hispanic American Historical Review* 34:
       1–19.
Rathbone, Richard
1985   Some Thoughts on Resistance to Enslavement in West Africa. In *Out of the
       House of Bondage*, ed. Gad Heuman, 11–22. London: Frank Cass.
Reis, João José
1982   Slave Rebellion in Brazil: The African Muslim Uprising in Bahia, 1835. Ph.D.
       diss., Univ. of Minnesota.
Robertson, Claire C., and Martin A. Klein, eds.
1983   *Women and Slavery in Africa.* Madison: Univ. of Wisconsin Press.
Rodney, Walter
1966   African Slavery and Other Forms of Social Oppression on the Upper Guinea
       Coast in the Context of the Atlantic Slave Trade. *Journal of African History* 8:
       431–43.
1972   *How Europe Underdeveloped Africa.* London: Bogle-L'Ouverture Publications.
Ryder, A. F. C.
1969   *Benin and the Europeans, 1485–1897.* London: Longmans.
Schuler, Monica
1980   *Alas, Alas, Kongo: A Social History of Indentured African Immigration into Ja-
       maica, 1841–1865.* Baltimore, Md.: Johns Hopkins Univ. Press.
Schwartz, Stuart B.
1977   Resistance and Accommodation in Eighteenth-Century Brazil: The Slaves'
       View of Slavery. *Hispanic American Historical Review* 57: 69–81.
1982   Patterns of Slaveholding in the Americas: New Evidence from Brazil. *Ameri-
       can Historical Review* 87: 55–86.
1985   *Sugar Plantations in the Formation of Brazilian Society: Bahia, 1550–1835.*
       Cambridge: Cambridge Univ. Press.
Scott, Rebecca J.
1985   *Slave Emancipation in Cuba: The Transition to Free Labor.* Princeton, N.J.:
       Princeton Univ. Press.
Scott, Rebecca J.; Seymour Drescher; Hebe Maria Mattos de Castro; George Reid
       Andrews; and Robert M. Levine
1988   *The Abolition of Slavery and the Aftermath of Emancipation in Brazil.* Durham,
       N.C.: Duke Univ. Press.
Sheridan, Richard
1986   The Maroons of Jamaica, 1730–1830: Livelihood, Demography, and Health. In
       Out of the House of Bondage, ed. Gad Heuman, 152–72. London: Frank Cass.
Silva, Eduardo
1993   *Prince of the People: The Life and Times of a Brazilian Free Man of Colour.* Lon-
       don: Verso.
Smith, Michael G.
1965   *The Plural Society in the British West Indies.* Berkeley: Univ. of California Press.
Sobel, Mechal
1979   *Trabelin' On: The Slave Journey to an Afro-Baptist Faith.* Westport, Conn.:
       Greenwood Press.

1987   *The World They Made Together: Black and White Values in Eighteenth-Century Virginia.* Princeton, N.J.: Princeton Univ. Press.
Solow, Barbara L., and Stanley L. Engerman, eds.
1987   *British Capitalism and Caribbean Slavery: The Legacy of Eric Williams.* Cambridge: Cambridge Univ. Press.
Sosa Rodríguez, Enrique
1982   *Los ñáñigos.* Havana, Cuba: Casa de las Américas.
Stern, Steve J.
1988   Feudalism, Capitalism, and the World System in the Perspective of Latin America and the Caribbean. *American Historical Review* 93: 829–72.
Stuckey, Sterling
1987   *Slave Culture: Nationalist Theory and the Foundation of Black America.* New York: Oxford Univ. Press.
Szwed, John F.
1974 [1969]   An American Anthropological Dilemma: The Politics of Afro-American Culture. In *Reinventing Anthropology,* ed. Dell Hymes, 153–81. New York: Vintage Books.
Tannenbaum, Frank
1946   *Slave and Citizen: The Negro in the Americas.* New York: Random House.
Terray, Emmanuel
1974   Long-Distance Exchange and the Formation of the State: The Case of the Abron Kingdom of Gyaman. *Economy and Society* 3: 315–45.
1983   Gold Production, Slave Labor, and State Intervention in Precolonial Akan Societies. *Research in Economic Anthropology* 5: 885–914.
Thoden van Velzen, H. U. E, and W. van Wetering
1988   *The Great Father and the Danger: Religious Cults, Material Forces, and Collective Fantasies in the World of the Surinamese Maroons.* Caribbean Series 9, Koninklijk Instituut voor Taal-, Land- en Volkenkunde. Dordrecht, Netherlands: Foris.
Thompson, Edgar T.
1932   The Plantation. Ph.D. diss., Univ. of Chicago.
Thompson, Robert Faris
1983   *Flash of the Spirit: African and Afro-American Art and Philosophy.* New York: Random House.
Thornton, John K.
1992   *Africa and Africans in the Making of the Atlantic World, 1400–1680.* New York: Cambridge Univ. Press.
Tomich, Dale W.
1990   *Slavery in the Circuit of Sugar: Martinique and the World Economy, 1830–1848.* Baltimore, Md.: Johns Hopkins Univ. Press.
Trouillot, Michel-Rolph
1982   Motion in the System: Coffee, Color, and Slavery in Eighteenth-Century Saint-Domingue. *Review* (Binghamton, N.Y.), vol. 3: 331–88.
Turner, Mary
1982   *Slaves and Missionaries: The Disintegration of Jamaican Society, 1787–1834.* Urbana: Univ. of Illinois Press.
1991   Slave Workers, Subsistence and Labour Bargaining: Amity Hall, Jamaica, 1805–1832. In *The Slaves' Economy,* ed. Ira Berlin and Philip D. Morgan, 92–106. London: Frank Cass.

Van Deburg, William L.
1979   *The Slave Drivers.* New York: Oxford Univ. Press.
Van den Berghe, Pierre L.
1967   *Race and Racism: A Comparative Perspective.* New York: John Wiley.
Van Lier, Rudolph A. J.
1971   *Frontier Society: A Social Analysis of the History of Suriname.* The Hague, Netherlands: Martinus Nijhof.
Wade, Richard C.
1964   *Slavery in the Cities: The South, 1820–1860.* New York: Oxford Univ. Press.
Wallerstein, Immanuel
1974–89   *The Modern World System.* New York: Academic Press.
Warner-Lewis, Maureen
1991   *Guinea's Other Suns: The African Dynamic in Trinidad Culture.* Dover, England: Majority Press.
Watson, James L.
1980   Slavery as an Institution: Open and Closed Systems. In *African and Asian Systems of Slavery*, ed. James L. Watson, 1–15. Berkeley: Univ. of California Press.
————, ed.
1980   *African and Asian Systems of Slavery.* Berkeley: Univ. of California Press.
White, Deborah Grey
1985   *Ar'n't I a Woman? Female Slaves in the Plantation South.* New York: Norton.
White, Shane. 1991. *Somewhat More Independent: The End of Slavery in New York City, 1770–1810.* Athens: Univ. of Georgia Press.
Wolf, Eric
1971 [1959]   Specific Aspects of Plantation Systems in the New World: Community Sub-Cultures and Social Classes. In *Peoples and Cultures of the Caribbean*, ed. Michael M. Horowitz, 163–78. Garden City, N.Y.: Natural History Press.
1982   *Europe and the People Without History.* Berkeley: Univ. of California Press.
Wood, Peter H.
1974   *Black Majority: Negroes in Colonial South Carolina, From 1670 Through the Stono Rebellion.* New York: Knopf.
1978   "I Did the Best I Could for My Day": The Study of Early Black History during the Second Reconstruction, 1960 to 1976. *William and Mary Quarterly* 35: 185–225.

1 | "Analyze the Sounds"

Frederick Douglass's Invitation to Modern Historians of Slavery

David W. Blight

In the past two decades, especially in the field of literature, the study of slave narratives has become a veritable industry. Slave autobiographies, particularly those as self-consciously artistic as Frederick Douglass's, have been mined by critics to uncover the meanings of every metaphor, every image, every silence or absence, the use of gendered language, and indeed the mastery of language itself. These works are seen as playing a role in the creation of an African-American literary tradition. Some critics have persuasively identified the influence of American and African-American religious traditions, particularly the jeremiad and the black chanted sermon, in the slave narratives. Still others have given the best of the slave narratives their place in the republic of American letters—as "songs of the self" and evocations of romantic individualism—while demonstrating that the narratives often were fierce critiques of the hypocrisy of republican America.[1] Literary critics, of course, have their own critical agendas, and they have done much to shape the direction of African-American studies in recent years. Their search for sources—texts—sometimes resembles and sometimes differs from the work of historians or anthropologists. Exactly how the uses of slave narratives (and interviews) in the projects of humanistic historians, social scientists, and literary critics do or do not overlap is a question I shall leave for another essay. My concern here is not so much the specific ways in which slave narratives do or do not allow us access to particular aspects of slave culture, but rather to indicate how Douglass's most famous autobiographical work all along has been pointing us toward the question at the heart of this volume, and especially to its historiographical and epistemological implications.

Did New World slavery foster slave cultures or cultures of slavery? Understanding the irony at the heart of this question is still the complex agenda of slavery studies. Was there an autonomous and creative slave culture through which slaves survived and resisted dehumanization? Or was slavery, in its huge variety of contexts, a system that rendered most slaves victims of irresistible power? Are we explaining African-American or Afro-Caribbean cultures that evolved within or because of oppression, or cultures that were inherently destructive of human personality altogether? How do we generalize about this question? Has the very nature of chattel slavery in the United States South, given all of America's national mythology of mission and republican virtue, caused North Americans persistently to discuss slavery in terms of ideal constructs: pure victims at one extreme and autonomously cunning and creative slaves at the other—"Sambos" or "Rebels," to go back to the way Kenneth Stampp urged us not to pose the question (Stampp 1971)? Are Americans sometimes just too teleological or too identity-conscious to understand that cultures are almost always in transition? Moreover, is there something about the way emancipation came about in the United States—through total war and social revolution—that has caused Americans to approach slavery as a totalizing institution, a world that was either evil or benign? "On the hard rock of racial, social, and economic exploitation and injustice," wrote Lawrence Levine, "black Americans forged and nurtured a culture" (Levine 1977: xi). But how hard was the rock? How mobile or immobile in different contexts? How did slaves maneuver or manipulate the sheer power or weight of that rock? Did the slaves pound on that rock with their labor by day, at most chipping away at the infinity of its weight, while walking around it by night living in an inner sacred world of music and folk belief that allowed them to sustain human dignity? How many were crushed by the rock? And how many survived by reshaping the rock itself? How many found a home in that rock, and how many lived only an enduring nightmare? The slave narratives are, indeed, replete with quests for a sense of "home" (Andrews 1986: 167–204).

Levine's work on the slave songs is one of the most fulsome responses to what we might call Frederick Douglass's invitation to modern historians. What, indeed, was it like to be a slave? What were the slaves' daily feelings, yearnings, crises, hardships? Douglass, like other authors of the best slave narratives, gave many answers to these questions. Despite the propagandistic nature of a work like Douglass's *Nar-*

rative (which is full of abolitionist sentimentalism as well as the language of the self-made hero ascending to his destiny), it allows us access to the psychological world of a slave. And that world, like the apparent paradox this volume explores, is full of antithesis and ironic reversals. Douglass's discussion of slave life constantly moves between horror and joy, between a totalitarian model of dehumanization and one in which slaves fashion creative resistance, between despotism and the quest for freedom, sometimes realized. Douglass's rich use of irony and oppositions can help us see the complex nature of slave resistance. On what Douglass called "The Great House Farm," his owner on the eastern shore of Maryland, Colonel Lloyd, had a magnificent garden. It was exotic and the object of awe and admiration among slaves, but it also offered an education in both the risks and the righteousness of "stealing fruit." The totalitarian capacity of masters to sell their slaves away for profit or spite is balanced by the slaves' control of their own language: the slaveholders' power was blunted by the slaves' "maxim, that a still tongue makes a wise head. They suppress the truth rather than take the consequences of telling it, and in so doing prove themselves a part of the human family" (Douglass 1993 [1845]: 48, 50). Thus, Douglass argues, the slaves' *humanity* manifests itself in a cunning accommodation to, and subversion of, evil authority.

Douglass makes this point most subtly, and anticipates modern historians' treatment of slave culture most directly, in his discussion of slave music. He portrays the slave songs as primarily expressions of sorrow and lament, but he also indicates the inseparability of the sacred and the secular in black folk music. Everyday life was mixed with appeals for deliverance in the most deeply spiritual tones. The slaves, wrote Douglass, "would sometimes sing the most pathetic sentiment in the most rapturous tone, and the most rapturous sentiment in the most pathetic tone." And "into all of their songs they would manage to weave something of the Great House Farm." The scene in which Douglass discusses music is that of a mass of slaves walking toward the Great House Farm on "allowance day." The "dense old woods . . . reverberate" with song as groups of selected slaves congregate at Colonel Lloyd's mansion for their periodic allotments of food and clothing. Here, Douglass juxtaposes the dehumanizing power structure of slavery with the slaves' own best means of inner relief and self-expression, their material sustenance with their spiritual sustenance. And he leaves an invitation for historians and folklorists: "If anyone wishes to be impressed with the soul-killing effects of slavery, let him go to Colonel Lloyd's plantation, and, on allowance day, place himself in the deep pine woods, and there let him, in silence, analyze the sounds that shall pass through the chambers of his soul." *Analyze the sounds*. Since the 1960s, this is precisely what a whole host of scholars have done with the lyrics and forms of slave music, as well as other forms of expressive culture. Scholars have found various ways to gain access to the piney woods, to listen to the slaves' own voices as they created an inner moral order out of potential chaos and forged what Levine has called an "improvisational communal consciousness." But Douglass's invitation, of course, was not to a concert, nor to any sort of Smithsonian celebration of folklife, nor in this case to a romantic a search for authentic culture. Embedded in an abolitionist polemic, this was an invitation to antislavery voters, and eventually to historians who might be willing or able to listen for the sheer range of ironic twists in the slaves' manipulation of hope and despair—to feel in their own souls, as Douglass put it, "the highest joy and the deepest sadness" (Levine 1977: 15; Douglass 1993 [1845]: 46–47). The best work of the revisionist culture-as-resistance school of slavery historiography has come from just such efforts.[2]

It might be said that the Douglass of 1845, who already was becoming the bourgeois man of letters and affairs, distanced himself from the "folk" in his comments on slave music. "I did not, when a slave," wrote Douglass, "understand the deep meaning of those rude and apparently incoherent songs." But even as he separated himself from the "wild songs," he admired his fellow slaves' spontaneous ability to "compose and sing as they went along, consulting neither time nor tune." Why should such ambivalence surprise us late-twentieth-century scholars? Just as Douglass had learned to negotiate the mine field of slavery's human relationships on the Great House Farm, and in the different environment of the streets of Baltimore, so as also an autobiographer he negotiated his way into the consciences of different audiences. Nowhere does he describe the slave songs (representative of a larger slave culture) as unworthy of attention or study. Quite the contrary. To the songs he traced his own "first glimmering conception of the dehumanizing character of slavery." Moreover, in the songs, slaves fashioned an art form out of daily life and "breathed the . . . complaint of souls boiling over with the bitterest anguish." A slave song, said Douglass, was a "prayer to God for deliverance from chains" (Douglass 1993 [1845]: 46–47). Such, precisely, were the slave narratives themselves: ex-slaves using the music of words, writing songs of abolitionism, sometimes like psalms of deliverance and sometimes in the tone of legalistic indictment.[3]

In recent years there have been numerous indications that the culture-as-resistance interpretation of American slavery may be undergoing a challenge, perhaps even a kind of post-revisionist critique, or a necessary correction. In a 1983 essay, Peter Kolchin (while writing his superb comparative study of American slavery and Russian serfdom) suggested that the culture-as-resistance paradigm forged in the 1970s had gone too far "toward celebration and even mystification of slave life" and perhaps had exaggerated the cohesiveness or autonomy of slave culture. Kolchin worried that the distortions posited in Stanley Elkins's "Sambo thesis" might have been replaced by new distortions, a myth of the slave community in which control of the quarters allowed slaves to fashion a world of "loving, cheerful, cooperative, and resourceful" families. Kolchin insisted that "playing down the injury slavery caused its victims is [as] questionable" as the overemphasis on that victimization in the Elkins thesis. Kolchin spoke for those who wanted the "pain, brutality, and disruption" of slavery put back on stage and given equal billing with slave resilience and cultural creativity (Kolchin 1983: 581–82).

Kolchin had a point. But whether he intended it or not, here again we see the risk of stark opposites: destruction over against a sometimes celebrated transcendence. Kolchin's larger target in that essay was the general aversion to comparative history among scholars of slavery in the United States South, a well-taken point about the entire American historical profession. His claims were based on his findings about the great differences among Jamaican, Russian, and American South slave "communities." He wanted to demonstrate just what illusive concepts "community" and "resistance" can be—a problem that this volume is once again illuminating. Kolchin challenged historians of the American South to observe the significance of *resident owners* in all areas save the great rice region of coastal South Carolina and Georgia (a situation very different from the Caribbean or Russian contexts). To the extent that slaveowner "paternalism" shaped the master-slave relationship in America, Kolchin argued, contrary to Eugene Genovese, that it obstructed black autonomy or cultural "breathing space," as Genovese put it. Constant intervention in the lives of slaves by their owners, however benign or brutal its motives, could have the effect of blunting collective forms of resistance. Kolchin—perhaps based on his reading of slave narratives like Douglass's, which are full of tales of heroic individual rebellion—argues that most slave resistance in America took an individual form. He concludes that the notion of culture as resistance not only needs a comparative perspective but also may sometimes be the product of historians' imaginations.

Heroic escape narratives, however, reflected only a small corner of slave life. Most slaves, of course, never even attempted physically to escape. Some, no doubt, were psychologically crushed by the system, but many more also managed to survive and live meaningful lives at least in part through "culture" that was no less real for being created in tragic circumstances (Kolchin 1983: 582–87; Genovese 1974: 3–7). Such has been the lot of most peasant cultures, and their conception of tragedy would not likely be the same as that of late-twentieth-century scholars. Whatever his differences with certain arguments and fellow historians, Kolchin, from a comparative perspective, posed the right questions.

Some 1970s scholarship doubtless romanticized the folk—a slave community imagined more, perhaps, out of modern civil rights or black power imperatives than real data. Kolchin's own favorite example of a book that went too far in such celebration is Thomas L. Webber's *Deep Like the Rivers: Education in the Slave Quarter Community* (1978). But when I started teaching in the early seventies, following the revolution in slavery historiography, I did not think I was reading about a myth of the "idyllic slave community" or a world, as Kolchin puts it, where "life as a slave must have been an enviable experience" (Kolchin 1983: 601). Robert Fogel and Stanley Engerman's *Time on the Cross* (1972) certainly stimulated that kind of public discussion.[4] But Genovese's compelling and moving discussion of slave religion in a world forged by slaves, not so much on a rock as out of possibly malleable clay, is not at all a world without pain. Indeed, the price of the reciprocity bought in the paternalistic relationship Genovese described (or theorized) might be a great deal of anguish. The risk of wearing the masks necessary to live in this bewildering world of emotional negotiation, as Genovese argued and as Nathan Huggins evoked so powerfully in *Black Odyssey* (1990 [1977]: 179–82), was that the masks might become permanent. There may have been victims on both sides of the master-slave relationship. I am reminded of C. Vann Woodward's classic essay, "The Irony of Southern History," in which he says: "The ironic interpretation of history is rare and difficult. In the nature of things the participants in an ironic situation are rarely conscious of the irony, else they would not become its victims" (Woodward 1968 [1960]: 138). As historians we probably should apply that maxim to ourselves as well as to our subjects.

An especially interesting recent example of a book that may indicate some kind of post-revisionist turn in American slavery historiography is Michael Tadman's *Speculators and Slaves: Masters, Traders, and Slaves in the Old South* (1989). Through remarkable new research in slave-traders' own papers, Tadman takes on the most sensitive questions about American slavery: the extent of the domestic slave trade in general and of forced family separations in particular (Tadman 1989). Tadman effectively revives this debate, which in the popular imagination is at least as old as the characters who argue about it on Ohio riverboats in Harriet Beecher Stowe's *Uncle Tom's Cabin.*[5]

In the American preoccupation with southern distinctiveness, it has been easy to forget that a massive westward movement was part of southern history as well. Tadman shows that in the 1820s alone an estimated 150,000 slaves moved from the Upper South to the Lower South, and in the even more expansionist 1850s, more than 300,000 slaves "migrated" to the cotton and sugar kingdoms of the Deep South. The question has always been: how much of this slave movement was due to planter migration westward, and how much to outright sale? Tadman concludes that, in the period 1820–60, fully 60 to 70 percent of all interregional slave movement was due to market-driven speculative trade. Tadman's typical migrating slaveholder moved westward with only a few slaves or alone and then, in time, purchased a large number of slaves in major trading centers such as New Orleans, where Tadman estimates that as many as 3,000 slaves were available in any given trading season (winter and spring). Some of Tadman's results are stunning: for the entire antebellum era, approximately 10 percent of Upper South slaves were forcibly removed to the Lower South each decade. For children and teenagers, the chance of being "sold South" to "Georgia men" was even greater. The vast majority of slaves were purchased alone as what he calls "very deliberately considered acquisitions." Moreover, as for forced separations of slave marriages (a question hotly contested in 1970s scholarship), Tadman concludes that approximately one in three first marriages were so "destroyed" among Upper South slaves. Tadman also skillfully illuminates the actual process of overland slavetrading—the long journeys of slave "coffles"; the highly organized, market-driven nature of this ugly business; slave "jails" and other holding stations along the routes; collecting and resale centers; pricing patterns and bargains; the forced dancing at auction time; the use of "paddles" rather than the lash as punishment so as not to scar valuable property; the advertising language of the traders; and so forth (Tadman 1989: 20, 141, 171). After a close reading of Tadman's evidence and his narrative, some readers may cast aside the works of Stuckey, Levine, Genovese, Gutman, et al.; they may once again "analyze the sounds" but hear in the slave songs only sorrow for its own sake.

But Tadman's book has a larger historiographical agenda. His ultimate aim is to establish that domestic slavetrading "unlocks" the mental worlds of masters and slaves, providing the "vital yardstick" by which blacks and their owners judged each other. This search for an essence in the master-slave relationship keeps Tadman busy determining responsibility for such a large traffic in human flesh, and he repeatedly reminds us that the charges must be leveled equally against the traders and their clients. He persuasively challenges the Old South's myth of the evil slave-trader who, with "Yankee" origins and instincts, preyed upon the well-meaning patriarchs of gracious plantations (Tadman 1989: 9, 179–210). Tadman is not much given to irony and ambiguity, and he treats mythology as though it were mere propaganda or disinformation.

Tadman's real target is Genovese's "paternalism" thesis. Slaves did have sufficient cultural space in which to sustain their beleaguered families, argues Tadman, acknowledging some of the findings of the culture-as-resistance school. But this was not due to any reciprocal bargain with their masters. Scholars will forever differ about the accuracy of Genovese's complicated view of paternalism in the Old South. Looking exclusively from the perspective of slavetrading, Tadman simply does not consider Genovese's notion of a "dialectic of accommodation and resistance" to be a historical reality at all. He believes evidence from slavetrading "specifically" will controvert "any broad theory" of paternalism and become its negating litmus test. What to Genovese was a rich web of dialectical paradox is to Tadman only elaborate mythology. Without acknowledging Genovese's own discussion of the deep racism and tragic consequences of paternalism and slavetrading, Tadman takes a blunt stand: scholars "should not take some compromise middle position along the spectrum of possible interpretations." (Tadman 1989: 218, 133, 211).

Such reasoning may find an appreciative audience these days, and not always for the right reasons. Today it would be a rare African-American studies, southern history, or comparative slavery course that did not give students a big dose of post-Elkins scholarship. In the early 1990s, however, one must wonder whether more than a decade of Reaganism, Thatcherism, resurgent racism, reactionary racial and ethnic chauvinism, warring nationalisms, and a deepening racial poverty on several continents has not led a new generation of scholars to ponder slavery anew, to answer the seventies' revisionists by putting, as Elkins ironically defined it, "the rhythm of right and wrong" back into the slavery debate (Elkins 1959: 1).

Writing in 1975, Willie Lee Rose hailed a "salutory new maturity" in the multitude of works published recently on slavery. After some very contentious years in the field of black history, Rose felt buoyed by a "new confidence that what long ago happened need not determine what will occur tomorrow" (Rose 1982: 176). There is room for disagreement over whether that mid-1970s context merited Rose's optimism. But her sanguine claim is worth reconsidering as we contemplate where we are in slavery historiography in the 1990s. With Kolchin's challenges ten years ago and especially Tadman's recent book as guides, it may be worth asking whether today or "tomorrow" once again is helping to shape "what long ago happened."

Finally, the Tadman-Genovese comparison might be further instructive. In tearing down the paternalism thesis, it seems to me, Tadman runs the risk of ignoring that the best analyses of slave culture and master-slave reciprocity are not merely "compromise middle positions"; they are a complex vision of human creativity and adaptability. Realism—and comparison—can offer valuable correctives in scholarship, and we would do well to look unflinchingly at the horror of those slave coffles, to *analyze the sounds* of the chains and the auctioneers shouting out, "No. 1 Negroes" or "Buying by the pound here!" But we still need the careful use of broad theory in the study of slavery across its many contexts, lest we return again to an uncomplicated victimization thesis that many of our students may find compatible with the world they are living in. Tadman and Genovese were using different "yardsticks" by which to make judgments. Genovese begins *Roll Jordan Roll* with the claim that slavery "bound two peoples together in bitter antagonism" and "organic relationship," while he ends the book with his evocative portrayal of slave religion as the anguished hope and sustenance, the "bright and morning star," of slave life. Tadman begins and ends his book with the claim that slavery was about destructive uses of power, and that masters and slaves lived in "separate, segregated worlds." As we once again witness the contrast of the bitter and destructive with the ironic and prophetic elements in slave experience—rooted now as before in differing assumptions and uses of opposites—we might keep watch for both parts of what David Brion Davis, in 1974, called the "rewards and perils of presentism" in slavery historiography (Genovese 1974: 660; Davis 1986 [1974]: 197). We might also, once in a while, take up Douglass's invitation, and listen for the tragedy *and* the transcendence in slave cultures.

Notes

1. For critical work on the slave narratives, see Andrews (1986), Charles T. Davis and Gates (1985), and Starling (1988 [1981]). For a survey of the revival of interest in slave narratives and an argument for their use by historians, see Blassingame (1977: xvii–lxv).
2. On Douglass's discussion of slave music, see Stuckey (1990: 32–35).

3. On the psalmlike qualities of Douglass's *Narrative*, see Blight (1993: 1–20).
4. On the reception of Fogel and Engerman's *Time on the Cross*, see Parish (1989: 32–41).
5. For a review essay on Tadman, see Blight (1991: 37–42).

References

Andrews, William L.
1986   *To Tell a Free Story: The First Century of Afro-American Autobiography.* Urbana: Univ. of Illinois Press.
John W. Blassingame, ed.
1977   *Slave Testimony: Two Centuries of Letters, Speeches, Interviews, and Autobiographies.* Baton Rouge: Louisiana State Univ. Press.
Blight, David W.
1991   The World the Slave Traders Made: Is There a Postrevisionism in Slavery Historiography? *Reviews in American History* 19: 37–42.
1993   Introduction. In Frederick Douglass, *Narrative of the Life of Frederick Douglass, An American Slave, Written by Himself,* ed. David W. Blight, 1–20. Boston: Bedford Books.
Davis, Charles T., and Henry Louis Gates, Jr., eds.
1985   *The Slave's Narrative.* New York: Oxford Univ. Press.
Davis, David Brion
1986 [1974]   Slavery and the Post–World War II Historians. In David Brion Davis, *From Homicide to Slavery: Studies in American Culture.* New York: Oxford Univ. Press, 187–206.
Douglass, Frederick
1993 [1845]   *Narrative of the Life of Frederick Douglass, An American Slave, Written by Himself,* ed. David W. Blight. Boston: Bedford Books.
Elkins, Stanley M.
1959   *Slavery: A Problem in American Institutional and Intellectual Life.* New York: Oxford Univ. Press.
Fogel, Robert, and Stanley Engerman
1972   *Time on the Cross: The Economics of American Negro Slavery.* Boston: Little, Brown, and Co.
Genovese, Eugene D.
1974   *Roll, Jordan Roll: The World the Slaves Made.* New York: Pantheon.
Huggins, Nathan I.
1990 [1977]   *Black Odyssey: The African American Ordeal in Slavery.* New York: Vintage.
Kolchin, Peter
1983   Reevaluating the Antebellum Slave Community: A Comparative Perspective. *Journal of American History* 88: 581–603.
Levine, Lawrence W.
1977   *Black Culture and Black Consciousness: Afro-American Folk Thought from Slavery to Freedom.* New York: Oxford Univ. Press.

Parish, Peter J.
1989   *Slavery: History and the Historians.* New York: Harper and Row.
Rose, Willie Lee
1982   The New Slavery Studies: An Old Reaction or a New Maturity? In *Slavery and Freedom,* ed. William W. Freehling. Baltimore, Md.: Johns Hopkins Univ. Press.
Stampp, Kenneth M.
1971   Rebels and Sambos: The Search for the Negro's Personality in Slavery. *Journal of Southern History* 37: 367–92.
Starling, Marion Wilson
1988 [1981]   *The Slave Narrative: Its Place in American History.* Boston: G. K. Hall.
Stuckey, Sterling
1990   "Ironic Tenacity": Frederick Douglass's Seizure of the Dialectic. In *Frederick Douglass: New Literary and Historical Essays,* ed. Eric J. Sundquist, 32–35. New York: Cambridge Univ. Press.
Tadman, Michael
1989   *Speculators and Slaves: Masters, Traders, and Slaves in the Old South.* Madison: Univ. of Wisconsin Press.
Webber, Thomas L.
1978   *Deep Like the Rivers: Education in the Slave Quarter Community.* New York: Norton.
Woodward, C. Vann
1968 [1960]   The Irony of Southern History. In C. Vann Woodward, *The Burden of Southern History,* 121–45. Baton Rouge: Louisiana State Univ. Press.

2 | Slave Life on Caribbean Sugar Plantations

Some Unanswered Questions

Sidney W. Mintz

Today, no serious student of New World slavery can ignore the violent, often inspiring, resistance with which slaves repeatedly confronted the armed defenders of the system under which both slave and master lived. Yet there was a time when, in order to establish that the slaves truly abhorred their condition, historians and anthropologists considered it absolutely essential to document such resistance (Aptheker 1943, Herskovits 1941). This may seem bizarre to us now; but it wasn't bizarre a half-century ago. People could not imagine what slavery had been like. That is why Herbert Aptheker, who often was asked why the slaves revolted, always gave the same answer: the slaves revolted because of slavery (Okihiro 1986, Paquette 1991). The truth about slave resistance had been thoroughly concealed by the time that the 1883 Civil Rights cases ended civil rights for African-American freedpersons in the United States. Soon, theories based upon the assumption of African-American racial predisposition to enslavement flowered. Among the apostles of such theories, for example, was the sociologist Albert Galloway Keller, who wrote that slaves of African origin were naturally fitted by temperament to servitude (Keller 1908: 145, 282). U. G. Weatherly, also a sociologist, was even clearer: "The Negro belongs perhaps to the most docile and modifiable of all races" (1923: 242). In 1908, the year that Keller's book appeared, eighty-nine African-Americans were lynched in the U.S. By 1923, when Weatherly's article was published, the number had fallen to twenty-nine. Perhaps the descendants of the slaves were becoming docile enough to avoid being lynched quite so often.

Whatever we make of this earlier period in the study of slave life, it nonetheless is a fact that during the nearly four centuries that slavery flourished in this hemisphere, only a tiny fraction of daily life consisted of open resistance. Instead, most of life then, like most of life now, was spent living; and most of it was lived in daily, even perfunctory, association with the holders of power. Hence to limit oneself to the study of violent resistance is to avert one's eyes from most of African-American history.

That said, it is true that a close look at the everyday is not always inspiring. What people sometimes were compelled to endure under slavery can make us wonder at times how such a system survived at all. Thomas Thistlewood's remarkable diaries, a record of his experiences during more than thirty years as an overseer in Jamaica, are one of many sources that provide a chilling counterpoise to the saga of violent resistance. Thistlewood wrote all sorts of things down, and many of his entries seem merely prosaic. The one for July 19, 1760, for example, reads somewhat wistfully: "Gave negroes molasses these three days past, yet they destroy cane [by eating it] sadly."

However, Thistlewood did not like the slaves destroying cane by eating it, and he was determined to maintain discipline. The entry for May 25, 1756, reads: "Derby [a slave] catched by Port Royal eating canes. Had him well flogged and pickled [vinegar or salt put on the lacerations], then made Hector shit in his mouth." This monstrous statement is recorded matter-of-factly. At Egypt plantation, where Derby worked, Ward tells us, "this treatment was subsequently referred to as 'Derby's dose'" (Ward 1988: 27). Thistlewood does not tell us how he "made" Hector do this to Derby, nor how Derby was immobilized so that it might be done to him. Here we are, amid the everyday life of the slaves, and we encounter an everyday form of plantation discipline— used not to punish insolence or violence, but to punish a slave for eating sugar cane. Yet the diaries do not provide evidence that Thistlewood was a maniac or even a sadist. We are merely gazing at one day in the life of an overseer, and one day in the life of a slave (Ward 1988).

But to look at the everyday surely does not mean to turn one's back on the study of resistance. No matter how inhumane the system, people *were* prepared to resist it, and did so in various ways. During the last half-century, in producing a broader picture of social behavior in New World slave societies, scholars also began looking at what has come to be called day-to-day resistance (Herskovits 1941, Bauer and Bauer 1942). Herskovits's students, Raymond Bauer and Alice Bauer, writing just a bit more than fifty years ago, documented behavior such as malingering, destruction of tools and farm animals, self-injury, and abortion, which they interpret as being among the ways that the slaves might fight back.

But the difficulty posed by what is called passive or covert resistance is precisely that we must *infer* the will of the actor. It is not that resistance has not been studied. Even though one scholar recently chose to call its study "fashionable" (Hanley 1987: 210), we have seen that Herskovits (1941) and Aptheker (1943), not to mention C. L. R. James (1938) and Eric Williams (1944), had long been its students. But if resistance is not violent, then we must divine intentions, for they are not told to us, and we cannot prove them. Recently Trouillot has suggested that resistance is a word that

> can be easily trivialized nowadays. Everything can become resistance to the point that we are not sure whether or not the word stands for an empirical generalization, an analytical category, or a vague yet fashionable label for unrelated situations. Unquestioned dichotomies such as "passive" versus "active," "overt" and "covert" may or may not be appropriate . . . Neither can we say *a priori* the extent to which resistance is dependent on the cognition, let alone the intentionality, of the subject. In some cases, we may never know the precise intentions or motives of the subject . . . In others, the unintended consequences of action may have greater impact on the future than the subject's state of mind at the moment of action. (Trouillot 1992: 9)

There are even different ways of saying what resistance is. It is often not easy to tell; and its definition may change with time and context. The enumeration by Bauer and Bauer is concerned with acts that look like resistance, even if the intentions of the actors are unprovable. Such deeds as suicide and abortion are violent, and doubtless hurt the planters, financially and possibly otherwise. Other acts might be judged "resistant" even though they were neutral in their consequences, so far as the planters were concerned—not hurting them, but not helping them, either.

Yet there are other categories of slave activity that, over the years, have come to be labeled "resistance" that may even have served to *help* the planters. These activities pose different problems. A highly tentative typology might end up with four categories:

(1) Violent resistance. We know what it is, and we are confident that we know the intentions of the actors.
(2) Nonviolent resistance. We don't really know whether it is resistance, if we have to base our judgment on intent alone; but the consequences lead us to believe that it is.
(3) Nonviolent nonresistance. We may not see how it can be resistance,

particularly if we have intent in mind; but it includes acts the consequences of which are not all predictable, some of which may be to
the noticeable disadvantage of the planters.

(4) Finally, that which, for lack of a better term, is here called "cultural
resistance," following arguments of Bastide 1978 [1960] and Mullin
1992, and to some extent of the present author (Mintz 1969, 1971,
1981).

In pursuit of the everyday, it is to the third of these—nonviolent nonresistance—that the argument turns.

In 1936, the Fabian socialist ex-governor of Jamaica, Sydney Haldane
Lord Olivier, referred in his book, *Jamaica the Blessed Isle,* to the cultivation tradition of Jamaican slaves:

> It was not generally realised in England that the slaves in Jamaica were in
> quite a different position from the wage-working classes at home, be-
> cause the estates did not either supply them with food, or provide them
> with cash to buy it. They grew it for themselves, so that, after emancipa-
> tion, provided they could occupy an acre or two of the land they already
> used, they did not need to work for wages to feed themselves. (Olivier
> 1936: 108)

Beginning around 1952, the present writer tried to find the links in
Jamaican history between the activities of those slaves who were engaged in the independent production and marketing of food, and general changes in their status and bargaining positions. In an early publication on this subject, slave production was described as the underlayer
of Caribbean marketing, long before freedom came (Mintz 1955). A
few years later (Mintz 1961), a preliminary classification of the rural
populations of the Caribbean was attempted, using for the first time
such terms as "proto-peasantry" and "*palenqueros*" (to describe the maroon runaway peasantries). These ideas were later enlarged upon (Mintz
1989 [1974]).

What has been most quoted in this connection was the claim that
Caribbean peasantries represented both "*a mode of response* and *a mode
of resistance* to imposed styles of life" (Mintz 1974: 132–33). This rendering appears to have caught the imagination of some scholars,[1] perhaps because it raises rather matter-of-factly the possibility that the same act may
turn out over time to be accommodative *and* resistant, no matter what
we choose to make of the slaves' personal motives or intentions.

But this formulation somewhat inadvertently opened the door to a wider vision of the forms that resistance might take. A good example of where this has carried us is provided in a recent paper by Gaspar:

> At the core of relations between masters and slaves was the subtle and complex interaction of slave resistance and the masters' quest for control. Slaves, individually or collectively, persistently pressed to open up the cracks in the system of slavery to achieve greater autonomy; slaveowners discovered that measured compromise and selective concession could be less counterproductive than vengeful punishment, although in extreme cases, such as slave revolt, conspiracy to revolt, or physical assaults on whites, slaves were punished to the fullest extent of the law. Slaveowners, recognizing the possibility of revolt, were persuaded to rely on methods other than brute force to win the cooperation of the slaves. The resistance of the slaves therefore contributed to their survival.
>
> Slave resistance must be broadly understood to include forms of slave behavior other than insurrection. Suicide, theft, lying, infanticide, insolence, insubordination, laziness, feigned illness—these were weapons that slaves possessed and used. Such day-to-day resistance, largely individual and nonconfrontational, was essential to survival. In fact, every willed response of the slaves to bend the system in their favor, to secure space for themselves within it, could be interpreted as resistance, even though such responses can also be interpreted as adaptation. Paradoxically, slave resistance involved some accommodation with slavery. (Gaspar 1991: 130–31)

The present writer was reminded by this passage of his own work on the same theme somewhat earlier (Mintz 1969, 1970, 1971) and agrees with much of it. But one aspect of Gaspar's formulation in particular deserves attention. To define resistance as including "every willed response of the slaves to bend the system" poses a dilemma precisely because we cannot tell when a response is willed nor what intention may lie behind it.[2] Hence this definition bypasses the problem of intent while making the specification of resistance tautological.

Recently Michael Mullin has widened still further the way in which resistance is to be defined; this brings the argument to the fourth category. Mullin divides those who look at slave reactions to oppression into two groups. There are those who see the slaves as victims, and those who see the slaves as rebels. Of the latter, he writes:

This approach amplifies the insight of the Brazilianist Roger Bastide that slave resistance was often cultural as well as political: the resistance of a people to being swallowed up by a foreign way of life. In this case resistance may be understood as a refusal to abandon one's values and traditions as well as—at another more familiar level—singular acts ranging from quiet sabotage to organizing and fighting back. (Mullin 1992: 2)

The concept of cultural resistance is real; its manifestations are certainly worthy of study. But we have come a great distance, conceptually, from Nat Turner and the Haitian Revolution. Have we come so far as to neutralize or invalidate the analytic value of the very concept of resistance?

Trouillot, taking his cues from Wolf and from Foucault, sees resistance as an exercise against power. But he is unwilling to stamp every act of defiance as resistance, arguing that such a blanket usage "makes the notion [of resistance] too general to be of any use" (1992: 10). I think that it is true that the constant widening of what is meant by resistance may eventually make the concept unworkable. Though some scholars wish to treat "resistance" as some sort of universal human essence, such broadening of meaning leads to other, perhaps even more serious, problems.

Paquette has urged "students of slave resistance to distinguish analytically between the resistance to enslavement and the resistance to slavery as a social system" (Paquette 1991: 682). He probably means here to draw on Genovese's distinction between escaping slavery and overthrowing it (Genovese 1980: 3).[3] Beyond this there is the obvious difference between individual and collective acts of resistance. We need to know in specific instances whether we are dealing with an individual act or a collective act; whether the act is directed against enslavement or against the system of slavery; and we need to begin to calibrate the consequences of such acts. There can be a vast difference between what individuals are doing to influence their own fates, and the consequences of what they are doing for the fate of the system of which they are parts. The same act may affect both the way a system of oppression operates, and an individual's fate within that system; but in most cases these will be different kinds of act.

In any event, the aim here is not to create a catalog. Suffice it to say that the variety of forms of what may be resistance is still not wholly charted. Even so, all of this is meant as an introduction. In arguing for a closer examination of the day-to-day character of slave life on Carib-

bean plantations, this writer hopes to keep in view the difference between a slave society, ideally conceived, and the way people actually
lived in such a society. The rules for social behavior and the social behavior itself are not the same thing. In the case of the Caribbean sugar
islands, the masters' ideas of the way slaves should behave never could
be perfectly imposed upon them in everyday life, no matter how hid-
eously repressive the system. The "space" between the code and the behavior is what must be understood. Such a space between real and ideal
might become particularly visible in the sphere of economic life. If the
slaves produced any part of their own subsistence without reducing their
input into plantation production, that part of their output constituted a
saving to their owners. Occasional famine, caused by interruption in
food imports induced by war, meant serious dollar losses to the planters—loss of capital in the form of dead laborers and hence in the loss of
crops. In many Caribbean islands, part-time subsistence production by
slaves saved their lives; it saved the masters' money, too. In some cases,
such as those of English Jamaica and French Saint Domingue, food
production by slaves soon sustained much of the free population. Slave
market earnings came to be retained by the slaves. Slave food production became a family enterprise, in which slaves could exercise many
skills that the ideology of slavery required their owners energetically to
deny that they even possessed (Mintz 1955, 1978a, 1978b; Mintz and
Hall, 1960). Accordingly, food production for subsistence and sale
could constitute a form of resistance, just by existing. But it could also
be a form of resistance in more tangible ways.

Clearly enough, it could also be a form of accommodation. The extent to which all of this made the state of slavery more bearable may
have in turn reduced the slaves' will to resist. Their labor saved the masters money. Their product fed the free population at large; indeed, in
Jamaica, slave marketers came to supply the garrison of British troops
quartered there expressly to suppress slave revolts! Yet that need be neither contradictory nor paradoxical. Revolts were probably planned in
markets; freedom to travel made knowledge of the terrain more useful
and contacts among slaves on different plantations easier. Why need we
assume that living better under slavery meant accepting slavery? Or that
accommodation at one point meant accommodation at later points?
The present writer once suggested that the cook who put ground glass
in her master's food first had to become the family cook. Was she resisting or accommodating? On what grounds dare we deny to the slaves
the same capacities for memory, deception, foregone pleasure, cruelty,
and violence that we are ready to accord the masters?

But then we are left asking ourselves just what subsistence production and marketing by slaves *did* mean. Was it resistance, or was it accommodation? And if it was both, does that mean that it was really neither? There are answers to these questions; and they have two parts.

First, to make sense of what may look like contradictory situations, we must deal with them as diachronic—that is, historical—processes. Second, such historical processes are specific and particular; each happens in some particular place, to people of some particular society; and it happens over time. Thus the temporal unfolding of the provision ground-marketing complex, which gradually came to typify Jamaican slavery between the closing decades of the seventeenth century and the Morant Bay Rebellion, contained within it powerful elements of both accommodation and resistance. In good measure, the capacity to resist had as its precondition some accommodation. But it is also the case that some measures of resistance led cumulatively to further accommodation. The historical process thus may involve a trading off through time, as each negotiation brings in its wake somewhat different conditions, which affect the manner in which the subsequent negotiation proceeds. The intentions of the negotiators in this lengthy process may not count for a great deal; but the system itself may change noticeably over time as a result.

Negotiated understandings can lead to new conditions, conditions unanticipated by the negotiators; that renegotiation may take account of these new conditions, and create yet newer conditions in its wake. If enough people are content with the way things are working, things are likely to continue working that way. But that also means that some people may end up bargaining for conditions they never believed they would ever have to bargain for. Sometimes, they may ask themselves: "How did we let ourselves get into this situation?" And make no mistake: at times they might be planters, not slaves.

It is immediately apparent, however, that this perspective locates the issue in place and in time. Students of slave resistance may wish to distinguish between interpreting events as disjunct frames—almost like slides—that can be compared without historical reference, on the one hand; and acts, interpreted as moments in a continuous, diachronic sequence, on the other. To put things this way is to rejoin an old battle. But if the varieties of resistance are better to be grasped, then the time frame becomes particularly significant. Students interested in the essential nature of processes and impatient with historical particulars tend to approach the things that they study in a nonsequential manner, even when dealing with past events, and even when the books they write have much "history" in them.

There are difficulties in reconciling the historically particular with a general rule, having to do with the annoying distinctiveness of the particular. Yet terms such as "resistance" and "accommodation" are difficult to understand as general phenomena, exactly because as general phenomena they have no specific cultural histories. Resistance may be thought to characterize humankind; but if it is studied as a universal, then it has no *history*, only a natural history. Much the same is true for "accommodation." This is a generic difficulty, inherent in the way we treat social facts. A familiar feature of so-called "grand theory" is the theoretical management of the historically particular so that it will create no classificatory dissonance for the classifier. But if they aspire to be more than ornate tautologists, large-scale theorists, in their fidelity to general sociological principles, must avoid becoming resolutely unhistorical or—to use Karl Marx's term—"super-historical."

A dozen years ago, commenting on the study of labor history, the present writer wrote:

> It seems likely that the near future will bring a somewhat different perspective to the study of labor and its history, a perspective that blurs distinctions among categories, rather than underlining them; that compares the superficially not comparable, that sees variant forms of exaction as tied to each other by market connections, so that status and color ["race"] are simultaneously reflectors and absorbers of larger social processes—a perspective, in short, impatient with definitions and disdainful of boundaries. It may be that periodic advances in understanding need their intermittent episodes of undisciplined imagination, if only to balance excesses in particularism and dogmatism. . . . perhaps it is time to see everything in everything else, only then to sort out the like and the unlike, with different—possibly even with better—criteria. (Mintz 1979: 566)

We may be in the midst of just such an episode; and perhaps when it is over, we *will* have better criteria for, among other things, studying resistance and accommodation in day-to-day life in slave societies.

Notes

I thank Michel-Rolph Trouillot for helpful comments on an early draft of this paper. However, I alone am responsible for errors of fact or interpretation.

   1. Berlin (1980), Besson (1985), Bush (1985), Fog Olwig (1985), Gaspar (1985), Tomich (1990), Berlin and Morgan (1991), Mullin (1992), etc.

2. Anthropologist Clifford Geertz, borrowing an analogy from Gilbert Ruyle, notes the problem of distinguishing between a wink and a blink. We may believe that we can determine which is which, particularly when we know the consequences; but making the identification is risky. Surely some have come to grief through not knowing the difference.
3. I had failed to make this point in an earlier draft of the paper. I thank Jean Besson for bringing this omission to my attention.

References

Aptheker, Herbert
1943   *American Negro Slave Revolts.* New York: Columbia Univ. Press.
Bastide, Roger
1978 [1960]   *The African Religions of Brazil: Toward a Sociology of the Interpenetration of Civilizations.* Baltimore, Md.: Johns Hopkins Univ. Press. 1978
Bauer, Raymond, and Alice Bauer
1942   Day-to-Day Resistance to Slavery. *Journal of Negro History* 28: 388–419.
Berlin, Ira
1980   Time, Space and the Evolution of Afro-American Society on British Mainland North America. *American Historical Review* 85 (1): 44–78.
Berlin, Ira, and Philip Morgan
1991   Introduction. In *The Slaves' Economy: Independent Production by Slaves in the Americas,* special issue of *Slavery and Abolition* 12 (1): 1–30.
Besson, Jean
1985   Land Tenure in the Free Villages of Trelawny: A Case Study in the Caribbean Peasant Response to Emancipation. *Slavery and Abolition* 5: 3–23
Bush, Barbara
1985   *Slave Women in Caribbean Society, 1650–1838.* Kingston, Jamaica: Heinemann.
Fog Olwig, Karen
1985   *Cultural Adaptation and Resistance on St. John.* Gainesville: Univ. of Florida Press.
Gaspar, David Barry
1985   *Bondmen and Rebels: A Study of Master–Slave Relationships in Antigua.* Baltimore, Md.: Johns Hopkins Univ. Press.
1991   Antigua Slaves and Their Struggle to Survive. In *Seeds of Change,* ed. H. Viola and C. Margolis, 130–37. Washington, D.C.: Smithsonian Institution Press.
Geertz, Clifford.
1973   *The Interpretation of Cultures.* New York: Basic Books.
Genovese, Eugene
1980   *From Rebellion to Revolution.* Baton Rouge: Louisiana State Univ.
Hanley, Eric
1987   Review of Fog Olwig, *Cultural Adaptation and Resistance on St. John. Man* 22: 210.
Herskovits, Melville J.
1941   *The Myth of the Negro Past.* New York: Harper and Bros.
James, C. L. R.
1938   *The Black Jacobins.* London: Becker and Warburg.

Keller, Albert Galloway
1908   *Colonization.* Boston: Ginn and Company.
Mintz, Sidney W.
1955   The Jamaican Internal Marketing Pattern: Some Notes and Hypotheses. *Social and Economic Studies* 4 (1): 95–103.
1961   The Question of Caribbean Peasantries: A Comment. *Caribbean Studies* 1: 31–34.
1969   Review of H. Orlando Patterson, *The Sociology of Slavery. Caribbean Studies* 8 (4): 65–70.
1970   Creating Culture in the Americas. *Columbia University Forum* 13: 4–11.
1971   Toward an Afro-American History. *Cahiers d'Histoire Mondiale* 13 (2): 317–32.
1978a   Was the Plantation Slave a Proletarian? *Review* 2 (1): 81–98.
1978b   Caribbean Marketplaces and Caribbean History. *Nova Americana* 1 (1): 333–44.
1979   The Dignity of Honest Toil. *Comparative Studies in Society and History* 21 (4): 558–66.
1981   Cultural Resistance and the Labor Force in the Caribbean Region. In *Latin America Today: Heritage of Conquest,* ed. D. Hazen, T. Holloway, and D. Jones, 28–42. Ithaca, N.Y.: Cornell Univ. Press.
1989 [1974]   *Caribbean Transformations.* New York: Columbia Univ. Press.
Mintz, Sidney W., and Douglas Hall
1960   *The Origins of the Jamaican Internal Market System.* Yale University Publications in Anthropology (New Haven: Dept. of Anthropology), vol. 57: 1–26.
Mullin, Michael
1992   *Africa in America.* Urbana: Univ. of Illinois Press.
Okihiro, Gary Y., ed.
1986   *In Resistance.* Amherst: Univ. of Massachusetts Press.
Olivier, Lord [Sidney Haldane]
1936   *Jamaica: The Blessed Isle.* London: Faber and Faber.
Paquette, Robert L.
1991   Social History Update: Slave Resistance and Social History. *Journal of Social History* 24 (3): 681–85.
Tomich, Dale
1990   *Slavery in the Circuit of Sugar: Martinique and the World Economy.* Baltimore, Md.: Johns Hopkins Univ. Press.
Trouillot, Michel-Rolph
1995   In the Shadow of the West: Power, Resistance and Creolization in the Making of the Caribbean Region. In *Born Out of Resistance: On Caribbean Cultural Creativity,* ed. Wim Hoogbergen. Utrecht: ISOR Press.
Ward, J. R.
1988   *British West Indian Slavery, 1750–1834.* Oxford, England: Clarendon Press.
Weatherly, U. G.
1923   The West Indies as a Sociological Laboratory. *American Journal of Sociology* 29: 290–304.

3 | African Cultural Principles in Caribbean Slave Societies

A View from the Danish West Indies

Karen Fog Olwig

The slave experience in the Americas often has been analyzed in terms of the concept of "resistant response." It has been documented how slaves established social and economic relations of their own which allowed them to survive physically and hence to adapt to the system of bondage. At the same time, these relations constituted important life contexts within which slaves could develop and consolidate cultural values and practices quite different from those of the slaveholders. By thus asserting themselves as African-American subjects with lives of their own outside the institution of slavery, the slaves negated and hence resisted their formal position as socially dead private property belonging to their owners.

This interpretation of the slave experience seems to derive mainly from the hindsight afforded by studies of the effects of slave behavior on slave societies. It is difficult, however, to attribute intentions and motives to slaves primarily on the basis of knowledge about the results of these actions. To understand how slaves dealt with their position in bondage, it is necessary to know more about how they viewed both the institution of slavery and their own possibilities for improving their situation. Comparative research on slavery shows great variety in the ways in which the institution of slavery was practiced and perceived in different societies. Thus the institution of slavery ranges from the chattel slavery associated with the plantation systems in the Americas to systems of patronage and dependency functioning as a means of incorporating strangers into kin-based polities in certain parts of Africa. Knowing about such varied forms of slavery is crucial for a more "emically" oriented understanding of the resistant responses displayed by slaves.

I argue that the slaves' resistant responses to slavery were, to a great extent, molded by cultural assumptions and social practices concerning slavery that were prevalent in those areas of West Africa from whence they came. I examine the manner in which slaves, informed by African cultural principles, carved out lives of their own in the slave society of the Danish West Indies. Finally, I suggest that an approach sensitive to African conceptions of slavery may offer important insights into the later development of African-American culture among the slaves and their descendants.

In this case study, the recent literature on Africa, which takes a more regional and historical approach to African culture, proved most helpful. It delineates notions of cultural identity and belonging which were radically different from those held in modern Western societies. These notions provide important insights into the nature of the Danish West Indian slaves' African background and its impact on African-American culture.

The Danish West Indies is admirably suited for a case study, primarily because of the work of the Moravian C. G. A. Oldendorp (see Meier, this volume). Based on interviews with slaves carried out during seventeen months' residence in the Danish West Indies in 1767–68, Oldendorp attempted to document the slaves' African background and their situation in the West Indies. His work, in highly edited form, was published in two parts in German in 1777. The second volume was devoted to an account of the history of the Moravian mission among the slaves. A few years later his work appeared in abbreviated form in other languages, such as Danish (1784) and Swedish (1784 and 1786); and in 1987 A. R. Highfield and V. Barac published a complete English translation of the German original.[1]

A useful supplement to Oldendorp's book, as far as the African background is concerned, has been found in letters written by the Danish medical doctor Paul Isert when he was in Danish Guinea and briefly in the Danish West Indies in the period 1783–87 (Raunkiær 1917).[2] With respect to the West Indies, useful additional information has been found in the eighteenth-century writings of Johan Lorentz Carstens, a planter on St. Thomas and St. John (1981 [ca. 1740]); Hans West, schoolmaster in Christiansted (1793); and Johan Christian Schmidt, a doctor at a plantation on St. Croix (1788).

Theoretical Approaches to African Culture

The importance of African culture in the New World was for many years a subject of heated controversy among scholars. Some viewed the persistence or reinterpretation of African cultural traditions as a major characteristic of African-American culture. Others argued that African culture, for all practical purposes, had been lost when the Africans were forcibly removed from their homes to become slaves in the New World; in consequence, a totally new culture, with a Western orientation, emerged. The retentionist position was propounded by American anthropologist Melville J. Herskovits, who did fieldwork on a number of Caribbean islands and in Dahomey in West Africa (Herskovits 1973 [1945]).[3] The neocultural position, on the other hand, was advocated primarily by the American sociologist E. Franklin Frazier, who did research among black Americans (Frazier 1966 [1939]; see also the debate in Rubin 1971 [1957]: 34–53).

The debate was inconclusive, largely because both sides concentrated on contemporary culture and society and paid little attention to the long history of blacks in the New World. Their levels of analysis also differed. Whereas Herskovits focused on particular cultural traits and traditions in different African-American communities, Frazier tended to look at social relations and institutions within wider societal contexts.

During the past decades, the impasse created by this cultural debate has been resolved, to a great extent, by a processual approach taking as its point of departure historical anthropological studies of specific slave societies. An important theoretical and methodological work in this connection has been *An Anthropological Approach to the Afro-American Past* by Sidney Mintz and Richard Price, which appeared in 1976. While it emphasized the importance of cultural creativity in the New World, it did not rule out the possibility of African influence. This influence, they argued, should not be seen in terms of the retention of specific traits or traditions of African origin—Herskovits's approach—because slaves derived from many different areas of Africa and so did not share a single culture. Nor should one expect to find recreated African cultural and societal systems, since it was extremely difficult, if not impossible, for slaves to reestablish them within the institution of slavery. Following Mintz and Price, one might rather argue that the African influence should be viewed in terms of "deep-level cultural principles" shared by all African slaves despite their origins in different parts of Africa. These principles helped slaves establish common cultural contexts of life and hence cultural identities of their own, which should not be interpreted as mere variants of Western culture.

In 1992, a new edition of Mintz and Price's book appeared, with the new title *The Birth of African-American Culture: An Anthropological Perspective*. In its introduction, the authors note that a processual approach to African-American cultural history has become generally accepted, even by those most concerned with the African heritage of the black population of the New World. Now African-American culture is likely to be viewed in terms of cultural mixture and blend, rather than particular, retained African cultural traits and traditions in the New World.

The concept of cultural resistance has become a central analytical tool in this study of cultural processes. African-American culture now is widely interpreted as the outcome of a complex interplay between processes of accommodation and resistance to systems of oppression on the part of the slaves and their descendants. This approach was first developed in Sidney Mintz's study of slave provision grounds, which in his view reflected both response and resistance to the plantation system. Response, or adaptation, in that the grounds provided slaves with food and nourishment and thereby enabled them to survive and to supply labor for the plantation owners; resistance, because the provision grounds constituted crevices in the plantation system within which slaves developed spheres of sociocultural and economic autonomy, and these, in the long run, made the slaves independent of their owners (Mintz 1974, 1985).

In an analysis of slave religious culture, Monica Schuler presents a parallel argument showing how African religious beliefs and practices became redefined in New World slave societies to provide new systems of values and interrelations that enabled the slaves to live with, yet also respond to, their situations as enslaved. Quoting Mintz and Price, she argues that "the processes by which enslaved Africans constructed their own societies occurred '*within* the parameters of the masters' monopoly of power, but *separate* from the masters' institutions'" (Schuler 1979: 121). Resistant response is also seen as a basic dynamic behind the formation of Caribbean peasantries after Emancipation. Jean Besson's work on family land is perhaps the clearest example of this (Besson 1984, 1987).

The concept of "resistant response" has proved useful in my analysis of slave culture on St. John, where the plantation system was weak and the slave population was able to develop a wide and fairly undisturbed sociocultural sphere of its own (Olwig 1985). Later historical anthropological research in the more developed plantation society of Nevis has made me aware, however, that resistant response may take many forms, depending on the nature of the slave society involved. Thus the slaves who lived in plantation societies controlled by a strong plantocracy of European background engaged in resistant response of a much more indirect nature than did those in the relatively weak plantation society of St. John. Resistance among slaves on Nevis appears to have been guided not only by struggle *against* the system of oppression, but also by struggle *within* the system. Slaves there made attempts to co-opt the system, including the masters' institutions, to make it serve their needs and desires. They also attempted to establish more independent spheres of social, economic, and cultural autonomy (Olwig 1993; cf. Karasch 1979). The slaves' resistant response therefore may have been quite different from that envisioned in modern-day Western concepts of resistance. Knowledge of some of the basic cultural principles that informed the way in which slaves experienced the institution of slavery thus seems crucial for a deeper understanding of African-American resistant response.

African Cultural Principles

A basic assumption concerning the slaves' African backgrounds was that the slaves could be classified according to clearly defined linguistic and cultural entities corresponding to tribes or ethnic groups. Historical research indicates that such tribes emerged later in time, largely as a result of changes that occurred in connection with European colonization of the continent (Sharpe 1986; Tonkin 1990). Since the bulk of the slaves were transported to the West Indies between the middle of the seventeenth century and the end of the eighteenth century (i.e., before the European colonial penetration of Africa began in earnest), most likely they did not belong to any permanent socioeconomic entities that can be defined as tribes in the later (colonial) sense of the term.

According to Kopytoff and Miers (1977) and others, in many parts of precolonial Africa a basic form of social organization consisted of more or less loosely organized alliances of polities competing for followers. People were regarded as vital resources, from political and social as well as economic points of view. Kinship provided an important means of incorporating strangers into a group. Such extension of kin ties to strangers could, under certain circumstances, incorporate slaves. In such cases, an individual forcibly was placed under the authority of a master in a kin group different from the one to which he or she originally had belonged. At the other extreme, such social strategies allowed the in-

corporation of persons who voluntarily placed themselves under the patronage of a particular person in a kin-like position of dependence, having given up membership in their own kin groups for such reasons as
"quarrels, threats, hunger, hope for a better life, or because they had
committed some crime." Kinship therefore provided "both the idiom
and the metaphor for social and political relations." The whole concept
of the person, then, was closely related to membership in a kin group
that conferred social, economic, and political rights, as well as ritual
protection (Kopytoff and Miers 1977: 12, 17, 22, 24).

This process of struggle and socioeconomic flux, in which political
control was sought by a number of competing patrons trying to enhance
their respective power bases as leaders of kin groups, seems closely related to African notions of the supernatural. Rowlands (1985) suggests
that, in much of West and Central Africa, there is an ambiguous perception of power, with deep historical roots, reflected in a belief that the
possession of a supernatural substance is a precondition for the assumption of leadership. If properly harnessed to communal goals, this substance is beneficial and works for the welfare of the community; if uncontrolled, the substance is used to amass individual wealth and
personal power and hence is dangerous and lethal for members of the
community. Power, in other words, involves substances that must be
controlled, and those leaders who show an ambition to centralize power
in their person will be regarded as demonstrating a lack of control of
this substance, which leads them to become involved with sorcery. The
power of such persons must be checked by any possible means.

Membership in secret cults, operating independently of kin groups,
offered protection against abuses of power. These cults were tied to certain places regarded as residences of particular spirits that could be wor-
shipped and invoked by human beings. Such local religious cults drew
their members from several different kin groups. Through secret rituals, a close, personal relationship was established with a guardian spirit.
This relationship was one of dependence and subordination to that
spirit, and for this reason cult members became partially freed from the
ties of subordination and dependence binding them to others, most notably to senior members of their lineage. Secret cults therefore often
came to challenge kin-based sources of power (Horton 1971: 102–13).
People in precolonial Africa, then, did not base their identities merely on
membership in a particular social and political group, but rather on "overlapping networks of association and exchange" (Ranger 1983: 248).

African cultural principles that may have guided the slaves' resistant
response revolved around *incorporation through ties of patronage and de-*

pendence, establishing *different sociocultural spheres,* and *harnessing super-natural forces* to generate, or challenge, a power base. Some of these ideas pertained directly to the status of slaves in Africa, which often was a temporary state of affairs that could be negated by establishing the status of belonging, typically through attachment to a kin group via a patron. This concept of slavery was, of course, markedly different from the institution of slavery as it existed in the New World, where slaves were regarded as private property possessed permanently by their owners.

The African Background of the Danish West Indian Slaves

There is evidence of the cultural principles outlined above in Oldendorp's work. One of the chapters, entitled "Geographical and Political Information about the African Nations from which the Slaves Were Principally Brought to the West Indies," describes the various peoples represented among Danish West Indian slaves. It was no easy matter to group the Africans into orderly, separate groups, explains Oldendorp, because misunderstandings over such problems as the usage of different names for "a single group of people" and several different pronunciations of the same name. Moreover, the slaves did not seem to identify strongly with nations, so, when asked the name of his nation, a slave often responded "with the name of the place where he lived in Guinea" (1987: 159).

Oldendorp also encountered many who were able to speak, and certainly to understand, the languages of several neighboring groups, giving the impression that Oldendorp expected to find clearly defined, sharply demarcated linguistic communities, corresponding to nations, where these may not have existed (1987: 159–63). A similar mixture was apparent in religious practices. Some "nations" had several different religions, including Islamic and Christian beliefs. Some of the people who lived close to a Danish fort—identified as the Akkran by Oldendorp—apparently at one time had attended Danish religious services but concluded "that it may be good for the Whites, but that it is not appropriate for the Negroes" (1987: 163–65). Isert notes that mulatto children of European fathers and African mothers were christened but practiced a mixture of religions, going to the altar one day and "eating fetish" the next (Raunkiær 1917: 149). These "fetishes" were lesser deities created by the great God to look after human beings. "Fetishes" were connected with what Isert terms "fetish temples," usually located in sacred groves and tended by priests or priestesses, who honored the "fetish" by singing and dancing adorned with magnificent decorations (Raunkiær 1917: 89–90).

Oldendorp also describes sacred groves that were "dwelling places of individual deities," adding that ordinary human beings were not allowed to enter them but instead made offerings via holy persons with special abilities to communicate with the gods. Such offerings were made in connection with major events in the life cycle, such as births and deaths; in the agricultural year, such as harvest celebrations; and in special life crises, such as sickness or other kinds of misfortune (1987: 187–99; see also Raunkiær 1917: 111–13). The tendency encountered by Oldendorp for people to identify with local places, rather than with nations, may be related to the significance of such holy places as *loci* of supernatural power fundamentally important for life.

The significance of the supernatural as a source of both evil and good is noted by both Isert (Raunkiær 1917: 111) and Oldendorp. Oldendorp reports a distinction made between those regarded as "enemies of the human race," because they used their supernatural power for evil purposes, and those seen as "beneficent, wise, and powerful friends of humanity," because they used their powers to relieve others of hardship. Whereas the former were destroyed if possible, the latter were honored and rewarded (Oldendorp 1987: 177). The importance of "fetish" in political matters is also apparent in the custom of "eating fetish," which Isert describes as a religious ceremony whereby a group of people made a covenant, the breaking of which was believed to result in death.

Whereas Oldendorp, understandably enough, shows great interest in African religious beliefs, he pays little attention to kinship and family relations, except for making brief reference to polygynous marriage practices. The role of kinship as the main organizing principle behind the "nations" that he sought to delineate is apparent, however, in his description of marriage regulations among the Kassenti. According to Oldendorp, they were not allowed to marry within the group because they all were considered to be blood relatives. For this reason, men "obtain their wives from the neighboring nations and give their daughters to them in marriage" (1987: 171). The prominence of kinship as a basic context of life is also apparent in Isert's statement that there were no "poor among the Negroes," because every family was obliged to care for its own, so that if one person suffered, the whole family suffered (Raunkiær 1917: 133). Some families might experience such extreme poverty, however, that it was necessary to sell one or several children into slavery, but only the most desperate resorted to this (131).

The fluidity of African social structure and the importance of attracting followers by establishing ties of dependency with them also are apparent in Oldendorp's work, especially in his description of African slavery. He notes that it was a common practice for persons "of lesser means or status [to] commit themselves to the service of the wealthier class, or even become their slaves, in order to earn their livelihood." Such dependents, he states, were treated much better than other slaves such as war captives or criminals, with whom a "black despot" did whatever he pleased (1987: 211).

Africans in West Indian Slavery

The slaves whom Oldendorp interviewed in the Danish West Indies had widely differing social, economic, and cultural backgrounds. However, as he notes, the state of slavery had "accomplished something similar to what is achieved by death in the destinies of all men, namely the removal of all external distinctions among them" (1987: 211). For the slaves, a vital mode of negating this involuntary situation of social death[4] was to create ties which would generate a basis of social and cultural distinction and hence a source of identity within slave society.

Ties of Incorporation

The main framework of life for most of the Danish West Indian slaves was the sugar plantation, headed by the planter. The hierarchical nature of the plantation is well known. At the bottom were the bulk of the slaves, who performed physically demanding field labor under the supervision of a slave driver, or *bomba*. Above them were the artisan slaves, who were trained to do skilled work; and the domestic slaves, who did fairly light housework and often developed a close relationship with the planter, which gave them certain privileges on the estate. The plantation system was unfamiliar to newly arrived African slaves, or *bussals*, and it was common for a planter to place them in the hands of older, experienced slaves who would take care of them and teach them the language and the plantation routine—including how to cultivate their own provisions. Oldendorp describes the relationship as one between parent and child, with the *bussal* respecting the experienced slave as a parent, addressing the mentor accordingly and assisting her or him in any way possible (1987: 220). Socialization into the plantation system therefore can be interpreted as taking place within the idiom of the inclusive African system of kinship.

This kin system seems to have been elaborated further by the slaves, in that they also performed a sort of baptismal ritual—apparently patterned after the Christian baptism—which served to institutionalize a kinlike tie between *bussals* and baptismal fathers and mothers, who promised to care for the *bussals* as if they had been their children. It is not clear whether these baptismal parents were identical with the experienced slaves assigned to the *bussals* by the planter. They may have been younger persons, since one of their most important obligations was to provide the *bussals* with a proper burial. These fictive forms of kinship could be extended still further, in that baptisms sometimes were attended by a number of godparents who also promised to assist in caring for the *bussals* (Oldendorp 1987: 263). A further extension of the kin system was found in the custom of forming fictive kin ties with those African slaves who had arrived in the West Indies on the same boat, or who derived from the same area in Africa. These fictive kinship relations were "inherited" by their offspring. My research in St. John turned up a case of a slave woman who was arranging a burial of an old African slave woman, because this woman had "come from Africa together with her parents" (Olwig 1985: 79).

The principle of inclusion through kinlike ties also seems to have operated between slaves and masters in certain cases. Hans West notes that it was not uncommon for strong ties of trust and confidence to develop between a master and one or two slaves on the plantation. This might result in the slaves' achieving a position of privilege on the estate whereby they, in effect, helped to supervise the work and secure an orderly state of affairs on the estate (West 1793: 130–40). West even claims that masters at times came to feel so close to these slaves that they regarded them as faultless and reacted to any criticism of them as if the slaves had been their own children (1793: 139–41).

Sexual relationships between female slaves and planters presented another means whereby close relationships developed between slaves and masters. Since slave women often were taken as wives in Africa, the African slave women may not have been surprised by such arrangements. Oldendorp asserts that they did not object to these sexual relations, but regarded it as an honor "to submit to the indecent demands of their masters." He adds, however, that, even if a slave woman should wish to resist the master's advances, she could do nothing about it (1987: 157). The mulatto children who resulted from such relationships usually became trained as artisan or domestic slaves. By the later part of the slave period, a significant number of slaves thus had improved their social and economic position in the plantation society, some of them even attaining freedom.

During the eighteenth century, the African slaves and their descendants were presented with another possibility to create a sense of belonging in the plantation society. This was the Moravian mission among the slaves, which in the Danish West Indies began in 1732. Oldendorp reports that African slaves had explained their desire to become Christian in these words: "We have come here such a long way across the sea from Guinea and have lost both father and mother. That is why we want to get to know the Father above and partake of His grace. Otherwise, we will remain miserable creatures" (1987: 584). Conversion to Christianity did not necessarily mean totally abandoning old religious beliefs and practices. It could be regarded as a supplement, adding yet another religion to draw on. This ability to combine different religions, too, can be related to the slaves' African background. As Monica Schuler, drawing on Robin Horton's work, notes, African cosmology can be seen to include two tiers of spirits—a microcosm of lesser spirits, concerned with local affairs; and a macrocosm of a "vague, generally non-providential supreme being" oriented towards the greater world (Schuler 1979: 122). It was therefore possible for slaves to defer to lesser spirits in matters concerned with the local slave society, while worshipping a more distant, Christian God connected with the wider, White world. That slaves combined African and European supernatural beings is apparent in Oldendorp's reference to a woman who was excluded from Moravian communion when it was discovered that she had in her possession items for the practice of witchcraft that she had inherited from relatives (1987: 551).[5]

Spheres outside the Plantation Regime

One must be careful, however, not to give an overly romantic impression of the institution of slavery as a basically benign, patriarchal institution composed of largely content slaves. Most of the slaves did not succeed in establishing particularly close ties with their masters but remained part of the large slave labor force toiling in the fields. Furthermore, even those who did establish close ties with their masters faced the harsh reality that they were part of a slave system that would not allow them full recognition as persons with social identities of their own. Most were kept in a position of social death in the plantation society and accorded a place in the plantation hierarchy under their owners' supervision and control. This system stood in contrast to the African system of slavery, which often functioned to facilitate incorporation of strangers into a new social order, such as a kin group (Kopytoff and Miers 1977). Most slaves therefore were not able to find their primary source of identity in ties to their owners, but sought to create other life contexts that might conduce to the development of other ties.

In my book on St. John (Olwig 1985), I have shown that one of the main contexts for the emergence of such ties was the slaves' subsistence economy, which enabled slaves to establish social and cultural identities outside the slave system. The subsistence economy involved slaves in such activities as cultivating provision grounds located in hilly areas on the margins of the plantations; fishing along the shores of the islands; burning lime; and trading these goods at the markets of St. Thomas and St. Croix. The slaves thereby became what Sidney Mintz (1974), in another connection, has termed proto-peasants, with established African-American communities of their own.[6] Similar fields for the creation of separate identities emerged in connection with the slaves' family relations, their music and dance, and their religious beliefs and practices. The latter also played an important role as a means whereby masters might be checked if they excessively abused their position of power.

The Harnessing of Supernatural Forces

The slaves, then, arrived in the West Indies with a notion of power as something based on supernatural forces. Whereas legitimate power indicated controlled supernatural power, abuse of power reflected uncontrolled supernatural power, or sorcery. It was necessary and legitimate to check the latter by recourse to countersorcery. It was not uncommon for slaves to practice witchcraft or sorcery in secret, and Johan Lorentz Carstens believes that there were among the slaves masters of witchcraft, who were able to project such things as a lump of hair, cut-off nails, and sharp, thin pieces of rusty iron into the bodies of human beings, causing them to die in a short time (1981 [c. 1740]: 85). Apparently many whites feared the supernatural abilities of their slaves, and Oldendorp encountered, for example, a woman on St. Thomas who attributed her illness to her slave's having bewitched her (Oldendorp 1987: 263). Such fear of the slaves' supernatural inclinations may have been behind an act published in 1701, making it mandatory that slaves be given instruction in Christianity in order that "their wild souls, old bad habits, idolatry, witchcraft, murder and evil would be weakened and broken by the transmission of Christianity." The act was not put into practice, however, due to protests on the part of the white population, who feared that imparting Christianity to the slaves might cause insubordination among them (Carstens 1981 [c. 1740]: 82).

The slaves' strong belief in the potency of the oath played a central role in the organization of slaves against their masters. The taking of an oath by sharing a piece of bread, according to Johan Christian Schmidt, constituted an important way in which rebels committed themselves to a plot—death was believed to be inevitable for those who revealed anything (1788: 234–35). Such oaths were taken before a conspiracy in 1759, when several thousand slaves on St. Croix had "sworn a bond of unity with one another, vowing to kill the white inhabitants of the island and to assume mastery over it" (Oldendorp 1987: 580). The conspiracy was discovered, but, despite long and intensive interrogation of slaves, the authorities did not succeed in finding the people behind it; the interrogated refused to reveal any information and thus break the oath (West 1793: 127).

There is evidence that the slaves' interest in the Moravian mission may have reflected a desire to gain knowledge of the supernatural forces that they believed granted the white man such a position of power. Robert Robertson, who was an Anglican priest on Nevis during the early part of the eighteenth century, wrote that newly arrived slaves regarded their master's ability to do things which to them were unknown and incomprehensible as proof of their masters' special powers: "When the *newer* Negroes observe that we can read and write (or as they word it, *make Paper speak*) and do many other things above their comprehension, they seem to take us for a sort of Superior Beings, made as it were on purpose to rule over them; they both admire, and fear, and hate us" (1730: 32). One of the main attractions of the Moravian mission certainly was its offer of education, and the Moravians purposely began their religious meetings with some instruction in reading and writing in order to attract more slaves to the mission (Oldendorp 1987: 318). Religious instruction as such may have appealed to many, because it gave an insight into the supernatural beliefs and practices of the whites, which were thought to be related to their position of power. Oldendorp states that the mission was particularly attractive to those slaves who had not succeeded in improving their position within the system of slavery, because "those slaves who enjoyed the greatest freedom and had to face the fewest obstacles were also the least likely to become converts" (1987: 361). The planters' persecution of the Moravians during the early years of their mission in the Danish West Indies—which, among other things, caused them to hold their meetings in secret in the bush (1987: 369)—may have contributed to the perception of their mission as offering an alternative source of supernatural power which might be useful against the planters.

Conclusion

In this paper I have discussed some of the ways in which African cultural principles may have informed the slaves' resistant response to their situation of bondage in the Danish West Indies. This resistant response should not be viewed primarily in terms of action against an oppressive system. More significantly, it should be seen as reflecting a wish on the part of the African slaves and their descendants to establish places for themselves, even though this had to occur "within the parameters of the masters' monopoly of power."

In their discussion of African slavery, Kopytoff and Miers (1977: 17) have concluded that, for Africans, *freedom* did not refer to personal autonomy, unhindered by social bonds, as tends to be the case in Western thinking. Rather, Africans conceived of freedom as the creation of ties of belonging that would negate their slave status. For those Africans who became slaves in the New World, it was natural to form a variety of ties within the hierarchical structure of the plantation society. These ties included kinlike relations of dependency with masters and more experienced slaves, both of whom might help improve a slave's position in the plantation society; and with missionaries, who offered a place of belonging, connected with the supernatural, that might help check the power of the slaves' master. Slaves also formed relations, extending outside the plantation society, with fellow small farmers, kinsmen, or performers of music and dance who came to provide important contexts of life for the slaves. And they attempted to harness supernatural forces to check abuses of power, much as they had known it to be done in Africa. The result was not the establishment of a clearly demarcated culture, based on African traditions and shared by all, but rather the creation by individual slaves of a multiplicity of ties, cutting across one another; the emergence of a number of different social, cultural, and economic fields; and the development of different sets of identities.

As long as the slave population was reproduced primarily through new imports from Africa, a great number of the slaves were, at any given time, undergoing processes of incorporation. For each new *bussal* this meant recreating ties of belonging in the Danish West Indies; establishing positions in the sociocultural spheres outside the plantation regime; and discovering the supernatural realms of significance in the slave society. With the end of the African trade, however, all new slaves were born into already existing African-American communities. These communities offered ties of belonging which constituted both sources of cultural identity and socioeconomic resources. The slave communities no longer had constantly to be recreated and reinvented by new *bussals* forced to establish for themselves a variety of ties to an assort-ment of available persons. Thus it became possible for African-Ameri-can contexts of life to become transformed into social frameworks of some permanence, such as farming communities connected with the provision grounds and, later, family land; networks of people related through kin or affinal ties; religious organizations; or performative groups. These contexts became primary *loci* for the further development of African-American culture and identity before and after freedom.

Notes

This is a revised version of a paper entitled "African Culture in the Danish West Indies: The Slave Trade and Its Aftermath," originally presented at a conference on the Abolition of Slavery, St. Croix, 18 Dec. 1992.

1. This English translation has been used in this paper. As early as 1843, long pas-sages from Oldendorp's work appeared in James Cowles Prichard's *History of Man*, and the latter book is believed to have been influential in the development of anthropological theory during the nineteenth century (Rupp-Eisenreich 1985). In 1983, a translation into English of some of the chapters in Oldendorp's book was published (Brown 1983).

2. An English translation of his work appeared in 1992 (Winsnes 1992). Unfortu-nately, this book was not available to me during the writing of this paper.

3. During the 1930s, the anthropologist J. C. Trevor carried out fieldwork on St. John and Tortola inspired by Herskovits's theoretical approach. He concluded that many traditions had been modified, largely due to the strong missionary influence (1950: 211).

4. See Patterson (1982) for a more elaborate discussion of this concept.

5. The Moravians clearly expected converted slaves to undergo a complete trans-formation, to abandon their former ways, and to become new, Christian human beings. This expectation was reflected in the assignment of a new name at bap-tism. Oldendorp mentions the example of a slave who refused to respond to his former name, November, after baptism, replying "November is dead" (Oldendorp 1987: 573).

6. The cultural significance of the system of provision cultivation is discussed in Olwig (1987).

References

Besson, Jean
1984   Land Tenure in the Free Villages of Trelawny, Jamaica: A Case Study in the Caribbean Peasant Response to Emancipation. *Slavery and Abolition* 5 (1): 3–23
1987   Family Land as a Model for Martha Brae's New History: Culture Building in an Afro-Caribbean Village. In *Afro-Caribbean Villages in Historical Perspective*, ed. Charles V. Carnegie. Kingston, Jamaica: African-Caribbean Institute of Jamaica, 100–132.

Brown, Soi-Daniel W.
1983   From the Tongues of Africa: A Partial Translation of Oldendorp's Interviews. *Plantation Society* 2 (1): 37–61.
Carstens, Johan Lorentz
1981 [c. 1740]   *En Almindelig beskrivelse om alle de Danske, Americanske eller West-Jndiske Ey-lande.* Copenhagen: Dansk Vestindisk Forlag.
Frazier, E. Franklin
1966 [1939]   *The Negro Family in the United States.* Chicago: Univ. of Chicago Press.
Herskovits, Melville J.
1973 [1945]   Problem, Method and Theory in Afroamerican Studies. In *Work and Family Life: West Indian Perspectives,* ed. L. Comitas and D. Lowenthal, 287–93. Garden City, N.Y.: Anchor Books.
Horton, Robin
1971   Stateless Societies in the History of West Africa. In *History of West Africa,* vol. 1, ed. A. Ajayi and M. Crowder, 72–113. London: Longmans.
Karasch, Mary
1979   Commentary on "Afro-American Slave Culture" by Monica Schuler. *Historical Reflections* 6 (2): 138–41.
Kopytoff, Igor, and Suzanne Miers
1977   African "Slavery" as an Institution of Marginality. In *Slavery in Africa: Historical and Anthropological Perspectives,* ed. S. Miers and I. Kopytoff, 1–81. Madison: Univ. of Wisconsin Press.
Mintz, Sidney W.
1974   *Caribbean Transformations.* Chicago: Aldine.
1985   From Plantations to Peasantries in the Caribbean. In *Caribbean Contours,* ed. Sidney W. Mintz and Sally Price, 127–53. Baltimore, Md.: Johns Hopkins Univ. Press.
Mintz, Sidney W., and Richard Price
1992 [1976]   *The Birth of African-American Culture: An Anthropological Perspective.* [*An Anthropological Approach to the Afro-American Past: A Caribbean Perspective.* Boston: Beacon Press. Originally published as ISHI Occasional Papers 2. Philadelphia: Institute for the Study of Human Issues.]
Oldendorp, Christian G. A.
1777   *Geschichte der Mission der evangelischen Brüder auf den caraibischen Inseln S. Thomas, S. Croix und S. Jan,* ed. Johann Jakob Bossart. Barby, [Saxony]: Christian Friedrich Laux.
1784   *Fuldstændigt Udtog af C. G. A. Oldendorps Geschichte . . . .* Trans. Niels Prahl. Copenhagen: J. R. Thiele.
1784   *Tillförlåtlig underrättelse om Negrene på Gvinea kusten. . . .* Uppsala: J. Edman.
1786   *Historiska Beskrifning öfwer Ewangeliske Brödernas Mißions-Arbete på Caraibiske Öarne St. Thomas, St. Croix och St. Jan.* Stockholm: P. A. Brodin.
1987   *A Caribbean Mission: History of the Mission of the Evangelical Brethren on the Caribbean Islands of St. Thomas, St. Croix, and St. John.* English ed. Trans. A. R. Highfield and V. Barac. Ann Arbor: Karoma Publishers.
Olwig, Karen Fog
1985   *Cultural Adaptation and Resistance on St. John: Three Centuries of Afro-Caribbean Life.* Gainesville: Univ. of Florida Press.

1987   Village, Culture and Identity on St. John, Virgin Islands. In *Afro-Caribbean Villages in Historical Perspective*, ed. C. V. Carnegie, 20–44. *African-Caribbean Institute of Jamaica Research Review* 2.
1993   *Global Culture, Island Identity: Continuity and Change in the Afro-Caribbean Community of Nevis.* Reading, Pa.: Harwood Academic Publisher.
Patterson, Orlando
1982   *Slavery and Social Death.* Cambridge, Mass.: Harvard Univ. Press.
Ranger, Terrence
1983   The Invention of Tradition in Colonial Africa. In *The Invention of Tradition*, ed. E. Hobsbawm and T. Ranger, 211–62. Cambridge: Cambridge Univ. Press.
Raunkiær, Ingeborg
1917   *Iserts Breve fra Dansk Guinea, 1783–87.* Copenhagen: G. E. C. Gad.
Robertson, Rev. (Robert)
1730   *A Letter to the Right Reverend of the Lord Bishop of London.* London: J. Wilford.
Rowlands, Michael
1985   Exclusionary Tactics in the Logic of Collective Dynamics. *Critique of Anthropology* 5 (2): 47–69.
Rubin, Vera, ed.
1971 [1957]   *Caribbean Studies: A Symposium.* Seattle: Univ. of Washington Press.
Rupp-Eisenreich, Britta
1985   Les Frère moraves, ethnologues de la condition esclave? (Isles Vierges, Petites Antilles, 1731–1768). *Naissance de l'Ethnologie? Anthropologies et missions en Amérique XVIe-XVIIIe siècles*, ed. C. Blanckaert, 125–73. Paris: Les éditions du Cerf.
Schmidt, Johan Christian
1788   Blandede Anmærkninger, samlede paa og over Ejlandet St. Croix i Amerika. *Samleven* 41: 225–40.
Schuler, Monica
1979   Afro-American Slave Culture. *Historical Reflections* 6 (2): 121–37.
Sharpe, Barrie
1986   Ethnography and a Regional System. *Critique of Anthropology* 6 (3): 33–65.
Tonkin, Elizabeth
1990   West African Ethnographic Traditions. In *Localizing Strategies: Regional Traditions of Ethnographic Writing*, ed. R. Fardon, 137–51. Edinburgh: Scottish Academic Press.
Trevor, J. C.
1950   Aspects of Folk Culture in the Virgin Islands. Ph.D. diss., Cambridge Univ.
West, Hans
1793   *Bidrag til beskrivelse over Ste Croix med en kort Udsigt over St. Thomas, St. Jean, Tortola, Spanishtown og Crabeneiland.* Copenhagen: Friderik Wilhelm Thiele.
Winsnes, Selena Exelrod, trans. and ed.
1992   *Letters on West Africa and the Slave Trade: Paul Erdmann Isert's "Journey to Guinea and the Caribbean Islands in Columbia," (1788).* Oxford: Oxford Univ. Press.

4 | A Taste for Human Commodities

Experiencing the Atlantic System

Stephan Palmié

According to the Portuguese chronicler Gómez Eannes de Azurara, one of the most tragic and certainly most portentous processes in modern history commenced on an unknown African beach in 1441. Only half a century before Columbus set sail for Asia, nine Portuguese sailors under the command of a certain Antam Gonçalves were roaming the coastal area in the vicinity of Cabo Bojador. Their voyage's objective was to gather skins and oils, but a different idea had occurred to the ambitious young captain Gonçalves: "Oh how fair a thing it would be," he reportedly said to his crew, "if we who have come to this land for a cargo of such petty merchandise, were to meet with the good luck to bring the first captives [i.e., from this region] before the face of our Prince" (Azurara, in Donnan 1930–35: vol. 1, p. 18). At first, this seemed easier said than done. After hours of aimless wandering in the scorching heat without finding so much as a human footprint, they set out to return to the ship. Just then it happened that they encountered a solitary man, walking with a camel. They pounced upon him, and, the chronicler relates, all fatigue suddenly left them. In the ensuing brief combat, they managed to wound and capture the man. Shortly thereafter, they picked up a woman in similar fashion; and by the time they reached Portugal, they could boast of a total of forty-six captives. There, the chronicler continues, it was happily discovered that these people were not yet "hardened" in Moorish aberrations; moreover, they proved to be excellent servants. That they also proved excellent merchandise seemingly goes without saying in Azurara's account.

Thus commences the documentary record of what arguably can be equated with the beginning of the transatlantic slave trade. Columbus, after all, acquired his navigational skills in similar African forays—ventures assessed by the German historian Friederici, in the 1920s, as follows: "The best that can be said about the great slave-catching enterprise of the Infant Henry, is encompassed in the fact that due to the need of this business to constantly enlarge its field of operation, geographical discoveries could not have been avoided" (1925–36: vol. 2, p. 35).

Unthinking decisions? Glib *post hoc* rationalizations? Perhaps both.[1] But whether one chooses to subscribe to the chronicler's view or Friederici's, it is the manifold outcomes of processes set in motion by just such historically situated decisions and rationalizations that we, today, tend to subsume under the rubric "modern slavery."

Already this common-sense terminology begs numerous far-reaching questions. For, unless one defines slavery in essentialistic terms, one faces the near-impossible task of accounting for the dazzling variety of historically known forms and definitions of socially institutionalized unfreedom. Moreover, the term "modern" only compounds the problem. For its use would seem to mandate distinguishing manifestations of slavery postdating the so-called "age of European expansion" both from previous ones, and from those for which the term "modern," in any other than a mere chronological sense, is of questionable applicability.[2] Were, for example, Antam Gonçalves or his seventeenth-century British colleague John Hawkins "slavers" in the same sense as—to name just two well-known nineteenth-century counterparts—Pedro Blanco or Francisco Feliz da Souza were?[3] What are we to make of men like Karfa Taura, Mungo Park's kindly Mande host, devout Muslim and vendor of human chattel (Park 1983 [1799]: 193ff.); or of Antera Duke, indigenous Cross River slave dealer, merchant prince, diarist, and statesman (Forde 1956)? How would we compare them to such contemporaries as Henry Laurens, Charleston slave trader and president of the American revolutionary Continental Congress during 1777–78? And what about the fate of those unfortunates whose bodies furnished the merchandise in which they dealt? Is there any transhistorical measuring rod by which to compare the lives and experiences of a black slave in early sixteenth-century Lisbon, a field hand in seventeenth-century Virginia, an eighteenth-century Afro-Jamaican slave driver, a slave in the boiling room of a mid-nineteenth-century Cuban *ingenio* (sugar mill), a worker on the "plantation" of a contemporary Old Calabar "river gentleman," a member of the retinue of a Yoruba warlord, a laborer in a gold mine of the Asante hinterland, a dweller in the slave village of a

Sokoto aristocrat, or a member of the household of a Luso-African merchant in Luanda?

How are we to weigh the peculiarities of such cases against their comparable features? Ought we perhaps—as Miers and Kopytoff (1977) have suggested in the African case—to replace altogether the concept of "slavery" with more manageable units of comparative analysis? Such units might be, for example, degrees of dependence combined with tendencies towards assimilation into (or continuing marginalization in relation to) social categories provided by local kinship structures. Indeed, might not this Africanist approach bear extension to other areas of inquiry? Were we, for instance, to suspend our knowledge of later developments, we might (with considerable justification) view the servile institutions in pre-1675 Virginia in a similar processual fashion, and posit a continuum from servant/slave to property holder, operating largely (though certainly not entirely) irrespective of social constructions of race (cf. Breen 1973, Breen and Innes 1980). Was "slavery," then, merely a mechanism of socialization or political differentiation, allowing for the mobilization of (at least initially markedly alien, and coerced or dependent) human resources for economic and/or political goals? A functional variable culturally elaborated into fairly "open systems" in some cases, taking on the features of rigidly closed "total institutions" in others (Watson 1980), and generally shading into other (perhaps coexisting) forms of dependence? Yet, unless we were to confine ourselves to matters of taxonomy, would not an analysis undertaken along such lines (whether in Africa *or* the Americas) lead us straight to questions about the nature of relations of production and reproduction, practices of surplus extraction, or commerce in human bodies *present within specific social and cultural contexts at specific times?*[4] And would we, then, not want to ask how such local political economies of slavery evolved and changed in articulation with shifts in the flow of goods, capital, and power within a larger "Atlantic" economic sphere?

Not that we could simply have recourse to a *radical* distinction between the social concomitants of slavery in "capitalist" (modern, closed, New World) and "noncapitalist" (premodern, open, Old World) contexts. Take a case such as that of Bartolomé de las Casas, a man who not only knew black slavery in both its Old and New World varieties, but also witnessed the institution's transition from Europe to America (and, thus, some would argue, from a late premodern to an incipiently modern stage). As Gordon Lewis (1983: 101) suggests, Bishop de las Casas's "Sevillan background may have been responsible for his initial acceptance of Negro slavery" as a solution to both the labor problem in the West Indies and the horrors of the *encomienda* system. To be sure, black slaves abounded in sixteenth-century Seville (cf. Pike 1972). But would not de las Casas's knowledge of the operation of the "peculiar institution" in Andalusia likewise account for his later (ironically, largely erroneous) rueful acceptance of historical blame for the institutionalization of a not less horrendous system of forced African labor? Much used to be made of the continuities of medieval slave laws in the Iberian colonies, in contrast to regions where the weakness of metropolitan cultural sanctions unleashed—as Elkins (1959) put it—the "dynamics of unopposed capitalism." To be sure, calling a sixteenth-century Hispaniola sugar mill a "capitalistic" enterprise would be problematical, if not an outright anachronism. Yet, apart from the fact that this line of reasoning has long been invalidated, is it not obvious that the good bishop might not have agreed with such a choice of variables? And although de las Casas could not have understood what he saw in such terms, was he not witness to the commencement of a process that, in due time, would engender the differentiation and, paradoxically, the increasingly mutual interpenetration and interdependence of free and slave-based, capitalist and non-capitalist economies on both shores of the Atlantic Ocean?

How, finally, are we to distinguish—on other than purely definitional grounds—the period of slavery from, e.g., the regime of the "workbook" in nineteenth-century Puerto Rico, the brutal exploitation of black tenants in the post-Reconstruction sharecropping systems of the United States' South, or the social and moral terms upon which rubber extraction was organized in the Congo Free State? Were we to go by a scale of grossness of exploitation, sheer cruelty, and human degradation (or, conversely, degrees of resistance to exploitation, or moral resilience in the face of terror), might we not have to dispense with much of that part of our analytic vocabulary geared towards discriminating historical befores and afters, cultural heres and theres? Or take the question of continuity and rupture on the ideological plane. We know that liberal abolitionist discourse quickly fizzled out after emancipation, only to resurface in the guise of the "white man's burden" and its various disciplinarian routines geared toward settling what Carlyle was to call the "Nigger Question" (cf. Hall 1992). What changed may have been the "idiom of power" (Patterson 1982). Much else remained the same—or went from bad to worse, from the victims' perspective. And even in structural terms, would not a bird's-eye view suggest little other than a shifting of gears (rather than a radical evolutionary discontinuity) within both local labor regimes and an increasingly global political economy? Still, does all this necessarily mean that the end of slavery marks a dif-

ference that made no difference (cf. Mintz 1992)? Certainly not. But
how do we go about measuring what really mattered?

These are momentous questions, and this volume does not proffer
easy answers. Rather, the aim of this book is to problematize the interior of the worlds—historically localizable aggregates of action and experience—that took shape, developed, and changed within the expand-
ing perimeters of an Atlantic economy based, in part at least, on trade
in human commodities and exploitation of unfree labor. So, instead of
developing a theoretically focused perspective on "modern slavery"—
how it came into being, what it entailed, how it worked, how it might
be conceptualized, what legacies it bequeathed to the social units affected by its operation—it may be sufficient to state provisionally that
slavery marks a phase in human history. This phase can be circum-
scribed with unusual precision: we know that the British abolished it in
1834, Denmark and France in 1848, the United States some seventeen
years after that, Brazil barely over a century ago, and so on, though the
legal chronology of emancipation tells us little about the continuity of
social and cultural patterns forged under slavery. This phase coincides,
perhaps not accidentally, with the emergence of the so-called "modern
capitalist world system." The reader may decide exactly what this might
mean and how this "coincidence" may relate to a concern with slave cultures and the cultures of slavery. Let us also leave untouched a number
of important questions about the validity of "systemic" perspectives
(Wallersteinian or other) and merely assume that the "careers" of some
of these cultures can profitably be viewed as both causally and functionally related to the developmental dynamics of this larger system. We
might then conclude that there was a time when the massive commodification of African people, their exchange through transcontinental
trading channels, and the exploitation of their productive capacities in
the Americas became crucial not only to the quantitative growth, but
also to the qualitative transformation, of an increasingly "systematized"
Atlantic world.

Great transformations, however, are truly great only in retrospect.
While they proceed, they thrive on incremental matter: contingent instances of behavior that—whether the actors intend it or not—cumulatively have momentous consequences. Viewed from that angle, the Portuguese chronicler's story quoted at the beginning of this essay appears
less teleological than that of the German historian Friederici. But is it
"history"? Did millions of Africans live through a 350-year nightmare
because of something that struck the fancy of an ambitious Portuguese
mariner? Sidney Mintz has taught us a powerful lesson in that respect

(Mintz 1985). How might something as politically and culturally important as, say, the rise of capitalist merchant empires, the emergence of Caribbean plantation economies, or the Industrial Revolution be related to something as trivial and seemingly "unhistorical" as the craving for sweet substances? Grossly distorting the subtlety of Mintz's argument, I would say this is so because a rather decisive variable intervenes not only in structuring relations of production and distribution, but also in structuring those social relations crucial for giving cultural form to the act of consumption. This variable is power—not only in its cruder aspects as physical force impinging upon people's lives, but also in those more subtle manifestations affecting their imagination and desires. The English working class, Mintz tells us, did not decide to change its dietary habits in order to foster the rise of a merchant class, help Caribbean planters amass fortunes, or contribute an economic rationale for the exploitation of enslaved Africans. It worked the other way around. Individuals, we might say, develop their own tastes, but they do so under circumstances that are not of their own choosing. With this in mind, I shall now mention a few less-than-obvious aspects of certain consumption processes around which the dynamics of the "cultures" central to the concerns of this volume have revolved—at least in part.

John Stuart Mill, who certainly knew a "world system" when he saw one, once pointed out that the West Indies were a place where England found it convenient to carry on the production of tropical commodities, much as it found it convenient to produce cloth in Manchester (Mill 1849: vol. 2, p. 230). He might have added: and much as it found it convenient to carry on the production of *human commodities* in Africa, when this particular commercial item still could be sold legally to its New World consumers. We do not normally think of labor as being "consumed," but given Mill's choice of Manchester and England's West Indian colonies as examples, the term may not be entirely inappropriate.[5] Unlike the Manchester mill, however, the Caribbean plantation, in practice *as well as* in economic theory, consumed not only labor, but also the laborer himself. There is a paradox here. To the planter, the death of a slave means loss of fixed capital; to the mill owner, however, the death of a mill worker has little economic meaning. He does not own his labor force. Yet, given conditions of steady supply, Mill writes elsewhere, "enlightened self-interest will recommend working the slaves to death, and replacing them by importation, in preference to the slow and expensive process of breeding them. Nor are," he sarcastically adds, "the slave-owners generally backward in learning this lesson" (Mill 1849: vol. 1, p. 303). Mill, of course, actively supported abolition. Yet

once one considers the writings of "truly enlightened" proslavery ideo-
logues such as the Cuban Francisco Arango y Parreña, Mills's wry comments about the seedy side of liberal economic thought take on a bitter
ring of truth. Under ideal conditions, maturing Caribbean plantation
regimes devoured both land and men—one in the form of a natural resource (limited and irreproducible), and the other in the form of what
one might call a commodity embodying labor yet to be extracted (limited but reproducible). As a social practice (and not a purely economic
one—if such a thing exists), consumption presupposes acquisition of
culturally relevant consumer skills. Hence, when the imaginations of
European actors grasped, as a feasible option and a desirable end, the
fantastic profits to be derived from involvement in what Philip Curtin
called the "South Atlantic System," they had to—and often did—"learn"
to consume men, with all the ghastly connotations this phrase implies.

Most of the Euro-American actors implicated in such patterns of
consumption have presumably gone through a process of "acquiring a
taste." Humans, at times, may be construed as things. But a "thing" is
not necessarily a "good," nor is it naturally good to consume every thing.
Even the perception of "use-value," as Trouillot (1992) points out, presupposes a process of cultural construction. More obviously still, demand and desire do not speak to relations between the consumer and
the object of his desire (quantifiable in such economistic constructs as,
e.g., "scarcity"); they rather refer to social and political relations between
consumers (or would-be consumers) within which "desirability" and access are negotiated. Quite aside from the—by now largely sterile—debate about European institutional precedents, nothing comparable to
the dimensions of full-blown American slave regimes ever existed in the
Old World. And the craving for "piezas de Indias"—as the Spanish
aptly called a mercantile unit of human flesh comprised sometimes of
more than one human being—is neither a biological given, nor an economic necessity. It is, if I may say so, an acquired taste.

To some the taste came more easily than to others. Take Matthew
"Monk" Lewis, recent inheritor of a Jamaican plantation, who shrinks
back when one of his servants introduces himself by saying "Massa not
know me; *me your slave*" (Matthew Gregory Lewis 1834: 62). Lewis
tells us:

> The sound made me feel a pang in my heart. . . . The lad appeared all
> gaiety and good humour, and his whole countenance expressed anxiety to
> recommend himself to my notice; but the word "slave" seemed to imply,
> that, although he did feel pleasure then in serving me, if he had detested

me he must have served me still. I really felt quite humiliated at the moment, and was tempted to tell him,—"Do not say that again; say that you are my negro, but do not call yourself my slave." (Matthew Gregory Lewis 1834: 62)

Lewis, of course, says nothing—not that it would have made any difference. For if it is true that "objectification" in the form of "goods" renders cultural categories tangible,[6] then—apart from the important question of what it might have meant to the servant—the change of labels, on Lewis's part, would have been irrelevant within the culture within which he had chosen to immerse himself. It was, to paraphrase Marx, one of those historical moments when "a negro" (and especially "my negro") is almost as automatically a slave as "a mule is a machine for spinning cotton."

Though certainly largely geared toward celebrating the romantic self in an exotic setting, Lewis's *Journal* is both a "Bildungsroman" of his education into a "culture of slavery," and—in a wider sense—exactly what its full title says: the journal of a West Indian *proprietor*, someone who derives the wherewithal for a luxurious existence from an economic unit in which the consumption of bought human beings miraculously engenders the wealth that he in turn consumes. Even in those moments when Lewis pines away in pleasant sexual fantasies about some sable Venus on his estate, Monsieur Le Capital and Madame La Terre do not stray from his side, implicating the poor man in his own culture's mystifications of a veritable cannibalistic feast.[7] The opportunity is there; he takes it. The rest is, perhaps quite aptly, "a process of seasoning"—although, in all fairness, one must say that Monk Lewis ultimately fails to live up to the standards of enlightened self-interest. The "Shylocky taste of raw flesh" (Matthew Gregory Lewis 1834: 50) that Lewis experienced when ingesting a bit of watermelon on his first day in Jamaica never seems quite to have left him.

All this may sound as if I am veering off in a somewhat odd direction. Did not the slaves themselves literally push their personhood upon their masters in exploiting the various contradictions—psychological, legal, economic—that the encompassing system engendered in local social practice? Did they not "singularize" (Igor Kopytoff 1986) themselves in myriad ways: by growing provisions for market exchanges, accumulating property, founding families, tracing descent, even committing crimes for which they had *individually* to be held responsible; or, conversely, by making themselves, *as persons*, psychologically indispensable to their masters? Did they not run away, rebel, kill their masters, or even kill themselves to avoid their eventual consumption by the plantation or the colonial state behind it? Most importantly, what about their agency in maintaining, manipulating, or cutting such ties as bound them to their masters (and, by implication to the merchants in Liverpool, Nantes, Amsterdam, or Rhode Island)? Did they not have a share in the making—and sometimes, as in St. Domingue, in the un-making—of whole worlds of slaveholding and slavery? All that is true, and the contributions to this volume highlight precisely such struggles and contradictions as characterized the societies and cultures that emerged within a globalizing economic order predicated upon funda-mentally antagonistic, but often strangely cooperative, human relation-ships, projects, and practices.

At this point, however, I am more concerned with a certain divi-sion of labor in the production of ideas about such worlds as slaves and slaveholders *perforce* had to share. So let me briefly approach this issue from an entirely different angle. Here is what Mungo Park has to say about images of such patterns of consumption fomented among the mass of human merchandise he was privileged to accompany on their way to a Gambian nexus with "the world system":

> They were all very inquisitive, but they viewed me at first with looks of horror, and repeatedly asked if my countrymen were cannibals. They were very desirous to know what became of the slaves after they had crossed the salt water. I told them that they were employed in cultivating the land, but they would not believe me. . . . A deeply rooted idea that the whites purchase Negroes for the purpose of devouring them, or of selling them to others, that they may be devoured hereafter, naturally makes the slaves contemplate a journey towards the coast with great hor-ror. (Park 1983 [1799]: 244)

Arriving in the West Indies about half a century before Matthew Lewis, Olaudah Equiano's "seasoning experience" proceeded on terms differ-ent from, though certainly not unrelated to, those of the poet-planter. "There was much dread and trembling among us, and nothing but bit-ter cries to be heard all night from these apprehensions," he tells us. "[A]t last the white people got some old slaves from the land to pacify us. They told us we were not to be eaten but to work, and were soon to go on land where we should see many of our country people. This re-port eased us much" (Equiano 1987 [1814]: 37).

It seems to have been fairly common in West Africa for the victims of the slave trade to think of the system into which they were to be incorporated as one of "cannibalistic consumption," though we should be careful to note the full semantic range of expressions, such as, e.g., the Kikongo phrase *dia bantu*, "to eat people" (cf. Laman 1962: 216). Often, these terms seem to relate to conceptions of ill-gotten gain, to ideas about the loss of the victim's personhood through witchcraft or other evil machinations designed to augment the sorcerer's power and wealth. The folk conception of the *zonbi* in Haitian *vodou* speaks to such processes of moral derailment, but so do the perceptions of modern-day Bakongo recorded by Wyatt MacGaffey (1968, 1972, 1978). In the latter case, Belgians or other Europeans are thought to transport stolen souls to a place variously called *mputo* (i.e., Portugal) or *Amérique* where they turn white and are made to produce cars, radios, and textiles for re-import into Africa. They think the driving force behind this all is witchcraft. We think it is world capitalism. "This is the price" says the mutilated slave who hobbles across Candide's path in Suriname, "at which you eat sugar."

All this ostensibly fits with the familiar *Tempest* scenario, except that, in our case, Alonso really would be the sorcerer, if one single such character ever could be read into the historical evidence. A second thought, even more disturbing, perhaps, is this: at times, even Prospero and Caliban are not that easy to tell apart. Take the fate that befell William Ellison, one of those sorcerer's apprentices whom James Johnson and Michael Roark made the subject of their monograph *Black Masters* (1984). Here we find an African-American Prospero—a self-freed, successful artisan, eventually a planter and substantial slaveholder. A man taking great pains to purchase no slaves lighter in skin color than any of his family members. Someone with an obvious stake in the magic that helped build his very own enchanted island near antebellum Charleston. Yet Ellison, too, falls victim to the plot of a morality tale that we, in the aftermath, might say his culture held in store for him. For, at the very acme of his remarkable success story, we find him agonizing over the likelihood that his son has fathered children of a slave woman, thus reducing Ellison's own grandchildren to a state of existence he had striven all his life to transcend: slavery. "Ellison built his refuge in Statesburg at a very high price," Johnson and Roark conclude:

> He enslaved other Afro-Americans, ignored most free people of color, dominated members of his own family, and spent all his life trying to please whites. The cost, however, did not include the sacrifice of his personality or the elimination of his will. He behaved deliberately, according to his judgement of the demands of his society. . . . He stood as far from

the river of heroic, militant black protest as any man in his era. He did not challenge Southern society, but he did seek to defend himself from the degradation it reserved for people of color. He contradicted the basic notions white Southerners had about Negroes. In that modest, quiet way he led a life of protest. (1984: 150)

Or did he? And did the maroons of Jamaica and Suriname who, after decades of successful warfare against the British and Dutch colonial states, signed treaties obliging them to return future fugitives—in exchange not only for their political sovereignty but also for payments they seem to have viewed as due tribute? And what about those black Moravian brethren, who not only knew but deeply felt that their elders had "bought" their persons in order to free their souls? What, we might ask, constitutes a "life of protest," after all? What are its "commensurabilities"? What are the "perils of the soul" it visits upon those embroiled in living it? dancing, as it were, with the enemy?

Take—as a last example—what Herskovits had to say about the ceremonies for the "unknown dead" he witnessed at King Behanzin's court in Abomey in the early 1930s. After the sacrifice, a priest intoned the following chant:

> Oh ancestors, do all in your power that princes and nobles who today rule never be sent away from here as slaves to Ame'ica, to Togbome, to Gbulu, to Kankanu [i.e., Dutch territory], to Gbuluvia, to Rarira. We pray you to do all in your power to punish the people who bought our kinsmen whom we shall never see again. (Herskovits 1966: 87)

But the priest continues: "Send their vessels to Whidah harbor. When they come, drown their crews, and make the wealth of their ships come back to Dahomey." And the participants in the ceremony enumerate exactly what such retribution is to be: "The English must bring guns. The Portuguese must bring powder. The Spaniards must bring the small stones which give fire to our fire-sticks. The Americans must bring the cloths and the rum made by our kinsmen who are there, for these will permit us to smell their presence" (Herskovits 1966: 87). That, then, may be what history—such histories, at least—is all about: the smell of a presence, an intimation. Reflected in, and refracted through, the odor of rum and gunpowder, the feel of fancy cotton, the taste of sugar. It is in the smile of a servant who turns out to be a thing one possesses, as it is in the sweat on the brow of a bunch of men roaming the coast near Cabo Bojador.

Notes

1. There is, of course, no question that Africans were held as slaves on the Iberian peninsula long before the Portuguese first achieved the crucial feat of circumnavigating Cabo Verde *and* returning. Neither was the trade in human beings anything but a time-hallowed, if perhaps declining, economic institution in late-medieval Europe. A market, as well as a demand for such import goods, in other words, already existed. Gonçalves's achievement (if it really was his) rather consisted in finding a way to eliminate the Islamic middlemen who monopolized the trade at the ends of the trans-Sahara routes. Incidentally, this was why Columbus's sponsors, too, invested in his project to find the passage to India: here the goal was to avoid the Muslim-infested eastern Mediterranean Sea and so gain direct access to valued Asian commodities.

2. In the African case, it is apposite to recall the numerous ramifications of the controversy—started by Rodney (1966) and Fage (1969)—concerning the external induction or indigenous character of slavery and slavetrading, especially since this controversy tends to merge with the substantivist-formalist debate in economic anthropology. Today few scholars would deny the pre-Atlantic existence of slavery and slavetrading in Africa. Still far from well understood, however, are the nature of the institution, its economic modalities and functions, and—perhaps worst of all—its role in the interplay of factors "relatively internal" to the economies of Africa, Europe, and the Americas in the shaping of what we have come to call the "*modern* capitalist world system." (See, e.g., the contributions to Solow and Engerman 1987 and Solow 1991.)

3. For Da Souza, see Verger (1953); Eltis (1987: 145–63) gives a good idea of the scale of their operations.

4. With respect both to overly sanguine views of "lineage slavery" in Africa and to the debate about Genovese's (1974) famous paternalism thesis, it may be worth recalling Wolf's insight that the relationships between owners and workers in what he calls "old-style plantations" *merely retain the form* of kin or other face-to-face relationships while serving different functions (Wolf 1971 [1959]).

5. The English word *consumption* probably continued—in keeping with its Latin root verb *consumere*—to carry the primary meaning of "destruction," "devastation," and "destruction through use" until the eighteenth century. Why its more "innocuous" economic connotations apparently acquired their present (relative) dominance in the course of that century might deserve further investigation.

6. See, e.g., Douglas and Isherwood (1979), McCracken (1988).

7. Here one might think of the strange semantic chain Adam Smith (1952 [1776]) creates, perhaps unwittingly, when talking about sugar as wine and the West Indies as a vineyard, then comparing wine with money as commodities whose scarcity engenders exaggerated demand and desire, and finally establishing a discursive linkage between engrossing or forestalling and witchcraft. If money could (metaphorically as well as literally) be "grown" in the Caribbean, and if restricting its consumption is evil, then liberal economics certainly provide a solution for satisfying the appetites of planters and merchants. But would not the free flow of sugar/wine/money, by implication, lead to intoxication? Smith says no, but some contemporaries with more direct experience of the addictive properties of this process knew better. Why was it that people like Tom Paine or

Thomas Jefferson, *who really knew better,* found it so exceedingly hard to kick the habit? Was it, as McCracken (1988: 132) puts it, because goods "seek not only to describe" the culture which constructed them, "but also to persuade" their consumer of the "inevitability" of such cultural arrangements? Could one of the key "problems of slavery in the age of revolution" have been based upon a conjunction, within a single communicative context, of the fairly straightforward language of the *droit des hommes* and a culturally far less determinate economic idiom, based on the exchange and consumption of human commodities? Though McFarlane's thesis (1987) strikes me as simplistic, his remarks on monetarization and the transvaluability of moral categories may be worth pondering in this context.

References

Breen, Timothy H.
1973   A Changing Labor Force and Race Relations in Virginia, 1660–1710. *Journal of Social History* 7: 3–25.
Breen, Timothy H., and Steven Innes
1980   *Myne Owne Ground: Race and Freedom on Virginia's Eastern Shore, 1640–1676.* New York: Oxford Univ. Press.
Donnan, Elizabeth
1930–35 *Documents Illustrative of the Slave Trade to America.* Washington, D.C.: Carnegie Institute.
Douglas, Mary, and Baron Isherwood
1979   *The World of Goods.* New York: Basic Books.
Elkins, Stanley
1959   *Slavery: A Problem in American Institutional and Intellectual Life.* Chicago: Univ. of Chicago Press.
Eltis, David
1987   *Economic Growth and the Ending of the Transatlantic Slave Trade.* New York: Oxford Univ. Press.
Equiano, Olaudah
1987 [1814]   *The Interesting Life of Olaudah Equiano.* Rpt. in *The Classic Slave Narratives,* ed. Henry Louis Gates, 1–181. New York: Mentor.
Fage, John D.
1969   Slavery and the Slave Trade in the Context of West African History. *Journal of African History* 10: 393–404.
Forde, Daryll
1956   *Efik Traders of Old Calabar.* London: Oxford Univ. Press.
Friederici, Georg
1925–36 *Der Charakter der Entdeckung und Eroberung Amerikas durch die Europäer.* Stuttgart-Gotha, Germany: Andreas Perthes.
Genovese, Eugene D.
1974   *Roll, Jordan, Roll: The World the Slaves Made.* New York: Pantheon.
Hall, Catherine
1992   Missionary Stories: Gender and Ethnicity in England in the 1830s and 1840s. In *Cultural Studies,* ed. Lawrence Grossberg, Cary Nelson, and Paula Treichler, 240–70. New York: Routledge.

Herskovits, Melville J.
1966 A Footnote to the History of Negro Slaving. In *The New World Negro,* ed. Frances Herskovits, 83–89. Bloomington: Indiana Univ. Press.
Johnson, James, and Michael Roark
1984 *Black Masters.* New York: Norton.
Kopytoff, Igor
1986 The Cultural Biography of Things: Commoditization as a Process. In *The Social Life of Things,* ed. Arjun Appadurai, 64–91. Cambridge: Cambridge UP.
Kopytoff, Igor, and Suzanne Miers
1977 Introduction: African "Slavery" as an Institution of Marginality. In *Slavery in Africa: Historical and Anthropological Perspectives,* ed. Suzanne Miers and Igor Kopytoff, 3–81. Madison: Univ. of Wisconsin Press.
Laman, Karl
1962 *The Kongo III.* Studia Ethnographica Upsaliensia No. 12. Lund, Sweden: Hakan Ohlssons Boktryckeri.
Lewis, Gordon K.
1983 *Main Currents in Caribbean Thought.* Baltimore, Md.: Johns Hopkins Univ. Press.
Lewis, Matthew Gregory
1834 *Journal of a West India Proprietor.* London: John Murray.
MacGaffey, Wyatt
1968 Kongo and the King of the Americans. *Journal of Modern African Studies* 6: 171–81.
1972 The West in Congolese Experience. In *Africa and the West,* ed. Philip Curtin, 49–74. Madison: Univ. of Wisconsin Press.
1978 African History, Anthropology, and the Rationality of Natives. *History in Africa* 5: 101–20.
McCracken, Grant
1988 *Culture and Consumption.* Bloomington: Indiana Univ. Press.
McFarlane, Alan
1987 Evil. In Alan McFarlane, *The Culture of Capitalism,* 98–122. London: Blackwell.
Miers, Suzanne, and Igor Kopytoff, eds.
1977 *Slavery in Africa: Historical and Anthropological Perspectives.* Madison: Univ. of Wisconsin Press.
Mill, John Stuart.
1849 *Principles of Political Economy.* London: Routledge.
Mintz, Sidney W.
1985 *Sweetness and Power.* Hammondsworth, England: Penguin
1992 Panglosses and Pollyannas; or, Whose Reality Are We Talking About? In *The Meaning of Freedom,* ed. Frank McGlynn and Seymour Drescher, 245–56. Pittsburgh, Pa.: Univ. of Pittsburgh Press.
Park, Mungo
1983 [1799] *Travels into the Interior of Africa.* London: Eland Books.
Patterson, Orlando
1982 *Slavery and Social Death.* Cambridge, Mass.: Harvard Univ. Press.
Pike, Ruth
1972 *Aristocrats and Traders: Sevillian Society in the Sixteenth Century.* Ithaca, N.Y.: Cornell Univ. Press.

Rodney, Walter
1966   African Slavery and Other Forms of Social Oppression on the Upper Guinea
        Coast in the Context of the Atlantic Slave Trade. *Journal of African History* 7:
        431–43
Smith, Adam
1952 [1776] *An Inquiry into the Nature and Causes of the Wealth of Nations.* Chicago:
        Encyclopedia Britannica.
Solow, Barbara L., ed.
1991   *Slavery and the Rise of the Atlantic System.* Cambridge: Cambridge Univ. Press.
Solow, Barbara L., and Stanley Engerman, eds.
1987   *British Capitalism and Caribbean Slavery: The Legacy of Eric Williams.* Cam-
        bridge: Cambridge Univ. Press.
Trouillot, Michel Rolph
1992   Banana Wars: The Sweetness of Commodities. Paper presented at the Annual
        Meeting of the American Anthropological Association, San Francisco, 2–6
        Dec. 1992.
Verger, Pierre
1953   Influence du Brésil au Golfe du Bénin. In *Les Afro-Américains,* 11–101.
        Mémoires de l'Institut Francais d'Afrique Noire, no. 27. Dakar, Senegal:
        Institut Français d'Afrique Noire.
Watson, James L.
1980   Slavery as an Institution: Open and Closed Systems. In *African and Asian Sys-
        tems of Slavery,* ed. James L. Watson, 1–15. Berkeley: Univ. of California
        Press.
Wolf, Eric
1971 [1959] Specific Aspects of Plantations in the New World: Community Sub-
        Cultures and Social Classes. In *Peoples and Cultures of the Caribbean,* ed.
        Michael M. Horowitz, 163–78. Garden City, N.Y.: Natural History Press.

5 | The Gold Coast, the Closing of the Atlantic Slave Trade, and Africans of the Diaspora

Richard Rathbone

The Gold Coast, as it was described by the British after their annexation of the coast and hinterland of what became Ghana in March 1957, was not exactly the area so denominated at the height of the Atlantic slave trade. The area from the mouth of the Tano River to the delta of the Volta River is roughly the area most commonly referred to in precolonial texts; the more modern, colonial definition extended beyond the coastal town of Keta.

Although the numbers of Africans exported from the Slave Coast or the Bight of Biafra far exceeded the numbers whose last sorrowing sight of Africa was the Gold Coast, the population of the latter region played an important role in the making of the Atlantic regional economy. Part of the evidence for this statement is still to be seen in the region today; the latter was—and remains—the site of some of the most spectacular trading forts on the entire West African coast. These awesome, if exceptionally grisly, reminders of a tragic past are to be found in widely differing states of repair from the western coastal borders of modern Ghana to the Volta mouth.[1]

The trade of these castles and forts always combined commodities and slaves. Thus the conduct of the Atlantic trade transformed the economic, social, and political lives not only of those African societies upon whom the trade preyed, but also of the more proximate coastal African communities. An appropriate urban historiography would recognize the widespread and profound impact on these societies, for three centuries, of supplying forts, castles, baracoons, and ships with foodstuffs, timber, and fresh water, as well as providing such services as blacksmithing, acting as porters or policemen, and numerous other craft and agricultural activities which facilitated the trade.[2] While African political sovereignty remained more or less intact until the 1870s—most of the European trading posts were, in effect, leasehold properties—it actually was a series of sovereignties over a variety of rapidly changing political economies and societies (Kea 1982).

As is well known, the slave trade was abolished by the three major participants in the international trade of this part of the West African coast between 1803 (Danish) and 1814 (Dutch). Such formal abolition took place following more than a half-century in which the volume of slave exports from these castles and entrepots had increased greatly. Abolition, however, did not end the trade. The region lacked deep-water ports;[3] trade goods and slaves always had been transferred by large canoes to merchant vessels anchored beyond the surf-line. After 1807, Africans continued to be shipped, especially to Brazil but also to the Caribbean, from "informal" gathering points along the coast, particularly those close to the Volta delta and the intricate lagoon system marking much of the coast east of the Volta. They also continued to be shipped from some of the forts under Danish and Dutch control. Complex shoal waters, treacherous tide-rips, and uncertain cartography impeded efforts by British naval antislaving patrols to harass the trade until the 1850s, when both the political situation and more accurate charts began to simplify their task. But their work before then was complicated by the fact that a proportion of Dutch human exports were, formally at least, free men who were "recruited" to the Dutch colonial military forces and eventually sent to the West Indies.

While it is widely agreed that the Atlantic and other intercontinental slave trades continued, albeit in contracting fashion, into the 1850s and even beyond, the history of slavery in the Gold Coast after, say, 1810 has received comparatively little attention. It is a commonplace to argue that slave use in the region both increased and intensified.[4] The full extent of this growth is unlikely to be determined satisfactorily and accurately. But it is clear that the slow and uneven transition to what, by the end of the nineteenth century, was a growing "legitimate" export economy[5] was undergirded in part by extensive use of unfree labor. One of the new colonial regime's first legal actions was to pass, in 1874, the Emancipation Ordinance, whose application was gradually and unevenly enforced over the following quarter-century.

The ending of the Atlantic trade in the course of the nineteenth century might have snapped the links between this part of Africa and the Americas, but it did not. Before British annexation of the entire coast in 1874, African-Caribbean and African-Brazilian peoples were beginning to play a small but important part in the post-abolition life of coastal communities.[6] Perhaps the earliest examples of those who made the return journey to the coast were some of the soldiers who had served in the Dutch East and West Indies, been repatriated by the Dutch, and settled between Elmina and Cape Coast. These were predominantly Moslems; although some may have been Moslem when recruited, not all of them were, and there is a strong suggestion in the oral material that a number of them had converted to Islam while serving the Dutch. Another element in the repatriated and largely Moslem population of coastal settlements were those Africans who were deported by the civil authorities in Brazil following a series of major slave revolts between 1831 and 1835. For reasons which remain unclear, a small segment of these communities, whose very recent African origins (most were African-born) were almost universally Moslem Hausa and Yoruba, had discarded Islam in favor of Christianity. Those who remained Moslem formed the socioeconomic cores of rapidly developing Moslem quarters—the Zongos, as they are called in Ghana—in the larger coastal towns like Cape Coast and Winneba. The Christians, or at least some of them, intermarried within the Western-educated coastal elite whose self-generation from the eighteenth century is such a vivid and important element in modern Ghanaian history.[7] In some cases, as with the Ribeiros, such families were to become leading members of the professional and administrative class in the twentieth century.

Although the "Brazilian" traders of Whydah, Porto Novo, and Lagos were more numerous and have attracted more scholarly attention (see, e.g., Verger 1976), Brazilians were active on the Gold Coast. Operating out of the eastern ports, they were active as agents of Bahian merchant houses in the import and export trades, which included slave transactions. As with their counterparts farther east, many sank the capital derived from private entrepreneurial activity into personal ownership of slaves, independent merchant careers, and, in some cases, small-scale oil-palm and coffee plantations.[8]

By the end of the eighteenth century, the Danes had been convinced that plantation agriculture could be established on the heights[9] which rise to the north of the Accra plains.[10] In 1843, twenty-five African-

Caribbean ex-slave settlers arrived from Jamaica. They had been recruited by the Presbyterian Basel Missionaries[11] from the Moravian community on the island. This group was to form the core of the community still referred to in Ghana as the "Jamaicans," who initially farmed around the mission station the Swiss had established in Akropong in 1842. The evidence, both oral and written, suggests that this was a very successful community. It provided a number of Christian activists who in part were responsible for the remarkably liberal attitudes exhibited by the Basel Mission in its operations in the southern Akan areas.[12] The distinguished Ghanaian scholar, Edward Reynolds,[13] himself a scion of this community, has shown me carefully researched evidence confirming the mission's record that some members of this proselytizing Christian farming and priestly community were slave owners at least until the formal British abolition of slavery in 1874 and in some cases after this.

By the first third of the nineteenth century, the Dutch were settling repatriates around the Accra area. Before 1874, there was also a small African-Caribbean presence drawn from the British West Indian colonies. The bulk of these individuals[14] were serving with the West India Regiment which, after 1844, was stationed in and around the town of Cape Coast and that sector of the Gā state which was called English Accra. British military campaigns against the large inland state of Asante in 1863–64 and especially in 1873–74 were carried out by forces composed in the main of local levies and allies, and a greatly enhanced number of troops from the West India Regiments.[15]

There is no doubt that a number of these soldiers made the Gold Coast their home. One of them, Edward Stewart, became a minister of religion and is remembered as the pioneer of the pro-temperance American Templar movement in the Gold Coast (Casely Hayford and Rathbone 1992). Another, J. B. Small, a Barbadian, who had served in the regiment in the 1860s, after leaving the army returned to the Gold Coast in the 1890s to establish the American Methodist Episcopal Zion Church there.[16]

The expansion of the British presence after the somewhat equivocal "defeat" of Asante in 1874 preceded a wave of racial discrimination in the colonial public service from the mid-1890s on. Before discrimination began to bite, African Caribbeans were recruited to serve in senior positions in the colonial state—for example, a puisne judge, one of the colony's select band of district commissioners, and a director of education—along with white officials with Caribbean backgrounds. This pattern persisted throughout the early colonial period. A surprisingly large number of African Caribbeans served the colonial state after being recruited in the West Indies.[17]

The "potted biographies" in the *Colonial Office Lists* demonstrate that a number of colonial officers, usually but not inevitably at the lower ends of departmental hierarchies, bore "English" surnames but in fact had been born and educated in the British Caribbean. This was especially notable in the Education Department. But the largely unofficial racial barriers that progressively prevented black people from ascending the career ladder, especially in the Political Service,[18] tended to push the children of successful families away from government service and into the private and professional sectors. Such an active choice is most obvious in the legal profession but also is clear in the frequency with which one encounters the descendants of most of these groups in medicine, business, and commerce. The close relationship between business and the law, and especially between concessionaire activity and the law, is obvious enough, and members of such families were involved in a variety of such activities in a single lifetime.[19]

On its own, this brief account of how and roughly when these groups went back to Africa is of merely antiquarian interest. That these coastal societies were complex, sophisticated, and culturally plural is well known, and outlining the precise provenance of each of their human building blocks produces nothing but laundry lists. The more intriguing issues—for example, the integration or reintegration of people of African descent into the region—remain largely unstudied. From the point of view of a historian of Ghana, this is a tragic byproduct of the rather remarkable absence of solid studies of Ghanaian coastal urban history.[20] In a broader perspective, intriguing questions about identity and culture arise. How, for example, were African Caribbeans and African Brazilians viewed by "host communities"? And how did repatriates view Africa?

It is striking how, several generations after these events, modern southern Ghanaian society is acutely aware of the provenance of these great (and not-so-great) families and of individual progenitors from the other side of the Atlantic. African-Brazilian and African-Caribbean genealogy assuredly is not alone in this awareness. Many of the significant coastal families have a European ancestor, a fact instantly evident in the proliferation of Dutch, Danish, and British surnames among the present-day elite.[21] Many of the single male traders on the coast in both eighteenth and nineteenth centuries took African wives.[22] Some of their descendants intermarried, while others married more obviously unalloyed Africans—those either indigenous to, or newly arrived in, these growing towns. The so-called "modern elite" in the Gold Coast never was a "closed" group, and it constantly recruited (and still recruits) from among those whose education, high birth, and wealth gave them access to their society (see, e.g., Gocking 1984).

While the family histories of those families with West Indian ancestry happily acknowledge the latter, it is no less clear that little distinction, if any, is made between West Indian and European progenitors. Both are regarded as somewhat exotic and socially desirable features of family escutcheons—sources of distinctiveness and pride. In the vernacular, West Indian forebears usually are not described as being racially different from those from Europe. Both are regarded as "other," and the otherness of the West Indians is not modified by their color, although both Twi and Gã languages have a rich vocabulary addressing skin color and "mixed ancestry."

There are, of course, many ways in which these modern recensions of ancestry can be read. It is certainly unclear that such present-day expressions have much in common with unrecorded recitals of ancestry 150 years ago. It is possible to argue, however, that the very history of these coastal towns—a history of long-term contact with the Atlantic, of in-migration from the hinterland as trade expanded, of intercontinental and inter-regional as well as inter-ethnic marriage—has categorized ethnicity, for lack of a better word, in ways which dwell less upon color than upon ideas such as "stranger." While the Twi word for a white man, *oburoni*, is used frequently, it can also be used to describe West Indian ancestors.

No less important for an understanding of how such strangers inserted themselves within these vibrant African communities is the utter lack of discussion of the slave origins of many of these African-Caribbean settlers. This cannot be simply the result of sweeping an uncomfortable reality under the carpet. Twi and Gã speakers are acutely aware of each other's genealogical origins. While it is abundantly clear that here, as in most communities, genealogy is constantly being constructed socially and that slave origins can be imputed to the weak and overcome by the strong, such origins are part and parcel of everyday discourse. Despite the strong traditional prohibition against invoking such elements of the past—a prohibition expressed in the normative avoidance of asking anyone where he or she comes from, a question which might imply doubt about free antecedents—such matters are, in reality, discussed frequently and openly. And from the way in which they are discussed, one might expect that the fact that the "Jamaicans," for example, had slave origins would be used against them by their enemies or rivals. But this appears not to have occurred.

It is impossible to be certain why this was so. It might be that such matters are socially inconvenient, but the robustness of contemporary Ghanaian discourse on slavery is such that this seems an unpersuasive argument. It is more intriguing and possibly more accurate to read this as the result of a distinction made between local slavery and slavery imposed far away. In Twi, the invocation of slavery connotes two major social burdens. The first is a particular kind of social distance. The term *odonkor* frequently is used not only for slaves or for those with a slave past, but also (regrettably, to this day) for people from northern Ghana,[23] the ancient slaving grounds for both local and export slaves. The second suggests extremes of poverty (which traditionally do not necessarily excite pity) and its usual cause, a lack of proximate, useful, and prideful kinship connections.

My guess is that African-Brazilian and African-Caribbean repatriates never were constructed within this complex, developed set of attitudes toward slaves and slavery. There clearly were several kinds of otherness which were, and sometimes still are, imagined by Twi speakers. The insertion of Europeans into these historical coastal societies—first as trading partners, then as husbands and sons-in-law, and ultimately as ancestors—created the usable precedents for repatriates. Their personally tragic family histories were discounted or brushed aside in view of their comparative wealth, their literacy in some cases, their styles of dress and address, and, for many, their profession of orthodox Christianity. The last, by the early nineteenth century, was a social as well as a confessional sign of being close to coastal "high society." It is noteworthy that the Moslem repatriates became far more thoroughly integrated into the poorer sectors of urban society, and at a more rapid rate, than their Christian equivalents. In southern Ghana, until recently Islam was largely the faith of some of the laboring poor and street traders and not of the elite.

The coastal communities, by the time of African-Brazilian and African-Caribbean repatriations, were firmly locked into international trade. They were already complex, cosmopolitan societies dominated by families who intermarried at a hectic pace and who commanded both economic life and what still was called, perhaps anachronistically, traditional power. They were habituated to the social, economic, and familial insinuation of eccentric figures from remote corners of the globe. By the mid-nineteenth century, these societies were using English as their trading, confessional, and in some cases even domestic *lingua franca*. "Race" seems to have played little part in these processes, and people of African descent—whether they came from the Americas or indirectly via Sierra Leone or what is today Nigeria—apparently were constructed as just another set of outsiders who could add social and other kinds of value by being allowed "inside."

But these outsiders were, at least initially, just that—outsiders. They were distanced from some of the more abidingly important aspects of African life by their ignorance of local languages, cosmology, and "customs," and they were not embedded in kinship structures. All such interlopers appear to have overcome such otherness in time. Almost all, it seems, became proficient in the relaxed and syncretic bilingualism of the coast. Some, through marriage, gained access to traditional offices, and almost all became subject to traditional obligations. Such transitions were differentially problematical. For "outsider" men marrying in the matrilineal, Akan-speaking Fante states to the west of Winneba, a wife's provenance would draw their children, especially, into the network of matrilineage rights and obligations inherited through their mothers; this connection was and is of far greater importance than the rights and obligations inherited through one's father. Strategic marriage placed many such *arrivistes* in advantageous positions within royal families; thus, by the end of the century, many "traditional rulers" were men whose ancestry included Europeans and repatriated Africans. Although the evidence is slight, it seems probable that such entry into patrilineal Gã society took rather longer when outsider men were marrying "insider" women. Overall, however, the overarching significance of family and family strategies in these coastal areas provided the mechanism by which integration could occur.[24]

It would be painting an incomplete picture to insist that such incorporation was a process in which "others" simply were sucked into a hegemonic African culture. That culture itself was being simultaneously deconstructed and reconstructed by processes profoundly influenced by the presence of aliens and their ideas and practices. The biographies of many coastal luminaries of the late nineteenth century illustrate the complexities of identity. Men like John Vanderpuije of Accra or B. D. Coker of Cape Coast simultaneously held positions such as minor chief, freemason, and important merchant. The great scholar, novelist, and lawyer J. E. Casely Hayford was Safohin Ahinnana Agyiman of Cape Coast Number 3 Asafo Company; there are innumerable other examples. The impacts of Christianity, literacy, and Western technology, and of the ideas that swirled around them, stood in constant and constructive tension with African thinking and practice. An unending dialectical process of appropriating, domesticating, and discarding took place.[25]

It is particularly difficult to discover what these repatriates thought of the Africa with which they had been reunited. What survives of their testimonies echoes, to some extent, the language of the Americo-Liberian settlers. They talk in the language of the day about "natives," and that expression, stripped of its later pejorative colonial connotations, was hardly inaccurate. Few if any of the repatriates, even if they were African by descent, were "natives" of the Gold Coast area, and they did not so regard themselves. There is a clear intersection of class and race in their discourse. Those who were made part of the colonial state in its early days regarded themselves as part of the governing class, distanced from those they ruled by dint of office but entwined with at least the elite among them through marriage and social practice. Their use of the words *native* and even *African* seems rooted in something like class consciousness and, it must be said, notable snobbery. But that statement needs periodizing. By the end of the nineteenth century, growing evidence of colonial exclusions on racial grounds led many of those with repatriate origins increasingly to identify themselves, especially in the politics of the Gold Coast, as African. This trend is visible in the iconographic record, where photography suggests that, more and more, people presented themselves in traditional cloth rather than in stifling stiff collars and three-piece suits. It is also clear in the use of given names, as more and more members of the coastal elite sought to be described by, for example, their African day names rather than by their baptismal and usually biblical given names. Literature has reflected a growing and decidedly assertive interest in the history of Africa (Jenkins 1990).

There is very little evidence suggesting that these new Gold Coasters found it easier to integrate in their adopted and adoptive societies because of any retained "Africanisms." As suggested above, few if any claimed even fictive origins in their eventual home. Because of the significant number of Akan words in Jamaican patois, simple vocabulary acquisition might have posed fewer problems for them than for other outsiders. Aspects of social life, including cuisine, might have been more familiar to them than to others. But there is no real evidence that they were perceived by their host societies as less foreign than other foreigners, nor that they were either more or less privileged in their integration process. But they were integrated by African communities which—given a specific history of pre-European incorporationist strategies and a later experience of the developing Atlantic economy—had created a set of complex and remarkable cultures and societies.

Notes

1. From the splendors of Elmina Castle, now used as a romantic if expensive tourist rest house; through Christiansborg, residence of the head of state; to the sadly crumbling ruins of Senya Beraku.
2. It is still the case that the primary material evokes this complexity more excitingly than the limited canon of secondary works. See, for example, the excellent new edition of *Barbot on Guinea,* ed. Paul Hair, Adam Jones, and Robin Law (1992). Fiction adds to the picture; Barry Unsworth's prize-winning novel *Sacred Hunger* (1992) deals with the coastal trade in the eighteenth century and relies heavily on the primary material.
3. Until the building of Tema harbor to the east of Accra in the late 1950s.
4. The most recent scholarship on this issue is neatly reviewed in Manning (1990).
5. Especially that in palm oil, a cash crop whose importance was to be eclipsed by the remarkable rise of the Gold Coast's cocoa industry in the first decade of the twentieth century.
6. Some of the best thinking on these questions is contained in an unpublished paper by Ray Jenkins (1988). Jenkins's tragic death in April 1993 robbed the field of a fine scholar and this author of a good friend.
7. For an excellent account of this process, see Priestly (1969). To this must be added the late Ray Jenkins's remarkable two-volume thesis "Gold Coast Historians and Their Pursuit of the Gold Coast Past, 1882–1917" (1985). The author's death makes publication of this massively detailed work unlikely.
8. On the more general issue of trade and traders, see Arhin (1979).
9. Which are not, it must be said, very high.
10. The plains are subject to a meteorological anomaly and, by contrast with much of the rest of the region, receive scant rainfall—only about 50 inches per annum. On the Danish proposition, see Winsnes (1992).
11. Who were to play a prominent part in the history of the southern Gold Coast until the First World War.
12. Such as their enthusiasm for transliterating African languages and for understanding rather than merely condemning African cultures. See Debrunner (1967).
13. Edward Reynolds wrote, among other works, *Trade and Economic Change on the Gold Coast, 1807–1874* (1974).
14. Not all were servicemen. The founders of the Ghanaian Methodist Church, Thomas Birch-Freeman and H. Wharton, have been claimed as West Indians. Freeman had discernible roots in St. Vincent, although his mother was English. Wharton's grandparents had been slaves on St. Vincent.
15. See Ellis (1885). For all its contemporary indifference to political correctness, this work is a valuable source.
16. For more on their role in the evolving cultures on the coast, see Casely Hayford and Rathbone (1992).
17. The pattern persisted. Sir Alan Burns, the Gold Coast's governor in 1942–47, was born in the West Indies.
18. Very early in the colonial period, Africans served in very senior positions, such as deputy-governor. By around 1895, racial prejudice was displacing them in favor of Europeans who frequently were less qualified. The first Africans appointed as

district commissioners in the twentieth century had to wait until 1942 for things to change.
19. See, e.g., the role of coastal lawyers in both land litigation and concession purchase in Rathbone (1993).
20. Some notable exceptions can be found in the work of Ray Dummet, Roger Gocking, and Larry Yarak.
21. Such as Bannerman, Capitein, or Ferguson. This is both intriguing and difficult for a scholar. As many of the coastal elite bear European surnames, it can be hard to discover whether some of the less prominent figures who surface in documentary sources were African or European.
22. Some of the more intriguing prosopographical possibilities of genealogical research are revealed in the recent doctoral thesis of my student Augustus Casely Hayford (1992), himself a descendant of a great Cape Coast family with a known set of European ancestors.
23. For whom exist an elaborate set of equivalents of demeaning and unkind "Polish jokes."
24. The overarching significance of families in decoding both political and social structures in the communities is strongly urged in Casely Hayford and Rathbone (1992).
25. For this reason the invocation of these historical actors as "African Victorians" always has seemed to me entirely to miss the point; that terminology suggests a "Western" hegemony that immediately dissolves upon serious inquiry.

References

Ajayi, Jacob F. A., and John D. Y. Peel, eds.
1992   *Peoples and Empires in African History.* London: Longman.
Arhin, Kwame
1979   *West African Traders in the Nineteenth and Twentieth Centuries.* London: Longman.
Casely Hayford, Augustus
1992   A Genealogical Study of Cape Coast Families. Ph.D. diss. Univ. of London.
Casely Hayford, Augustus; and Richard Rathbone
1992   Politics, Families and Freemasonry in the Colonial Gold Coast. In *Peoples and Empires in African History,* ed. Ajayi Jacob F. A. and John D. Y. Peel, 143–60. London: Longman.
Debrunner, Hans
1967   *A History of Christianity in Ghana.* Accra: Waterville Publishing House.
Ellis, Alfred B.
1885   *A History of the First West India Regiment.* London: Chapman and Hall.
Gocking, Roger
1984   Creole Society and the Revival of Traditional Culture in Cape Coast during the Colonial Period. *International Journal of African Historical Studies* 17: 601–22.
Hair, Paul E.; Adam Jones; and Robin Law, eds.
1992   *Barbot on Guinea.* London: Hakluyt Society.

Jenkins, Ray
1985   Gold Coast Historians and Their Pursuit of the Gold Coast Past, 1882–1917. Ph.D. thesis, Univ. of Birmingham, England.
1988   West Indian and Brazilian Influences in the Gold Coast—Ghana, c. 1807–1914: A Review and Reappraisal of Continuities in the Post-Abolition Links between West Africa and the Caribbean and Brazil. Paper presented at the 12th Annual Conference of the Society for Caribbean Studies. London.
1990   Intellectuals, Publication Outlets and "Past Relationships": Some Observations on the Emergence of Early Gold Coast–Ghanaian Historiography in the Cape Coast–Accra–Akropong Triangle, c. 1880–1917. In *Self Assertion and Brokerage: Early Cultural Nationalism in West Africa*, ed. Paulo F. de Moraes Farias and Karen Barber, 68–77. Birmingham, England: Center for West African Studies.
Kea, Ray A.
1982   *Settlement, Trade and Politics in the Seventeenth-Century Gold Coast.* Baltimore, Md.: Johns Hopkins Univ. Press.
Manning, Patrick
1990   *Slavery and African Life: Occidental, Oriental and African Slave Trades.* Cambridge: Cambridge Univ. Press.
Priestley, Margaret
1969   *West African Trade and Coast Society: A Family Study.* London: Oxford Univ. Press.
Rathbone, Richard
1993   *Murder and Politics in Colonial Ghana.* New Haven, Conn.: Yale Univ. Press.
Reynolds, Edward
1974   *Trade and Economic Change on the Gold Coast, 1807–1874.* London: Longman.
Unsworth, Barry
1992   *Sacred Hunger.* New York: Doubleday.
Verger, Pierre
1976   *Trade Relations Between the Bight of Benin and Bahia from the Seventeenth to the Nineteenth Century.* Ibadan, Nigeria: Ibadan Univ. Press.
Winsnes, Selena A., ed.
1992   *Letters on West Africa and the Slave Trade: Paul Erdmann Isert's Journey to Guinea and the Caribbean Islands in Columbia (1788).* Oxford: Oxford Univ. Press.

6 | Preliminary Remarks on the Oldendorp Manuscripts and Their History

Gudrun Meier

In the holdings of the Central Archives of the Moravian Church[1] in Herrnhut, Upper Lusatia, eastern Germany,[2] there exist two lengthy manuscripts by Christian Georg Andreas Oldendorp concerning the journey he undertook to the Danish West Indies in 1767–68. As one of the first academically trained members of the Moravian Church, Oldendorp had been commissioned to visit the mission stations that had been established there in 1732, for the purpose of writing a history of the mission. In late 1768, he returned to Herrnhut after seventeen months in the West Indies and a brief stay at the Moravian stations in Bethlehem, Pennsylvania. In 1769, Oldendorp submitted a report of approximately three thousand pages (the "Orginalmanuskript I," or OMS I)—far more than the Moravian Church was willing to publish.

Evidently Oldendorp was too much of a scholar to restrict himself to recording the mission's history; the manuscript brims with descriptions of the islands' geographical and biological characteristics and the ethnographic, linguistic, medical, and legal features of their societies. The work is divided into two parts. The first covers the islands' Arawak past and their discovery and colonization by different European nations. This part contains Oldendorp's remarkable firsthand observations concerning the slaves' African origins, their languages, physical anthropology, common illnesses, the plantation labor regime, the life of house slaves, patterns of kinship and marriage, and so forth. Also described are the environment, geology, plants, animals, wind and weather conditions, agriculture, fishing, and common routes of travel between the islands. Only the second part of this manuscript concentrates on the history of the Moravian mission on St. Thomas, St. Croix, and St. Jan (St. John), from its inception in 1732 until 1768.

Asked by the Unity Eldest Conference (UAC) in Herrnhut to reduce his report to "essential matters," Oldendorp produced another manuscript (the "Reinschrift," or OMS II) of nearly equal length. In its present form, this manuscript contains a multitude of insertions and additions in colored pencil, many of which clearly are not in Oldendorp's handwriting. Since this second manuscript also apparently failed to conform to the UAC's intentions, the head of the church archives, Johann Jakob Bossart, was entrusted with the task of reducing the manuscripts to publishable size. Bossart did so, but in a manner which the author considered arbitrary, haphazard, and distorted. The results—featuring a largely intact version of the second part of the manuscript but only a fairly short section on the "natural history" of the islands—were printed in Barby (in the Kingdom of Saxony) in 1777. Though Bossart's edited version, the *Geschichte der Mission der evangelischen Brüder auf den caraibischen Inseln S. Thomas, S. Croix und S. Jan*, still contained almost 1,100 printed pages, Oldendorp was most dissatisfied. In a long and carefully drafted letter to the UAC, he protested the manner in which his observations and findings had been distorted, while nevertheless bowing to the wisdom of the UAC's decision.

Oldendorp's contribution cannot be understood except against the background of the Moravian Church's Caribbean missionary endeavors. In 1732, only ten years after the founding of Herrnhut by exiles from Bohemia and Moravia under Count Zinzendorf's auspices, Zinzendorf inaugurated the Caribbean mission of the Herrnhuter Brüdergemeine or Moravian Brethren. While attending a royal wedding at the Danish Court—to which he was linked by kinship—Zinzendorf became acquainted with the fate of the black slaves in the Danish West Indian possessions. In line with their Christian self-concept, the Moravians felt called to the task of conducting missions among the "poorest of the poor." Nitschmann, a carpenter, and the potter Dober were sent to St. Thomas in 1732. The published version of Oldendorp's mission history reports that these young missionary artisans seem initially to have considered trying to sell themselves into slavery in order to share the lot of blacks—a testimony to both their idealism and their fundamental ignorance of local social conditions. Neither were their attempts to find gainful employment as craftsmen graced with success. Furthermore, Dober's attempts to live and work with the slaves failed, and their missionary endeavors soon met with resistance on the part of the planters

(Oldendorp 1777: vol. 2, chap. 4). Dober and Nitschmann barely scraped by, and their successors came to the conclusion that entering the plantation business was the only way to keep the mission afloat economically. In 1738, a new group of missionaries under the leadership of Friedrich Martin bought a plantation on St. Thomas, thereby turning themselves into the missionary masters of nine enslaved congregants.

By then, according to contemporary reports, about three hundred whites and three thousand black slaves were living on some eighty plantations in St. Thomas. The whites—"die Blanken," Oldendorp calls them—were mostly Reformed Dutch and Lutheran Danes. Their common language was Dutch, the official language Danish. Among the slaves, however, a creole idiom ("Cariolisch" or "Negerhollands") had developed, encompassing elements of African, Dutch, English, and other languages. At Oldendorp's time, the black population customarily was divided into *Bussalen* (slaves born in Africa) and creoles (those blacks and mulattos born in the island from unions of white men and black women). The major social divisions within the slave sector were house slaves, skilled workers, and field slaves, positioned along a continuum of diminishing social rights and privileges.

In the eyes of the missionaries, the slaves' living arrangements represented a "moral wreckage, for neither marriage, nor family and parentage were recognized by the slaveholders," and "every religious, moral, and emotional sentiment of the negroes was intentionally and systematically killed off." Several dramatic conflicts ensued as the missionaries endeavored to counteract the widespread and generally accepted practice of treating the slaves as mere chattel. For example, in 1738–39, preaching-grounds were closed off by the local authorities—a state of affairs that was alleviated only temporarily when Count Zinzendorf initiated negotiations in the course of his personal visit in 1740. With respect to this visit, it is worth noting that Zinzendorf preached his farewell sermon in creole. For, in the aftermath of Spangenberg's 1736 visitation, use of the creole language in missionary work already had become mandatory among the Moravians.[3]

With the islands' transition to full Danish possession in 1754, a governor general in Christiansstadt on St. Croix assumed power over all of the islands. In the same year, the mission station Bethanien was founded on St. John; in 1757—despite vehement protests by local whites—Friedenthal opened on St. Croix; and in 1771 and 1819, there followed Friedensberg on the island's west coast, and Friedensfeld in the center of the island. In 1771, the mission station Niesky was inaugurated on St. Thomas; and in 1782, the station Emmans began its operation at the eastern tip of the island. By 1800, the mission had become largely self-sufficient economically; plantations, mills, and foundries assured its economic viability. The mission's relations with the local planter elite had improved considerably. As the missionaries themselves now owned plantations and slaves, they seem to have been perceived less as a threat to the established social order. Moreover, their endeavors generally had come to be regarded as beneficial; the planter elite appears to have reasoned that Christianized blacks were far less prone to rebellion.

Oldendorp's history of the mission covers only the period up to 1768, the era of the founding fathers, with their manifold difficulties and setbacks. As the proper historiography of the mission (part 2 in each of the manuscripts) deals with a short time span, it is particularly valuable. For it covers many details that had to be omitted in later, more concise histories of the Moravian missionary work. This information would be lost, were it not for the existence of these manuscripts. Yet the value of Oldendorp's manuscripts goes far beyond its usefulness for missionary historiography.

Oldendorp, who had begun his studies at the University of Jena, now in eastern Germany, around 1740, was well versed in the natural historical scholarship of his day. His detailed descriptions of plant and animal life, soil consistency, meteorological phenomena and their impact upon man, and methods of agricultural production—especially in relation to sugar cane processing—establish him as a talented and meticulously attentive observer. In cataloguing biological specimens, Oldendorp was keenly aware of the most recent scholarly advances in taxonomic systematics. He already used Linné's classificatory system, and he appended a wide variety of observations to his descriptions—such as, for example, concerning the edibility or poisonous character of local plants and animals, nesting habits of birds, physiology and colors of fish, different structures of shells, and much more. Further proof of Oldendorp's scholarly versatility is seen in his account of tropical diseases and their different incidence and symptomatology among the white and black populations; and his notes on medical plants and modalities of prophylaxis and treatment. Moreover, he was a talented draftsman; the manuscript corpus includes a series of drawings and watercolors that form an invaluable supplement to the written documentation.

An unusually "modern" empiricist attitude characterizes Oldendorp's ethnographic observations. Unlike the authors of many contemporary travel accounts, he derived information mainly by questioning slaves directly—partly in the local creole dialect, which he appears to have mastered, and partly with the assistance of Africans acting as interpreters.

He thus claims to have conducted "conversations with negroes of almost thirty different nations" (Oldendorp 1777: 270; cf. Brown 1983).[4] On this basis, he compiled collections of lexical items and comparative word lists of twenty-six different African languages, many of which were still spoken on St. Thomas or at least recalled by first-generation Africans. Just as stunning are Oldendorp's insights into the complexity of African ethnic divisions. Hardly any contemporary author discerned as clearly the terminological confusion arising out of the conjunction, caused by the slave trade, of indigenous African ethnic autonyms and heteronyms, place names, and designations used solely by the traders (cf. Rupp-Eisenreich 1987; Palmié 1991, 1993; Olwig, this volume).

Oldendorp's excursions into the islands' past relate to theories of the origin of the Antilles, prehistoric Arawak migrations, the islands' settlement, the Columbian discovery, and the islands' post-Columbian history. He critically surveys the treatment of the native population by Spanish, French, and English colonizers and rejects these various colonizing ventures as inhumane. He goes on to describe the changing colonial regimes up to the time of the Danish takeover and finally focuses on the islands' enslaved population. Oldendorp notes the varied African origins of the slaves and describes modalities of the slave trade, as well as the present living condition and productive employment of field slaves, slave artisans, and house slaves. He offers detailed observations on their legal disabilities (prohibiting, e.g., the recognition of familial ties among them), their native religious cultures, and the development of the creole language ("Negerhollands") that had emerged among them via a fusion of African, Dutch, English, French, and Spanish elements.

Even a superficial comparison of the tables of contents of Oldendorp's manuscripts (which consist of several thousand closely-written pages) and the published version suggests that Bossart made drastic reductions particularly in the area of natural history. This is understandable, given the publication's intended readership and the goals of the Moravian Church— to promulgate information about the mission and garner support for its activities. In this context, it is remarkable how much of Oldendorp's scholarly reportage actually was included in the published volume.

Initially, Bossart's edition attracted some attention among late-eighteenth- and early-nineteenth-century scholars—such as, for example, Paul Jakob Bruns, Christoph Meiners, and James Cowles Pritchard (cf. Rupp-Eisenreich 1985)—who were engaged in the speculative natural historical and anthropological research of the age. After the mid-nineteenth century, however, Oldendorp's work was virtually forgotten. The Dutch philologist Hesseling, investigating Danish Virgin Island creole (his work was published in 1905), was first to recognize the significance for linguistic scholarship of the published version of Oldendorp's mission history. In 1942, Herskovits emphasized its importance for African-Americanist research and described it as equaling the quality of much more widely known accounts, such as those of Labat, Du Tertre, and Moreau de St. Mery (French Antilles); Hartsinck and Stedman (Dutch Guyana); and Edwards and Long (Jamaica). Still, Oldendorp's *Geschichte der Mission* has been largely neglected by African-Americanist anthropology. The few studies that have made use of the published account include two short articles on slave resistance on St. Croix (Pope 1972, 1975), Danish anthropologist Karen Fog Olwig's monograph *Cultural Adaptation and Resistance on St. John* (1985),[5] an essay on Moravian perceptions of African Americans (Rupp-Eisenreich 1987), and discussions of Oldendorp's views on African ethnicity (Rupp-Eisenreich 1989; Palmié 1991, 1993). In addition, Soi-Daniel W. Brown (1983) has published a brief translation of selections from Oldendorp's notes about interviews he conducted with slaves.

As far as historiography is concerned, the published account has been widely used by Moravian missionary historians—such as, for example, von Dewitz (1882), J. Taylor Hamilton (1900), J. E. Hutton (1922), and, more recently, Hartmut Beck (1981). In addition, it was consulted by colonial historians such as Westergaard (1917) and Degn (1974); and by the late historian of Danish West Indian slavery, Neville Hall (1992). Oldendorp's importance for the linguistic history of Africa has been acknowledged by Hair (1963, 1966), Fodor (1975, 1977), and Jones (1990). Finally, Stein (1984, 1985a, 1985b, 1989), Stolz (1986), and Stolz and Stein (1986) made use of Oldendorp's account and some Moravian archival materials as unique primary sources for creole linguistics, particularly for the reconstruction and analysis of the (now extinct) "Negerhollands" of the Danish Virgin Islands.

Publication of an English translation of Bossart's edited version, made by Highfield and Barac (Oldendorp 1987), has been hailed as the recovery of a first-rate historical and ethnographic document on the eighteenth-century Caribbean (cf. Price 1987, Olwig 1989, and Dillard 1990). Unquestionably, however, the manuscripts are qualitatively superior to the published text. In fact, the existence of a (truncated) printed version may well have kept scholars from taking full cognizance of the larger manuscripts. Written as they are in Old German script and tucked away in a corner of the world where few Caribbeanists would expect to find a major repository of regionally relevant primary sources, the manuscripts have remained virtually unstudied.

In 1986, the linguist Gilbert—one of the very few authors who had access to the original manuscripts in the Herrnhut Moravian archives— reported first impressions concerning significant divergences between the original texts and Bossart's edition, concluding: "Unfortunately, the original work, which may be the finest surviving 18th century description of any part of the West Indies, remains unpublished" (Gilbert 1986: 5). Similar judgments have been voiced by Rupp-Eisenreich (1985), Price (1987), and Olwig (1989). All three agree that the archival sources accessible in Herrnhut must be regarded as highly superior to the published text, indispensable to regional scholarship, and valuable in relation to more general anthropological and historiographical concerns.

The staff of the Staatliches Museum für Völkerkunde Dresden (Dresden Ethnographic Museum) has been working toward publication of these materials since the early 1970s. Under the directorship of the African-Americanist Peter Neumann, efforts were initiated to create a historical-critical edition of the manuscripts and related materials, to be published in German and English. As envisioned by Neumann, the project's goal was both to return to the people of the Virgin Islands a significant record of their history, and to publicize and honor Oldendorp's unique scholarly achievement. Neumann himself had begun to analyze the ethnographic aspects of the materials, and attempts were made to establish cooperation with members of the Moravian Church of the Virgin Islands, in order to integrate local experts in different scholarly disciplines into the project. First contacts of this nature were initiated by correspondence in 1983. In 1985, an agreement was negotiated in Herrnhut between the museum and the Reverend Dr. Charles Peters, a Moravian historian and theologian from St. Thomas. The contract specified the rights and obligations of the collaborators and restated the dual goals of the project. The manuscripts and related archival materials were reproduced on microfilm and shipped to St. Thomas.

Subsequent progress of the project has been hampered by three major problems. First, a serious illness soon forced Neumann—who had been the project's driving force—gradually to withdraw. Second, difficulties arose when some collaborators and interested but unaffiliated scholars attempted to publish parts of the manuscripts and/or other archival holdings relevant to the Oldendorp corpus. Though permission to do so initially was granted by the management of the archives in Herrnhut, Neumann steadfastly refused to give his consent, because he feared that such excerpting would violate the integrity of the materials and interfere with publication of the entire corpus. To this day this problem continues to plague the project. Third, the interest of the collaborators in St. Thomas significantly diminished after Highfield announced his intention to publish an English translation of the Bossart edition. Personnel changes in the Unitäts-Direktion (Unity Directorate) of St. Thomas further contributed to the decline in interest. Meanwhile, however, the St. Thomas–based sociologist Helga Berger was granted access to the filmed materials by the St. Thomas Unitäts-Direktion and independently began to transcribe parts of the manuscript onto diskette, as well as to translate portions of it into English. Since 1990, she has been part of the project staff that was formed after Neumann's death in 1989.

In 1991, the directors of the Staatliches Museum für Völkerkunde Dresden and the Evangelische Brüderunität in Herrnhut agreed to resume working on the manuscripts. As just noted, by then a new project staff had formed under the directorship of Dr. Heinz Israel, representing the museum; and the Moravian Archiv-Dezernent (head archivist), representing the Moravian Church, legal owner of the manuscripts. This new project staff currently includes archivist and theologian Ingeborg Baldauf, creole linguist Peter Stein, African-Americanist Stephan Palmié, sociologist Helga Berger, and anthropologist Gudrun Meier as permanent collaborators. In addition, there is a staff of affiliated scholars, including anthropologists Karen Fog Olwig (Copenhagen), Michael Harbsmeier (Copenhagen), Adam Jones (Leipzig), and Britta Rupp-Eisenreich (Paris); and several natural scientists who have agreed to cooperate in compiling a critical apparatus and preparing commentaries to be included in the eventual publication.

In spring 1992, a proposal for funding was submitted by the Staatliches Museum für Völkerkunde to the German National Research Foundation (DFG). In November 1992, the project's first stage—mainly the creation of a computerized transcription of the texts—was granted two years of financial support; work began in July 1993. Six research assistants are currently working on a paleographic transcription, to which will be added copious documentation and scholarly apparatus. This preliminary task should be finished by mid-1995. After that, specialists in relevant fields will provide critical annotation and commentaries. Publication of the first volumes most likely will commence by 1998. Accordingly, we finally have a realistic hope of seeing the fruits of several decades of labor.

Notes

I would like to thank Stephan Palmié for his assistance in writing and translating this article.

1. Also known as *Evangelische Brüdergemeine, Evangelische Brüder Unität,* or *Unitas Fratrum.*
2. Situated in the southeastern part of the former German Democratic Republic, the area is now part of the Federal German Free State of Saxony.
3. As Stein (1984) notes, the Moravians were unique in regarding the creole idioms spoken in the Danish West Indies, in Suriname, and in Mauritius not as mere dialects or corrupted versions of the European idioms of the master class, but as *bona fide* languages. Their pragmatic efforts to communicate the Christian message thus led them to a conclusion not reached by academic linguists until well into the present century.
4. Since hardly any direct quotations appear in the published account, it is likely that Bossart regarded these important data as irrelevant and eliminated them. Accordingly, only close scrutiny of the manuscripts will allow us to assess Oldendorp's "fieldwork" techniques and, hence, the validity of the data presented in the published version.
5. See also Olwig (this volume).

References

Beck, Hartmut
1981   *Brüder in vielen Völkern.* Berlin: Evangelische Verlagsanstalt.
Brown, Soi-Daniel W.
1983   From the Tongues of Africa: A Partial Translation of Oldendorp's Interviews. *Plantation Society* 2: 37–61
Degn, Christian
1974   *Die Schimmelmanns im atlantischen Dreieckshandel.* Neumünster, Germany: Wachholtz.
Dillard, J. D.
1990   Review of Highfield and Barac, *C. G. A. Oldendorp's History of the Missions . . . Journal of Pidgin and Creole Languages* 5: 309–15.
Fodor, István
1975   *Pallas und andere afrikanische Vokabularien vor dem 19. Jahrhundert.* Hamburg: Helmut Buske.
1977   Zur Geschichte des Gã (Accran): Protten (1764) und Oldendorp (1777). In *Zur Sprachgeschichte und Ethnohistorie in Afrika,* ed. Wilhelm Möhling et al., 47–56. Berlin: Reimer.
Gilbert, Glen G.
1986   Oldendorp's History and Other Early Creole Materials in the Moravian Archives in Herrnhut, East Germany. *Carrier Pigeon* (Apr.): 5–7.
Hair, Paul E. H.
1963   The Languages of Western Africa, c. 1700: A Note and a Query. *Bulletin of the Society for African Church History* 1: 17–20.

1966   Collections of Vocabularies of Western Africa before the Polyglotta: A Key. *Journal of African Languages* 5: 208–17.
1989   A Further Note on Oldendorp's Interviews. *Plantation Society* 2: 343.

Hall, Neville T.
1992   *Slave Society in the Danish West Indies.* Mona: Univ. of the West Indies Press.

Hamilton, J. Taylor
1900   *A History of the Church Known as the Moravian Church.* Bethlehem, Pa.: Times Publishing.

Herskovits, Melville J.
1989 [1941]   *The Myth of the Negro Past.* Boston: Beacon Press.

Hesseling, D. C.
1905   *Het negerhollands der deense Antillen. Biyydrage tot de Geschiedenis der Nederlandse taal in Amerika.* Leiden, Netherlands: A. W. Sijthoff.

Hutton, J. E.
1922   *A History of the Moravian Missions.* London: Moravian Publishing Office.

Jones, Adam
1990   *Zur Quellenproblematik der Geschichte Westafrikas, 1450–1900.* Stuttgart, Germany: Franz Steiner.

Oldendorp, Christian G. A.
1777   *Geschichte der Mission der evangelischen Brüder auf den caraibischen Inseln S. Thomas, S. Croix und S. Jan,* ed. Johann Jakob Bossart. Barby, [Saxony]: Friedrich Christoph Laux.
1987   *A Caribbean Mission: History of the Mission of the Evangelical Brethren on the Caribbean Islands of St. Thomas, St. Croix, and St. John.* English edition and translation [of Oldendorp 1777] by Arnold R. Highfield and Vladimir Barac. Ann Arbor: Karoma Publishers.

Olwig, Karen Fog
1985   *Cultural Adaptation and Resistance on St. John: Three Centuries of Afro-Caribbean Life.* Gainesville: Univ. of Florida Press.
1989   An Eighteenth-Century Ethnographer of the Danish West Indies. *Plantation Society* 2: 337–42.

Palmié, Stephan
1991   *Das Exil der Götter: Geschichte und Vorstellungswelt einer afrokubanischen Religion.* Frankfurt: Peter Lang.
1993   Ethnogenetic Processes and Cultural Transfer in Afro-American Slave Populations. In *Slavery in the Americas,* ed. Wolfgang Binder, 337–63. Würzburg, Germany: Königshausen and Neumann.

Pope, Polly
1972   A Maroon Settlement on St. Croix. *Negro History Bulletin* 35: 153–54.
1975   Danish Colonialism in the West Indies: A Case of Transculturation Failure. In *War: Its Causes and Correlates,* ed. Martin A. Nettleship, R. Dale Givens, and Anderson Nettleship, 573–82. The Hague, Netherlands: Mouton.

Price, Richard
1987   A Caribbean Mission: Blood, Sweat, and Tears—and More Blood. *Nieuwe West-Indische Gids* 61: 175–81.

Rupp-Eisenreich, Britta
1985   Les Frères Moraves, ethnologues de la condition esclave? (Iles Vierges, Petit Antilles, 1731–1768). In *Naissance de l'ethnologie?* ed. Claude Blanckaert, 125–73. Paris: Les èditions du Cerf.

1987   Les "informateurs" africains des missionaires pietistes et moraves. In *Images de l'Africain de l'antiquité au XXe siècle,* ed. Daniel Droixhe and Klaus H. Kiefer, 45–61. Frankfurt: Peter Lang Verlag.

1989   L'ethnicité, critère descriptif au XVIIIe siècle: Le cas de la traite danoise. In *Les ethnies ont une histoire,* ed. Jean-Pierre Chrétien and Gérard Prunier, 49–60. Paris: Karthala.

Stein, Peter

1984   Die ersten "Kreolisten": Die Herrnhuter Missionare im 19. Jahrhundert auf St. Thomas. *Unitas Fratrum* 15: 53–63.

1985a   Die Anfänge der Verschriftung einer Kreolsprache: Das Negerhollands im 18. Jahrhundert. In *Entstehung von Sprachen und Völkern,* ed. P. Sture Ureland, 437–57. Tübingen: Niemeyer.

1985b   Bemerkungen zur Edition der "Sklavenbriefe" aus St. Thomas, 1737–1769 (Kurzfassung). In *Akten des 1. Essener Kolloquiums über 'Kreolsprachen und Sprachkontakte' vom 26.1.1985 an der Essener Universität,* ed. Norbert Boretzky, Werner Enninger, and Thomas Stolz, 135–42. Bochum, Germany: Brockmeyer.

1989   When Creole Speakers Write the Standard Language: An Analysis of Some of the Earliest Slave Letters from St. Thomas. In *Wheels Within Wheels: Papers of the Duisburg Symposium on Pidgin and Creole Languages,* ed. Martin Pütz and René Dirven, 153–78. Frankfurt: Peter Lang.

Stolz, Thomas

1986   *Gibt es das kreolische Sprachmodell? Vergleichende Grammatik des Negerholländischen.* Frankfurt: Peter Lang

Stolz, Thomas, and Peter Stein

1986   Language History in the Former Danish Antilles: Non-Linguistic Evidence for a Diachronic Description of the Negro-Dutch Language. *Amsterdam Creole Studies* 9: 103–22

von Dewitz, August Karl Ludwig

1882   *In Dänisch-Westindien: Hundert- und Fünfzig Jahre der Brüdermission in St. Thomas, St. Croix und St. Jan.* Niesky, Germany: Direction der Brüdergemeine.

Westergaard, Waldemar

1917   *The Danish West Indies under Company Rule.* New York: Macmillan.

7 | Slavery and Slave Cultures in a Hydraulic Society

Suriname

Gert Oostindie and Alex van Stipriaan

Among the major themes in the emerging historiography of New World slavery, the intraregional comparison of variants of slavery has long been a favorite. Initially "idealistic" interpretations held sway, linking presumed variations in systems of slavery to differences in metropolitan cultures. Such constructions often were colored by nationalistic interests or by domestic concerns. Later, "materialistic" readings of slavery came to dominate the debate, convincingly urging cross-colonial analyses dealing with fixed time periods.

At the same time, the debate became far more sophisticated. As scholars started to untangle the various dimensions of slavery, it became increasingly evident that there was no necessary link between the distinct parameters of slavery in any given slave colony. Working and living conditions, demography, levels of repression, opportunities for manumission, limits to cultural autonomy, etc., all formed dimensions of a matrix in which crucial relationships are anything but straightforward. The more sophisticated the analyses became, the less useful a ranking of variants of slavery on a harsh-to-mild continuum seemed. Consequently the question—perhaps posed less clearly in recent scholarly writings—arises as to whether we may still interpret the distinct dimensions of any given slave system in terms of one "unified field theory." Should we simply accept the elusiveness of some posited hidden crucible and interpret the various dimensions of a given slave system each in its own right, without imposing the rigidity of a presumed encompassing theoretical model?

Perhaps surprisingly, in view of this somewhat rhetorical question, we *do* advocate analyzing variants of New World slavery from a unifying perspective. Neither elusive nor hidden, the crucible put forward in this case study is quite an obvious one: ecology, and, more precisely, the physical environment shaping a particular plantation economy. This choice of perspective is informed by the down-to-earth conviction that, rather than comparing systems of slavery at an abstract level, one should begin by coming to grips with the immediate material world surrounding the slaves and so shaping their lives. In describing this material world, one has to take a series of variables into account, including the availability of natural sources of energy, climatic conditions, natural vegetation, type and wetness of soils, geographical relief, and specific crop-related labor regimes. A few scholars of Caribbean slavery, notably Higman (1984) and Watts (1987), have recognized the importance of ecology; yet, so far, no attempt has been made to use ecology as the main frame of reference. This essay attempts to place ecology at the center, by discussing the impact of one particular ecological factor: water.[1]

The place is Suriname, a Dutch plantation colony in the Caribbean, to which both contemporary observers and subsequent scholarship have attributed particularly harsh conditions of slavery. Analyzing the emergence and perpetuation of the disgraceful fame of Suriname slavery is not our concern here. Suffice it to state that much of the traditional argument suffered from a poor grasp of the dynamics of Suriname slavery and, moreover, from sheer ignorance and inconsistency (Oostindie 1993b). Remarkably, virtually no authors on Suriname slavery have probed the one crucible which we think gave slavery in Suriname (and in the Guyanas in general) a measure of uniqueness: the omnipresence of water, both free-flowing and harnessed for the plantation economy. Readers may suspect a Wittfogelian inspiration in our attempt to reflect on the importance of "water" in the emergence of specific conditions of slavery and of a distinct slave culture (Wittfogel 1957). Rather than suggesting an encompassing model, however, we highlight the heuristic gains to be made by taking seriously the "hydraulic" qualities of Suriname slavery.

Working and Living Conditions

"How is it possible that the human body can endure this [hardship]? [Even] the strongest are undermined" (quoted in Siwpersad 1979: 90). This observation by G. S. de Veer, an official discussing slavery conditions on Suriname sugar plantations in 1838, was anything but unique. Over the previous century and a half, the demanding regime of the

Suriname slave plantation had exacted a high toll in human lives. This sad fact had not gone unnoticed. The chronically negative demographic growth rates of the slave population had induced observers—without benefit of intraregional comparisons or a grasp of the gradual improvement over time—to portray the colony's system as an extremely harsh variant of New World slavery. Contemporary authors overestimated the annual natural decrease to be a staggering fifty per thousand. Hence John Gabriel Stedman's chilling observation in the 1770s that in Suriname "the Compleat number of negro Slaves consisting in 50,000 Healthy people is Exactly Extinct one every 20 Years Which is truly Shocking to Human Nature" (Stedman 1988 [1796]: 533).

Another author commenting on Suriname in this period was fascinated by other features of the colony. According to Raynal, "Les Hollandais ont eu la gloire de dompter l'Océan dans le nouveau monde comme dans l'ancien [The Dutch have had the glory to tame the ocean in the New World just like in the Old]" (Raynal 1774: vol. 4, p. 336). Indeed, with its neighboring, lesser Dutch colonies in the Guyana's (Berbice, Demerara, and Essequibo), Suriname stood out for its sophisticated technology adapted from the Dutch *polder* (a tract of low land reclaimed from water by means of high embankments) system.

Most of the colony's plantation area was located on the shores of mighty rivers and subsidiaries linked to the Atlantic. Over time, the plantation area continued to spread across the colony's territory; and in most locations *polder* technology provided the backbone for the plantation sector. The application of hydraulic technology had made possible the construction of hundreds of *polder* plantations whose irrigation and drainage systems were effectively linked to the rivers. Moreover, on the large sugar plantations, a second system of waterworks provided a relatively easy means of transporting sugar cane to the mill, which in turn was propelled by tidal energy. Most of the surface of an "impoldered" plantation—to use the anglicized Dutch term—initially was left uncultivated. Only the parcels nearest the river were utilized for growing the tropical staples and foodstuffs and for the location of industrial buildings, planter's house, and slave huts. Over time, in response to (temporary) soil exhaustion, the area effectively in use within the impoldered plantation tended to recede from the river.

Without this technology, the natural conditions of Suriname were not suitable for plantation agriculture; with it, the colony's competitive powers were enviable. In our calculations, eighteenth-century Suriname emerges as one of the most productive areas within the Caribbean. Sugar output per unit of labor or land compare favorably to results obtained else-where, as does productivity of the other major plantation product, cof-fee. For a number of reasons, some of them technological and agricul-tural in character, nineteenth-century figures are slightly less impressive. But even as the colony's technological edge eroded, the technical feasi-bility of the Suriname *polder* plantation was not endangered (Oostindie 1993a, van Stipriaan 1993a: 128–44).

What were the links between the particular *polder* technology of the Suriname plantation and its conditions of slavery? Hypothesizing that the implications of the *polder* regime went beyond mere efficacy of the agricultural system, we first probe the implications of "hydraulic slavery" for material life, particularly for working and living conditions.

The very construction of a *polder* demanded an enormous invest-ment of hard labor. A typical plantation might stretch for half a mile along the river and extend up to three miles or more inward. This area had to be fenced off by dikes. Within these dikes, the system of irriga-tion and drainage channels easily covered five to ten miles. On sugar plantations, the waterworks for transport and tidal energy for the mill added a second set of channels. And this was only the beginning. The *polder* area itself was divided by miles and miles of smaller trenches, cut-ting the plantation domain into hundreds of small rectangular plots. This construction required an enormous amount of manual labor. For example, by the third quarter of the eighteenth century, the length of the two major waterworks on a sugar plantation averaged ten miles. Departing from average norms for width and depth, the construction of these canals would have entailed moving some 150 metric tons of heavy alluvial clay. And then, of course, digging the narrower trenches remained to be done.

Once the initial infrastructure had been put in place, the *polder* com-plex called for continuous labor to keep the dikes from caving in and the canals and trenches from silting up. Naturally, the fact that the area effectively under cultivation tended to move inland implied extra work, particularly the extension of extant waterworks, and thus more digging for the slaves.

It is not difficult to see—although it is impossible fully to grasp—the implications of this particular technology for the slavery regime. Digging and keeping up the dikes, waterworks, sluices, etc., with noth-ing but manual labor must have been formidable tasks. One is hard pressed to find comparable labor demands on plantations in other parts of the Americas. Not surprisingly, the number of slaves required for the average *polder* plantation was considerable. By the late-eighteenth century, the average sugar plantation had some 120 to 140 slaves, which by Caribbean standards was a high but not extraordinary figure.

The coffee sector, which in this period dominated the Suriname economy, offers a useful contrast to the sugar sector. As the coffee plantations were equally *polders,* they could not do with a much smaller labor force than the sugar plantations. The *polder,* rather than the requirements of the crop, dictated the organization of the estate. In the last decades of the eighteenth century, the average Suriname coffee plantation had 110 to 120 slaves. This situation was is striking contrast to that of the then-dominant Caribbean coffee producer, St. Domingue, a French colony. Of over three thousand coffee estates there, the bulk were situated on hills and mountain slopes and employed no more than 40 slaves each.[2]

On the typical eighteenth-century sugar plantation, the management of the *polder* system imposed extreme labor demands. As the sugar mill was propelled by tidal energy, milling schedules were dictated by the calendar of the Atlantic Ocean. The period in which milling was feasible varied with the location and efficiency of a plantation. On average, milling with tidal energy was possible during approximately half the month, in periods around the new moon and the full moon. In contrast to those in other parts of the Americas, the particular ecological conditions of Suriname allowed for harvesting virtually all year long. While periodic peaks in production and therefore in demand for labor characterized sugar production elsewhere, here sugar production was nearly continuous. The presumed "dead season" may well be an erroneous or at least an exaggerated construction for other areas of sugar production; but it is evident that the Suriname sugar plantation's operation allowed its slaves no "break." On the contrary, at high tide, planters tried to maximize the use of tidal energy by operating the mill day and night. This implied that gangs of slaves, in alternation, were supposed to work continuously for thirty-six hours.

These characteristics have given the Suriname sugar plantation a particularly bad reputation. Actually, the Dutch official's judgment quoted above was correct in regard to the labor regime on those sugar plantations that used tidal energy. It seems telling that, whereas elsewhere—e.g., in Cuba (Moreno Fraginals 1978: vol. 1, p. 214, and vol. 2, pp. 27–29)—the introduction of steam engines ostensibly increased labor exploitation, the same innovation was welcomed by virtually all contemporaries in Suriname as a major step toward ameliorating the slaves' working conditions. The omnipresent hydraulic technology indeed must have been a major factor shaping Suriname slavery.

Some further data may serve at once to underscore this conclusion and to propose some nuance. First, what about the demographic record? Contemporaries thought of Suriname as the nadir in New World slave demography. In fact, the demographic performance of the Suriname slave population over time was less unfavorable than had been believed. It was long thought that annual growth deficits were around 50 per thousand, and total slave imports to the colony about 300,000 to 350,000. Recent research, however, has reduced these figures significantly. Demographic growth was indeed negative, standing at 50 per thousand in the mid-eighteenth century. But this figure improved over time, coming down to around 23 in the period 1775–1830 and to only 3.5 in the 1850s. Moreover, the total number of slaves imported into Suriname probably should be seen as about 215,000 (Postma 1990: 186–212, van Stipriaan 1993a: 313–14). These figures are anything but indications of a mild slavery regime, but they do serve to place Suriname in a more usual Caribbean context.

Insofar as we should still place Suriname demographics in a relatively grim category, we should look beyond the stereotypes of overexploitive and brutal planters and reckon more seriously with the colony's unfavorable ecological conditions and disease environment. This, of course, returns us to the weight of the ecological factor, including the omnipresence of water, in the slaves' lives.

There is a convincing method of substantiating the claim that material conditions, and particularly the hydraulic factor, determined slave demography. Our calculations pinpoint significant contrasts in demographic performance between slave populations on sugar plantations and those working in other sectors (see table 7.1). Up to the last decades of slavery, Suriname slave populations in all sectors experienced negative demographic growth rates. Yet, on sugar plantations, demographic decrease was consistently higher than in other sectors. These hard figures substantiate the eighteenth-century planters' wisdom that, in comparison to a coffee plantation, working conditions on a sugar plantation "are infinitely more demanding" and that therefore "these slaves are worn out at a higher pace."[3]

Here we have firm grounds for a "hard" conclusion. Yet we do face a methodological conundrum. From the 1760s to 1820, most Suriname slaves worked in the less dramatically "hydraulic" coffee sector, rather than on sugar plantations. As particularly the first part of this period witnessed high rates of demographic decrease, the "hydraulic" explanation does not seem to hold. Closer inspection, however, solves the puzzle. Whereas most sugar plantations were established in the earlier part of

Table 7.1

Plantation Type, Work on Canals, and Demographic Performance

Plantation Type	% of Total Slave Population (1830–39)	Transport Canals Dug and to Be Maintained (ca. 1810)	Frequency of Night Labor after Full Day Shift	Mortality per Thousand Slaves (1830–39)	Fertility per Thousand Slaves (1830–39)	Natural Growth per Thousand Slaves (1830–39)
Sugar	38	10 km	Often	42.5	25.9	-16.6
Coffee	28	3 km[a]	Sometimes	36.8	25.3	-11.5
Cotton	14	—	Almost never	20.8	20.8	0.0
Timber	5	—	Never	28.0	36.3	+8.3[b]

SOURCES: Van Stipriaan 1993a; CBBS & Lands Archive: Slave Registers.
[a] Average length for coffee plantations with canals for transportation; few coffee plantations possessed such canals, however.
[b] 1839–42, n = 5 plantations with a total of approximately 700 slaves

the century, most coffee estates were laid out in 1740–70. The expansion of the area under cultivation on these coffee plantations continued even into the 1780s. Therefore, in this period, hundreds and hundreds of completely new *polders* were laid out, taking a heavy toll on the slaves. As the expansion of the coffee sector came to a halt in the last quarter of the eighteenth century, demographic performance of the slaves in this sector immediately improved. At that stage, the demographic contrast between average sugar and coffee plantations became evident once more and continued so afterward.

At the risk of undermining the proposed linkage of "hydraulic slavery" with the conditions of Suriname slavery, we do propose a few caveats. First, even if the *polder* complex was extremely demanding in terms of labor, this in itself does not prove that the Suriname slave was particularly overworked. Short of systematic analyses of the typical labor force on plantations elsewhere in the region, it remains impossible to substantiate any significant differences in average workload, particularly since everywhere planters had a vested interest in getting as much as possible out of each slave during a variable lifespan. Next, in exploring possible links between the hydraulic complex and slave life, we should distinguish between working and living conditions. For instance, digging and keeping up the waterworks were strenuous tasks, implying a need for enormous caloric intake. Yet the same vast and remarkably fertile *polder* that dictated these workloads also allowed for relatively ample and rich provision plots, possibly securing for the Suriname slave more and better food than her or his contemporaries on many Caribbean islands. The surrounding waters provided another source (fish) with which slaves might upgrade their food supply. Moreover, the use of plantains ("coffee mamas") to shade coffee trees provided the slaves on these plantations with an important caloric asset. Indeed, there is very little report of famines during the period of slavery in Suriname. Ironically, archival sources do suggest frequent shortages of drinkable water (van Stipriaan 1993a: 356–57).

Finally, it may be worthwhile to ponder for a moment the effects of the *polder* technology on social relations, both during and after slavery. The hydraulic complex was at once sophisticated, costly, and vulnerable to both neglect and sabotage. Its maintenance therefore required strict supervision, but at the same time must have given prudent planters incentive to entrust essential tasks to elite slaves. The same, of course, happened with the sugar mill. Some scholars have linked the early modern emergence of democracy in the Netherlands to the need for all social classes jointly to participate in the preservation of the essential Dutch *polder* landscape. It may not be farfetched to think of the Suriname *polder* complex likewise as an institution tending to stimulate compromise rather than excessively violent rule. Obviously, here we are very much at odds with Wittfogel's "oriental despotism" and more in tune with the findings of, say, Joyner on slavery in South Carolina (Joyner 1984).

The complexity of the Suriname *polder* plantation also may have been a major factor in the abortive history of an Afro-Suriname peasantry. The late abolition of slavery (1863) and the following decade of apprenticeship culminated in the virtual withdrawal of the freed population from a declining plantation sector. The importation of some seventy thousand indentured laborers from British India and Java substituted Asian labor for the former slaves. This period of transition, and particularly the vicissitudes of the black peasantry, have been largely neglected in modern historiography. Perhaps future scholarship may uncover another direct link to the prevailing ecology. It may well have been nigh impossible to subdivide deserted *polder* plantations into technically and administratively manageable clusters of viable provision plots. After all, as soon as this *morcellement* had been institutionalized, the problem arose of how to insure the maintenance of the previously centrally supervised infrastructure. The failure to establish procedures to make up for the collapse of the plantation's mechanisms well may help to explain the faltering development of the black peasantry. In fact, a successful peasant transition was made in the Para and Coronie districts, where, because of atypical ecological circumstances, the *polder* technology was of lesser importance.

Social Relations

Evidently "water" in the broadest sense played a prominent role in slaves' lives. After the traumatic experience of the Middle Passage, African slaves brought to Suriname would pass their lifetimes in a physical milieu dominated by water. How did slaves experience this predominance of water in their lives? Our initial hypothesis is that water formed an important element in the process of creolization and in the formation of slave culture. We test this hypothesis through an analysis of social relations along with several cultural institutions: language, oral tradition, music, dance, and religion.

The implications for social relations of the physical milieu and its technological domestication in the hydraulic system were manifold.

First, because of the *polder* system, almost every plantation formed an island, with the river on one side and trenches along the other sides. A watershed literally separated the slaves from the rest of society. If a slave wanted to have contact with slaves on other plantations, or attempted to run away, he or she always had to cross water and/or use water as his means of transportation. Water therefore signified both isolation and an escape route.

The hardships imposed by the *polder* plantation system, particularly on sugar estates, was a prime factor stimulating slave resistance. Both small-scale uprisings and marronage posed constant threats from the first to the last days of slavery. Water continued to play a prominent part therein. Oral tradition, for example, suggests that the arduous digging of *polder* canals and trenches in the heavy sea clay of the coastal plains provoked deep resentment and overt slave resistance. More than two centuries *post hoc*, Saramaka and Ndjuka Maroons still recall abhorrence of this work as a prime factor motivating their forebears to escape from the plantations to the hazardous environment of the tropical forest.[4] Likewise, recollections of broken sluices and dikes surface in recorded oral traditions of the freed slaves' descendants (*De slaventijd in odo's* 1960). The negative impact of water-related labor is also underlined by the fact that, during the second half of the eighteenth century, the number of slaves running away from sugar plantations was two to four times as high as that from coffee estates (van Stipriaan 1992: 128–29).

Furthermore, without agreeing on the underlying causes, several historians have observed that eighteenth-century plantation uprisings in Suriname nearly always occurred during the dry season. Maroon raids on plantations, in contrast, most often took place during the rainy season, which provided perfect conditions for guerrilla tactics (de Beet 1984: 29–31). Maroons also made ingenious strategic use of rivers, creeks, and especially swamps to evade pursuers and/or to protect their villages. Indeed, during the Suriname civil war of the 1980s, thousands of Maroons fled from Bouterse's army to the protection of the Marowijne River in French territory.

One of the most frequent causes of rebellion among nineteenth-century slave groups in Suriname was owners' attempts to move slaves to another plantation. Most of the time, slaves simply refused to leave "their" plantation. Earlier examples indicate that, as creolization progressed, a slave's loyalty became tied ever more closely to her or his home plantation, and this last phenomenon too harks back to differences in the material milieu. Attempts to move slave populations invariably involved relocating slaves from coffee or timber estates to sugar plantations (van Stipriaan 1993a: 389–92). The fact—shown by our de-mographic analysis—that the hydraulic sugar plantation imposed the harshest conditions for the slaves assumes direct relevance here.

Like slaves elsewhere in the Americas, the Suriname slaves struggled to improve their lots through a range of more subtle strategies. As creolization progressed, their bargaining position improved. This is shown by—to quote just two examples—the increasing number of work strikes and the expansion of subsistence-related versus plantation-related activi-ties. Increasingly, slaves supplemented their plantation rations with food produced on their own time. They also entered economic activi-ties by trading their surpluses. Again, water was of vital importance, as part of the slaves' produce was fish. The plantation provided nets, as well as large quantities of salt to preserve the fish. The planters there-fore actively contributed to the growing slave self-sufficiency. Fish be-came a vital element in Afro-Suriname culinary tradition.

Geography also helped to shape regional loyalties. Even today, one finds a sense of oneness among people from the same district in Suriname, i.e., from along the same river or seashore. People from the same river share a common history and culture dating back to slavery, and this common identity created bonds that transcend the solidarity of all Afro-Surinamers, not to mention national identification.

On a more personal level, the impact of water may not be traced directly, but it did serve as a significant contextual factor in the articu-lation of Afro-Suriname social relations. In one sense, this is true for New World slavery generally; for example, two terms still used today to symbolize kinship and/or friendship refer to the bonds that developed between two persons of the same sex on the same slave ship sailing across the Atlantic (Mintz and Price 1992 [1976]: 43–44). One vari-ant, *sipi* (ship), is adopted by two people who have had similar misfor-tunes or traumatic experiences; the other, *mati* (mate), may refer to a special friend or a homosexual relationship. It remains a puzzle whether the word *mati* is a creolization of *shipmate* or of *mate* more generally.

Water played a prominent role in the love lives of the many slaves who, despite strict prohibitions, had partners on other plantations. To arrange meetings, slaves probably had to wade through water for long periods of time before reaching their loved ones, an obstacle they must have resented. If, however, they had a canoe at their disposal, they surely welcomed the water that made the trip so much shorter. The lat-ter situation probably was observed by a nineteenth-century colonist who drew this almost idyllic scene (Focke 1858: 95–96): "Being on a plantation, one may often hear at night some negro,—passing alone in his canoe, probably on his way to one of his wives on a far-off plantation,—bawling a song with all his heart alternated by whistling the melody."

Slave Culture

Not surprisingly, the vocabulary of the slaves' creole language, *Sranan Tongo*, evinces the influence of the physical milieu. Water is the most frequently used noun in multiple constructed words, covering a variety of facets typical of Suriname. For example, *watra* (water) may be found in descriptions of natural phenomena such as *draywatra* (whirlpool) or *farawatra* (ebb or low tide); and of flora and fauna such as *watraguyaba* (*Psidium actuangulum*), *switwatrakrarun* (*Hydrolea spinosa*), *swampuwatradagu* (*Lutra ennudis*, a small swamp otter typical of Suriname), or *watra-aboma* (*Eunectes murinus*; anaconda). *Watra* is heard in the kitchen, as in *peprewatra* (pepper soup) or *fayawatra* (hot water as well as coffee or tea); in and on the human body, as, for instance, in *sturuwatra* (diarrhea) and *watray* (tears); and in religion, as in *watramama* (water goddess), *watrawenu* (water spirits), *switwatra* (magic liquid for purification bath), and *seygiwatra* (holy water) (cf. Sordam and Eersel 1985).

Of course, vocabulary alone is no sufficient criterion. A crucial part of spoken Sranan consists of *odos*, i.e., sayings, proverbs, or aphorisms, many of which were recorded during slavery.[5] Water and water-related phenomena make a frequent appearance, e.g., in the collection of *odos* compiled by Teenstra:

> *Broko boto tjari en masra na foto*—"a leaking boat [also] brings the master to town": anyone can do it
> *So langa yu no pasa liba, yu no kosi kayman*—"so long as you have not been on the river do not curse the cayman"
> *Ala de alen fadon gi liba, oten liba sa fadon na alen?*—"everyday the rain falls into the river, when will the river fall into the rain?": you always call on me, when can I call on you? (1835: vol. 2, pp. 210–42)

However, despite such examples taken from a nineteenth-century collection of several hundred *odos,* and in contradiction to our hypothesis, less than 10 percent of these *odos* refer to water, whereas, for example, 20 to 30 percent relate to the animal world. Similar collections compiled in the 1930s suggest the same conclusion (Herskovits and Herskovits 1969 [1936]: 151–490). Water apparently had a stronger impact on the *description* than on the *interpretation* of slave life.

The same observation may be made regarding oral history. In stories handed down from slavery times, water is frequently present, but seldom in a leading role. There is, for example, a story about an extremely cruel planter on the Cottica River who, time after time, was confronted with broken sluices and leaking dikes. This was the warning of the gods that he had to change his ways. As he did not obey, the gods retaliated. He almost drowned near his own plantation's sluice, then ran as a madman into the woods to find his death there (Guda 1985: 39–48). Even in this tale, and in oral traditions more generally, water is little more than a scene in which a story is enacted. In oral history, the only exceptions to this rule are the Maroon tales regarding the excruciating labor demands of the *polder* complex.

Music was essential to slave culture, and part of the Afro-Suriname musical tradition was directly related to water—if not spiritually, at least materially. Until quite recently, for example, a prominent percussion instrument in a Suriname orchestra was the "water drum," beaten with two sticks (*ondro-watra-agida/godo*). It consisted of one or two big hollow calabashes filled with water, inside which a much smaller calabash floated upside down. Calabashes were used in daily life for practical purposes such as fetching water from the creek and storing it. The instrument was probably played during death ceremonies; contemporary authors maintained that the slaves believed that man was created out of water (van Breugel 1842: 53, Wooding 1972: 267, IJzermans 1987: 57). Slaves reputedly also blew a "water horn" (Focke 1855: 139).

Of more importance than these water-related instruments were the *botosingi* and *stréboto*, boat songs and boat races respectively. As water was the predominant means of transportation in the colony, boat traffic on the rivers was intense. Slaves rowed these boats, and, much like gang labor in fields and factories, rowers sang songs while working. The rhythm was beaten on the water with their oars. Through structured call-and-response songs, slaves commented on plantation life and also ridiculed the masters' behavior. In contrast to field songs, these call-and-response songs also served as means of cross-plantation communication. The songs were sung while passing plantations and other boats rowed by slaves; social commentary, news, and messages therefore were woven into the songs (van Stipriaan 1993b: 160–61).

Boating entailed competition, testing strength. Rowing matches between boats going in the same direction were taken so seriously that slaves reputedly sometimes died of exhaustion. Joining and, most important, winning a race were means of showing off masculine strength. At the same time, rowers defended the honor of their home plantation, because a race was always between one plantation and another. All this well illustrates the paradoxes of slave life. During the boat trip, the slaves were exploited for the transport of plantation products. At the same time, their behavior during the trip undermined the system in several ways: through the slaves' open or covert criticism, through their communication with other slaves about their situation, and through their voluntary display of combined physical power. This masculine strength, however, was inspired by defending "their" plantation's name—the symbol of their subjugated status.

Likewise, as time passed, the plantation itself, although it was the property of whites, was appropriated culturally and emotionally by the slaves. They were the ones who were born there, knew every hidden corner of the estate, and used every possibility it offered to generate some income of their own; their umbilical cords were buried in plantation ground, and their forebears still lived there as part of the local spirit world. In short, the plantation had come to symbolize their growing rootedness as Afro-Surinamers.

A decisive part of this cultural creolization was inspired and stimulated by, or coincided with, the growth of Afro-Suriname religion. Religion probably was the most important cultural institution in slave society, and water seems to have played a prominent role in slave religion. In some cases, such as in the use of libations and ritual bathing, there is little to suggest that Suriname religious practices were decisively influenced by the natural environment. After all, such rituals are characteristic of a wide range of religions. Yet for other elements of Afro-Suriname religion, a link with the omnipresence of water may be made. This is particularly the case with the so-called *Watramama* cult, which was most likely established fairly early from various West African elements.

A short digression on the ethnic composition of the Suriname slave population seems appropriate here. As in most Caribbean plantation colonies, the Suriname slave population was composed of all the major West African peoples between Senegal and Angola. As the mixture of different ethnic groups varied by colony and over time, the cultural outcome of creolization in these societies depended on both the development of the ethnic and cultural mixture over time, and on the specific local circumstances to which slaves had to adapt, such as, in Suriname, the dominance of water.

During the first half-century of Dutch slave importation, about 55 percent of slaves were so-called Papa (a generic name for slaves shipped between West Nigeria and Togo), 30 percent Luangu (from the Congo-Angola area), and 15 percent Cormantin/Kromanti (from present-day Ghana). Only after this period did Kromanti and, increasingly, Mandingo slaves (the latter shipped between Senegambia and the

Ivory Coast) come to dominate. Papa slaves were hardly imported any-
more, while the Luangu share remained stable (van Stipriaan 1993b:
145). By that time, however, much of Afro-Suriname religion, or *winti*
as it came to be known, already had been established. A crucial element
in this religion, and perhaps even the basis of *winti* itself during slavery,
was the Watramama cult, with its inflammatory *watramama* dance.

According to a 1775 manuscript written by Nepveu, the Watramama
cult, which he equates with *winti*, was introduced by the "Papa,
Nago, Arada and other slaves commonly shipped under the name of
Ouidah slaves [*Fidase Slaaven,*] [who] have introduced certain develish
practices in their dancing, which they have transferred to all other slaves"
(Nepveu 1775: 232). Apparently, by the time importation of the Papas
declined and Cormantins and Mandingos became the overwhelming
majority, Watramama already held a central position in slave religion.
This at least is suggested by the fact that it is the most frequently mentioned cult and/or religious dance in both eighteenth- and nineteenth-
century reports, and the only one explicitly forbidden in the colonial
laws because of its "dangerous effects on the slaves" (Nepveu 1775: 235;
West Indisch Plakaatboek 1973: 896; Blom 1787: 389).

The Watramama lived in the rivers, from whence she often appeared before the people, ordering them to bring her sacrifices, such as
the blood of a white hen. If such persons did not obey, she quickly
would bring about their death, or the death of one or more of their family members (*Ontwerp* 1744: 317). In the course of the nineteenth century, the picture of this horrific goddess changed into a more lovely one,
according to the descriptions of some slaves, who envisioned her "as a
beautiful [Amer]indian woman with a child wreathed with water-lilys,
humming-birds fluttering around her, their feathers glittering in the
setting sun like gem stones" (Iets over Suriname 1854: 156).

It can hardly be a coincidence that this Suriname Watramama has
much in common with the today's *Mammy Wata* cult in West Africa
(Brain 1980: 48). The latter cult is found mostly along the sea and river
shores from what is now the Ivory Coast to Cameroon. Its center, however, is between Togo and southwestern Nigeria, i.e., former Papa
country. In this region, a beautiful, long-haired [East] Indian-type goddess, who lives in the water, is held responsible for accidents that happen to people. The present cult is still quite young but is said to have
centuries-old roots. One explanation advanced for the existence of this
cult is the presence of seacows (*Trichechus senegalensis*) in some West
African waters. The females of this mammal have pronounced breasts,
which make a humanlike impression. The presence of this intriguing

animal could have been the basis for the old-time Mammy Wata cult (Salmons 1979: 125).

As seacows (*Trichechus manatus*) also occur in Suriname waters, one can imagine Papa slaves introducing the Watramama in Suriname and adapting it to local circumstances and other culture groups. Indeed, in Suriname oral tradition and especially in the *Anansi-tori's*, Watramama frequently makes her appearance; and although Anansi is one of her best friends, she also punishes him severely for his greediness (Helman 1978: 96–99).

Trustworthy observers recently have noted that the most powerful gods in Afro-Suriname religion today are the earth gods and the Kromanti or air gods (see, e.g., Wooding 1972: 308–10, Voorhoeve and Lichtveld 1975: 51–52, Stephen 1983: 43–47). We may have to take into account the possibility that this already was the case during slavery. Watramama may only have been practiced when whites were around, as a kind of decoy to attract attention and so protect the more secret and powerful elements of winti culture, such as *Kromanti* or *Gron winti*. Perhaps in this way whites came to view Watramama and slave religion as identical, labeling every religious dance a Watramama dance and forbidding the category, rather than making separate laws against every single religious dance or "dangerous" ceremony. This interpretation, however, points to another methodological problem. If whites indeed used the term *Watramama* to describe any manifestation of slave religion, there is little chance of charting the development of the Watramama cult from their reports.

Even with this caveat in mind, we do find some ground for attributing a dominant position to the Watramama in the formation of Afro-Suriname religion. During most of the first half-century of Dutch presence in Suriname, Papas were the numerically dominant ethnic group. They probably introduced Watramama, a religious cult fitting in well with the general plantation experience of the slaves, as well as the specific ecology of Suriname. Of course the emergence of Watramama coincided with the massive expansion of the *polder* complex, which made the hydraulic factor of dominant importance in the slaves' lives. Particularly after the initial stages, cultural influences of other ethnic groups who became numerically dominant added new elements to the cult, which slowly became a full-blown religious complex known by the name of *winti*. An increasing part of this acculturation and creolization process was hidden from white observers, who, to say the least, were not very interested in these developments. Therefore, Watramama and slave religion became synonymous and for a long time would remain so.

During the nineteenth century, land was of growing importance to the slaves and became especially important for the ex-slaves after Emancipation. In the final decades of slavery, the slaves were transforming into a proto-peasantry, increasingly producing agricultural products for themselves as well as for the market. Over the next decades, large segments of the former proto-peasantry settled in and around the capital of Paramaribo. A disproportionate share of the permanent Afro-Suriname ("creole") peasantry settled in the Para and Coronie districts, where the *polder* complex was not as dominant as elsewhere. Consequently, the influence of "water" in the slave world diminished, and that of "earth" increased. This transformation may have augmented the power of the earth gods at the expense of the water gods. Today, Watramama is no longer the most powerful god. Neither is she marginalized. In the hierarchy of appearances during a winti ceremony, Watramama holds a middle position.[6] Moreover, water spirits, or *watra winti*, still are very popular with the now urbanized creole population, the direct descendants of the majority of the former slaves. Therefore, in Afro-Suriname religion the hydraulic factor has lost its dominance, but not its influence.

A final instance of "water" as a formative element in Afro-Suriname culture is of a more social-psychological nature and refers once more to the geography of the Suriname plantation complex. Conceptualizing the geographical setting of the plantations as hundreds of islands in a green sea—metaphorically, a very Caribbean image—one wonders whether this location shaped an island mentality. Whatever their communalities, island populations tend to adhere to their own cultural horizons. Considering each plantation as an island, which the slaves officially were forbidden to leave, one imagines the surrounding water as a kind of cultural barrier. Within a general slave culture, the plantations can still be conceptualized as separate cultural entities. Personal contacts and kinship ties did develop among slaves of neighboring plantations. The move beyond the immediate environment, however, was thwarted by water, more than in plantation areas where roads provided the major means of communication (e.g., Beckles 1989: 72–90, Kulikoff 1986). Easily controllable as they were, the Suriname rivers remained virtually the only means of communication all through the slavery period. This not only retarded processes of cultural homogenization across the colony, but also denied most slaves direct access to Paramaribo. Slaves' produce usually was brought to the capital's market by smugglers and professional traders rather than by the producers themselves, as became accepted practice in Caribbean islands. Such geographic immobility reproduced insularity.

Indeed, every slave community had its own village god, its own spirits, and its own interpretation of the hierarchy of the higher gods. Furthermore, every plantation probably had its own style of drumming in respect to the village *winti*, and this specific style was forbidden to be played by a nonvillage drummer (see, e.g., Price and Price 1980: 179, Voorhoeve and Lichtveld 1975: 51–52, Wooding 1972: 259–60). Boat races between the rowers of different plantations could underpin an "island mentality." Maroon clans were organized principally among slaves who had belonged to the same plantation. During Maroon raids or slave uprisings on a particular plantation, slaves on neighboring plantations often chose not to join the protest. They did so for various reasons, but the point is that slaves on different plantations apparently continued to define their positions primarily as inhabitants of relatively isolated "islands," rather than as members of one undifferentiated slave class.

Conclusion

How far does an emphasis on ecology, and in particular on the "hydraulics" of Suriname plantation slavery, carry us? In terms of hard demographic data, working and living conditions, etc., the evidence uncovered seems inconclusive. We have been able to demonstrate some significant variations of material conditions *within* the Suriname *polder* complex; the contrasting demography of sugar and coffee plantations is a case in point here. These contrasts do emphasize the relevance of strictly materialist interpretations at this level of analysis. Even in this sphere, however, there is little evidence to support broad generalizations. Some specific labor demands of *polder* plantations were extremely strenuous; but there is no conclusive evidence that these translated into harsher labor conditions across the board. There is much less hard evidence that the average workload on a Suriname plantation compared unfavorably to conditions in other Caribbean locales.

Whatever the specific consequences for workloads and hence possible slave demography, there is no doubt that ecology, and the *polder* environment in particular, marked the Suriname slaves' working and living conditions. We suggest a substantial difference here with slavery in most other slave systems of the Americas. Much of this paper attempts to substantiate this claim by pointing to the many spheres of life in which the Suriname slave confronted challenges and options different from those facing her or his contemporary peers. The direct result of this analysis is to suggest some contours of a particular variant of slavery. Yet this outcome too is rather trivial. In a way, we merely rescue from oblivion the all-too-obvious fact that the ecological factor, and more specifically the omnipresence of water and hydraulic technology, strongly marked the material conditions and responses of Suriname slaves.

At the same time, it remains indeterminate how far we may venture beyond this somewhat commonplace conclusion. The grounds for a firm conclusion regarding the influence of "water" on slave culture remain somewhat shaky. And even if we cannot understand Afro-Suriname culture without taking into account the importance of ecology during its formative period, this does not imply that water was the only relevant ecological phenomenon. It is tempting to consider the Suriname tropical forest—to cite Fernando Ortiz's seminal and suggestive but equally elusive model (Ortiz 1940)—as a cultural "counterpoint" to water. In this metaphor, to the Maroons the forest symbolizes freedom, and on timber estates a relatively light slave regime. It is the other home of religion (gods, holy animals, and trees). It plays a prominent role in oral tradition (Anansi and other animal stories, proverbs, etc.). It is extremely important in music (wooden instruments, woodcutter songs). And the tropical forest surrounded the plantations like a green sea that gives and takes. Again, the challenge of analyzing slave culture and creolization from an ecological point of view is evident.

Notes

1. This paper departs from our own previous research on Suriname slavery (e.g., Oostindie 1989, 1993b; van Stipriaan 1993a, 1993b). For comparative purposes, see Joyner (1984).
2. The figures for slave populations at Suriname sugar and coffee plantations are taken from the samples in van Stipriaan (1993a: 128, 135).
3. An administrator quoted in Oostindie (1989: 229). Indeed, on the two plantations under his administration, both owned by the same absentee Dutch family, the sugar estate had consistently higher demographic losses than the one producing coffee (Oostindie 1989: 251–59).
4. See Price (1983: 48) on the Saramaka. Among the Ndjuka Maroons, similar recollections are transmitted (H. U. E. Thoden van Velzen, personal communication, 26 Feb. 1993).
5. The following analysis is based on Teenstra (1835, vol. 2, pp. 210–42), Cohen Rodríquez and Hesseling (1935), Herskovits and Herskovits (1969), *De slaventijd in odo's* (1960), and Guda (1984, 1985).
6. Likewise, in neighboring Guyana—a Dutch plantation colony until around 1800, and one with similar hydraulic characteristics—the "Watermama" is still an important spirit or goddess. See Reinders (1993).

References

Beckles, Hilary McD.
1989   *Natural Rebels: A Social History of Enslaved Black Women in Barbados.* London: Zed Books.
Blom, Anthony
1787   *Verhandeling van den landbouw in de Colonie Suriname.* Amsterdam: Smit.
Brain, Robert
1980   *Art and Society in Africa.* New York: Longman.
Cohen Rodríguez, P., and D. C. Hesseling
1935   Papiamentse en Negerengelse spreekwoorden. *West-Indische Gids* 18: 161–73.
de Beet, Chris
1984   *De eerste Boni-oorlog, 1765–1778.* Utrecht, Netherlands: Centrum voor Caraïbische Studies, Rijksuniversiteit Utrecht.
De slaventijd in odo's
1960   *De slaventijd in odo's: Een boekje over Suriname's heden en verleden.* Paramaribo: Radhakishun.
Focke, H. C.
1855   *Neger-Engelsch woordenboek.* Leiden, Netherlands: Van den Heuvel.
1858   De Surinaamsche Negermuzyk. *West Indië* 2: 93–110.
Guda, Trudy, ed.
1984   *Aleks de Drie: wan tori fu mi eygi srefi.* Paramaribo: Ministerie van Onderwijs, Wetenschappen en Cultuur.
1985   *Aleks de Drie: Sye! Arki tori!* Paramaribo: Ministerie van Onderwijs, Wetenschappen en Cultuur.
Helman, Albert, et al.
1978   *Cultureel mozaïek van Suriname.* Zutphen, Netherlands: Walburg Pers.
Herskovits, Melville J., and Frances S. Herskovits
1969 [1936]   *Surinam Folklore.* Colombia University Contributions to Anthropology. New York: Colombia Univ.
Higman, Barry W.
1984   *Slave Populations of the British Caribbean, 1807–1834.* Baltimore, Md.: Johns Hopkins Univ. Press.
Iets over Suriname
1854   Iets over Suriname. *Globe* 12: 151–61.
IJzermans, Jan
1987   Ontstaan en ontwikkeling van de creoolse populaire muziek in Suriname: 1800–1940. *OSO: Tijdschrift voor Surinaamse Taalkunde, letterkunde, Cultuur en Geschiedenis* 6: 49–66.
Joyner, Charles
1984   *Down by the Riverside: A South Carolina Slave Community.* Urbana: Univ. of Illinois Press.
Kulikoff, Alan
1986   *Tobacco and Slaves.* Urbana: Univ. of Illinois Press.
Mintz, Sidney W.
1979   The Role of Water in Steward's Cultural Ecology. *Journal of the Steward Anthropological Society* 11: 17–32.

Mintz, Sidney W., and Richard Price
1992 [1976]   *The Birth of African-American Culture: An Anthropological Perspective.*
Boston: Beacon Press.
Moreno Fraginals, Manuel
1978   *El ingenio: Complejo económico social cubano del azúcar.* Havana, Cuba: Editorial
de Ciencias Sociales
Nepveu, Jean
1775   "Annotaties op het boek van J. D. Herlein 'Beschryvinge van de volkplantinge
Zuriname.'" Manuscript, Amsterdam Municipal Archives, collection
Marquette 230.
Ontwerp tot een beschryving van Surinaamen
[1744] *Ontwerp tot een beschryving van Surinaamen.* N.p.
Oostindie, Gert
1989   *Roosenburg en Mon Bijou: Twee Surinaamse Plantages, 1720–1870.* Dordrecht,
Netherlands: Foris.
1993a   The Economics of Suriname Slavery. *Economic and Social History in the Nether-
lands* 5: 1–24.
1993b   Voltaire, Stedman, and Suriname Slavery. *Slavery and Abolition* 14 (2): 1–34.
Ortiz, Fernando
1940   *Contrapunteo cubano del tabaco y el azúcar.* Havana, Cuba: Montero.
Postma, Johannes Menne
1990   *The Dutch in the Atlantic Slave Trade, 1600–1815.* Cambridge: Cambridge
Univ. Press.
Price, Richard
1983   *First-Time: The Historical Vision of an Afro-American People.* Baltimore, Md.:
Johns Hopkins Univ. Press.
Price, Sally, and Richard Price
1980   *Afro-American Arts of the Suriname Rain Forest.* Los Angeles: Museum of Cul-
tural History, Univ. of California.
Raynal, G. F.
1774   *Histoire philosophique et politique des établissements et du commerce des Européens
dans les deux Indes.* Amsterdam: n.p.
Reinders, Marileen
1993   De Watermama. *CAhier* 2 (4): 43–51.
Salmons, Bill
1979   Mammy Wata: Wassergötter in Nigeria. In *Moderne Kunst aus Afrika,* ed.
Sabine Hollburg, 125–34. Berlin: Berliner Festspiele GmbH.
Siwpersad, J. P.
1979   *De Nederlandse regering en de afschaffing van de Surinaamse slavernij (1833–
1863).* Groningen, Netherlands: Bouma's Boekhuis.
Sordam, Max, and Hein Eersel
1985   *Sranantongo/Surinaamse taal: Een korte inleiding tot het Sranantongo, met
uitgebreide woordenlijst.* Baarn, Netherlands: Bosch and Keuning.
Stedman, John Gabriel
1988 [1796]   *Narrative of a Five Years Expedition against the Revolted Negroes of
Surinam.* [Ed. Richard Price & Sally Price.] Baltimore, Md.: Johns Hopkins
Univ. Press.

Stephen, Henry J.
1983   *Winti: Afro-Surinaamse religie en magische rituelen in Suriname en Nederland.* Amsterdam: n.p.
Teenstra, M. D.
1835   *De landbouw in de kolonie Suriname voorafgegaan door eene geschied- en natuurkundige beschouwing dier kolonie.* 2 vols. Groningen, Netherlands: Eekhoorn.
van Breugel, G. P. C.
1842   *Dagverhaal van eene reis naar Paramaribo en verdere omstreken in de kolonie Suriname.* Amsterdam: Sulpke.
van Stipriaan, Alex
1992   Het dilemma van plantageslaven: Weglopen of blijven. *OSO: Tijdschrift voor Surinaamse Taalkunde, letterkunde, Cultuur en Geschiedenis* 11: 122–41.
1993a *Surinaams contrast; Roofbouw en overleven in een Caraïbische plantagekolonie, 1750–1863.* Leiden, Netherlands: KITLV Uitgeverij.
1993b "Een verre verwijderd trommelen . . . ": Ontwikkeling van Afro-Surinaamse muziek en dans in de slavernij. In *De kunstwereld: Produktie, distributie en receptie in de wereld van kunst en cultuur,* ed. A. Bevers et al., 143–73. Rotterdam, Netherlands: Faculteit der Historische en Kunstwetenschappen, Erasmus Universiteit Rotterdam, Uitgeverij Verloren.
Voorhoeve, Jan, and Ursy M. Lichtveld, eds.
1975   *Creole Drum: An Anthology of Creole Literature in Surinam.* New Haven, Conn.: Yale Univ. Press.
Watts, David
1987   *The West Indies: Patterns of Development, Culture and Environmental Change Since 1492.* Cambridge: Cambridge Univ. Press.
West Indisch Plakaatboek
1973   *West Indisch Plakaatboek: I Suriname: Plakaten, ordonnantiën en andere wetten, uitgevaardigd in Suriname, 1667–1816,* ed. J. A. Schiltkamp and Th. de Smit. Amsterdam: Emmering.
Wittfogel, Karl A.
1957   *Oriental Despotism: A Comparative Study of Total Power.* New York: Yale Univ. Press.
Wooding, Charles J.
1972   *Winti: Een Afroamerikaanse godsdienst in Suriname: Een cultureel-historische analyse van de religieuze verschijnselen in de Para.* Meppel, Netherlands: Krips Repro.

8 | Female Slave-Owners on the Gold Coast

Just a Matter of Money?

Adam Jones

When British troops were about to invade Asante in 1873, Mrs. Swanzy of Cape Coast sent "80 of her people" to assist in the preparations. A sympathetic English observer wrote:

> This term *people* is a vague one, but so is the connection between Mrs. Swanzy and these 80 women. . . . It is possible that among the number there were half a dozen slaves, but the rest are exactly in the position of the Roman clients. The clients include freed men and women and their children and descendants, together with a number of others who have . . . chosen one or other of the great houses as their protector. It is, indeed, a good deal the same position which the other natives occupy towards their chiefs, except that, in the cases of persons like Mrs. Swanzy and Mrs. Barnes, the actual assistance and kindness shown to their clients is greater than that which the chiefs can afford to dispense. (Henty 1874: 205–7)

The author of this passage was at pains to minimize the number of slaves involved; yet it seems likely that a substantial proportion of those women to whom he referred as "people" ought more properly to have been termed slaves.[1]

Despite their un-African names, neither Mrs. Swanzy nor Mrs. Barnes was a European. Nor was the ability of such women to acquire large numbers of slaves and other dependents altogether atypical for sub-Saharan Africa. Women possessed slaves (or at least profited directly from slave labor) in many parts of the West African coast, in several societies of the West Sudan, in what is now Zaire, in Mozambique, and in Mombasa (Robertson and Klein 1983; Miers and Kopytoff 1977).

In recent literature this phenomenon has generally been explained in terms of production and trade. Many slaves helped women in the production of food, cloth, or gold; others served as carriers or earned wages which they handed over to their mistresses. Thus, it is argued, slaves produced surplus value for their mistresses just as they did for their masters: "Women, especially in commercially developed societies, utilized the slave labor of their less fortunate sisters" (Robertson and Klein 1983: 13).

Yet we still know little about the kind of woman who possessed slaves or the reasons for her doing so. In comparison with the documentation for slave societies of the New World, that for sub-Saharan Africa is meager and fragmentary. In particular, we lack the statistical data which have enabled New World historians to analyze the demography and productivity of such societies.[2] Moreover, we possess hardly any autobiographies, songs, diaries, or similar material which might indicate how slaves and slave-owners perceived their positions.

In this paper I propose to examine one case—that of the Gold Coast (i.e., the coast of what is today Ghana)—where, in comparison with other parts of sub-Saharan Africa, the documentation is fairly good. Even here, however, in order to say anything useful about female slave-owners, it is necessary to draw together fragments of material from the seventeenth, eighteenth, and nineteenth centuries—a dangerous procedure, since in doing so I am likely to give insufficient weight to the historical changes that took place during this period.[3] I shall confine myself mainly to the sources predating the British abolition of slavery and the slave trade in 1874.[4]

First, a word about the nature of these sources. Attracted by the possibility of purchasing gold, the Portuguese built their first fort on the Gold Coast, São Jorge da Mina (later known as Elmina), in the late fifteenth century. In the course of the seventeenth century, slaves began to supersede gold as the principal export, and the Portuguese were replaced by the Dutch, English, and Danes, all of whom established their own forts. Following the abolition of the Atlantic slave trade in the early nineteenth century, the European traders resident on the Gold Coast were joined by a growing number of administrators and missionaries. As a result of this European presence, we possess a substantial body of travel literature in English, Dutch, German, French, and Danish, as well as numerous commercial and administrative records. Only seldom, however, do the sources deal specifically with slaves as individuals, and they mention women comparatively rarely (see Jones 1989).

I shall attempt to answer two questions. First, what made it possible for women on the Gold Coast to own slaves? And second, what did they want slaves for?

One reason why it was more common for women to own slaves on the Gold Coast than in many other parts of Africa is that the Gold Coast was a highly commercialized area. Indeed, apart from sea-fishing (by men) and the preparation of dried fish (by women), commerce was probably the main economic activity, especially on the central Gold Coast. Records from throughout the period concerned indicate that women, although less important than men in European commerce (notably the gold trade), played an important role in retail. In general, husbands and wives were economically independent of one another; but during the nineteenth century, something resembling a patrilineal nuclear family began to establish itself at the expense of existing kin networks, and thus "husbands and wives became partners on the path toward primitive accumulation" (Kaplow 1978: 27).

The majority of women owning slaves were of Afro-European descent; the British called them mulatresses, while Dutch documents usually refer to them as *tapoeyerinnen* (for a discussion of this term, see Yarak 1989: n. 2). This descent may be deduced from eighteenth-century documents, which refer to slave-owners by their Christian names,[5] while nineteenth-century sources are more explicit, naming women from virtually all of the major Afro-European families (Huydecoper, Swanzy, Reindorf, Bannerman, etc.).[6] Other slave-owners were the African wives, *mulheres* (common-law wives), or widows of Europeans.[7] In some cases it was through marriage to a European that the women were in a position to obtain slaves. In 1851, for instance, it was reported that John Marman, a merchant resident in British Accra, had a large household of slaves whom he employed in domestic service. Marman himself claimed that the slaves belonged to the African woman with whom he cohabited; yet he had redeemed her from a slave-dealer, and whatever property she had since accumulated had been derived from capital supplied by him.[8]

Often these two groups overlapped, since, given the virtual absence of European women on the Gold Coast, European men were most likely to marry an Afro-European. There can be no doubt that some Afro-European women who were wives of Europeans owned large numbers of slaves. In 1841, when British officials were looking for a way to abolish slavery within the territory they controlled on the Gold Coast, the colonial secretary in London received a petition from seven women resident in Cape Coast, protesting that they were "without the least warning to be deprived of their rights and property, and in one moment to lose the services of the whole of their slaves." All had European names, yet described themselves as "natives of Africa" (and apparently were illiterate).[9]

Only occasionally do the sources mention slave-owning women who fell into neither of these categories. Some were clearly rich, such as Coffiba, an Elmina trader who sold maize and oil to the Dutch in exchange for cloth in the early eighteenth century (Feinberg 1969: 142). But we also find a few slave-owners at the opposite end of the socioeconomic scale. A century later another Elmina woman, Amma, who owned one female slave, was described as follows: "She is a poor woman, and lives from one day to the next . . . Each day she buys enough salt and other things to eat for that day, which is then consumed on the same day. The next day she again buys what she needs for the day, because she is too poor to buy a lot at once" (Dutch record dated 1827, trans. in Yarak 1986: 40). Women became slave-owners in several different ways, none of them unique to women. Often they inherited slaves, generally (in the Akan region) from their mother, brother, or mother's brother.[10] They might also buy or sell slaves.[11] Others acquired slaves or pawns in return for writing off debts due to them.[12] It was not uncommon for a family to pawn a girl with the intention (often never fulfilled) of redeeming her later.[13] In 1863 one of the Basel Mission's members living near Accra explained his inability to manumit a slave woman by saying that his sister had once paid his debts and therefore would claim the slave woman as her own if he tried to manumit her.[14]

This brings us to our second question: What did women want slaves for? A number of women possessed male slaves, who performed a wide variety of tasks. One was described as a "fetish priest" (Yarak 1986: 38); another was once hired by a woman to carry her baggage;[15] others were allowed to earn money by working for the British authorities in Cape Coast or for the Basel Mission.[16] One woman had her slaves cultivate cotton, coffee, and plantains but also allowed them three days a week to grow maize and yams for their own consumption (Yarak 1989: 51). It is impossible to generalize about the uses to which male slaves were put, given the fragmentary nature of the documentation.

The majority of slaves owned by women, however, appear to have been female. Robertson (1983) has argued that in late nineteenth-century Accra female slaves were considered desirable because of their "productive value": they were bought "to help women with their tasks," and it was because of their economic value, particularly to female owners, that the British proclamation outlawing slavery and the slave trade in 1874 failed to achieve its aims. Gā women, Robertson argues, used female slave labor mainly in productive tasks (farm labor, making pottery, making soap, processing beads, or preparing food for local trade and fish for long-distance trade). Thus they themselves were enabled to "devote more of their time to marketing" (1983: 224).

This all sounds plausible; but since Robertson offers hardly any evidence on this point, some caution is warranted. Certainly slave women helped their mistresses with household chores such as winnowing, cooking, smoking fish, baking *kenkey*, and collecting firewood (see, e.g., De Marees 1987 [1602]: 20a, 89b). Yet production does not figure prominently in the sources that mention the labor of female slaves. Far more important was petty commerce. One document mentions a slave woman sent from Elmina to sell goods in Anomabu, which she continued to do for two years.[17] Another slave woman in Elmina took cheese to sell in Cape Coast market.[18] Women in Accra sent their slaves to sell rum and other commodities in neighboring villages.[19]

Meillassoux and others have argued against the notion that female slaves were desired because of their reproductive (rather than productive) capacity (Robertson and Klein 1983: passim). Yet in the case of the Gold Coast, at least, this notion does not appear totally unwarranted. Among both the matrilineal Akan and the patrilineal Gā, sons and daughters of slave women became the property of the women's owners. Female owners took full advantage of this, even to the extent of circumventing "traditional" rules of inheritance by writing a will. Thus, in 1748, an Elmina woman of Afro-Dutch descent bequeathed three female slaves and the children of one of them to her niece.[20] Two decades later, an African woman in Sekondi successfully claimed twenty-seven slaves living at Takoradi; all were offspring of her mother's brother by another African woman, whom he had purchased (rather than married).[21] These examples suggest that the rate at which slaves were "incorporated" or "integrated" into the lineage of their owners may have been slower than some anthropologists have assumed.

Unlike male slave-owners, women were probably not in a position to take advantage of their female slaves' sexuality. Men on the Gold Coast sometimes used female slaves or pawns to lure unwary men and extract "adultery payments" (Kaplow 1978: 33–34), but this would have been virtually impossible for a female owner to do. Nor could she be the owner of the "village whores" described in a number of sources relating to the western Gold Coast in the seventeenth and nineteenth centuries (see Jones 1990). On the other hand, a woman could expect to receive bridewealth if a free man wished to marry one of her female slaves (see appendix to this essay, "A Tale of Two Women").

It is clear that women on the Gold Coast drew some economic benefit from the labor of their slaves and pawns, as well as from the children to whom their female slaves gave birth. Yet if we acknowledge that production and reproduction were important reasons for women to own slaves, we ought not to neglect other motives.

One function of slaves, to which Robertson in my view attaches too little importance, was that of caring for the very young and the very old. Several documents mention slave women who nursed infants.[22] Likewise, old women without children needed someone to look after them. In Accra, for instance, one woman paid a younger woman's debts, saying "I am old, stop with me and care for me," after which the ceremony for slave-buying was performed.[23]

Even more important was a desire for prestige. With reference to "centralized state systems" on the Gold Coast, Dumett and Johnson (1988: 77) have pointed out that "every chief or 'big man' needed a retinue of subordinates to follow him as he made his regular rounds of the community." The same applied to "big women." Thus, at the beginning of the seventeenth century, a Dutchman noted that when women of high status went out, they leant on the shoulder of "other women who serve them and are their slaves" (De Marees 1987 [1602]: 48a). Two centuries later, another Dutchman described how, when free women danced together in a circle, the slave of one woman might run behind her waving a handkerchief and crying out "*Mó! Mó!*" (a form of congratulation) (De Marrée 1817–18: vol. 2, p. 90).

In addition to performing such honorific gestures, slaves might assist a mistress by lending her moral or physical support in her relations with other women. In 1862, for instance, a quarrel arose between Adjuwa Crampo and Amba Praba, both of Elmina, concerning an overdue debt. Both women instructed their slaves (also referred to in the same report as "serfs" and "maids") to shout insults at the other party, and eventually the two sides came to blows. The dispute was finally settled by the town elders in consultation with the Dutch.[24] In such disputes, slaves were probably of more use to a woman than relatives, simply because they were more dependent on her.

In order to enhance the status of their mistress, slave women themselves sometimes had to be dressed as finely as possible. This, on the Gold Coast, meant above all displaying gold. In nineteenth-century Elmina, where it was customary for a girl to be decorated in gold when she reached puberty, responsibility for decorating slave girls, who of course had no kin to do this, was assumed by the mistress. Thus one observer reported after attending a wedding dinner:

> One of the lady's slave girls had just reached this state of jubilation, and she served us at table, having on her body [jewelry] worth more than 6,000 gold guilders, which the good mistress had fastened all over her body, to such an extent that in serving us she was handicapped by it. This lady, moreover, could scarcely contain her joy at having been able to make us witnesses of such a touching ceremony. (Douchez 1839: 109, my translation)

If a woman wore gold ornaments, so did her "maids" (Jeekel 1869: 32); thus one might see a wealthy woman going through the streets of Elmina followed by ten of her slave women, all finely dressed and wearing gold ornaments (Kerdijk 1978: 181). A woman of high status might spend hours dressing her female slaves and arranging their hair (Gramberg 1861: 90; cf. Kerdijk 1978: 168).

We may conclude that women valued female slaves not merely as a factor of production but also as vendors of merchandise, as potential mothers of slaves, as nurses of young and old, and above all as sources of prestige and moral support. This, of course, does not necessarily mean that Gold Coast women treated their slaves better than men did.[25] Some observers, including the Englishman quoted at the beginning of this paper, believed that this was the case, but others were of a different opinion. One of the earliest extant records concerns an old woman, probably resident at Mouri (just east of Cape Coast), to whom the Dutch gave two sick male slaves as a present in about 1621. Subsequently, finding one of them lying near the fire, she decapitated him, saying: "*Siempre Comeer y non [i.e., Sempre comer e não] trabalhar, nada nada*" ("Always eating and never working, it just won't do").[26]

Appendix

A Tale of Two Women

The following account is adapted from a memorial written in Elmina by an officer of the Dutch West India Company in 1762.[27] Although Aquassiba was (according to this source) *not* a slave, her story illustrates several points relevant to this paper, especially the fact that a woman who owned a female slave could expect to receive bridewealth if a free man wished to marry her.

The "Prince" of Great Comany had a "grand-daughter"[28] named Aquassiba and a male "serf" named Abouwelo. The latter gained considerable influence in serving his master, and when the Prince died, Abouwelo inherited much of his wealth, including some slaves. He entrusted Aquassiba to the care of a woman in Elmina called Tetjeba Casse, who had been Abouwelo's concubine.

When Abouwelo died, Tetjeba claimed that he owed her the sum of 1 ounce and 8 engels in gold, which she had given him to buy a young female slave for her. Abouwelo's family, however, refused to recognize this debt and ordered Aquassiba to leave Tetjeba and return with them to Great Comany. Thereupon Tetjeba took some earth from the ground, sprinkled it over Aquassiba, and said: "If you run away to your relatives [*vrinden,* literally "friends"] before I have received my payment, you must die." Aquassiba, who hitherto had been content to live with Tetjeba and was frightened by this oath, remained with her.

Eventually she married. Tetjeba refused to accept the bridewealth for this marriage, saying that Aquassiba was not her slave and the bridewealth should be taken to Aquassiba's family instead: "I ask for my payment and nothing more."

Most members of Aquassiba's family were unwilling to have anything more to do with her, because she had refused to go with them. But her nephew reached an agreement with Tetjeba: the latter would receive 1 ounce and 2 engels (instead of 1 ounce and 8 engels), and a goat would be sacrificed when she died. Upon Tetjeba's death, Aquassiba's nephew sacrificed the goat; but Tetjeba's daughter and heir refused to accept the sum of 1 ounce and 2 engels, demanding a slave woman instead. A slave woman was brought, but Tetjeba's daughter considered her too old.

Thus the dispute remained unsettled, and eventually Tetjeba's daughter died, leaving her grandson as heir. The latter refused to accept even a slave, insisting that Aquassiba herself was his slave. His reason for doing so may have been connected with the fact that, by this time, Aquassiba had borne several children to a Dutchman, the author of the report, who was anxious lest she and her children be sold if he were to die. Apparently the dispute was settled when this Dutchman agreed to pay two male slaves in return for official recognition that Aquassiba and her children were free.

This story illustrates the extent to which the position of a woman who was dependent upon other women might be ambiguous. Whereas Aquassiba's status was relatively comfortable as long as Tetjeba and her daughter were alive, it remained essentially insecure and subject to renegotiation.

Notes

Abbreviations

ARA   Algemeen Rijksarchief (General State Archives), The Hague, Netherlands
BMA   Basel Mission Archive, Basal
GNA   Ghana National Archive, Accra

1. Slavery is usually defined in terms either of a particular property relationship or of the lack of kin. For the purposes of this paper, I adopt the rather broad definition used by Robertson and Klein (1983: 3–4): "The slave is involuntarily servile, has a marginal position within her social unit, and is subject to the control of another."
2. For European-language coverage of precolonial sub-Saharan Africa, see Heintze and Jones (1987). The different nature of the documentation for the Caribbean may be seen, for example, by comparing any work on women in precolonial Africa with Gautier (1985).
3. This criticism has been leveled against several works on African slavery, especially Miers and Kopytoff (1977). It has been suggested that, in the nineteenth century, slavery on the Gold Coast was becoming "increasingly oppressive" (McSheffrey 1983). This, view, however, has been strongly contested; see, especially, Dumett and Johnson (1988) and Yarak (1989).
4. Some of the evidence for the 1870s and 1880s has been studied by McSheffrey (1983), Robertson (1983), and Dumett and Johnson (1988). But McSheffrey and Dumett and Johnson say little about gender, while Robertson deals mainly with female slaves rather than with female owners. Peter Haenger's forthcoming dissertation at the University of Basel, based largely upon the records of the Basel Mission and those held in the Ghana National Archive, may throw further light on this subject.
5. ARA, NBKG 295 Nr. 104, Jan van Voorst 27.11.1749. ARA, NBKG 297 Nr. 33, Akoffy and Tonwa 21.9.1757.
6. Yarak (1986: 41) and (1989: 51–52). Swanzy (1956: 100n). BMA, D-1, 3, Ussu 1851 Nr. 13, Zimmerman 4.10.1851. BMA, D-1, 13a, Schrenk 19.5.1862 to Widman. Report by Bohner dated 3 Apr. 1868, Christiansborg, *Jahresbericht der evangelischen Missionsgesellschaft* 53 (1868): 95. Kaplow (1971: 145, n. 3).
7. ARA, NBKG 239, minutes of 13.1.1737. British Parliamentary Papers, 1842, vol. 12, p. 52, Maclean 15.5.1841. GNA, SCT 5/1/11, anonymous, 31.12.1865. Kaplow (1971: 148). Feinberg (1989: 117). For a discussion of Anglo-Fante marriages in the early nineteenth century, see McCarthy (1983: 36–47).
8. GNA, SCT 5/1/6, Cruickshank 24.11.1851 to Hill. Marman had been suspected of slave-dealing as early as 1842; McCarthy (1983: 158). In the nineteenth century both European and African merchants on the Gold Coast exploited the differences between Akan custom and British law regarding the property and the debts of spouses. They also tried to convince the British authorities that their slaves belonged to their wives, who were not British subjects; see Kaplow (1978: 27–28, 30).
9. British Parliamentary Papers, 1842, 551-II, Report of the Select Committee, p.

138, petition by Fanny Smith, Mary Jackson, Elizabeth Swanzy, Mary Hutton, Sarah Crosby, Catherine Bannerman, and Helen Coliver, 29.3.1841. Most, but not all, were of Afro-European descent.

10. GNA, SCT 5/1/2, Clanston 26.6.1846 to Derx.
11. ARA, NBKG 193, Fennekol 9.1.1770. BMA, D-1,13a, Schrenk 19.5.1862 to Widman. Kaplow (1971: 148).
12. In about 1818, Carolina Huydecoper acquired six male slaves belonging to Carel Ruhle of Elmina, who had died while still in debt to her father; Yarak (1989: 51).
13. See, e.g., GNA, SCT 17/4/2, case dated "7.11.1875."
14. BMA, D-1, 14, Africa 1863 Nr. 41, Sclaven-Emancipations-Commission 24.7.1863.
15. GNA, SCT 5/1/2, Maclean 8.4.1847 to Derx.
16. Gordon (1874: 26). BMA, D-1, 3 Ussu 1851 Nr. 13, Zimmerman 4.10.1851.
17. GNA, SCT 5/1/6, Schomerus 6.5.1850 to Fitzpatrick.
18. GNA, SCT 5/1/5, Van der Eb 21.8.1851 to Bannerman. Cf. Kaplow (1971: 145, n. 3).
19. GNA, SCT 17/4/2, pp. 66–67, case dated 2.8.1875. GNA, SCT 17/4/2, pp. 276–78, case dated 3.11.1875.
20. ARA, NBGK 295 Nr. 66, Helena van den Burgh 18.8.1748.
21. ARA, NBKG 242, pp. 71–72, Huydecoper 14.5.1767. In principle, the payment offered for a women or girl as a slave was quite distinct from bridewealth, and the accompanying ceremonies differed. In practice, though, there seems to have been a number of borderline cases which subsequently became matters of dispute.
22. GNA, SCT 5/1/9, Corner 8.6.1860 to Brew. BMA, D-1, 14, Africa 1863 Nr. 41, Sclaven-Emancipations-Commission 24.7.1863.
23. GNA, SCT 17/4/2, Addookey v. Accosuah 29.10.1875. It is possible, as Robertson (1983: 225) claims, that in some cases such court statements were designed to offer "extenuating" reasons for slave-owning and to downplay the labor value of slaves.
24. ARA, NBKG 776, palaver of 22.9.1862. One woman slave, asked why she had called Adjuwa Crampo a "she-devil" and an "ugly *tapoeyerin*," replied that "her grandmother [Amba] Praba was offended."
25. In the mid-nineteenth century, when the British began to take an interest in slave runaways, a number of cases were recorded of slave women who had escaped from their mistresses: GNA, SCT 5/1/6, passim (1849); SCT 5/1/8, Roe 6.6.1855 to Runckel and Clarke 17.11.1858 to De Ruvignes.
26. Lange (1658: 44). For an instance of cruel punishment meted out by a woman to a slave boy, see report by Bohner dated 3 Apr. 1868, Christiansborg, *Jahresbericht der evangelischen Missionsgesellschaft* 53 (1868): 95. Yarak (1989: 51) describes a case in which a woman tried to make her male slaves work harder and threatened to take away the wives she had given them; they responded by conspiring to murder her.
27. ARA, NBKG 298 Nr. 115, Walmbeek 16.1.1762.
28. This term need not necessarily have signified a biological relationship; compare n. 24 above, which documents a slave woman's calling her mistress "grandmother."

References

De Marees, Pieter
1987 [1602]   *Beschryvinge ende historische verhael vant Gout Koninckrijck van Gunea.*
Amsterdam: Cornelis Claesz. English version is *Description and Historical Account of the Gold Kingdom of Guinea,* ed. Albert van Dantzig and Adam Jones.
Oxford: Oxford Univ. Press for the British Academy,. 1987 [1602].

De Marrée, J. A.
1817–18   *Reizen op en Beschrijving van de Goudkust van Guinea.* 2 vols.
's Gravenhage, Netherlands: Gebroeders van Cleef.

Douchez, F.
1839   *Causeries sur la côte de Guinée, à propos de l'expédition du général Verveer pendant l'été de 1838.* La Haye and Amsterdam.

Dumett, Raymond, and Marion Johnson
1988   Britain and the Suppression of Slavery in the Gold Coast Colony, Ashanti, and the Northern Territories. In *The End of Slavery in Africa,* ed. Suzanne Miers and Richard Roberts, 71–116. Madison: Univ. of Wisconsin Press.

Feinberg, Harvey M.
1969   Elmina, Ghana: A History of Its Development and Its Relationship with the Dutch in the Eighteenth Century. Ph.D. diss., Boston Univ.
1989   Africans and Europeans in West Africa: Elminans and Dutchmen on the Gold Coast during the Eighteenth Century. Philadelphia: *Transactions of the American Philosophical Society* 79, part 7.

Gautier, Arlette
1985   *Les soeurs de Solitude: La condition féminine dans l'esclavage aux Antilles du XVIIe au XIXe siècle.* Paris: Editions Caribéennes.

Gordon, C. A.
1874   *Life on the Gold Coast.* London: Baillière, Tindall, and Cox.

Gramberg, J. S. G.
1861   *Schetsen van Afrika's Westkust.* Amsterdam: Weijtingh and Brave

Heintze, Beatrix, and Adam Jones, eds.
1987   *European Sources for Sub-Saharan Africa before 1900: Use and Abuse.*
(= *Paideuma* 33).

Henty, G. A.
1874   *The March to Coomassie.* London: Tinsley.

Jeekel, C. A.
1869   *Onze bezittingen op de kust van Guinea.* Amsterdam: C. F. Stemler.

Jones, Adam
1989   Schwarze Frauen, weisse Beobachter: Die Frauen der Goldküste in den Augen der europäischen Männer, 1600–1900. In *Der europäische Beobachter aussereuropäischer Kulturen: Zur Problematik der Wirklichkeitswahrnehmung,* 153–68. (= *Zeitschrift für Historische Forschung,* Beiheft 7).
1990   Prostitution, Polyandrie oder Vergewaltigung? Zur Mehrdeutigkeit europäischer Quellen über die Küste Westafrikas zwischen 1660 und 1860. In *Aussereuropäische Frauengeschichte: Probleme der Forschung,* ed. Adam Jones, 123–58. Pfaffenweiler, Germany: Centaurus.

Kaplow, Susan B.
1971   African Merchants of the Nineteenth-Century Gold Coast. Ph. D. diss., Columbia Univ.

1978   Primitive Accumulation and Traditional Social Relations on the Nineteenth-Century Gold Coast. *Canadian Journal of African Studies* 12: 19–36.
Kerdijk, Lodewijk
1978   *Reisjournaal van Lodewijk Kerdijk: West-Afrika, 1857–1858,* ed. A. F. Schepel. Schiedam, Netherlands: Interbook International.
Lange, Jacob [Jacobus Langius]
1658   *Daemonomanie ofte der Moore wonderheden.* Amsterdam: B. Schouwers.
McCarthy, Mary
1983   *Social Change and the Growth of British Power in the Gold Coast.* Lanham, New York: Univ. Press of America.
McSheffrey, Gerald M.
1983   Slavery, Indentured Servitude, Legitimate Trade and the Impact of Abolition in the Gold Coast, 1874–1901: A Reappraisal. *Journal of African History* 24: 349–68.
Miers, Suzanne, and Igor Kopytoff, eds.
1977   *Slavery in Africa: Historical and Anthropological Perspectives.* Madison: Univ. of Wisconsin Press.
Robertson, Claire C.
1983   Post-Proclamation Slavery in Accra: A Female Affair? In *Women and Slavery in Africa,* ed. Claire C. Robertson and Martin A. Klein, 220–42. Madison: Univ. of Wisconsin Press.
Robertson, Claire C., and Martin A. Klein, eds.
1983   *Women and Slavery in Africa.* Madison: Univ. of Wisconsin Press.
Swanzy, Henry
1956   A Trading Family in the Nineteenth-Century Gold Coast. *Transactions of the Gold Coast and Togoland Historical Society* 2: 87–120.
Yarak, Larry W.
1986   Murder and Theft in Early Nineteenth-Century Elmina. In *Banditry, Rebellion and Social Protest in Africa,* ed. Donald Crummey, 33–47. London: James Currey.
1989   West African Coastal Slavery in the Nineteenth Century: The Case of the Afro-European Slaveowners of Elmina. *Ethnohistory* 36: 44–60.

9 | Dangerous Ancestors

Ambivalent Visions of Eighteenth- and Nineteenth-Century Leaders of the Eastern Maroons of Suriname

H. U. E. Thoden van Velzen

Maroon Leaders Celebrated

Maroon societies are extolled by Surinamese nationalists, as well as by most citizens of the Republic of Suriname as communities of proud, free people. So, too, are the maroon leaders of the eighteenth-century revolt against the planters. In the rhetoric of the modern nation-state, a triumvirate of rebels stands out: Boni, Baron, and Jolicoeur. De Kom (1971 [1934]: 75), the best known of Suriname's early nationalists, formulates it thus: "Baron, cheated and mistreated; Joli Coeur, reviled and badgered; opened contacts with Bonni, the fear of the Whites. These chiefs succeeded in establishing a regime of discipline and order, and to form an army that for many years proved itself equal to the well organized force of the Dutch." The freedom fighters found their way into present-day discourse through Stedman's well-known eighteenth-century "Narrative of a Five Years Expedition against the Revolted Negroes of Surinam" (1988 [1790]). Stedman's account of the defense and capture of Boekoe, an ingeniously built maroon fortress in the swamps of the coastal plain, has been enshrined in modern nationalist rhetoric as well: *Membre Boekoe* (Remember Boekoe) is the name given to the barracks of the Surinamese army in Paramaribo, capital of Suriname.[1]

Maroons

At the end of the seventeenth century, insurgent slaves ("runaways" or maroons) escaped from Suriname's plantations to take refuge in the rain forest of the Guyanas. Around the middle of the eighteenth century, several consolidated maroon groups emerged in different parts of Suriname's interior. In 1760, after decades of deprivation and war, the Ndyuka maroons of eastern Suriname became the first group to gain its freedom by concluding a peace treaty with the Dutch colonial government. In the central part of Suriname, treaties followed with the Saramakas (1762) and the Matawais (1767). A century before the abolition of slavery in Suriname (1863), thousands of maroons had won their freedom. In official documents they were referred to as "pacified maroons." Estimates of their numbers at the times of the treaties vary considerably, but to estimate Ndyukas and Saramakas at between 2,500 and 3,000 each would not be far off the mark; Matawais probably numbered about 300.

The main result of the peace treaties was to transform erstwhile foes into vassals. In return for autonomy and the promise of providing them with most of the goods they could not make themselves, such as guns, gunpowder, iron utensils, clothes, and many other objects, maroons pledged to refrain from acts of aggression against the "plantation colony"—the area actually occupied by the plantations—and not to enter into negotiations with other groups, whether Amerindians, other Europeans, or other maroons, without the approval of these authorities. In other words, these maroons were not allowed to conduct an independent foreign policy. Particularly galling, and a cause of considerable friction later, were those articles of the treaty demanding that maroons deliver all later runaways into the hands of their former masters. To restrict and control their movements beyond their own territories, a pass system was devised: only small groups of maroons were allowed entry into the plantation colony. An official with the title of *posthouder* (literally, postholder) took up residence with each of the maroon groups to supervise the implementation of the peace treaty. This *posthouder* served as a liaison between the maroon chiefs and the colonial authorities; he issued passes to maroons traveling to the plantation colony and was also instructed to gather "intelligence."

Firm ties of dependence connected the plantation colony with the pacified maroons. The three or four yearly shipments of goods—in official documents named "the distribution of presents" but viewed by maroon leaders as tribute, or obligatory payments, to their people—represented one of these links. Economic transactions between planters and maroons soon forged even stronger bonds. Maroon communities were kept from withdrawing deeper into the interior, or severing links with the plantation colony, by their economic dependence on coastal society.

In eastern Suriname, however, a war continued with other runaways. In 1768, hostilities between the government of planters and the Alukus, a coalition of smaller groups of maroons under the leadership of Boni, began to pose a formidable threat to the plantations (Hoogbergen 1990: 52). Between 1768 and 1777, an army of mercenaries drove them out of the plantation colony. In 1789, when the Alukus hit the plantations again, the colonial army followed the Alukus to their new villages along the Maroni River, the border river separating Dutch from French territory. The colonial troops destroyed one settlement after another, until they finally defeated them with the help of the Ndyukas in 1793. Other smaller groups of runaways, such as those later known as Paramakas, were left in peace by the planters' army. Although the Ndyukas, by supporting the planters in their war with the Alukus, had behaved as a Dutch vassal nation, this did not keep them from secretly establishing relations with "nonpacified maroons," i.e., with Paramakas and other smaller groups of runaways. In 1805, they went even further by granting asylum to a group of mutinous Black Rangers, former slaves who had won their freedom by serving as mercenaries in the Dutch army. At the confluence of Tapanahoni and Lawa rivers, Ndyukas offered the Rangers a place to settle, with the obligation to stand as sentries at the entrance to the main Ndyuka area of settlement, the Tapanahoni River.

The Construction of History as Maroon Praxis

This essay deals with the visions that contemporary maroons have of their past leaders. My examples are taken from all three eastern groups, i.e., Alukus, Ndyukas, and Paramakas. Present-day maroons in most cases envision maroon leaders of the eighteenth and nineteenth centuries as despotic. Once maroons begin to relate their historical knowledge, pronounced ambivalent feelings about these famous ancestors soon come to the surface. This is true for both maroon historians and all other maroon adults. When I refer to historians, I have in mind those individuals who are known and admired throughout Ndyuka territory for their knowledge of the past. Although much of that learning is specific for locality and kin group, a reputation as a historian can be gained only by those who have succeeded in collecting information about events that are considered crucial to the development of the Ndyuka nation as a whole. To offer one example: all historians are expected to have obtained special knowledge on the Ndyuka-Aluku war of 1793, regardless of whether their own clans took part in the hostilities. How Ndyuka historians practice their craft and how they manage to collect such information are not the subject of this paper. In many ways the training and practice of Ndyuka historians resembles those of the Saramaka maroons (cf. Price 1983: 8–11).

This maroon historiographical tradition should be understood within the egalitarian context characteristic of the tiny village republics that were (and still are) the functioning units of their societies after the struggle for freedom had secured a large measure of political autonomy.

Maroons today speak with admiration of their war leaders, shamans, and headmen. However, they also feel free to express sentiments about these same persons that are extremely negative, at times painting them as irascible and irresponsible or even as murderers or witches. Various mechanisms are employed to create these portraits. Some maroon historians, for example, would contrast the account of a good leader with that of the evil one: "My ancestor X was such a bad man! Fortunately my ancestor Y was always at his side to protect the people from his evil colleague."[2]

Others would start out with the glorious deeds of a leader in the war of independence and then suddenly begin to elaborate on that same man's allegedly bloodthirsty nature. They would relate in great detail, for example, how each afternoon, when taking a bath, a great war leader could not feel content unless he had had a chance to kill one of the children of his own group. Ordinarily, such behavior is associated only with witches. In a society where children were few and were the only means by which the group might survive, these murders must have been considered particularly horrific.

Another technique often depicts the feared leaders as strangers to established maroon society, as individuals who "imported" awesome powers from the wilderness or from untrustworthy groups of "backwoods people" (*Bakabusi sama*) and who never were fully accepted as equals by the pacified maroons. Of a notorious Ndyuka shaman it was said that he was sired by an extremely dangerous forest spirit. Other leaders were born and raised among the backwoods people but brought unknown and powerful new *obeahs* with them when they settled among Ndyukas or other eastern maroons. (*Obeahs*, or *obias*, are those supernatural forces that have become available to humankind. At times Ndyukas use these terms to designate objects charged with supernatural power; at other times, for invading spirits.) But even shamans or headmen who were fully accepted in the world of the pacified maroons felt it necessary to make a "grand tour"—that is, they would be away for months on trips to other maroon communities, learning the lore and practice of new types of obeahs from other inhabitants of the interior. When returning to their native villages, news would spread quickly about dangerous obeahs being imported into the world of the pacified maroons. People were given to understand that the obeahs imported by a shaman were treated and refined for use in civilized society. However, uncertainty about the extent of such domestication was an essential part of this process, giving a dangerous edge to the powers of their leaders. I will offer examples of such dubious imports in later sections.

Before examining the ambivalent views that present-day maroon historians hold concerning former maroon leaders, the main stages of maroon history should be clearly established. The beginning of all maroon history lies in the African past. Maroon historiography, however, has little to offer in this respect; few myths or other accounts refer to events that took place on the other side of the Atlantic. It remains a distant and remote past. The first developed stage of maroon historiography deals with their experiences as slaves on the plantations in Suriname's coastal plain. Maroons are never ambivalent in their condemnation of slavery. Whatever doubts maroons might voice about some of their ancestors and former leaders, Ndyuka historians, like all other maroon historians, keep alive the memory of their predicaments as slaves. They tell their children how their ancestors were dragged off in chains to the slavers' ships, about the agony of the transatlantic crossing in the holds of ships, and about the cruelty of the planters. One Ndyuka historian told me: "We can never forget what happened on the plantations; they made us dig these ditches, all day long under the burning sun without rest; this should never happen again."[3] Young people are told by elders not to forget these times and to cherish their freedom.

Ndyukas distinguish quite clearly three stages and two generations. The stages are: *katibo ten*, the time of their suffering as slaves; *lowe ten* (runaway time), the years of the great escape into the forest and the ordeals awaiting them in that hostile environment; and finally *a fii*, the time after the peace treaties. *Katibo* and *lowe ten* are stages fixed in maroon thought, anchored in a number of standard historical episodes. The period after the treaty, *a fii*, is seen as changeable in quality; for a few decades, their new freedom seemed to them extremely precarious. But then they began to grow confident about the new situation; *a fii dipi* ("peace settled"), people will say of the time when they felt assured that they were relatively safe. "Relatively," because maroons hold that only fools indulge in complete trust in the *bakaa* (outsiders or aliens), be they black or white. The enjoyment of freedom, however, was great. It is still celebrated today. Ndyukas constantly remind one another that they live in a free state. When they visit each other, before their boats come to a stop on the sandy beaches of their island fortresses, they exchange greetings. A host welcomes his visitor with the old sentry challenge: "Wadaa, wadaa . . . ooo!" (This comes from the German *Werda!* meaning "Who is there?"). The visitor responds: "Fiiman!" (free person).

The generations distinguished by maroons are: *fositen sama* (first-time people), the founders of the Ndyuka nation; and the *baka kio* (latter-day people), the founders' descendants. All that is valuable, Ndyukas assert, has been created by these "first-time people"; their descendants came to enjoy what had been won at great cost.

Taking into account this basic framework of all Ndyuka historical thinking, let us turn to our subject, the ambivalent sentiments of maroons concerning their leaders. Let us begin with the case of several war chiefs of the Aluku maroons.

Aluku Guerrilla Chieftains

The vision that maroons have of their early history is different from the one cherished by Surinamese nationalists. The triumvirate of Boni, Baron, and Jolicoeur, which figures so prominently in Paramaribo's[4] historical discourse, is absent in the accounts given by maroons. To be sure, Boni occupies an important place in maroon history. Baron, however, is mentioned only occasionally, and Jolicoeur is not mentioned at all. Interestingly, this maroon emphasis is consonant with the findings of Hoogbergen's (1990) comprehensive study of archival documents on the wars between the Alukus and the Dutch. Hoogbergen (1990: 62) found the first reference to Boni as a guerrilla leader in the year 1769. From then until 1793, the year of Boni's death, he appears continuously in reports of the colonial troops. Hoogbergen (1989: 181), however, has reason to believe that Jolicoeur spent only one or two years with the guerrillas and probably never was accepted as a leader. Baron was somewhat more important but could not hold a candle to Boni. Kwadyani, also known as Aluku, the other guerrilla chieftain of the late eighteenth century, never is referred to by Stedman and, probably for that reason, has not found his way into modern historical discourse.[5]

When discussing Boni, maroons first pay tribute to his role as a war leader. Spectacular and even superhuman feats are attributed to him.

Toward his enemies Boni acted ruthlessly and cruelly. Once, it is said, Boni traveled under water to an enemy vessel. When he emerged from the ocean, he stealthily climbed aboard the schooner and killed everybody in sight; not a single crew member was spared. Ndyuka historians told me that he skinned whites alive to get covers for his drums. Stories such as these need not surprise us; naturally they form part of the myths woven around a guerrilla fighter.[6]

Another quality of the Aluku chieftain is revealed in archival documents, where Boni is given the honorific name of "krutu" (Hoogbergen 1990: 64). The word probably used by maroons when talking to the colonial scribes is *kuutuman*, meaning counselor or judge, a testimony to Boni's reputation as a sagacious man. When Boni was still paramount chief of the Alukus, a war erupted between Alukus and Ndyukas, ending in Boni's death at the hand of the Ndyukas. Several Ndyuka historians blame the intrigues of the Dutch for the estrangement and violent conflict, and archival evidence shows them to be correct.[7]

Surprisingly, oral history repeatedly draws attention to another dimension of this famous guerrilla leader's character: Boni's alleged cruelty and at times even murderous behavior toward his own people. Some (but not all) maroon leaders are treated similarly by oral historians. The accounts presented in this section deal with four maroon leaders, all of them Alukus: Boni; his "father" (stepfather or, rather, foster father) Kwadyani (usually named "Aluku" in the literature); Balon [Baron in Dutch spelling]; and Boni's son Agosu.

Kwadyani and Boni Escape

Two very good friends, Kwadyani and Boni, were planning to "run away" [to escape from the plantations]. When they had a set a day for their escape, Boni had second thoughts. He feared domination by Kwadyani. . . . Although Boni was about the same age as Kwadyani, and although both were well-versed in the obeahs, Kwadyani had the edge on him. The latter possessed the gift of clairvoyance. Well in advance, Kwadyani knew where dangers lurked; he knew that even across great distances, . . . he also knew where the animals of prey were skulking. Kwadyani possessed a "luku obia" [an oracle]. Boni was painfully aware of Kwadyani's magical superiority. To annul this advantage, he decided to escape without giving notice to Kwadyani. [To hatch a plan for escape, and then to break one's commitment, was one of the most serious sins runaways could think of] There was only one thing on Boni's mind: to take the leadership away from Kwadyani. He knew Kwadyani would overtake him, but he

[Kwadyani] then had to recognize that he, Boni, was now in charge. . . . Boni's escape made it much harder for Aluku to "run away." When the opportunity finally presented itself, he had little difficulty in following Boni's trail. Soon he arrived in Boni's camp where he was greeted with a show of enthusiasm. Boni offered Kwadyani apologies for his sudden departure, but claimed that this was necessary because he had to prepare a base camp. Boni: "I now have everything we need for the near future: houses, fire. Let's stay here before we move on." But Kwadyani was far from enthusiastic about this proposal. Suspicion had settled in his mind, and it only increased when Boni pleaded with him to stay in his camp. Kwadyani was now determined; it was as if he could read Boni's mind. He established a camp a few hundred yards away from Boni. Kwadyani wished to stay independent from Boni. His feeling was that his descendants should never be able to blame him for becoming indebted to Boni. He did not want people to say at a later time: "Kwadyani had to accept fire from Boni to cook his food or warm his cold body." From that moment on, Kwadyani and Boni kept each other at arm's length. (Ajax, *De West*, 10 Nov. 1961; English translation by H. U. E. Thoden van Velzen)[8]

Boni Kills Kwadyani

Kwadyani "ran away." He was Boni's foster father; we don't know the name of Boni's real father because that one remained in Africa.[9] During his escape, Kwadyani went upstream until he arrived at Salua Creek [middle course of the Maroni River]. While he was at Salua, Boni's knowledge of the obeahs increased steadily. One day, when the obeahs were strong in him, he followed Kwadyani to the latter's private washing place in [what is now called] the Boni Creek. Boni crept up to him while his foster father was taking his bath. Kwadyani's obeah warned him of impending danger. He startled! Boni offered his apologies [to Kwadyani]. Well, on another occasion the same incident happened, and then once again, until three times. Gradually Kwadyani grew careless. It was on the third occasion that Boni surprised Kwadyani while the latter was taking a bath without his obeahs. Boni hit Kwadyani with a club, and then butchered him. After that Boni took over the command of those Runaways; he moved them to Bofoo Creek and then Sipawini Creek. There he lived for many years, causing a lot of trouble for everyone. It was because of his bad behavior that war came to this river. (Asawooko, Ndyuka historian, interview by H. U. E. Thoden van Velzen, at Diitabiki, Suriname, May 1981; English translation by H. U. E. Thoden van Velzen)

Boni the Tyrant

Soon Boni showed himself to be just as cruel as his former master [the European planter]. He was notorious for his cruelty. Very soon the number of his followers started to dwindle. The poor, helpless followers were slaves again, but this time it was worse than on the plantations. In Boni's group no one was certain of his life. It goes without saying that to defect to Kwadyani's camp was always on people's minds. One day, for a minor transgression, Boni mistreated one of his followers by cutting off one of his ears. Kwadyani then decided to intervene. Boni backed down, and promised never to do this again. Kwadyani placed Boni's following under his protection. Boni acquiesced and the combined group [of Boni and Kwadyani] began to prosper. But Boni hated to see Kwadyani and his followers thrive. . . . This period of calm ended when Kwadyani fell ill and died. For a second time Boni held absolute sway over the group; he was accountable to no one. At Selua Creek Boni made camp. Once a month he took a bath in a nearby creek; he used to stay under water as long as he possibly could. He did this three times. When diving for a second time he would call a boy to rub his back and then, when going down for the third time, he took him under water until the boy didn't move any more. He flung the dead body at his people to bury it. After such a murder Boni brought a sacrifice to the gods. No one dared to protest against this [the murder], and the scene was repeated month after month. When the time of Boni's bath approached, all mothers lived in fear. Nobody knew who was going to be the next victim. (Ajax, *De West*, 11 Nov. 1961; English translation by H. U. E. Thoden van Velzen)

Boni Takes Children to the Graveyard

Da Tikidai, a Ndyuka man, had married Ma Weemina, an Aluku woman. He went to live with her among the Alukus. They had two children, two boys. But one evil person lived there; he was called Damboni [fusion of *Da* (father) and *Boni*]. Boni saw these two boys. He took them to the graveyard. It was his purpose to decapitate them. One of the boys understood that Boni was about to kill them. He started crying calling his mother's name aloud: "Weemina! Weemina!" Boni was surprised: "Are you Ma Weemina's children? Then I'll save you. Ma Weemina and I have one mother and one father; I cannot kill my own sister's children! Go back to where you came from." They went home and told their mother. Weemina warned her husband. Tikidai immediately returned to his Ndyuka village. And that's how the war between Alukus and Ndyukas started.[10] (Da Afuyee, a Ndyuka of Benanu village and Dikan clan, interview by H. U. E. Thoden van Velzen, Stoelmanseiland, June 1961; English translation by H. U. E. Thoden van Velzen)

A Son Kills a Father

One of Boni's sons was called Agosu. In Agosu arose the thought to kill Boni, his father. For this purpose he took an old and worn machete. Day after day Agosu secreted himself to prepare his weapon. He needed to have a fine, sharp point to his machete to pierce through Boni's back in one thrust. On a certain day Agosu moved to Boni's washing place, and waited for him to come. When Boni had sufficiently cooled his body, he dived. When he surfaced again, he mumbled a few words. Again he dived, but now for the last time in his life. Agosu jumped at him, and pierced his body with his weapon. Boni wrestled, but he could only offer resistance for a short while. Agosu won the struggle. In the village people were waiting for Boni to tell them to bring a human sacrifice. Agosu returned to the village to tell them he had killed Boni. How could that be possible?, people asked him. His mother stepped forward and demanded an explanation. "I have killed him," Agosu replied. "Boy, keep your mouth shut," cautioned his mother; "your father shouldn't hear this!"

And all the same it was true. A few men decided to convince themselves. Boni's blood, which had discolored the water, proved that Agosu spoke the truth. They crowned Agosu as their new leader, and prepared him for his task by giving him obeahs. Later they named him "Agosu Boni" or "Boni the Second." . . . Unfortunately, Agosu soon turned out to be even more bloodthirsty than his predecessor. [Then follow stories of atrocities committed by Agosu.] (Ajax, *De West,* 11 Nov. 1961; English translation by H. U. E. Thoden van Velzen)

Balon Kills His Mother's Brother

A European was Balon's father. You could see that because he had long hair. The Europeans loved to whip him [Balon]. Adueke was born in Africa; he was the leader when his people ran away. His people referred to Adueke as "Kwadyani Klonton Amusu." Adueke didn't fight and he didn't kill people. One day, when they were trekking through the jungle, Adueke asked Balon: "Who are you?" Balon gave his mother's name. Adueke replied: "Then you are my sister's child!" From then on they traveled together. Later the two men had an argument. Adueke felt Balon was killing too many Europeans. Balon told Adueke that he wasn't responsible. It were his obeahs who made him kill all these whites. While bathing Adueke loved staying under water for long periods. When Balon saw this the idea occurred to him to kill Adueke. Balon waited until Adueke surfaced after staying under water for considerable time. Balon pierced Adueke with a lance. It took a long time for Adueke to die. Then Balon shouted: "I have killed my uncle (*tiu*). I am no longer suppressed (*Mi komoto a sitafu*)." The Ndyuka chief of that time told

Balon that he was no longer welcome on the Tapanahoni as he had
killed too many people. Otyee [famous Ndyuka ancestor of the Dikan
clan] helped Balon get rid of this evil obeah. But still you couldn't trust
him. He sneaked to Puketi [ancient capital of the Ndyukas] to do evil
things." (Da Kasiayeki, a historian of the Dyu clan, Fisiti village,
Suriname, interview by H. U. E. Thoden van Velzen, 1977; English
translation by H. U. E. Thoden van Velzen)

Village Republics

Ndyuka villages were (to a large extent they still are) tiny republics; daily
affairs were settled through lengthy palavers (*kuutu*). A strongly democratic and egalitarian atmosphere pervaded village life. In reality, however, relationships were egalitarian only within the social category of
older men. Nevertheless, the opinions of women and younger men were
seldom disregarded. Younger people sometimes might show their dissatisfaction with the skewed pattern of decision making, by following a
course of action different from that of their elders. But consensus remained greatly prized and a key ideological tenet. Cooperative and har-
monious living, and sharing among kinsmen and affines were believed
to be essential for a decent form of social life. In the past, such village
democracies offered little encouragement to the eccentric or the economically successful; small-scale agricultural entrepreneurs and medicine men with lucrative businesses were obliged to sustain the cooperative ideology of the village community in word and deed, and had better
not estrange themselves from their kinsmen by behavior that diverged
too clearly from standards of custom or propriety.

The core of this village democracy was formed by one or a few
matrilineages. These were corporate groups that shared a common fund
of possessions: titles to particular tracts of forest, fishing rights, and political offices. Other possessions were immaterial but not of lesser importance: knowledge of medicinal plants and, above all, belief in a special relationship with particular spirits. Of significance, too, were the
ritual possessions of the group. Central among these were two shrines,
both of them for the veneration of the ancestors: one resembling a flag
pole (*faaka tiki*) and the other a mortuary (*kii osu*). Revealing for the
egalitarian pattern of relationships, the rites conducted at these shrines
were a collective enterprise, demanding the presence of all the elders in
a village. Elders took turns making libations and offering their prayers.
The mortuary was not under the exclusive control of one or a few shrine

keepers. It was the collective property of the village community, or rather of the elders of a village's matrilineages.

Another binding element was the notion of a collective curse, an avenging spirit (*kunu*) that haunted a lineage. These religious beliefs tended to create a well-demarcated community, as its members were obliged to share the burden of responsibility for an avenging spirit. Although the misdeed of a single individual usually was enough to provoke the spirit avenger, all lineage members were to suffer equally from the consequences. The required feast of atonement for the avenger was a collective responsibility; it was believed that only joint worship would placate the spirit. Ideas such as these greatly enhanced the corporate character of the lineage.

The Growth of Inequality and the New Maroons

Quite early, perhaps already during the formative state of maroon societies, forces were at work undermining these egalitarian relationships. The most important of these processes was the growth within this matrilineal society of groups (*foloku*, or following) centered around powerful individuals. A development of this kind usually started when some elders proved successful in attracting persons other than their close matrilineal kin. They might, for instance, succeed in persuading their sons to take up residence with them, or matrilineal kin who normally would have been considered too remote to reside near the elder concerned. Those elders who enjoyed prestige as medicine men commanding powerful obeahs were particularly suited to become Big Men, persons who were in a position to attract and consolidate their followings. People accused or suspected of witchcraft in other villages or regions often would apply for membership in such a following. These alleged witches had in common that they were totally dependent on their protectors and hence were considered more reliable than some of the Big Man's own close kin. These dependents represented sources of cheap labor as well.

A novel opportunity for mobilizing followers emerged when waves of new runaways (*lowe sama*) started to compound the situation in the interior. During the peace negotiations of the 1760s, a major concern for the authorities in Paramaribo was the possibility that the villages of the "pacified bush Negroes" would become havens for a new generation of fugitive slaves. Two key articles in the peace treaties of the 1760s reveal these apprehensions and show the direction of the colonial authorities' thinking. Articles 4 and 5 of the peace treaty between the Dutch and the Ndyukas run as follows.

> If any slave should defect to them after Amnesty and the Treaty and the signing thereof, they, the Maroons, shall be bound to return the same and surrender them to the whites without exception, for which they shall receive a due reward in money and kind. . . .
>
> They, the pacified Bush Negroes and their successors, shall do everything in their power to capture any slaves running away after the conclusion of this treaty, as well as any hostile Indians, and shall surrender the same [and], if necessary, kill them. Furthermore, they shall be bound to try and track down and capture any runaway slaves immediately. (Translation in de Groot 1977: 11–12)

The Dutch colonial government had good reason for its concern. Each year slaves fled the plantations, hoping to find a life free from yoke and whip. Some of these turned to the "pacified bush Negroes" for shelter. It is hard to generalize about the reception that these runaways received. A few were handed over almost immediately to military posts or to *posthouders*, i.e., representatives of the colonial government resident in maroon territory. A considerable number of runaways, however, did find asylum with Ndyukas or Saramakas. Although their presence in Ndyuka villages was well concealed, the *posthouders*, assisted by a few spies, would get wind of at least some of these refugees.

> In 1808, when a *posthouder* protested with Ma Akuba, a Ndyuka woman of the village of Mainsi, against the presence of four Runaways in her village, she replied that she did not feel like handing them over to the Europeans as long as the Paramount Chief hid many more in his village. In his report the *posthouder* confirmed this by adding that he knew about at least eight Runaways in the Chief's residence. From another *posthouder's* report of 1809 it is apparent that practically all villages harbored a few refugees; in one village fifteen Runaways were reputed to have found shelter.[11]

Usually, the information available to a *posthouder* was less precise. Besides, this official had only one assistant and no means of enforcement at his immediate disposal. Therefore, it turned out to be next to impossible to compel Ndyuka chiefs to deliver runaways to the government. Dependent as he was on Ndyuka boatmen for his travels, there was little the *posthouder* could do but bring his complaints to the chief. At such

times, the *posthouder* usually left the Ndyuka paramount chief's residence with every assurance that the matter would be looked into carefully and that if, by any chance, the chief's investigations should reveal
the presence of runaways, the fugitives would be handed over instantly.
More often than not, little resulted from such maneuvers. When the
posthouder obtained reliable information and the government was resolved to put pressure on the chief, Ndyuka leaders sometimes would
send runaways to farm in Poligudu, the village of the "Black Rangers,"
those rebel soldiers. At Poligudu, the runaways performed odd jobs for
their benefactors.[12] Undoubtedly, many fugitive slaves found refuge
with Ndyukas in the period before Emancipation (1863). In 1829, several Ndyuka headmen, including the paramount chief, were employing
runaways. Those new maroons who were later known as the Paramakas
are mentioned specifically as a group whose members worked for
Ndyuka chiefs.[13] Ndyuka headmen, who had settled in the coastal region, also succeeded in sheltering and exploiting new maroons.[14]

The refugees were gradually incorporated into existing Ndyuka kin
groups, thus concealing their humble—in the eyes of Ndyukas—origins. The sheltering of refugees was a cause of constant friction between
the Dutch and Ndyukas, and occasionally would result in tense political situations. These difficulties transpire in the articles of the renewed
Peace Treaty of 1837. The instructions for the *posthouder* reveal the
anxiety of the authorities regarding the problem of the runaways: "The
postholder is emphatically urged to investigate with the greatest possible secrecy and discretion who are the chiefs of the villages guilty of
harboring runaway slaves or in league with runaways" (translation in de
Groot 1977: 18). The "runaway question" did more than strain relationships between Tapanahoni Ndyukas and Paramaribo; it had repercus-
sions for internal relations within Ndyuka society as well. Some influential Ndyuka elders were particularly successful in sheltering refugees:
doing so boosted their status and provided them with dependents more
compliant than other followers. Some of these elders exploited the runaways as cheap and readily available labor, all the more important as so
many young Ndyuka males had left for the coast to work as lumbermen.
They would clear a Big Man's gardens, make dugout canoes for him, or
work as his trusted assistants when consulting oracles or at other moments when the need for discretion was considerable. Most village
chiefs and the paramount chief had recourse to this source of labor. But
over and beyond this, reliable followers were worth a great deal in a
matrilineal society where an elder knew that his claims on the allegiance
of younger kinsmen were always contested: fathers would endeavor to

keep their sons with them, or a mother's brother would put pressure on his sister's son to show where his loyalties lay by taking up residence with his own matrilineage. With refugees, one had secured a group of people who had nowhere else to go.

A Big Man's following could usurp many ritual functions that ordinarily were the prerogative of the matrilineage. Ancestor worship, for example, rather than being the duty and privilege of the collectivity of elders of a matrilineage, would become of central concern to a Big Man and his assistants. The responsibility for avenging spirits, however, remained the exclusive concern of the lineage. A following was a residential group; it became most visible on the northern frontier, near the plantations and the capital city. This area was a land of new opportunities for maroons. There a Big Man could leave his imprint by forming a following without too much interference on the part of lineage elders.

During the last decades of the eighteenth century, and for the better part of the nineteenth century, Big Men usually were medicine men serving as intermediaries for *Kumanti* spirits, the gods of war and medicine. According to legendary tales, *Kumanti* medicine men had formed the backbone of armed resistance against the planters and their mercenaries in the war of independence that ended in 1760. Ndyukas attributed the downfall of war leader Boni (1793) to the powerful and fearless assault of their medicine men. These *Kumanti* specialists had supplied warriors with obeahs granting them invulnerability to bullets and machetes. Their reputations, forged in war, also depended on entrepreneurial qualities demonstrated in times of peace. *Kumanti* medicine men seldom contented themselves with the inspiration received from seizure by a possessing spirit; they also would seek sacred knowledge elsewhere. The best repository of *Kumanti* knowledge—war obeahs, medicinal knowledge, sacred texts—was believed to be in the lands of the Aluku maroons, where superior *Kumanti* obeahs could be bought from renowned medicine men. A Ndyuka medicine man with high aspirations therefore would have to make a pilgrimage and business trip to the Alukus. The transfer of sacred knowledge took months and required a considerable outlay of money and goods. After such a trip, a *Kumanti* medicine man's reputation was established beyond doubt. His return from "Aluku"—the land of the Alukus—would mark the beginning of a career as an independent *Kumanti* priest (*basi*), who himself could start training acolytes.

Kumanti medicine men, backed by a loyal following, formed the only fairly secure islands of power in a sea of egalitarian relationships. Some would earn the reputation of tyrants. If their group was tightly organized, and if their following proved loyal, such Big Men could get away with braggadocio, intimidation, and even despotism.

Life on the Northern Frontier

Elsewhere the presence of the runaways was felt in a quite different way. The no-man's-land between plantations and the maroon villages of the interior had shrunk, as a result of two forces eroding it: maroons coming from the south and establishing anything from temporary shelters to permanent villages in the coastal area, and the waves of runaways who settled in these regions after the peace treaties. This second group built fortified villages and hidden storage dumps in places as far apart as the Tempati Creek, the swamps between the Cottica River and the ocean, and the Surnau Creek. Some of these hidden settlements were quite close to the capital, Paramaribo; difficult to reach and well concealed in mangrove swamps, some were less than twenty miles from the city. Almost yearly, military expeditions attempted to track down runaways. The upstream part of the Surnau Creek became the scene of a vicious little war between the Dutch and the runaways; the violence dragged on for decades. The last military engagement in that area took place in 1862, only months before the abolition of slavery (Hoogbergen 1978: 31–34, 1983: 105–6).

The Ndyukas' attitudes toward the runaways varied. Much depended on the manner in which the first contacts were established; on incidents that had then occurred; and, of course, on the personalities of the people involved. Cases are known in which runaways owed their survival as a group to Ndyukas who had incited them to revolt when they were still slaves and assisted them after they had escaped.[15] In other instances, Ndyukas cultivated social contacts with runaways, traded with them, or hired them for clearing fields or felling trees. Those slaves who managed to reach the Tapanahoni River and had to beg Ndyuka elders for shelter were put to work by their patrons, doing all sorts of odd jobs with little or no recompense.

Often, however, Ndyukas feared the hideouts of runaways as threatening nests of vipers full of dangerous obeahs. The term *backwoods people* (*bakabusi sama*), used as a general name for these last waves of maroons, assumed an ominous cast: these were people living too close to dangerous forest spirits (*ampuku*) to feel comfortable with. The settlements of these runaways were raided by Ndyukas. In some instances they also informed the colonial government of the location of these "backwoods people's" villages. On the Cottica River and the Sara and Surnau creeks, Ndyukas repeatedly participated in military expeditions against runaways or took the initiative by asking the colonial authorities to commission their patrols against these people.[16] Motives seem to have been mixed: the appeal of handsome rewards promised by the planters for successful expeditions must have played a powerful role. But at other times, runaways were fought because they posed a threat to a Ndyuka settlement or to the security of Ndyukas moving along one of the rivers, one of the few lines of communication with the outside world.

Two Highway Robbers

The small band led by the runaways Amawi and Nelo is a case in point. First, the band terrorized the Paramakas, a group of runaways whom the Ndyukas considered friendly neighbors. Stories about the tyrannical rule of the twosome reached the Tapanahoni, engendering dismay. But when Amawi and Nelo's band began to ambush Ndyukas in the Wane Creek, a vital water link connecting Maroni with the Cottica River, crucial Ndyuka interests were felt to be at stake. In reprisal, an expedition against them was mounted. It clashed with Amawi and Nelo's followers in the central part of the Maroni, finally breaking the back of the group by killing its two leaders. Of this episode two accounts exist, one collected among Ndyukas, the other among Paramakas.

Ndyuka Account

Endiikii (Hendrik) Amawi was evil! He did all sort sorts of bad things among the Paramakas. He also killed Ndyuka people near Anpoma [central section of the Maroni]. If you were not courageous, and if you didn't have strong obeahs, this was no place for you to go. This man (Amawi), with his assistant Nelo, would soon get the better of you, and kill you. The only way to escape death was to give them everything you had bought in Paramaribo. When these two men began to occupy part of Ndyuka territory, our ancestors called a great meeting. They selected a group of good warriors to remove these evil persons. Anike from Poligudu was appointed their leader. They fought with Amawi and Nelo at Anpoma. Anike was wounded, but the two ruffians were killed. Then we could do our shopping in Paramaribo in peace, and we had liberated the Paramakas.[17] (Da Kasiayeki, interview by H. U. E. Thoden van Velzen, Fisiti Village, 18 May 1981; English translation by H. U. E. Thoden van Velzen)

Paramaka Version

Endiikii Amawi, a Paramaka, courted a married woman, and thus provoked the traditional retaliation by the husband and his kinsmen, who have the right to beat the seducer, as long as they do so with their bare hands. But Amawi did not play by traditional rules: he fought back, and defended himself with a club against their fists. He would certainly have been found guilty and punished by the council of elders, but Amawi did not wait for their judgment. He made his way through the jungle until he reached the Ndyuka village of Poligudu. He married a Ndyuka woman, and settled in Poligudu. But then the Ndyuka Paramount Chief got wind of this. The Chief decided to turn him over to the Europeans for money. One night, on the way to the coast, Amawi managed to untie his ropes, and escape into the forest. He returned to the Paramaka settlement. Shortly after his return a Ndyuka delegation arrived there to request Amawi's deliverance. The Paramaka chief, Da Dofen, promised the Ndyukas to hand over the man. Amawi overheard this conversation, went into hiding until the Ndyuka delegation had left, and then murdered Dofen in his makeshift garden hut. Amawi cut off his victim's genitals and placed these into Dofen's mouth. By ambushing and killing a Ndyuka, Amawi obtained a gun, and machetes. With these arms he returned to the Paramakas who, in the first part of the nineteenth century, had no weapons to speak of. From this position of power, Amawi could order them to accept his friend Nelo as their Paramount Chief. When the Ndyukas heard about the events among the Paramakas, they decided to intervene. An expedition was mounted, and two men from Poligudu killed Amawi. (Condensed version of Lenoir's account of the life of Hendrik Amawi: Lenoir 1973: 68–72)

A Man Burnt at the Stake

The history of the two tyrants was situated in a frontier zone, a dangerous land between the "plantation colony" and the territory of Ndyukas. Let us now investigate the fate of extraordinary individuals within Ndyuka society itself. Such a person, unless protected by devoted followers, was in a vulnerable position. Tales from the preceding centuries abound with entrepreneurs and shamans who fell victim to the leveling pressures of matrilineages. Some were burned at the stake, while others simply gave up and turned their attention to more modest occupations. The following sections illustrate acts of arrogance and intimidation by Ndyukas who felt sufficiently protected by their followings and their own resources. However, first let us look at the fate of those who, after many years of prominence and lucrative occupations, were thwarted by their kin.

During the 1830s, Atokwa, a Ndyuka man, had left his Tapanahoni village and settled in the coastal plain, in the Cottica region, to grow food for the market in the capital and for the plantations. He was fairly successful. Soon, when demand began to outstrip production, Atokwa had to hire laborers to help him tend his banana plantation. The people he hired were Caribs, Amerindians, and that practice likely irritated his fellow Ndyukas. But what certainly irked them was the financial success of his enterprise. He was making a good deal more money than the lumbermen around him. Attempts by others to follow him in growing food for the urban market ended in failure. Rumors began to circulate that Atokwa's accomplishments owed much to his witchcraft. Things came to a head when some Ndyukas claimed that they had taken a few overripe bananas from Atokwa's garden, but that "evil things" installed by Atokwa made them fall ill. Neighboring Ndyukas of several matrilineages reached agreement that Atokwa should have to undergo the tribal poison ordeal, so that the accusations of witchcraft could be looked into properly. This consortium first obtained the cooperation of Atokwa's Carib workers. The Caribs informed Atokwa of the impending danger and offered to smuggle him out of the area, beyond the reach of the Ndyuka investigators. Atokwa entrusted himself to his workers, who hid him under banana leaves in their boat. According to prearranged plan, the boat was stopped on the river by Atokwa's Ndyuka enemies; they tied him and then brought him back to the interior, to the village of Puketi, the ancient Ndyuka capital where the Ndyuka poison ordeal of *Sweli Gadu*[18] was situated. Shortly after drinking the potion, Atokwa fell ill; this was considered definitive proof that he was a witch. Subsequently, Atokwa was burned at the stake. This happened in 1845. In 1848, another Ndyuka man, named Aboma Gadu, was saved in the nick of time by colonial government officials. Others were less fortunate. Until the beginning of Da Aban's paramount chieftaincy (1867), more than a dozen entrepreneurs and village headmen were executed.

Atokwa was posthumously rehabilitated. This was achieved when Atokwa's ghost visited the living to tell his descendants that they had burned him, while he had never harmed them. "Where are my bones?" the ghost would ask through the mouth of a medium. Today Ndyukas explain that the fire had been so intense that Atokwa's bones had been destroyed. Even today, Atokwa's ghost haunts three Ndyuka matrilineages.

The Tale of the Arrogant Shaman

What could happen to an arrogant and eccentric shaman is demonstrated by the life of Dikii Pambu. Dikii was born around 1800. He was well versed in the lore and practice of all spirit medium cults familiar to Ndyukas. But he was known and feared above all as a shaman who claimed to enjoy a special relationship with forest spirits (*ampuku*). Such deities have an ambivalent relationship with human beings. On occasion they may help people, but one should never be caught off guard. Other factors made Dikii's position precarious, however. First, Dikii seemed unable to remain long in one place; he wandered through the no-man's-land between plantation colony and maroon territory. What was he doing there, in that dangerous forest where malevolent spirits and treacherous runaways lived? What Dikii was doing there becomes plain when one learns from Dutch colonial archives that Dikii was instrumental in organizing raids against camps of runaways.[19] These manhunts took place in the 1830s and 1840s; he was a bounty hunter who worked for the planters. Nowadays most Ndyukas have little good to say about such runaways, and they probably felt similarly a century ago, when danger lurked everywhere between the colony and maroon territory. On the other hand, Dikii's hunting down refugees for the hated former masters and thereby amassing considerable wealth likely engendered mixed feelings in Ndyukas, themselves the erstwhile victims of the whites.

It was when Dikii started to make a nuisance of himself that public opinion turned against him. Several unpleasant characteristics combined to make him highly unpopular. First, his lust for women began to exceed the attraction he aroused in them. When he realized his waning popularity, he started threatening females: if they were not compliant, he would unleash his forest spirits to punish them. Increasingly he played the tyrant. He demanded that some married men hand over their wives. Any resistance meant quick retaliation: usually death would strike down the noncompliant husband. Women who withheld their favors were given somewhat more time. But if they continued to refuse him, death would also be their fate. "All of this undermined his position," I was told by a medium of Dikii's ghost whom I came to know quite well. This medium added: "He made himself unbearable. He started to act as a tyrant over all Twelve Clans [a term for the Ndyuka nation]".

This was perhaps the most galling of Dikii's peculiarities. But other personality traits also irked his neighbors. When someone excelled in some capacity or other, Dikii would do his utmost to prove that he

could do better. It did not matter what the arena was; whether in dancing or in the *agi* game (a board game derived from Africa), he would
have to outshine all rivals. He would trick people into competing with
him, usually by giving them a head start. He could, for example, let an
adversary win twice but then, the third time, he would beat him and
shout: "I have killed you! And what is dead remains dead! [*Kii tan kii*]."
His rival would be dead within three days. When people were dancing
susa (a traditional funerary dance requiring virtuoso footwork), Dikii was
wont to look around for competitors. He baited these by letting them out-
perform him for awhile. Then he would strike back. Usually he won. Dikii
would then shout the traditional "I have killed you! [*Bada, bada, hee!*]." If
Dikii lost, his rival was in even more direct danger. Dikii would tell him:
"The trap flattens the rat, but the rat will flatten the earth!" And Ndyuka
historians add: "Within three days his rival would be gone."

Gradually Dikii's position in Ndyuka society became untenable.
When his relatives delivered him to the poison ordeal at Puketi village,
perhaps with his elder brother as first witness for the prosecution,[20] it
was not the end of his life. No visible malady or other tell-tale signs
manifested themselves. But it meant the end of his career. The humili-
ation, and suspicions that could not be allayed, eventually made things
so miserable for Dikii that he lost all zest for life. Today's legends say
that, before he died, he roamed through the forest, dejected. Nonetheless, for a few decades, Dikii tyrannized Ndyukas with impunity. There
may not have been many like him, but the fact that such people could
cow their fellow Ndyukas into subjection is pertinent to my argument.

Medicine Man and Despot

A few decades later, another medicine man by the name of Menisaki
achieved great fame, both for his knowledge of the obeahs and for his historical learning. During the 1880s, Menisaki had acted as a kingmaker,
pushing the candidacy of Oseyse (1888–1915) for the paramount chieftaincy and obstructing that of Da Labi Agumasaka ("Saka" for short), the
head of the most prominent of Ndyuka cults. Menisaki, who was from
the village of Benanu and was a member of the respected Dikan clan,
used the Poligudu people as his servants. He demanded tribute in the
form of part of the produce of their gardens (swidden plots) and ordered
them to perform odd chores for him, to build a house or make a canoe.
Resistance was dealt with brutally. The Poligudu people were in a vulnerable position. They were the descendants of mutinous soldiers who

had fled to the Tapanahoni in 1805, after having killed their officers. For many years this desertion caused friction between the Ndyukas and the Dutch. The Dutch demanded that the rebels be sent back. The Ndyukas did not refuse outright but rather stalled and sabotaged until, ten or fifteen years later, the Dutch lost interest. The Poligudu people's relationship with the Ndyuka chiefs was not as favorable as such support against the colonial regime may suggest. The Poligudu village is only a few hundred meters away from the confluence of Lawa and Tapanahoni rivers; officially the Poligudu runaways had been given the task of standing guard over the entrance of the Tapanahoni. But the Poligudus had to perform various services for the "established" Ndyukas. What Menisaki did with the Poligudu people therefore differed only in degree from what others did.

> Menisaki, that was a man in a quite different league from the medicine men of today. He was born in the village of Benanu. From Poligudu to Godo Olo—at that time the first and the last of Ndyuka villages on the Tapanahoni—no one could stand up to him. He knew everything; when making a libation he would pray to all of our ancestors, naming them; from the beginning of our society to the present-day. No decision could be taken without him. [*Then my interlocutor wanders off to an account of how Menisaki terrorized the village of Poligudu.*] (Da Babe, interview by H. U. E. Thoden van Velzen, Diitabiki Village, 19 Oct. 1970)

Menisaki inspired great fear among the people of Poligudu. Particularly his assistants plagued their village. If the Poligudu people were disobedient or aroused Menisaki's displeasure in any other way, the assistants would go into their gardens and destroy their crops. Menisaki acted in a rough and even brutal way. The Poligudu people had nowhere to run to. Finally, people from another village apprised the paramount chief of what was going on. Paramount Chief Oseyse ordered Menisaki to stop pestering these people: "They are my sentries," he said, "and you should let them live in peace." A few days later Menisaki died (ca. 1900) (Da Babe, interview by H. U. E. Thoden van Velzen, Diitabiki Village, 19 Oct. 1970).

The Trojan Horse

Saka was another man unusual in the Ndyuka context. To my knowledge, no one ever compared him with the tyrannical and somewhat childish Dikii. But he ruled the Ndyukas with a firm hand. Some even claim that he hanged people who violated his rules. All Ndyuka historians stated that he could be tough, not given to leniency. Between around 1860 and 1914, the year of his death, Saka undoubtedly was the most powerful man in Ndyuka society. What claim did he have to such prominence?

The most surprising thing is that Saka was not born to a prestigious lineage; in fact, no Ndyuka that I spoke to ever managed to trace Saka's lineage. It proved impossible to link Saka, one of the greatest names in Ndyuka history, to any of the existing lineages in that society. Later I learned that Saka's mother could have been a member of a small group of runaways or "backwoods people" (*bakabusi sama*) who had settled in the Cottica region and later, after many years of hostilities with Ndyukas, mingled with their erstwhile foes. These were the so-called "Kaabu Olo Maroons" (Hoogbergen 1993). In 1834, the year when Ndyukas from the Cottica region organized a raid against their camp, there were about forty of them, hiding in the forest between the Cottica and Marowijne rivers and the ocean.[21] I surmise that Ndyukas from the Cottica offered shelter to Saka's mother. Saka was born about 1825, and probably a Ndyuka family adopted him when still an adolescent. Saka's father is reputed to have been a Creole from Paramaribo; and Saka's grandfather a Jew, "a man from Israel," as people explained to me. I present these details surrounding Saka's extraction in some detail, as they reveal the openness of Ndyuka society to newcomers—at least to some of them.

Saka settled in the Tapanahoni region around 1860 (de Goeje 1908: 66). He was invited to come to the Tapanahoni by the foremost Ndyuka priestess of the nineteenth century, Ma Dyemba. Saka behaved in every respect like an adopted son. He had been working in the Cottica as a lumberman before, and he continued to return to the area for stints of lumber work. With the proceeds, he took care of all Ma Dyemba's material needs; my sources volunteer long lists of goods (salt, kerosene, clothes, sugar) bought by Saka for the priestess. In return, Dyemba initiated him into the secrets of the obeahs. Saka was groomed for succession as the first custodian of the tribal *Sweli*[22] cult. The teaching deliberately went slowly; bit by precious bit, the information was passed on to Saka. Dyemba's obvious and, for Ndyukas a legitimate, purpose was to let Saka pay for the information. It is feared that, once such a pupil decides that he has learned all there is to learn, gifts and contributions to the teacher's household budget will be discontinued. But Saka's record on this score is impeccable and today is still recalled in great detail. As time wore on, however, this apprentice—as eager as he was to learn and to ingratiate himself—would confront Ma Dyemba with problems of a far more serious nature.

It is pertinent to discuss the reason why Ma Dyemba picked Saka, instead of someone from her own lineage, as her most trusted protégé. Historians mention several reasons. At the time of his arrival on the Tapanahoni, sources explain, Saka already had achieved a reputation as a formidable medicine man. This was unusual but not impossible for a thirty-five-year-old man in Ndyuka society. He had impressed Ma Dyemba with his courage; his shrewdness and his command of obeahs were common knowledge.

Dyemba certainly would have weighed these qualities when she chose him as her successor. Another consideration, not mentioned by the historians I consulted, may have been Saka's insecure status. Dyemba may have thought that Saka, given his humble origins as a "backwoods man" and his position as a stranger to the society of Tapanahoni Ndyukas, would be more pliable and accommodating than any of her own relatives. To rely on a kinsman for succession to the office of *Sweli* priest would be tantamount to inviting him to oust his teacher after the training period had passed. To Dyemba, Saka had the great advantage of being a "nobody"; he could not base his aspirations on any legitimate claim to succession.

Saka, however, embarked on a career of expansion; he began to build a following and enhance his reputation as a medicine man through additional learning. He enticed a number of his relatives, who still resided in the Cottica region, to settle with him at the Ndyuka capital of Diitabiki. When the headman of a nearby village died, part of that following joined Saka's new group. Within a decade Saka had secured the stable core for his own following. To enhance his knowledge of the obeahs, Saka made three trips to the Saramaka maroons on the Suriname River. This was the classic "grand tour" of a Ndyuka medicine man, now directed to the west rather than to the east where enterprising Ndyuka medicine man had gone in the past to buy *Kumanti* obeahs from Aluku maroons. Such trips were costly and took many months to complete. Weeks before his return to the Tapanahoni, a spate of rumors would hint at spectacular advances in Saka's understanding of new and more powerful obeahs. After these Saramaka trips, Saka's position in Ndyuka society was secure. He had a following of his own; in fact, he was the headman of the most populous quarter of Diitabiki. There was no one in the whole of Ndyuka who could stand up to Saka and challenge him; he was the leading medicine man in the area, as well as the main beneficiary of the teachings of priestess Dyemba. Paramount Chief Aban (1868–82) came to rely heavily on Saka's support.

At the end of the 1870s, the triumvirate of Dyemba, Aban, and Saka began to fall apart. Friction developed between Dyemba and the two men about their handling of the obeahs. The precise reason for this dispute is unknown. But at least two issues divided Aban and Saka from the old guard represented by Dyemba. First, Saka enlisted Aban's support for the merger of several older rites and obeahs into a new cult. Second, Aban and Saka "went public." Whereas formerly the custodians of Ndyuka cults would repair to the seclusion of a shrine, at Saka's insistence divination was now performed in the middle of the village. Dyemba's opposition to these innovations was silenced with: "Women have no say in these matters!" Dyemba cursed the new holders of power: "Now that you have come to tell me women have no say in these matters, I will wash my hands of you and your innovations!"

When Chief Aban died in 1882, there was no one in the whole of Ndyuka society who could stand up to Saka. He was the supreme custodian of the tribal cults, now merged under his direction. After a few years of bickering, Saka managed to force the new Chief Oseyse (1888–1915) to accept his supervision. In the early 1890s, Saka had more trouble with a witch-cleansing movement that had the support of affluent river transporters. It took him several months to bring the witch-finders to heel and incorporate this movement in the tribal cult of which he was high priest. At this period his authority was no longer contested. In an egalitarian society, a conglomerate of tiny village democracies, Saka was the law of the land. After Saka's death (1914), many Ndyukas were nostalgic for the period of his rule. He had been "bad," he had been tough, he had ruled Ndyuka with the whip and the hangman's cord, but, thanks to him, people had behaved decently:

Saka was an extremely strict elder. [Informant reiterates this several times. Asks me to write it down.] Take the case of the village headman Pankuku. This headman was courting his own "sister" [a classificatory sister; probably someone from his own lineage. This is considered incest in Ndyuka culture.] He was brought to the center of Puketi village, Ndyuka's ancient capital. They whipped him; they cut him with a razor, but Pankuku didn't bleed. His skin was too thick. Well you know, the man was an accomplished medicine man after all. Now Chief Oseyse and our father Saka were the only ones who hadn't tried it yet. Oseyse took the razor, but he couldn't cut through Pankuku's skin. This upset Father Saka; he shouted at Oseyse: "You thin shit boy!" He grasped the razor, kicked Pankuku's legs, and spit him in the face. Then, in one slash, he cut through the skin of Pankuku's thigh and opened an artery. He was beyond himself and had to be restrained by bystanders. Saka shouted: "Next time I will chop off his head!" (Da Papa,[23] Saka's grandchild, interview by H. U. E. Thoden van Velzen, in Albina, Suriname, Apr. 1978; English translation by H. U. E. Thoden van Velzen)

Despots as Condensation Figures

Why do maroon historians so often paint their most prominent ancestors in such an unfavorable light? One might guess that these bleak portraits were painted by the opposition, by rival maroon groups, and not by the descendants themselves. But most Aluku maroon leaders were depicted by *both* Ndyuka and Aluku historians as "cruel" or "murderous." The same is true of Endiiki Amawi and Nelo, the Paramaka "highway robbers," described negatively, as we have seen, by both Paramaka and Ndyuka historians. The Paramaka account is much more elaborate and concrete but no less critical than the Ndyuka one.

To this should be added the accounts of prominent Ndyuka leaders and entrepreneurs given by *Ndyuka* historians: for example, the portraits of Atokwa, the witch burned at the stake; of Dikii, the eccentric shaman; of Menisaki, the man who had no equals; and, finally, of the founder of the modern Ndyuka religious cult of the Great Father, Da Saka. All these portraits are two-sided. Atokwa was a witch who jealously guarded his overripe bananas and would not shrink from killing trespassers in his fields. Only after his death was he vindicated on the score of witchcraft. But the fact that he was a wealthy man who stingily clung to his property never changed. Dikii was perhaps the greatest shaman enshrined in Ndyuka oral history, but—and now I quote his latter-day prophet, Akalali, a man I came to know quite well—"he made himself impossible; he put all Twelve Clans in a difficult position." Of Menisaki, another source, almost in one breath, said: "Menisaki had no equals, his knowledge of our ancestors was immense; his obeahs were astounding," but he treated the descendants of the mutinous Black Rangers very badly, brutally. Perhaps the picture given of Saka is the most favorable one, but still some of the personality characteristics mentioned hardly seem flattering. It was said of him that he was irascible to the point of losing control of himself. This contrasts sharply with the model always held up as befitting a respectable Ndyuka elder; such a person should be capable of a high degree of self-control.

Only one historical figure seems to have escaped this general tendency to regard leaders ambivalently: Aluku, or Adueke, also called Kwadyani Klonton Amusu. But Kwadyani was what in North American Indian ethnography is referred to as a "peace chief," and Boni would

fit the role of a "war chief." In 1776, for example, Boni attacked a plantation, while Aluku reportedly brought the women and children to a place of
refuge (Hoogbergen 1989: 183). If this was the general pattern, then it
might explain the fact that Kwadyani was exempt from condemnation.

Hoogbergen (1989: 187), discussing Kwami, a maroon leader who
terrorized his own group by accusing many of them of witchcraft and
executed no less than twenty-eight of his fellow villagers, suggests that
such despots would merge in the historical imagination with leaders
whose records looked much better to their contemporaries. Kwami, as
Hoogbergen points out, was only one of a number of early maroon leaders, many of whom seem to have disappeared from the oral history records.
Some of them joined forces with Boni's group and others clashed with him,
but most were close to Boni's band of guerrillas. A condensation process, whereby images of all these various leaders fused, could be responsible for the end-product, the dark portrait expressing strong ambivalent feelings. It is an attractive explanation, but it cannot explain why
nineteenth-century leaders such as Endiiki Amawi and Nelo would be
represented in a similar way. These surely were not "condensation figures."
Prominent Ndyuka maroons of that same century—for example, Dikii,
Atokwa, Menisaki, and Saka—did not give rise to the horror stories
that were associated with Amawi and Boni, yet they too were often
painted in an unfavorable light.

All Power Is Suspect

The past is a foreign country. They do things differently there.
—L. P. Hartley, Prologue, The Go-Between

One can think of at least three processes that might be responsible for
these "dark portraits." First, one may conjecture that the blend of veneration and abhorrence reflects both the excitement and the apprehen-
sion of people who lived in these small-scale communities—people who
had nowhere else to go. Leader-follower relations always engender fantasies, but being firmly shackled to these chieftains might have presented an ideal breeding ground for ambivalent sentiments. If the leaders were "dangerous" (*ogii*), it seemed to signify that their headmen were
in touch with powerful if evil forces; only then were they felt to have
the extra assets needed to steer them through difficult terrain. At the
same time, the followers continued to live in suspense, for these same
persons possessed capacities beyond the control of ordinary mortals.

But these are conjectures about communities that existed two centuries ago and therefore more hazardous than speculations grounded in recent fieldwork in modern maroon communities. On the basis of fieldwork experience,[24] I suspect that the web of egalitarian relationships characteristic of maroon communities restricts the "social leeway" enjoyed by maroon elders. Probably well before 1800, tiny village republics had evolved, dominated by the elder males through the mechanism of the *palaver*. A paramount chief could ask elders in another village to comply with him—he could plead his case—but he lacked the means of coercion (cf. Hostmann 1850 and Kappler 1881). The situation is little different in recent decades. One can wield power only if a large majority of the elders assent. Unusual individuals—eccentrics or successful and arrogant persons who have aroused the community's envy and distrust—are prime targets for today's "leveling coalitions," just as they were in the past.

Maroon historians are working under an "egalitarian regime." While depicting the singularity and forcefulness of some of their ancestors, they also must listen to the voices of distrust rampant in their own communities. Contradictory evaluations cause both the zigzag of public judgment and, in the long run, its lack of resolution. Dikii, the shaman, we may recall, was first a superman and a hero loudly applauded, and only later a martyr and a wishy-washy man. Such contradictions are resolved when we understand both negative and positive affects as coming from the same knot of ambivalence. To bring forward notions about the past that are not felt to be "politically correct" could be a risky operation. Can one honestly expect Ndyuka maroons, who know that the way to full acceptance as an elder is "to humble oneself" (Köbben 1979; Thoden van Velzen 1984), to bring forward historical information that glorifies strong leadership and eschews comments concerning the perils of such personal regimes? History is dangerous; it uses the past to deliver a commentary on the present.

One should view these historians as being limited by their egalitarian environment, but also allow for the possibility that they are constantly making diagnoses about fateful events in the past that could recur in the present. Saramaka historians confided to Richard Price (1983: 11–12) their fear that the horrors of the past could return in full force: "This is the one thing Maroons really believe. It's stronger than anything else. . . . This is the greatest fear of all Maroons: that those times [slavery and the struggle for freedom] shall come again." In 1987, only a few years after Price took down this statement, the Surinamese army brutally killed a number of Saramaka civilians who did not even take part in the civil war.[25] Ndyukas, when commenting on the killings of about forty Ndyuka civilians at Moi Wana in 1986, said exactly the same: "*Katibo* [slavery and persecution] times have returned." On a somewhat different level, the same holds true for the arrogance of power within their own societies. Some of their ancestors had abused their position; was it likely that such a thing could never happen again? Those who tasted power might wish to acquire more of it; one should never let down one's guard. For maroons, the past is *not* a foreign country.

Notes

Abbreviations

ARA	Algemeen Rijksarchief (General State Archives), The Hague, Netherlands
CIB	Commissariaat voor de Inlandse bevolking van Suriname (1828–45), in ARA
GJ	Gouvernements Journaal, in KOL (below)
HVP	Hof van Politie en Criminele Justitie (Court of Policy and Criminal Justice), in ARA
KOL	Archief van het Ministerie van Kolonien, 1813–49
NWI	Archief van het Nederlandsch West-Indisch Bezit, in ARA

1. *Boekoe* is written as *Boucou* in Stedman (1988 [1790]). In 1986, ironically, it was from the Membre Boekoe barracks that the special army unit was directed that spread terror through Ndyuka settlements in Suriname's coastal plain, killing women and children. The campaign led thousands of maroons to flee to neighboring French Guiana and reminded them how justified the warnings of their elders had been "never to forget these times [of slavery and the liberation fight], as these may return." The quotation is from Richard Price's *First-Time* (1983).

2. "My ancestor X" is the standard way of referring to prominent ancestors, whether these are from one's own group or from other clans or lineages.

3. Da Kofi Atyaukili, captain of Mainsi Village (Dyu clan), interview by H. U. E. Thoden van Velzen, 1977. Throughout the interview, Atyaukili emphasized the suffering of the slaves. He stressed that it was a holocaust that should never be forgotten—certainly not by whites. It is interesting to compare Atyaukili's remark concerning the heavy toil of trench digging with the following statement in Price's (1983: 48) account of Saramaka historiography: "The heaviness of canal-building labor is cited as the specific motive for escape in the traditions of several Saramaka clans." (Cf. Oostindie and Van Stipriaan, this volume.)

4. Paramaribo is not only the capital of Suriname but also, when one includes its suburbs, the place where approximately 70 percent of the country's population is concentrated. It is a "city-state," in the sense that it is a fairly self-contained political unit. From the capital, the coastal districts and the interior constitute a periphery. In addition to de Kom (1971 [1934]), many other sources stress the significance of the triumvirate. See, e.g., van Kempen (1989: 62–64) on Baron,

the "Surinamese Spartacus." Hoogbergen (1988; 1990: 62) presents evidence that Maroons like Jolicoeur and even Baron were of lesser stature than Boni and some of the other guerrilla leaders of their time. On the basis of Hoogbergen's data, one may even doubt that such a triumvirate ever existed. Stedman's (1988 [1790]) influential book, first issued in 1790, undoubtedly delivered the material for the myth of the triumvirate. Stedman held a commission as an officer in the Dutch colonial army in Suriname in 1773–77.

5. Hoogbergen (1989) has collected whatever is known on Aluku from archival sources.

6. Asawooko, Diitabiki Village, interview by H. U. E. Thoden van Velzen, May 1981. Asawooko presented an elaborate account of Boni's assault on the schooner. Stedman (1988 [1790]: 188–89) describes Boni's cruelties in some detail. Incidentally, Stedman also describes the cruelties of his own superior, Colonel Fourgeoud.

7. Da Afanyaka of Puketi Village and Da Aida of Mainsi Village interviewed jointly by H. U. E. Thoden van Velzen, 29 May 1981. Many references in Hoogbergen's (1990) work, based on archival sources, support the view of Ndyuka historians that Dutch scheming was instrumental in causing the Ndyuka-Aluku war. Saka, the most influential man of the Ndyuka nation between about 1860 and 1914, was among those who held the same opinion. Information from his grandson, Da Papa, interview by H. U. E. Thoden van Velzen, Albina, May 1981.

8. Ajax is a pseudonym of the missionary A. J. Axwijk. Axwijk published the data he collected on Alukus and Ndyukas in the Paramaribo-based newspaper *De West* in November 1961. Axwijk, a Moravian, worked as a missionary and schoolteacher among the Alukus and Ndyukas from 1937 until 1963. As I personally observed on several occasions, he had an excellent command of the eastern maroons' language. An account almost identical to Axwijk's version was given by Da Kasiayeki, a historian of the Dyu clan, Fisiti village; interview by Bonno Thoden van Velzen, 1987. This part of Axwijk's account is widely believed to be the authentic record of the clashes between Aluku and Boni. Kasiayeki usually referred to the first guerrilla leader as Kwadyani Klonton Amusu, reason for me to substitute Kwadyani for Aluku.

9. In 1769, a captured maroon from Boni's group told his interrogators that Boni was a *bosch creool* (bush creole; one born in Suriname in freedom) (Hoogbergen 1989: 180, 185).

10. The priority given in this myth to matrilineal ties is pronounced.

11. For 1808, see HVP, code 1.05.10.02, letter #967; letter of Callenburgh Kelderman, 15 Nov. 1808; HVP, 967, 15 Feb. 1809; HVP 196, 24 June 1809.

12. That Ndyukas sought shelter for runaways at Poligudu is mentioned in a letter to the Court of Policy at Paramaribo, HVP 189, Minutes of Defense, 1807.

13. Compare CIB, code 1.05.11.06; filed under 1: 83, 18 Nov. 1829.

14. For the Cottica River, see CIB 1: 31, 19 June 1829. For the Commewijne River, see CIB 1846, letter of Heemraad to Paramaribo, 28 July 1846; and NWI: 816, no. 66b, 16 Jan. 1833.

15. CIB 1846, letter of Heemraad Niefeld, 28 July 1846.

16. For the Cottica, see NWI 810: 491, 13 Aug. 1831; NWI 820: 66, 29 Jan. 1934; CIB 3, 31 Mar. 1834; NWI 308, 27 Aug. 1845; KOL 3417, GJ, 13 Sept. 1847. For the Sara Creek, see NWI 820: 36, 13 Jan. 1834; and CIB 4, 8 Jan. 1835.

For the Surnau Creek, see NWI 804: 502, 4 Nov. 1830; NWI 807: 502, 26 Oct. 1830; NWI 808: 61, 28 Jan. 1831; NWI 310, Oct. 1845.

17. Loth (1880: 253) too mentions the actions of "the ruffians Amani and Nero" and tells how they threatened to stop all traffic through the Wane Creek. The Amani and Nero mentioned by Loth undoubtedly are the same as Amawi and Nelo. Kassiayeki emphasizes the tyrannical rule of the two men over the Paramaka maroons, whom they had joined at a fairly late stage.

18. The poison ordeal was one of the few "tribal" institutions of the nineteenth century. Its rulings were considered authoritative. However, the priests administering the poison ordeal would only work if the relatives of the suspect had asked for it and brought the person to their shrine.

19. A "Dicki" or "Dicki Pambu" appears in the government correspondence (NWI 804: 52, Nov. 1830; NWI 807: 502, 26 Oct. 1830; NWI 808: 61, 28 Jan. 1831; NWI 808: 22a 37, 11 Jan. 1833).

20. Close relatives should always be the first to accuse someone of witchcraft. Without such accusations from the immediate kin, a person need not be afraid of being condemned of witchcraft.

21. The only group of "new runaways" in the Cottica region in the early nineteenth century was the Kaabu Olo group. Around 1834, these "runaways" started negotiations with Ndyukas working in lumber camps along the Cottica. In that same year, Paramount Chief Beeyman gave the Cottica Ndyukas permission to track them down and hand them over to the colonial authorities (CIB 3: 68). The Kaabu Olo Maroons, however, were not defeated, as shown by the fact that the colonial government organized new patrols against them in 1836, 1844, and 1846. The Kaabu Olo people were in frequent contact with Ndyuka and with plantation slaves (NWI 819: 725; 819: 747; 820: 55). Dr. Hoogbergen kindly provided me with archival documents on the Kaabu Olo group.

22. The poison ordeal that condemned Atokwa but found no cause for convicting Dikii.

23. Da Papa did not know his age, but he told me he was among the first children to be born in the village of Gaan Boli. The village was founded in 1888 or 1889.

24. Fieldwork started with an eighteen-month period in 1961 and 1962. It was resumed in 1965 and continued with shorter trips in the 1970s and 1980s. These latter stints of fieldwork varied in time from one to three months. Most of the archival data were collected in the Netherlands in the 1970s. As a result of the exodus of many Surinamers to the Netherlands, I was in a position to interview several Maroon historians in the Netherlands.

25. On the civil war in Suriname, see Polimé and Thoden van Velzen (1988), Price (n.d.), and Thoden van Velzen (1994).

References

Ajax [A. J. Axwijk]
1961　De vlucht van Boni en Aloekoe. *De West* (Suriname), 10 Nov. and 11 Nov. 1961.
de Goeje, C. H.
1908　*Verslag der Toemoekhoemak-expeditie (Tumuc-Humac-expeditie)*. Leiden, Netherlands: Brill.

de Groot, Silvia W.
1975   The Boni-Maroon War, 1765–1793: Surinam and French Guiana. *Boletín de Estudios Latinoamericanos y del Caribe* 18: 30–48.
1977   *From Isolation towards Integration* Verhandelingen van het Koninklijk Instituut voor Taal-, Land- en Volkenkunde 80. The Hague, Netherlands: Martinus Nijhoff.
1988   Het Korps Zwarte Jagers in Suriname: Collaboratie en opstand 1. *OSO: Tijdschrift voor Surinaamse Taalkunde, letterkunde, Cultuur en Geschiedenis* 7 (2): 147–60.
1989   Het Korps Zwarte Jagers in Suriname: Collaboratie en opstand 2. *OSO: Tijdschrift voor Surinaamse Taalkunde, letterkunde, Cultuur en Geschiedenis* 8 (1): 7–21.
de Kom, Anton
1971 [1934]   *Wij slaven van Suriname.* Amsterdam: Contact.
Hartley, L. P.
1968   The Go-Between. In *The Collected Stories of L. P. Hartley*, ed. David Cecil. London: Hamish Hamilton.
Hoogbergen, Wim S. M.
1978   *De Surinaamse "Weglopers" van de 19e eeuw.* Bronnen voor de Studie van Bosnegersamenlevingen, no. 1. Utrecht, Netherlands: Center for Caribbean Studies.
1983   Marronage en Marrons, 1760–1863: De niet-gepacificeerde Marrons van Suriname. In *Suriname: De schele onafhankelijkheid*, ed. Glenn Willemsen, 75–110. Amsterdam: De Arbeiderspers.
1984   *De Boni's in Frans Guyana en de Tweede Boni-oorlog, 1776–1793.* Bronnen voor de Studie van Bosnegersamenlevingen, no. 10. Utrecht, Netherlands: Center for Caribbean Studies.
1988   Boni, Aluku en Kormantin Kodjo: Over de vroegste Boni-geschiedenis. *SWI-Forum* 5 (1): 59–86. Paramaribo: Stichting Wetenschappelijke Informatie.
1989   Aluku. *New West Indian Guide* 63 (3 and 4): 175–98.
1990   *The Boni Maroon Wars in Suriname.* Leiden, Netherlands: E. J. Brill.
1993   De verdwenen Marrons van Krabbeholle. *OSO: Tijdschrift voor Surinaamse Taalkunde, letterkunde, Cultuur en Geschiedenis* 12 (1): 6–27.
Hostmann, F. W.
1850   *Over de beschaving van negers in Amerika door kolonisatie met Europeanen.* Amsterdam: J. C. A. Sulpke.
Kappler, A.
1881   *Holländisch-Guiana: Erlebnisse und Erfahrungen während eines 43 jährigen Aufenthalts in der Kolonie Surinam.* Stuttgart, Germany: Kohlhammer.
Köbben, André J. F.
1979   *In vrijheid en gebondenheid: Samenleving en cultuur van de Djoeka aan de Cottica.* Bronnen voor de Studie van Bosnegersamenlevingen, no. 4. Utrecht, Netherlands: Center for Caribbean Studies.
Lenoir, J. D.
1973   The Paramacca Maroons. Ph.D. diss. New York: New School for Social Research.
Loth, W. L.
1880   Verslag van eene expeditie tot het traceereu van een weg van de Tempatiekreek

naar de rivier Suriname. Rapport aan Z. E. den Gouverneur van Suriname. *Tijdschrift van het Aardrijkskundig Genoofschap* 4: 250–55.

1904–5   Rapport over de exploratie van het Lawa-gebied. Handelingen der Staten Generaal [Minutes of Parliament.] *Koloniaal Verslag*, 1905, appendix no. 5: *Suriname.* s'Gravenhage: Staatsuitgeverij.

Polimé, T. S., and H. U. E. Thoden van Velzen

1988   *Vluchtelingen, opstandelingen en andere Bosnegers van Ooost-Suriname, 1986–1988.* Bronnen voor de Studie van Afro-Surinaamse Samenlevingen, no. 13. Utrecht, Netherlands: Instituut voor Culturele Antropologie.

Price, Richard

1983   *First-Time: The Historical Vision of an Afro-American People* Baltimore, Md.: Johns Hopkins Univ. Press.

n.d.   *The Killings.* Forthcoming.

Stedman, John Gabriel

1988 [1790]   *Narrative of a Five Years Expedition against the Revolted Negroes of Surinam.* Edited, with introduction and notes, by Richard Price and Sally Price. Baltimore, Md.: Johns Hopkins Univ. Press.

Thoden van Velzen, H. U. E.

1984   The Djuka Civilisation. *Sociologia Neerlandica* 20 (2): 85–97.

1994   Priests, Spirit Mediums, and Guerrillas in Suriname. In *Transactions: Essays in honor of Jeremy F. Boissevain,* ed. Jojada Verrips, 209–28. Amsterdam: Het Spinhuis.

Thoden van Velzen, H. U. E, and W. van Wetering

1988   *The Great Father and the Danger: Religious Cults, Material Forces, and Collective Fantasies in the World of the Surinamese Maroons.* Caribbean Series 9, Koninklijk Instituut voor Taal-, Land- en Volkenkunde. Leiden, Netherlands: KITLV Press.

van Kempen, Michiel

1989   *Surinaamse schrijvers en dichters.* Amsterdam: De Arbeiderspers.

10 | Indian-Black Relations in Colonial and Antebellum Louisiana

Daniel H. Usner, Jr.

In 1920, Carter G. Woodson declared that relations between African Americans and American Indians were "one of the longest unwritten chapters of the history of the United States" (1920: 45). Today the history of Indian-black relations is still, at best, only an uneven outline. As Woodson himself illustrated, the subject cannot be confined geographically to the South. Even in the colonial Northeast, where the black populace remained relatively small, American Indians and African Americans developed significant ties. Yet historians of that region continue to neglect them.[1] Among historians of the Southeast, where the proximity of numerous blacks and Indians is obvious, the emphasis has been on the institution of slavery as it evolved within Indian nations during the early nineteenth century. Intercultural relations during the colonial period—the dynamic and diverse interaction that occurred over the sixteenth, seventeenth, and eighteenth centuries—are just beginning to be explored. But the bulk of new scholarship remains compartmentalized, with works concentrating on either African Americans or American Indians and missing the wider scope of contacts and influences between groups.[2]

By examining Indian-black relations in the Lower Mississippi Valley during the entire eighteenth century and into the nineteenth century, I hope to highlight a fuller range of cross-cultural interaction than studies of single Indian nations or of slavery in single colonies have portrayed. Through exchanges among seemingly disparate sites within the region—Indian villages, hunting camps, plantations, runaway camps, and port towns—people took advantage of flexible and fluid relations. This economic interdependency hampered efforts by colonial officials to draw racial boundaries across a population that was ethnically heterogeneous. Throughout the eighteenth century, Indians and blacks interacted in a variety of spheres, ranging from slavery in colonial settlements to trade in Indian villages, where intercultural influences helped shape a unique region of North America (Hall 1992, Usner 1992). But as the Lower Mississippi Valley was developed into an agricultural export economy, its inhabitants found these spheres constricting, due to the work of lawmakers who were dedicated to strengthening prohibitions against interracial exchange. An understanding of the real complexity in Indian-black relations in the American South must take into account the causes and effects of this transformation.

Not surprisingly, contact between Africans and Indians in Louisiana originated in the context of slavery. During the first two decades of the colony's life, however, Indians—not Africans—comprised the majority of slaves. As of 1708, the colonial population numbered only 122 soldiers and sailors, 77 settlers (24 men, 28 women, and 25 children), and 80 Indian slaves. Most of these Indian slaves were Chitimachas and Alibamons captured in warfare by the French and their Indian allies. For two hundred livres each, colonists purchased a score of prisoners taken by Lt. Louis Juchereau de Saint-Denis when he attacked a Chitimacha village of Bayou Lafourche in 1707. Enslaved in small numbers and too close to their communities of origin, however, Indians proved to be an insufficient and recalcitrant labor force. The few colonists willing to consider developing this isolated outpost into a productive colony felt their only hope was to acquire African slaves "to clear the land." Gov. Jean-Baptiste Le Moyne de Bienville proposed that, since the Indians being captured by Frenchmen and their allies deserted too easily, although they were "very good for cultivating the earth," settlers should be allowed to "sell these slaves in the American islands in order to get negroes in exchange." But the French minister of marine affairs prohibited Louisiana officials from allowing this pattern to develop, wishing to avoid the degree of disorder and animosity instilled among southeastern Indians by English shipment of Indian slaves from Carolina. Before 1718, only a few African slaves reached Louisiana (*Mississippi Provincial Archives* 2 [1929]: 32–34, 38–39; *Mississippi Provincial Archives* 3 [1932]: 38–39, 115–16; Jay Higginbotham 1977: 93–94, 288–93, 302, 541).

Between 1718 and 1731, the Company of the Indies shipped about 7,000 slaves from West Africa to Louisiana. During this same period of spirited investment, a roughly equal number of Europeans traveled to the Gulf Coast colony. High mortality, due to disease and hunger suffered by migrants during the 1720s, limited growth of the colonial population to only 4,500 people by 1732, with African Americans comprising nearly 75 percent of the total. But the perpetuation of Indian slavery during these years brought a smattering of individual Indians into close contact with Africans and Europeans. Thirty of the colony's 159 Indian slaves in 1726 lived at New Orleans, in a variety of household arrangements. On Rue Royalle, 2 Indian and 4 black slaves lived with carpenter Thomas Dezery. At Bayou St. John and Gentilly, on the northeastern outskirts of the capital, 8 Indian slaves worked beside white and black laborers on several different farms. At the settlement of Chapitoulas, just above New Orleans along the Mississippi River, 11 Indian slaves lived on four separate plantations along with 11 European servants and 302 black slaves. Two large plantations farther upriver at Natchez employed 4 Indian and 56 African slaves in addition to 29 indentured servants (Maduell 1972: 50–76).

A significant percentage of Indians and Africans living in Louisiana households as slaves were women. As in most frontier regions during their formative years, in Louisiana the white populace had a high ratio of men to women—especially in the towns of Mobile and New Orleans and the garrisons of Natchez and Natchitoches. Women of all nationalities and classes, therefore, were invaluable partners, sexually and otherwise. In a memoir written after his return to France in 1710, a former pastor of Mobile denounced many soldiers and settlers for preferring, over legitimate marriage, "to maintain scandalous concubinages with young Indian women, driven by their proclivity for the extremes of licentiousness. They have bought them under the pretext of keeping them as servants, but actually to seduce them, as they in fact have done" (Archives des Colonies 3: 390). Beginning in 1724, the Code Noir prohibited sexual intercourse between slaves and settlers. But cohabitation across this legal barrier, like so many other acts forbidden by colonial laws, certainly did not end, since many Indian and black women lived with Frenchmen as mistresses or common law wives. "Although the number of those who maintain young Indian women or negresses to satisfy their intemperance is considerably diminished," the Capuchin Vicar General of Louisiana complained in 1726, "there still remain enough to scandalize the church and to require an effective remedy" (Archives des Colonies 10: 46).

A more serious threat to the designs of colonial officials than cohabitation was the potential for collaboration between enslaved Indians and Africans. Despite the odds facing strangers in a foreign land, some

African slaves took the initiative to seek freedom in Indian societies. Given their knowledge of the terrain and familiarity with local tribes, Indian slaves held the key to unlocking mass rebellion against slavery and colonial rule. Following reports of "marrons sauvages" raiding cattle and attacking the black public executioner, a maroon camp was discovered outside New Orleans in 1727. An Indian slave named Sancousy, after losing his owner's ox, fled to this makeshift village, where he met about fifteen African and Indian fugitives. These escaped slaves possessed enough guns and ammunition to defend themselves against pursuers. The arrest of other runaways who apparently had seen this community influenced Gov. Etienne Boucher de Périer to request that the trade in Indian slaves be terminated. Not only did this traffic incite costly wars between tribes, but "these Indian slaves being mixed with our negroes may induce them to desert with them, as has already happened, as they may maintain relations with them which might be disastrous to the colony when there are more blacks" (Records of the Superior Council 1: 109, 3: 414, 3: 443–44; *Mississippi Provincial Archives* 2 [1929]: 573–74).

As in other slave colonies situated amid Indian societies, Louisiana officials employed local Indians to catch runaway slaves as an effective device for keeping separate peoples who otherwise might have conspired against a common enemy, the white planter. Once ships began depositing enslaved West Africans on the Gulf shore, Indian villagers situated around colonial settlements were offered bounties of munitions and alcohol for capturing and returning runaways. In order to restore peaceful relations with the French after a brief conflict, the Natchez in 1723 were expected to "bring in dead or alive a negro who has taken refuge among them for a long time and makes them seditious speeches against the French nation and who has followed them on occasions against our Indian allies." Alarmed by robbery and arson being committed by numerous bands of runaways in 1726, Attorney General François Fleuriau, himself the owner of eight blacks, urged the Superior Council to "take prompt and sweeping action against runaway slaves" by hiring "neighborhood Indians" to pursue them (Records of the Superior Council 3: 414; Le Page du Pratz 1975 [1774]: 29).

Various dimensions of Indian-black relations in early Louisiana converged in the Natchez Indian War of 1729. The presence of slaves in colonial settlements vividly illustrated to Indian observers the desire that the colonists had to dominate others. "Before the French came amongst us," one Natchez elder declared to an assembly of chiefs, "we walked with boldness every road. . . . But now we go groping, afraid of meeting thorns, we walk like slaves, which we shall soon be, since the French already treat us as if we were such." Warning that the French, for the least fault, will tie young Natchez people "and whip them as they do their black slaves," the orator asked the war council, "is not death preferable to slavery?" (Le Page du Pratz 1975 [1774]: 81–84).

When the Natchez struck on November 28, they killed nearly two hundred fifty settlers and captured nearly three hundred black slaves along with some fifty white women and children. Many of these black captives aided the Natchez in the ensuing battles. On January 27, 1730, five hundred Choctaw allies of the French besieged the Natchez, killing about one hundred warriors and recovering most of the white women and children and about one hundred slaves. But as Périer later discovered, "this defeat would have been complete if it had not been for the negroes who prevented the Choctaws from carrying off the powder and who by their resistance had given the Natchez time to enter the two forts." On February 8, the Choctaws were joined by two hundred troops from New Orleans, including fifteen blacks. After protracted bombardment of the Natchez forts, the besieged Indian rebels agreed to return all remaining hostages to the French. Within a few days, the Natchez managed to slip by the French and cross the Mississippi. As the colonial army pursued the Natchez into the Ouachita River basin, the Choctaws returned to their villages with about thirty of the Negroes released from the fort.

The Choctaws wanted to guarantee themselves indemnity for their military services to the colony and understood the market value of slaves to colonial Louisianians. Anxious to regain these slaves, Louisiana officials sent Capt. Joseph Christophe de Lusser to the Choctaw nation to negotiate for them. The fate of all those African Louisianians captured by the Choctaws during the Natchez War is indeterminate, but available evidence about some illuminates how distressing the status of slavery was for people caught between colonial and Indian societies. Eventually, at least twenty were purchased back into the colony, either by the government or by individuals. Others reportedly fled to the Chickasaw villages or were sold to English traders. At Mobile in late October, Choctaw spokesmen told Governor Périer that several Negroes whom they tried to return to Louisiana "killed themselves on the way." In the following spring, three blacks being taken to Mobile by a chief known as Alibamon Mingo asked Ensign Regis de Roullet to take them because, they told him, "the Indians make us carry some packages, which exhausts us, mistreat us much, and have taken from us our clothing." The French officer noticed that one "had a tomahawk wound on the head which went as far as the bone" (Usner 1992: 72–74).

The colonial government did everything possible, of course, to encourage fear and hostility between Indians and blacks. When news of the Natchez attack first reached New Orleans, Périer dispatched a group of armed black slaves downriver from the capital on December 5, 1729, to destroy the Chaouachas, a neighboring village of only thirty warriors. This expedition, according to his report, "kept the other little nations up the river in a respectful attitude." Commending the slaves for their prompt and secret mission, the governor boasted, "If I had been willing to use our negro volunteers I should have destroyed all these little nations which are of no use to us, and which might on the contrary cause our negroes to revolt." He did not further employ these black soldiers "for fear of rendering [them] . . . too bold and of inclining them perhaps to revolt after the example of those who joined the Natchez" (*Mississippi Provincial Archives* 1 [1927]: 64–65, 71).

Encouraging enmity between racial groups without delivering to any one of them enough power to overthrow the colonial order was indeed walking a thin line. In summer 1730, while the French were mobilizing several regiments upriver against the Natchez, African-American slaves in the New Orleans area plotted their own rebellion. Hints of a slave conspiracy did not take long to appear, as on the day when a black woman, after "receiving a violent blow from a French soldier for refusing to obey him," shouted that "the French should not long insult negroes." Once the plot became known, several black men, including the overseer of the company plantation named Samba Bambara, were broken on the wheel, while one of the women conspirators was "hanged before their eyes" (Le Page du Pratz 1975 [1774]: 77–79; Dumont de Montigny 1853 [1753]: 99–100; *Mississippi Provincial Archives* 4 [1984]: 82, 104). Meanwhile, the French sent three Negroes accused of playing "the most active part" in the Natchez War to be burned by the Choctaws. This effective use of a divide-and-rule policy, as Father Le Petit reported from New Orleans on July 12, "has inspired all the Negroes with a new horror of the Savages, but which will have a beneficial effect in securing the safety of the Colony" (Thwaites 1900, vol. 68, p. 198).

Bondage of American Indians was not officially prohibited in Louisiana until Spain acquired the province, but factors shared with other North American colonies did slow down the rate of Indian enslavement. The decimation of Indians by disease, the desire to secure stable trade relations with neighboring tribes, the availability of African slaves, and the ease with which Indian captives could abscond all contributed to a declining number of Indian slaves in colonial Louisiana after 1730.

A campaign against the Natchez during the winter of 1730–31 produced five hundred Indian captives, mostly women and children, but most were shipped away from the colony to the Caribbean. Also influencing the decline in Indian slavery was the tendency in both custom and law to classify slaves automatically as Negro or mulatto. Liaisons between Indian and African-American slaves produced children who were ascribed with increasing regularity to Negro or mulatto identities. Some Indians were assimilated into the free segment of colonial society, as the offspring of Indian slave women and freemen grew up as free people of color or as whites (Maduell 1972: 113, 123; Archives des Colonies 15: 105; Dominguez 1986).[3]

Efforts by Louisiana slave-owners to exploit the labor of a black majority in a colony surrounded by an even larger Indian populace required that enforcement of a racially divided law and order be continued and even intensified. Because of its peripheral situation in the French colonial empire, Louisiana received only a trickle of settlers and slaves from abroad over the mid-eighteenth century. General Commissioner Honoré Michel de La Rouvillière called his financial charge in 1752 "the best land that there is in the world and the finest colony that the King could possess," but colonists "are all asking for negroes and really cannot succeed without that" (*Mississippi Provincial Archives* 5 [1984]: 115–16). As the colonial population increased and commercial production expanded—both gradually—Louisiana depended heavily upon stable relations with Indian nations, especially the populous and powerful Choctaws. "None of those who have come to the country," the commandant of troops at New Orleans explained, "fail to be aware of the impossibility of keeping a country as vast as the one we occupy with the few troops and settlers who are there and who would soon be obliged to depart from it if the Choctaws refused us their assistance and decided to act against us" (*Mississippi Provincial Archives* 4 [1984]: 262).

But from 1746 to 1750, a large faction of Choctaws did revolt against the French alliance, heightening fears of simultaneous, and possibly even coordinated, black and Indian rebellions. When some Choctaw warriors attacked a settlement just upriver from New Orleans in spring 1748, they killed a settler and captured his wife, daughter, and five slaves. In April, a colonial force of about fifty soldiers and militiamen marched after the raiders. Across Lake Pontchartrain from the city, this detachment mistook a peaceful Choctaw hunting camp for the rebels and opened fire in panic. Not until one soldier was killed and another two wounded did the two sides calm down. The head of the Choctaw party apologized for the incident but argued that some runaway Negroes actually had fired the fatal shots. Groups of slave maroons were indeed camped in the area (*Mississippi Provincial Archives* 4 [1984]: 318–21).

Literally caught in the crossfire of slave resistance and Indian war, a young Louisiana-born black named François recently had fled into the woods behind the Boisclair plantation. His encounter with Choctaw rebels offers a glimpse of the ongoing network of marronage through which many Louisiana slaves, African-American and American Indian, came and went during the eighteenth century. François had been sold to a New Orleans merchant and did not want to leave family and friends. Running away, he survived in the forest by taking provisions from the slave cabins and milking his former owner's cows. In May 1748, he met five other runaway blacks, some of whom had come downriver from Pointe Coupée. Together they fed off cattle and poultry stolen from farms in the German Coast settlement. François soon joined up with a Chickasaw Indian named Joseph, a slave captured in one of many raids against his people and now determined to return to them. Joseph, a black named Cezard, and an Indian woman earlier had rowed a pirogue into Lake Pontchartrain. At Bayou Tchefuncte, these marrons were hailed by a band of about ten Choctaw rebels en route to raid the German Coast settlement. Fearing the consequences of such an open attack against the French, Joseph separated himself from these warriors and eventually was captured along with François (Records of the Superior Council 19: 768–71).

Day-to-day relations between American Indians and African Americans never actually conformed to the wishes of colonial officials and planters. Spheres of interaction in colonial Louisiana remained too varied and dispersed for government ordinances to enforce intercultural divisions. Even in those settlements most closely tied to the commercial export economy, exceptional circumstances defied uniformity. Tobacco farms at Pointe Coupée by the mid-1740s included a population of nearly three hundred whites, over four hundred blacks, twenty-three Indians, and fifteen mulattos. The household of Philippe Haynault, before his death in 1743, contained two Africans, an Indian woman, and her daughter—all slaves—and a European overseer. Another Pointe Coupée farm, worked by seven black slaves, was owned by a free Indian woman named Marie (Records of the Superior Council 5: 466–77).[4] Further diversifying the ethnic combinations within this incipient plantation world were camps of runaway slaves and Indian hunters that moved through the backcountry. Barter among slaves living on plantations, runaways hiding in the swamps, and Indians traveling on winter hunts created a significant exchange network along Louisiana's bayous and trails. Official efforts to extinguish the marketing of stolen goods through this network repeatedly were frustrated by the persistence of the participants themselves and by many slave-owners' resignation to its utility as a supplemental means of livelihood (Usner 1992).

Indians in the several villages scattered along the Mississippi and Red rivers during the eighteenth century shared many economic roles with slaves on the plantations. Despite the depopulation and displacement suffered during the early years of colonial contact, Chitimachas, Houmas, Bayogoulas, Taensas, Tunicas, and other Lower Mississippi Valley Indians managed to hold themselves together in small communities. These "petites nations" provided colonists with the slave-catchers already mentioned, but also with rowers, sailors, cattle drivers, soldiers, and hunters. Blacks and Indians often worked side by side at these tasks, along with white employees. Techniques for farming, hunting, fishing, gathering, and traveling appropriate to the local environment were transmitted from Indian inhabitants to colonial slaves and settlers.

Participation in the regional food economy also involved intercultural relations. In the street and riverside markets of New Orleans and other towns, slaves sold food items grown in their own gardens or those of their owners. Indians from neighboring communities also brought produce and game to the same places. Social interaction and intercultural influence in this sphere of exchange had long-term effects on the foodways of the Gulf Coast South (Usner 1986, 1989).

Relations between blacks and Indians even extended farther inland, since numerous slaves and free people of color participated in Louisiana's deerskin trade. African Americans traveled widely among interior Indian villages as packhorsemen, rowers, and sometimes even interpreters. Six slaves owned by Marthe Frémont, for example, were hired out to merchant André Fabry in 1744 for his trade with the Atakapas and Opelousas Indians of southwestern Louisiana (Records of the Superior Council 6: 283, 10: 258, 13: 309, 16: 334–35; *Mississippi Provincial Archives* 1 [1927]: 204; *Mississippi Provincial Archives* 3 [1932]: 556). In 1787, two African-American slaves were arrested near the Arkansas post for trading rum and brandy to some Delaware Indians. Louis, a slave born in New Orleans who spoke their language, testified that he only "did what his master ordered him to do" (Kinnaird 1949: vol. 3, pp. 203–7). Some free blacks also traded with Indians in the Lower Mississippi Valley. During the 1770s and 1780s, they included: a mulatto trader named Jeanot who dealt with the Caddos, a man called "Louis Mulatto" who worked for Simon Favre among the

Choctaws, and a mulatto woman named Nelly Price who operated along the Mississippi River at Grand Gulf (fifty miles upriver from Natchez). The Mobilian trade language, used extensively in this eighteenth-century Indian commerce, endured into the twentieth century as a patois spoken by scattered blacks and whites in southern Louisiana (Usner 1992: 255, 258–59, 267).

The frontier exchange economy that sustained such variety and flexibility in Indian-black relations underwent drastic transformation during the late eighteenth and early nineteenth centuries. The size and composition of the colonial populace in the Lower Mississippi Valley began to change after 1763, when Spain and Great Britain divided the region into their respective provinces of Louisiana and West Florida. In order to improve economic productivity, as well as to secure political control, both powers implemented vigorous colonization schemes that drew new waves of settlers and slaves to the Gulf Coast. The colonial population tripled and became more ethnically diverse by the mid-1780s (16,000 slaves; 13,000 whites; and 1,000 free people of color). As desired by officials, plantation production of export crops expanded along with this demographic growth. The Indian population actually began to increase during these years, following generations of decline, but for the first time it began to be outnumbered by the more rapidly growing non-Indian population. The regional deerskin trade, upon which Indians had become dependent, concomitantly became overshadowed by the agricultural export economy. These processes of change continued after Spain assumed sovereignty over the entire Gulf Coast in 1783 and then accelerated when the United States established the Mississippi Territory in 1798 and purchased Louisiana in 1803.

During this volatile period, governments escalated efforts to control interaction between blacks and Indians. As measures to restrict the activities of slaves to plantation production intensified, fear of slave rebellion heightened. The means of livelihood and the mobility of Indians likewise encountered more aggressive regulation under Spanish and American regimes. To mold the racial order that eventually undergirded the cotton economy of the Deep South, governments continued to rely on familiar divide-and-rule strategies. In November 1785, for example, the New Orleans Cabildo paid one hundred pesos to an unidentified group of Indians, as promised by the governor, for killing a runaway black slave (Records and Deliberations of the New Orleans Cabildo, 25 Nov. 1785).[5] Although citizen patrols became the principal means of vigilance against slave defiance, Indians in Louisiana occasionally were called to help retrieve runaways throughout the antebellum period. In

Twelve Years a Slave, Solomon Northrup recounted how a mill owner in Avoyelles Parish "hastened straightway to the Indian village" for assistance in capturing two runaway slaves (1968 [1853]: 184–85). The daughter of a planter in Donaldsonville recalled a search for a runaway camp when the sheriff went to "'Blow-Gun' John's, a Goula Indian living on a cane ridge some distance up the bayou, to seek information and canoes" (Ailenroc 1903: 41–43).

Local ordinances and legislative acts passed in the Orleans and Mississippi territories included a spate of laws designed to tighten restraints around Indian and slave activity in the Lower Mississippi Valley—following a pattern that had been set under Spanish administration. Through federal Indian law, United States officials exerted pressures within the Choctaw, Chickasaw, Quapaw, and Caddo nations to arrest runaway slaves and other fugitives and to minimize Indian movement around towns and plantations (Usner 1985). Territorial regulations were aimed at types of exchange occurring outside Indian territory, which seemed increasingly subversive of the norms of a stratified racial order. Tavernkeepers and other citizens were prohibited from selling liquor to Indians and slaves. Purchasing livestock from either group was proscribed (McMurtrie 1942: 4; Martin 1816: vol. 2, pp. 434, 438; McCain 1948: 237–40). The general marketing activities of slaves came under tighter restrictions, while peddlers faced mounting vigilance concerning their visits to plantations and Indian communities. A law passed by the Orleans territorial assembly in June 1806 specified that if an Indian or free person of color "should maliciously steal any slave, he or she shall forfeit the value of said slave and shall be condemned to two years imprisonment at hard labor" (Martin 1816: vol. 1, pp. 648–50).

The intercultural fluidity that Indians and blacks had managed to retain during the colonial period decreased significantly by the 1820s. State laws in the Deep South erected legal barriers that proved difficult to surmount, imposing a magnitude of social control that authorities back in French Louisiana could scarcely have imagined possible. But, while the range and frequency of contacts diminished, American Indians and African Americans continued to share experiences within southern society. Although the spheres of interaction narrowed in the Cotton South, the legacy of Indian-black exchange endured in some important ways.

Well into the nineteenth century, Indians and blacks openly participated together in certain public activities. Indian families traveled regularly to New Orleans and other towns to trade foodstuffs and wares. Amid the predominantly black assembly of peddlers at New Orleans markets, small groups of Indian men, women, and children sold game,

herbs, spices, firewood, baskets, and cane blowguns. When not ped-
dling in the marketplace, these Indians joined free and enslaved blacks,
as well as working-class whites, at taverns, parades, dances, and games
on the outskirts of town. All of this face-to-face contact, which often
troubled city officials, resulted in a continuing influence between cultures. The most notable public evidence of these Indian relations was
the widespread popularity among nineteenth-century Louisianians of
the ball game called "raquettes." Early in the century, Indian, Negro,
and white teams competed against each other in this ancient Indian
sport. New Orleans raquettes was perpetuated into the twentieth century by black teams, whose style of play and celebration—as observed
by ethnologist Steward Culin in 1901—closely resembled that of the
Choctaws (Usner 1984).

The persistence of some Indian people inside slave communities
also facilitated personal relationships with African Americans for a long
time. After Spain's Laws of the Indies reached Louisiana, no more Indians
could be enslaved in the colony, and those already living under slavery could
not be sold by their owners. Avenues to emancipation available under
Spanish law contributed somewhat to the eventual disappearance of an
Indian slave population in Louisiana, as shown in numerous petitions for
freedom made by slaves who claimed Indian identity. Gradual absorption
into the rapidly growing non-Indian population—especially African-
American slaves—and a tightening racial structure, in which any combination of mixed ancestry was classified as "people of color," further diminished the visibility of Indian slaves by the early nineteenth century. But
Indian ancestry had a lasting effect on the culture and identities of many
African Americans. Alice Dunbar-Nelson, New Orleans civil rights and
feminist activist of the late nineteenth and early twentieth centuries,
learned from her slave-born mother that most slaves on the Opelousas
plantation where she had lived before the Civil War "were of mixed Indian blood" (Hull 1988: 34–35). Several early jazz musicians identified
some Indian ancestry in their families. George Lewis's paternal grandmother was a Choctaw from the New Orleans area. Gus Perryman,
born in Hattiesburg, Mississippi, told an interviewer that his father "was
colored and part Creek Indian" (Bethell 1977: 14–17, 46–47;
Cortinovis 1974: 72–78).

The proximity of several American Indian communities to plantation areas in the Gulf South also meant that some African-American
slaves and runaways still entered Indian society. The young slave
woman who was arrested by an Avoyelles Parish patrol in 1800 for trying to elope with an Indian certainly was not the last person to attempt

such a passage (Saucier 1943: 444–45). An indeterminate number of blacks were adopted into Choctaw, Tunica, and Houma families during the nineteenth century, while some multiracial families formed separate communities (Posey 1979). Slaves often visited neighboring Indian villages just to watch or participate in seasonal celebrations, to socialize with acquaintances, or to buy and sell goods (Northrup 1968 [1853]: 71–73; McDermott 1940: 58).

Under these various circumstances, boundaries between Indians and blacks remained blurred in scattered parts of the Louisiana countryside. On a journey from Lake Charles to Opelousas in 1854, Frederick Law Olmsted stumbled into this still complex world: "At a rude corn-mill belonging to Mr. Béguin, we had noticed among the negroes an Indian boy, in negro clothing, and about the house were two other Indians—an old man and a young man; the first poorly clad, the other gaily dressed in a showy printed calico frock, and worked buckskin leggings, with beads and tinsel ornaments, a great turban of Scotch shawl-stuff on his head." Olmsted discovered that the two men were Choctaws ("of whom a good many lived in the neighborhood") who hired themselves out as farm laborers for thirty-seven cents a day, and that the old man "had a field of his own in which stood handsome corn." But the keen observer of antebellum southern life showed little understanding of this margin of society. He noted that some of these Indians "were industrious, but none were steady at work"—merely touching upon the economic means by which many Indians across the South maintained their autonomy. Inquiry about the boy at the mill yielded the information that "he lived there and did work, getting no wages, but 'living there with the niggers.'" "They seldom consort," Olmsted quickly concluded, since "our host knew but one case in which a negro had an Indian wife" (1862: vol. 2, p. 38).

As racial bifurcation deepened over the nineteenth century, relations between American Indians and African Americans became more strained within the communities and more disapproved by outside observers. United States removal policy drastically reduced the Indian population in the Deep South, yet many Indian people remained. More than ever before, the survival of small Indian communities still scattered across Louisiana and Mississippi depended upon maintaining social boundaries. Laws designed to protect slavery and to enforce white supremacy made intercultural relations riskier. In order to avert official efforts that endangered their autonomy and identity, Indians distanced themselves from blacks and whites. So, within the predominant context of an intensifying white-black distinction, Indian people became less conspicuous in the landscape. Customary forms of interaction, however, were not abandoned entirely. Livelihood and amusement continued to bring Indians and blacks together on the margins of plantation society. Mostly hidden from the suspicious view of others, but occasionally in open defiance of authority, exchange between African Americans and American Indians testified to the endurance of pre-cotton outlooks and customs in the Cotton South.

Notes

1. From the 1930s to the 1950s, Kenneth W. Porter published almost all the important works on Indian-black relations. Among his various essays, the most notable in scope is "Relations between Negroes and Indians within the Present Limits of the United States" (1932). For a recent narrative that presents the subject to a wider audience, see Katz (1985).
2. Perdue (1979) and Wright (1981) are exceptional studies of American Indians in the context of African-American slavery because they delve into the colonial background of Indian-black relations. Merrell (1984), Braund (1991), and Joel W. Martin (1991) signal new directions that emphasize the colonial experience. The persistent compartmentalization and isolation of American Indian studies in colonial scholarship is sharply criticized in Merrell (1989).
3. The conjunction of demographic and legal changes in Indian slavery among English colonies is investigated in A. Leon Higginbotham, Jr. (1978), Wright (1981), and Kawashima (1986).
4. In Hall (1992), see chapter 8 for an especially discerning exploration of race relations at the frontier settlement of Pointe Coupée.
5. For further inquiry into slavery during this period of Louisiana history, see McGowan (1976) and Kerr (1983).

References

Ailenroc, M. R.
1903   *The White Castle of Louisiana.* Louisville, Ky.: John P. Morton.
Archives des Colonies. Archives Nationales, Paris. Series C13A, Louisiana General Correspondence. 54 vols.
Bethell, Tom
1977   *George Lewis: A Jazzman from New Orleans.* Berkeley: Univ. of California Press.
Braund, Kathryn E. Holland
1991   The Creek Indians, Blacks, and Slavery. *Journal of Southern History* 57 (4): 601–36.
Cortinovis, Irene E.
1974   Jazz on the Riverboats: The Way a Piano Player Tells It. *Journal of Jazz Studies* 1 (2): 72–78.

Dominguez, Virginia R.
1986 *White by Definition: Social Classification in Creole Louisiana.* New Brunswick, N.J.: Rutgers Univ. Press.
Dumont de Montigny, Jean François Benjamin
1853 [1753] Historical Memoirs of M. Dumont. *Historical Collections of Louisiana.* Vol. 5. New York: Lamport, Blakeman and Law.
Hall, Gwendolyn Midlo
1992 *Africans in Colonial Louisiana: The Development of Afro-Creole Culture in the Eighteenth Century.* Baton Rouge: Louisiana State Univ. Press.
Higginbotham, A. Leon, Jr.
1978 *In the Matter of Color: Race and the American Legal Process: The Colonial Period.* New York: Oxford Univ. Press.
Higginbotham, Jay
1977 *Old Mobile: Fort Louis de la Louisiane, 1702–1711.* Mobile, Ala.: Museum of the City of Mobile.
Hull, Gloria T.
1988 Shaping Contradictions: Alice Dunbar-Nelson and the Black Creole Experience. *New Orleans Review* 15 (1): 34–37.
Katz, William Loren
1985 *Black Indians: A Hidden History.* New York: Atheneum.
Kawashima, Yasuhide
1986 *Puritan Justice and the Indian: White Man's Law in Massachusetts, 1630–1763.* Middletown, Conn.: Wesleyan Univ. Press.
Kerr, Derek Noel
1983 Petty Felony, Slave Defiance, and Frontier Villainy: Crime and Criminal Justice in Spanish Louisiana, 1770–1803. Ph.D. diss., Tulane Univ.
Kinnaird, Lawrence, ed. and trans.
1946–49 *Spain in the Mississippi Valley, 1765–1794.* 3 vols. of materials from the Spanish Archives. Washington, D.C.: United States Government Printing Office.
Le Page du Pratz, Antoine
1975 [1774] *The History of Louisiana,* ed. Joseph G. Tregle, Jr. Facsimile reproduction of 1774 edition. Baton Rouge: Louisiana State Univ. Press.
McCain, William D., ed.
1948 *Laws of the Mississippi Territory, May 27, 1800.* Beauvoir Community, Miss.: Book Farm.
McDermott, John Francis, ed.
1940 *Tixier's Travels on the Osage Prairies.* Norman: Univ. of Oklahoma Press.
McGowan, James Thomas
1976 Creation of a Slave Society: Louisiana Plantations in the Eighteenth Century. Ph.D. diss., Univ. of Rochester.
McMurtrie, Douglas C., ed.
1942 *Regulations to be Observed by the Syndic and Alcads of the Jurisdiction of Baton Rouge.* Evanston, Ill.: Printed privately.
Maduell, Charles R., ed.
1972 *The Census Tables for the French Colony of Louisiana from 1699 through 1732.* Baltimore: Genealogical Publishing Company.

Martin, François-Xavier, ed.
1816   *A General Digest of the Acts of the Legislatures of the Late Territory of Orleans and the State of Louisiana.* 3 vols. New Orleans: Peter K. Wagner.
Martin, Joel W.
1991   *Sacred Revolt: The Muskogees' Struggle for a New World.* Boston: Beacon Press.
Merrell, James H.
1984   The Racial Education of the Catawba Indians. *Journal of Southern History* 50 (3): 363–84.
1989   Some Thoughts on Colonial Historians and American Indians. *William and Mary Quarterly* 46 (1): 94–119.
Mississippi Provincial Archives
1927–32   *Mississippi Provincial Archives: French Dominion.* Vols. 1–3, ed. Dunbar Rowland and Albert Godfrey Sanders. Jackson: Mississippi Dept. of Archives and History.
1984   *Mississippi Provincial Archives: French Dominion.* Vols. 4–5, ed. Patricia Day Galloway. Baton Rouge: Louisiana State Univ. Press.
Northrup, Solomon
1968 [1853]   *Twelve Years a Slave,* ed. Sue Eakin and Joseph Logsdon. Baton Rouge: Louisiana State Univ. Press, 1968.
Olmsted, Frederick Law
1862   *The Cotton Kingdom.* 2 vols. New York: Mason Brothers.
Perdue, Theda
1979   *Slavery and the Evolution of Cherokee Society, 1540–1866.* Knoxville: Univ. of Tennessee Press.
Porter, Kenneth W.
1932   Relations between Negroes and Indians within the Present Limits of the United States. *Journal of Negro History* 17 (3): 287–367.
Posey, Darrell A.
1979   Origin, Development and Maintenance of a Louisiana Mixed-Blood Community: The Ethnohistory of the Freejacks of the First Ward Settlement. *Ethnohistory* 26 (2): 177–92.
Records and Deliberations of the New Orleans Cabildo, Louisiana Division, New Orleans Public Library.
Records of the Superior Council of Louisiana.
1918–39   French judicial records published intermittently in *Louisiana Historical Quarterly* 1: 109, 3: 414, 3: 443–44, 5: 466–77, 6: 283, 10: 258, 13: 309, 16: 334–35, 19: 768–71. Trans. Heloise H. Cruzat.
Saucier, Corinne
1943   *The History of Avoyelles Parish, Louisiana.* New Orleans: Pelican Publishing Company.
Thwaites, Reuben Gold, ed.
1896–1901   *The Jesuit Relations and Allied Documents.* 73 vols. Cleveland, Ohio: Burrows.
Usner, Daniel H., Jr.
1984   "Fragment of This Erratic Race": American Indians in Nineteenth-Century New Orleans. Paper read at American Society for Ethnohistory meeting in New Orleans.

1985   American Indians on the Cotton Frontier: Changing Economic Relations with Citizens and Slaves in the Mississippi Territory. *Journal of American History* 72 (2): 297–317.

1986   Food Marketing and Interethnic Exchange in the Eighteenth-Century Lower Mississippi Valley. *Food and Foodways* 1 (3): 279–310.

1989   American Indians in Colonial New Orleans. In *Powhatan's Mantle: Indians in the Colonial Southeast*, ed. Peter H. Wood, Gregory A. Waselkov, and M. Thomas Hatley, 104–27. Lincoln: Univ. of Nebraska Press.

1992   *Indians, Settlers, and Slaves in a Frontier Exchange Economy: The Lower Mississippi Valley before 1783.* Chapel Hill: Univ. of North Carolina Press, for the Institute of Early American History and Culture.

Woodson, Carter G.

1920   The Relations of Negroes and Indians in Massachusetts. *Journal of Negro History* 5 (1): 45–57.

Wright, J. Leitch, Jr.

1981   *The Only Land They Knew: The Tragic Story of the American Indians in the Old South.* New York: Free Press.

11 | Native American Tribes and Their African Slaves

Renate Bartl

One of the least discussed subjects in the voluminous literature on slavery in North America is the enslavement of African Americans by Native American tribes. For various reasons—some pertaining to scholarly neglect, others to the politically sensitive nature of the issue—this topic tends to arouse reactions of incredulity or denial. On a popular level, it is simply a non-issue. Just to mention a recent case, Ken Burns's television documentary series on the Civil War, broadcast in the United States in 1991, did not contain a single word on African slaves living among the Indians, or on Indian troops fighting on the side of the Confederacy.

Even among historians and anthropologists, the consensus seems to be that Native American slaveholding either was too marginal a phenomenon or is too controversial a subject to warrant exhaustive treatment. Specialized monographic treatments of the issue are few, and it hardly ever is discussed in general historiographies of slavery in North America.[1] Nonetheless, we cannot ignore the historical record: Native Americans did enslave black people and made them work for them.

Some initial clarification is in order here. In the literature on Native Americans, terms such as *slavery, slave, adoption,* or *prisoner* often are used interchangeably. Moreover, they tend to refer to social relations between individuals of different Native American tribes, as well as to those between Indian and non-Indian persons. Not uncommonly, one author speaks of an individual as the adoptee of an Indian tribe, while another author may classify the same individual's social status as that of a slave or prisoner. These terms express Euro-American conceptions applied to social institutions of Indian tribes, who often did not possess a word for *slave* in their own language. As Halliburton notes, "Though the Cherokees practiced slavery, there is no word for 'slave' or 'Negro' in their language. The closest word for slave is "ah-hutsi" which signifies "captive" and was used frequently in reference to Indian prisoners of war and black slaves" (Halliburton 1974/75: 483). All this makes it very difficult to determine the exact status of a person within a certain tribe, as is shown by the following example concerning the Mohawks of Ontario, Canada:

> The famous Mohawk, Captain Brant . . . is by some thought to have been a slaveholder. It was shown by reference to history and to enquiry now made of living descendants of Brant that such was not the case. He had large estates at Burlington Bay and on Grand River. Here many runaway negroes from the States had come, were treated hospitably, and remained working and living with the Indians, often adopting their customs and mode of living. (Hamilton 1889/90: 107)

There is no way to assess, on the basis of such statements, the freedom or unfreedom of the blacks working on Captain Brant's estates. But apart from the difficult question of what Brant himself may have thought about his relation to these people, whether or not an Indian tribe is classified as slaveholding obviously depends, to some degree, on the viewpoint and bias of the classifier. Furthermore, not all Native American tribes practiced the enslavement or adoption of Indian and/or non-Indian persons. Among those tribes that did, the forms of enslavement, adoption, or holding of prisoners were very diverse and differed from one tribe or band to another.[2]

Rather than surveying Native American slaveholding in general, the present article is concerned with the enslavement of African Americans by Native American groups who assimilated the model of the Euro-American plantation economy, including the exploitation of unfree black labor.[3]

It is often thought that conditions of slavery under Indians usually were not as onerous as those under whites and that the African slaves preferred Indians as owners. This assumption, however, is disputable. A popular account thus claims, in relation to the Five Civilized Tribes:

> Most observers found that the chains of slavery were fitted rather loosely on black people owned by Indians. Only the Chickasaws had a reputation for treating their slaves as badly as did white masters. The other na-

tions practiced such a mild form of bondage that it upset U.S. slave owners. The Seminoles . . . infuriated white and Indian masters with their gen-
erosity, fairness, and a level of equality towards their "slaves." . . . Whites
who visited slaveholding Indians described slave men and women who
were well-treated, adequately fed and cared for. (Katz 1985: 136)

Here, the Chickasaws are characterized negatively as "tough slaveholders,"
while Seminole slaveholding is described in a more positive manner. Such
impressionistic generalizations about this or that tribe abound in the literature. Unless qualified aggregate data are available, however, such
generalizations are dangerous, for extrapolations from single known
cases where individual slaveholders within certain tribes treated their
slaves more or less well cannot be applied to the whole tribe without reflection. Compare, for instance, Halliburton's view of Indian slaveholding with Katz's statement quoted above:

It is often alleged that the lives of Black slaves owned by the Cherokees
were considerably easier than those owned by White masters. Moreover,
it has frequently been reported that the Indians regarded the Black as a
fellow human being; that the slave enjoyed much more "freedom" and
that intermarriage was not uncommon. There appears to be little evidence to support such conclusions. (Halliburton 1975: 23)

Indeed, closer scrutiny of the sources reveals that, more often then not,
what is paraded as historical fact actually is rash generalization from
meager data, unqualified assertion, or sheer preconception.

The enslavement of African Americans by Indian tribes was not confined to the southern states, as one would expect. In 1765, Lt. Alexander
Fraser—a decidedly prejudiced observer—wrote about the Illinois Indians
living in Illinois: "They have a great many Negroes, who are obliged to labor very hard to support their masters in their extravagant debauchery"
(cited in Dillard 1972: 170). But the South was the area where Indian tribes
practiced the enslavement of African Americans on a larger scale. An
anonymous 1859 article reports: "The four leading tribes now located in
our Southwestern region—the Cherokees, Choctaws, Creeks, and Chickasaws—had adopted slavery on a large scale, and . . . it also prevailed to
some extent among the Shawnees and Delawares" (C. [pseud.] 1859: 333).

Many reasons could be adduced to explain why southern Indian
tribes adopted African slavery. It may be that adopting the southern plantation economy and enslaving blacks made the surrounding white southern society view Indians as "civilized." Especially in the eastern and south-

eastern states of the United States, those Indian groups who selectively bor-
rowed aspects of southern culture and consequently came to be labeled
"civilized" had significantly better chances of surviving than others. Slaveholding Indians no longer seemed dangerous to southern society, because
they were no longer seen as attractive to runaway slaves; this fact diminished the likelihood that these tribes would be persecuted and extinguished.

That the Cherokee, Chickasaw, Choctaw, Creek, and Seminole
were called "The Five Civilized Tribes" was only partly because they
had developed their own writing system or invented legal codes very
close to white legal codes. A more important reason was that they had
copied the social system of the South and had introduced elements of the
southern plantation economy and African slavery into their tribes: "Civilization among the Indians was the result of their adoption of negro slavery"
(C. [pseud.] 1859: 333).

As mentioned above, slavery was not unknown in some North American Indian tribes before the arrival of the first Europeans. Of the pre-
Columbian situation of the Cherokee, Halliburton writes:

> Apparently the slaves were usually prisoners taken in wars with other tribes
> and there appears to have been a regular commercial traffic in slaves in some
> areas. In addition, among some Indians, slavery was the basis of consider-
> able wealth. As a result, raiding expeditions were sometimes launched for
> the express purpose of capturing slaves. . . . Nonetheless slavery, as the term
> is usually understood today, probably did not exist among the Cherokees
> before the arrival of the Europeans. (Halliburton 1974/75: 484)

Thus African slavery was grafted onto pre-existing forms of institutionalized unfreedom. This might explain why the Cherokees "exhibited no
moral bias against slavery and were quick to accept numerous accoutre-
ments of European Civilization—including the institution of black slavery"
(Halliburton 1974/75: 486). Additionally, Cherokee women appear immediately to hàve approved of the enslavement of blacks, because it lightened
their traditional role in agricultural production (Halliburton 1974/75: 486).
Step by step, the Cherokees' value system changed: "The example of white
plantation owners in the surrounding colonies gradually induced many progressive Cherokees to view the planter as an occupation worthy of honor
and refinement" (Halliburton 1974/75: 486). The steady flow of new
settlers into the area of the Cherokee Nation, causing the gradual loss
of Cherokee lands, finally transformed their social and economic system from a semi-nomadic to a sedentary and agrarian one. Halliburton
describes the ensuing development:

Slowly abandoning the communal cultivation of land, they began to operate their farms on an individual basis. Black slavery both contributed to and made possible such change. So much that by 1790, the institution had spread throughout the Cherokee Nation. Some full-scale Southern-type Cherokee plantations existed in northern Georgia by the end of the eighteenth century. . . . Most of the well-known Cherokees were becoming slaveowners. (Halliburton 1974/75: 489)

A further effect of this development was that slaveholding divided each of the Five Civilized Tribes into a wealthy slaveholding minority and a poorer non-slaveholding majority. The slaveholding Indians within these tribes were predominantly *mixed-bloods* with some white ancestry, while the *full-bloods* usually formed the non-slaveholding part. This finally engendered a racial ideology in parts of these nations, resembling that prevalent in the white South (Katz 1985: 135–38). In addition, slaveholding threw the whole social ranking and prestige system within these ranking societies into disorder. This is shown by the following example. Around 1825, the Creek chief William McIntosh, a mixed-blood cousin of the governor of Georgia, owned some 120 black slaves. At the same time, the higher-ranking Tustunugge Hopoi, a full-blood Creek, had only six black slaves (Feest 1976: 285). Examples such as this make clear that the invention of black slavery affected the social system of these tribes to a high degree.

As mentioned above, plantation slavery emerged among the Cherokee in the late eighteenth century. Cherokee plantations were established on Cherokee land in Georgia and Tennessee. In 1811, 12,395 Cherokees, 341 whites, and 583 black slaves were counted in Cherokee country (Halliburton 1974/75: 490–93). By 1835, 209 Cherokees owned almost 1,600 slaves (Perdue 1982: 322). In the year 1819, the Cherokee Nation began to pass slave codes. While in the beginning these slave codes regulated only the slave trade within the nation, they became more inclusive and severe over the course of time. Eventually, intermarriage between black slaves and Indians or whites came to be forbidden, as was ownership of private property by slaves. The codes also imposed punishment upon runaway slaves. Similar slave codes were enacted by the Choctaw, Chickasaw, and Creek Nations (McLoughlin 1974: 381; Littlefield and Underhill 1977: 124).

The need for more farmland in the states east of the Mississippi urged the United States government in 1830 to pass the Indian Removal Act, which ordered the deportation of all Indian tribes living east of the Mississippi to the Indian Territory west of the Mississippi (today's Kansas-Oklahoma area). The Choctaws were deported in 1832, the Cherokees in the years 1835–39. On the whole, some 60,000 Native Americans and African Americans were deported from the east to the Indian Territory after 1830 (Katz 1985: 136–38). The Indian Removal Act effected enormous changes in the lives of the deported tribes. Not only were they expelled from an agricultural area with fertile soil into a wilderness area, but also they incurred heavy population loss:

> Between 1830 and 1860 the population of the Four Nations declined sharply, Cherokees by 31 percent, Choctaws by 27 percent, Chickasaws by 18 percent, and Creeks by 43 percent. At the same time the number of members of white blood increased and so too did the number of slaves each nation held. By 1860 Cherokees had 2,511 slaves, Choctaws 2,344, Creeks 1,532, and Chickasaws 975. (Katz 1985: 138)

Nonetheless, with the help of their black slaves, the deported slaveholders were very quick to clear the land and establish plantations as soon as they arrived in the Indian Territory. The Cherokees began to reinstate the slave codes that had existed before removal and passed further restrictions on their slaves (Littlefield and Underhill 1977: 125).

The whole situation seems to have become worse for the black slaves of the Indians after the deportation: "We . . . find scattered accounts which tell of Indian slaveowners who whipped, maimed, hung and burned slaves as late as the 1850s in the Indian Territory (now Oklahoma)" (McLoughlin 1974: 368). Such behavior and the enforcement of the Indian slave codes seem to have been the reasons for the Cherokee slave revolt of 1842. In November 1842, a number of Cherokee slaves left their plantations near Webbers Falls, Indian Territory, and headed southwest, presumably toward the Mexican territory. During their flight they were joined by a few Creek slaves, making a total of some thirty-five persons. Members of the Cherokee and Creek nations pursued the runaway slaves and a few days later caught twelve of the slaves and killed two others. The rest of the group was able to flee again. This group later was joined by eight Choctaw slaves. At the end of November 1842, these runaway slaves were finally caught by Cherokee and Creek slave-hunters and brought back to their masters. During the 1840s, several further cases of runaway slaves were reported in Indian Territory. By 1851, nearly three hundred blacks had tried to escape from there; some had succeeded and made it to the Mexican territory (Littlefield and Underhill 1977).

The situation of the African Americans among the Seminole Indi-

ans of Florida differed considerably from the lot of those living among
other southern tribes. The Spanish colony Florida always had been very
attractive to African slaves from Alabama, Georgia, and the states farther north, because its dense and nearly impassable forests and swamps offered perfect hiding places for runaway slaves. In addition, Spanish laws
were more lenient concerning race, miscegenation, and slavery than those
of the British colonies or, later, the United States. The Seminoles, a conglomerate of different tribes and bands, immigrated from Georgia into
Florida around 1750, at the time when the first maroons established
their settlements in Florida.[4]

The Africans fleeing into Florida mainly sought protection against
slave-hunters from the North, who tried to bring them back to their
masters. The Seminole blacks lived in their own villages, were protected
by the Seminoles, and got land for agriculture from them. In return,
they paid tribute to the Indians by delivering parts of their harvest, and
they fought on their side in the three Seminole Wars. The Seminoles
alone among the Five Civilized Tribes rejected large-scale slaveholding,
although some of the Seminoles owned slaves and made them work in
their fields. In 1843, after the Second Seminole War, a large part of the
Seminoles and their blacks had to leave Florida and move to the Indian
Territory (Katz 1985: 69). Here the Seminole blacks were still able to
retain their relatively free status as friends and allies of the Seminoles
and settled down in their own villages.

Within the Indian Territory, the United States government had
tried to resettle most of the southern slaveholding tribes south of the
Missouri Compromise line and northern tribes north of this line. Even
so, slaveholding was allowed in the whole Indian Territory:

> Within the Indian country, . . . slavery was allowed, at least on suffer-
> ance, both north and south of the interdicted line. It was even encour-
> aged by many white men who made their homes or their living there, by
> interlopers, licensed traders, and missionaries; but it flourished as a le-
> gitimate institution only among the great tribes planted south of the line.
> (Abel 1915–25: vol. 1, p. 22)

The situation of the free blacks and half-breeds living in Indian Territory differed from that of the black slaves there:

> Among the Creeks and the Seminoles, the status of the free negro was
> exceptionally high, partly due, with respect to the latter, to conditions
> growing out of the Second Seminole War. . . . the Creeks had no aver-

sion whatsoever to race mixtures, and intermarriage between negroes and Indians was rather common. The half-breeds resulting from such unions were accepted as bona fide members of the tribe by the Indians in the distribution of annuities, but not by the United States courts—another source of difficulty and a very instructive one as well, particularly from the standpoint of reconstructionist exactions. (Abel 1915–25: vol. 1, p. 23, n. 14)

With the outbreak of the Civil War, many tribes in Indian Territory chose to affiliate with the Confederacy. One reason for this surely was that, while the United States government had promised the deported tribes that they would always be protected on Indian Territory by government troops, at no time had the army been able to keep this promise. The government had deported the tribes and had left them alone, hoping they would remain neutral. Of this false assessment of the situation by the United States government, Abel writes:

They were slaveholding tribes . . . yet were supposed by the United States government to have no interest whatsoever in a sectional conflict that involved the very existence of the "peculiar institution." Thus the federal government left them to themselves at the critical moment and left them, moreover, at the mercy of the South, and then was indignant that they betrayed a sectional affiliation. (Abel 1915–25: vol. 1, p. 14)

In addition, many of the federal Indian agents supervising the reservations and other people living on and around Indian lands in the South at that time were southern-born slaveholders and proslavery advocates, who influenced the Indians according to their interests (McLoughlin 1974: 375; Abel 1915–25: vol. 1, p. 22).

The Confederacy very early realized the huge potential, in population and land, of the southern tribes living in Indian Territory. It tried to win them as allies and partners in the establishment of the independent Confederate States. In 1861, the Confederacy negotiated nine treaties with the Creeks, Choctaws, Chickasaws, Seminoles, Cherokees, Osages, Senecas, Shawnees, Quapaws, Wichitas, Comanches, and some smaller tribes. The treaties guaranteed to these nations territorial and political integrity, representation by delegates in the Confederate Congress, and a prospect of ultimate statehood in the Confederate States. Such treatment differed markedly from the experience these tribes had had with the United States government. The latter seemed to regard the Indians more as transportable goods than as human beings, had deported them by force from their fertile plantations in the east to the western wilderness, and always had looked upon them as wards or enemies, never as citizens of the United States. In contrast, the Confederacy treated them as independent nations and offered them citizenship and statehood, as the example of the Choctaw and Chickasaw Treaty of 1861 shows:

> ARTICLE XXVIII. In consideration of the uniform loyalty and good faith, and the tried friendship for the people of the Confederate States, of the Choctaw and Chickasaw people, . . . it is hereby agreed by the Confederate States, that whenever and so soon as the people of each nation shall . . . declare its desire to become a State of the Confederacy, the whole Choctaw and Chickasaw country . . . shall be received and admitted into the Confederacy as one of the Confederate States, on equal terms, in all respects, with the original States, without regard to population; and all the members of the Choctaw and Chickasaw Nations shall thereby become citizens of the Confederate States (Confederate Statutes/Official Records, 4th ser., vol. 1; cited in Abel 1915–25: vol. 1, p. 160, n. 265)

It has to be noted here that, at the time these treaties were signed, the Africans slaves living among these tribes were not enrolled members of the tribes and therefore would not have become citizens of the Confederate States, had a tribe decided to join the Confederacy.

The signing of these treaties caused the Native American tribes to split into secessionist and non-secessionist factions, the former consisting mainly of slaveholding mixed-bloods, the latter of non-slaveholding full-bloods and African slaves and free blacks living among the Indians (Abel 1915–25: vol. 1, pp. 157ff. and 216; Katz 1985: 142–43). This social division conditioned their involvement in the Civil War: "Indians fought on both sides in the great sectional struggle, . . . they were moved to fight, not by instincts of savagery, but by identically the same motives and impulses as the white men, and that, in the final outcome, they suffered even more terribly than did the whites" (Abel 1915–25: vol. 1, p. 17).

In the end, the Indians lost greatly in this war. Defeated by the North, all Indian tribes that had signed treaties with the Confederate States lost their right to federal aid and protection by the United States, as well as the title to their land. After the Civil War, in 1866, they had to sign treaties with the United States government bringing the Five Civilized Tribes back into the Union. The Cherokees had freed their slaves voluntarily in 1863. The treaties with the remaining four tribes abolished slavery and emancipated the African Americans living among them (Abel 1915–25: vol. 3, p. 187ff.; Andrews 1965: 367–68).

But what to do with the freedmen who now were in Indian Territory? This problem caused these tribes many difficulties all during Reconstruction. The treaties left open several possibilities:

> Freedmen were either to be admitted to citizenship or to be "given compensation in the form of separate lands." The Seminole, Creek and Cherokee treaties conferred directly upon their former slaves all the "rights and privileges of native citizenship." The Choctaw and Chickasaw treaty, however, provided those two nations with an alternative: a choice between adopting the freedmen as citizens or having them removed by the United States. (Andrews 1965: 368)

After the war, the federal government had trouble enforcing these treaties, including full enrollment of the African Americans in the Indian tribes. Some tribes were willing to emancipate their black slaves but did not want them as full members of their tribes. They were, with some justification, afraid of someday being classified as colored and consequently of losing their status as an Indian tribe, along with the titles to their reservations.

The Chickasaw and Choctaw cases especially were resolved only after a long and wearisome process. From the beginning, the Chickasaw and Choctaw tribes wanted to be relieved of their freedmen; and their freedmen several times petitioned Congress to be removed from these nations. Congress, for unknown reasons, ignored these requests and petitions and remained silent on this problem. In 1869, the freedmen changed their minds and wished to remain in the Choctaw and Chickasaw Nations permanently. The freedmen in the Indian Territory—like the Indians—were under the direct protection of the federal government; they would have lost this status by removal from the territory. It was not before 1882 that Congress started to resolve the issue. After passing the "Indian Appropriation Act," which guaranteed both nations the payment of a huge sum of money if they should adopt their freedmen, the Choctaw Nation reacted and enrolled their freedmen as members of their tribe in 1883. In the case of the Chickasaw Nation, the matter was not settled before 1894 (Andrews 1965, James 1967).

As these examples demonstrate, the history of the African Americans living among Native American tribes is a long and complicated one that still awaits adequate scholarly treatment. In many publications on southern Indian tribes and on southern history in general, this subject is—almost studiously—avoided. Yet, in my opinion, the history of the South—and of the African Americans and Native Americans living there—cannot be fully appreciated as long as we keep silent on this topic.

Notes

The research for this article was made possible in part by a 1991 fellowship from the German Marshall Fund of the United States, for study in the United States (Grant No. RG 8-90588-07).

    1. Here it is appropriate to mention some scholars whose research has focused on African slavery among Indian tribes. Annie Heloise Abel published the first comprehensive description of the enslavement of African Americans by Indian tribes, in a three-volume work entitled *Slaveholding Indians* (1915–25). The first two volumes were reprinted in 1992 (Abel 1992a [1915], 1992b [1919]).

    Kenneth Wiggins Porter supplied us with a large number of publications on the situation of African Americans living among the Seminoles (e.g., Porter 1932, 1933, 1941, 1943a, 1943b, 1945, 1946a, 1946b, 1951a, 1951b, 1956, 1964). Many of Porter's original field notes and manuscripts are housed in the archive of the Schomburg Center, New York, and have been used by many scholars for their publications. It must be noted that Porter used sources such as military papers, diaries, official statements, etc., written by soldiers, politicians, and other persons involved in the war against the Seminoles and their blacks. Usually these sources were biased, tending to exaggerate the number and strength of the enemy. In the case of the Seminoles of Florida and their blacks here—who fought in three wars against the U.S. Army—they surely falsify and exaggerate the strength, interaction, and relations of the Seminoles and the blacks in Florida. Southern white society feared nothing more than an alliance between Indians and blacks against whites (see Willis 1963), and this fear of Indian-black alliances often was used by the military for its own ends—for example, to justify the invasion of Florida or to secure financial aid and moral support in fighting the Indians. One must, then, be very cautious in evaluating and using Porter's statements and papers.

    Daniel Littlefield wrote on the situation of African slaves and freedmen among the Seminoles, Cherokees, Creeks, and Chickasaws (Littlefield 1977, 1978, 1979, 1980; Littlefield and Underhill 1977). Finally, Theda Perdue (1979a, 1979b, 1982, 1988) specialized in the Cherokees, as did many other researchers (e.g., Halliburton 1974–75, 1975, 1977; Roethler 1964; and Griffin n.d.).

    Literature marked by obvious racism has not been used for this article, because its truthfulness is highly questionable. A great number of publications contain such statements as the following one on the Indians of Texas: "Some were possessed of money . . . and had purchased Negro slaves for working their farms, for even the half-civilised Indians have a rooted aversion from manual labour. . . . The possession of Negroes, by rendering the Indians idle and dependent on slave-labour, has confirmed the defects of their character" (Kennedy 1974 [1841]: 337 and 337n.) For obvious reasons, such literature has been neglected, except for illustrative purposes.

2. Many North American Indian tribes were familiar with the possession of "human property" before the arrival of the Europeans. War captives could be adopted or enslaved, and individuals could lose the rights in their person to another person by gambling. Especially the ranking societies of the Northwest Coast and the Southeast had developed economic and social systems based on acquisition of property, including "human property." Within these systems, however, slaves raised their master's prestige predominantly by their mere existence and number—not by their labor. Moreover, most of these Indian slaves were kept in an unfree status only for a limited period of time and afterwards were released (Feest 1976: 286). For literature on the forms of adoption and slavery among Indian tribes, see the respective subjects or index entries in Hodge (1975 [1907–10]) and Trigger (1978–).

3. In this regard, the involvement of eastern Indians in the slave trade and the hunting and catching of black slaves might be of some interest. From the beginning, eastern Indians were involved to a large degree in slavetrading and slavecatching businesses. Of the Indians of South Carolina, the following is reported: "Indians were excellent slave catchers. The Settlement Indians in particular were regularly employed to track down fugitive slaves, indeed, slave catching was so profitable to them that they readily agreed in 1727 to move their villages so that they could do a better job" (Willis 1963: 163). For each slave brought in, an Indian slave-catcher usually got paid in money or goods that amounted, e.g., to the value of a certain number of deerskins, which would have required several months of hunting to amass (Willis 1963: 168).

Moreover, eastern Indians had developed a well-organized network for trading black slaves within their tribes and to white slaveholders. On the frontier, slavetrading was a lucrative business: "In time, this trade became well organized. Negroes were stolen from one part of the Indian frontier and carried into the Indian country and there traded about among Indians, and between Indians and Whites, until they ended up in slavery on another part of the Indian frontier. Indians had little trouble selling these Negroes. Whites in the frontier settlements never had enough slaves. Moreover, law enforcement was lax. . . . This trade extended outside the South. The Cherokees sold Negroes north of the Ohio River, and Shawnee traders came from the North into the Creek country to buy Negroes" (Willis 1963: 172–73).

4. Information on maroons and their settlements and alliances with Native Americans can be found in Aptheker (1939) and Price (1979 [1973]).

References

Abel, Annie Heloise
1915–25   *Slaveholding Indians.* 3 vols. Cleveland: Arthur H. Clark.
1992a [1915]   *The American Indian as Slaveholder and Secessionist.* Rpt. of *Slaveholding Indians,* vol. 1. Lincoln: Univ. of Nebraska Press.
1992b [1919]   *The American Indian as Slaveholder and Secessionist.* Rpt. of *Slaveholding Indians,* vol. 2. Lincoln: Univ. of Nebraska Press.
Andrews, Thomas F.
1965   Freedmen in Indian Territory: A Post–Civil War Dilemma. *Journal of the West* 4 (3): 367–76.

Aptheker, Herbert
1939   Maroons within the Present Limits of the United States. *Journal of Negro History* 24 (2): 167–84. Rpt. in *Maroon Societies,* ed. Richard Price, 151–67. Baltimore, Md.: Johns Hopkins Univ. Press, 1979 [1973].
Bartl, Renate
1986   Die Beziehungen zwischen Schwarzen und Indianern in Nordamerika. Master's thesis, Dept. of American Cultural History, Univ. of Munich, Germany.
C. [pseudonym]
1859   Slavery among the Indians. *Southern Literary Messenger* 28: 333–35.
Dillard, Joey Lee
1972   *Black English.* New York: Random House.
Feest, Christian.
1976   *Das rote Amerika: Nordamerikas Indianer.* Vienna: Europaverlag.
Griffin, Larry D.
n.d.   Black Slaves in the Cherokee Nation. Manuscript in Cherokee Nation Collection, John Vaughn Library, Northeastern State College, Tahlequah, Okla.
Halliburton, Richard, Jr.
1974/75   Origins of Black Slavery among the Cherokees. *Chronicles of Oklahoma* 52: 483–96.
1975   Black Slave Control in the Cherokee Nation. *Journal of Ethnic Studies* 3 (2): 23–35.
1977   *Red Over Black: Black Slavery Among the Cherokee Indians.* Westport, Conn.: Greenwood Press.
Hamilton, J. C.
1889/90   Slavery in Canada. *Transactions of the Royal Canadian Institute* 1: 102–8.
Hodge, Frederick Webb
1975 [1907–10]   *Handbook of American Indians North of Mexico.* 2 vols. Washington, D.C.: U.S. Govt. Printing Office.
James, Parthena Louise
1967   Reconstruction in the Chickasaw Nation: The Freedman Problem. *Chronicles of Oklahoma* 45 (1): 44–57.
Katz, William Loren
1985   *Black Indians: A Hidden Heritage.* New York: Atheneum.
Kennedy, William
1974 [1841]   *Texas: The Rise, Progress and Prospects of the Republic of Texas.* Book 2. Clifton, N.J.: Kelley.
Littlefield, Daniel F., Jr.
1977   *Africans and Seminoles: From Removal to Emancipation.* Westport, Conn.: Greenwood Press.
1978   *The Cherokee Freedmen.* Westport, Conn.: Greenwood Press.
1979   *Africans and Creeks: From the Colonial Period to the Civil War.* Westport, Conn.: Greenwood Press.
1980   *The Chickasaw Freedmen.* Westport, Conn.: Greenwood Press.
Littlefield, Daniel F., Jr., and Lonnie E. Underhill
1977   Slave "Revolt" in the Cherokee Nation, 1842. *American Indian Quarterly* 3: 121–31.

McLoughlin, William G.
1974   Red Indians, Black Slavery and White Racism: America's Slaveholding Indians. *American Quarterly* 26: 367–85.
Perdue, Theda
1979a *Slavery and the Evolution of Cherokee Society, 1540–1866.* Knoxville: Univ. of Tennessee Press.
1979b Cherokee Planters: The Development of Plantation Slavery Before Removal. In *The Cherokee Indian Nation: A Troubled History,* ed. Duane King, 110–28. Knoxville: Univ. of Tennessee Press.
1982   Cherokee Planters, Black Slaves, and African Colonization. *Chronicles of Oklahoma* 60 (3): 322–31.
1988   *The Cherokee.* New York: Chelsea House.
Porter, Kenneth Wiggins
1932   Relations Between Negroes and Indians within the Present Limits of the United States. *Journal of Negro History* 17: 287–367.
1933   Notes Supplementary to Relations between the Negro and Indian Within the Present Limits of the United States. *Journal of Negro History* 18: 282–321.
1941   Abraham. *Phylon* 2 (2): 105–16.
1943a Three Fighters for Freedom. *Journal of Negro History* 28: 51–72.
1943b Florida Slaves and Free Negroes in the Seminole War, 1835–1842. *Journal of Negro History* 28: 390–421.
1945   Negroes and the East Florida Annexation Plot. *Journal of Negro History* 30: 9–29.
1946a John Caesar: Seminole Negro Partisan. *Journal of Negro History* 31: 190–207.
1946b Negroes on the Southern Frontier, 1670–1763. *Journal of Negro History* 33: 53–78.
1951a Negroes and the Seminole War, 1817–1818. *Journal of Negro History* 36: 249–80.
1951b The Seminole in Mexico, 1850–1861. *Hispanic American Historical Review* 31: 1–36.
1956   Negroes and Indians on the Texas Frontier. *Journal of Negro History* 41 (3): 185–214; and (4): 285–310.
1964   Negroes and the Seminole War, 1835–1842. *Journal of the Southern History* 30 (4): 427–50.
Price, Richard, ed.
1979 [1973]   *Maroon Societies.* Baltimore, Md.: Johns Hopkins Univ. Press.
Roethler, Michael
1964   Negro Slavery among the Cherokee Indians, 1540–1866. Ph.D. diss., Fordham Univ., New York.
Trigger, Bruce G., ed.
1978– *Handbook of North American Indians.* 20 vols. Washington, DC: Smithsonian Institution.
Willis, William S.
1963   Divide and Rule: Red, White, and Black in the Southeast. *Journal of Negro History* 48 (3): 157–76.

12 | Theft, Moral Economy, and the Transition from Slavery to Freedom in the American South

Alex Lichtenstein

Several years ago, in an article on slave crime (Lichtenstein 1988), I took issue with Eugene Genovese's contention that slaves' defense of theft "could not arise simply as an alternative morality," since stealing necessarily contributed to African-American self-contempt. I argued, to the contrary, that when slaves stole from slaveowners, they engaged in an act of resistance rooted in what I (following E. P. Thompson and other historians of eighteenth-century Britain) called a moral economy that did indeed pose an alternative view of property relations. This moral economy helped, in the words of James Scott, to "mitigate or defeat appropriation" within the plantation economy (Genovese 1974: 608, Scott 1986: 18–19); it took on special significance when petty pilfering led slaves to the market, where they could participate in autonomous exchange relations beyond the ambit of their masters' control.[1]

Since the appearance of this article on slave theft and moral economy, I have pursued the history of southern punishment rather than crime, by examining the history of the convict lease system in the New South. Here, however, I return to the questions posed in that article, assessing the "supply side" of the postbellum criminal justice system, as it were; weighing my conclusions against recent challenges; and, most significantly, considering how the idea of a moral economy of theft may apply in the postbellum period in the South.

How relevant, in fact, is the concept of a "moral economy" in studying the postbellum era? First, the usefulness of such a concept tends to be inversely proportional to the breadth of its applicability. Thus, if African-American slaves, eighteenth-century British poachers, nineteenth-century London dock workers, twentieth-century Southeast Asian peasants, African diamond miners, Atlantic pirates, South Carolina Sea Island freedpeople, and modern factory workers all are moral economists in the eyes of historians, then who isn't?

Second, it may be that Genovese's cautionary remarks were particularly relevant in the context of the new responsibilities and struggles of a free people whose solidarity and moral fortitude were their greatest assets. He himself notes that "evidence of blacks' stealing from blacks after the war suggests that for too many it had become a way of life."

Third, given the ravages suffered by contemporary African-American communities beset by crime, would not a sympathetic account of postbellum criminality be arrogant, insensitive, and perhaps even "politically incorrect"? A study of postbellum crime cannot be detached from such considerations, since the current problems of the so-called underclass increasingly are being linked to the transmission of a culture of poverty rooted in southern sharecropping. Perhaps Robert Paquette's admonition that "to succeed, oppressed peoples, unlike some social historians, can ill afford to misconstrue license as moral economy" applies especially in the case of the freedpeople (Genovese 1974: 607, Naison 1992, Lemann 1991, Paquette 1991: 684).

Perhaps. But after reviewing some of the most compelling literature on the postbellum rural social order (particularly Joseph Reidy's recent book *From Slavery to Agrarian Capitalism in the Cotton Plantation South* (1992), and the works of Jonathan Wiener, Steven Hahn, and Eric Foner) and after looking for evidence in postbellum prosecutions of petty crime, I think a strong case can be made for the following proposition: the dynamic interaction between postbellum changes in legal definitions of agrarian property rights, on the one hand, and violations of criminal law by rural freedpeople, on the other, made petty theft an absolutely *classic* example of moral economy, narrowly defined. Moreover, what postbellum planters regarded as the unbreakable habit of pilfering carried over from slavery was, for black plantation workers, a distinctive tool of resistance to sharecropping and other inequitable forms of postbellum land tenure and labor.

I began a consideration of the new conflicts engendered by emancipation with a revealing piece of "folklore" offered by a man who had experienced the transition to freedom firsthand. This former slave told a Works Progress Administration (WPA) interviewer in the 1930s that, when he was freed, "I figguered [*sic*], like de balance of 'em, dat ole

massa wus jes' tryin' to get outen feedin' us." As a result, he continued
to help himself, as he thought was his right, to his master's corn crib
and potato kiln—"collectin'," as he put it. His master asked him to do
some plow work, offering to pay him in corn and potatoes, but he of course
refused, continuing his "collectin'." One night, however, the freedman put
his hand in the corn crib and was caught in a raccoon trap his former master had placed there. In the morning the planter arrived and said, "I is
free too." He stated that he was no longer obligated to feed his former
slave, so the latter should "start plowing, or I'll land you in de chain
gang fur stealin', or set the Ku Klux on you."

"Dat's how come I ain't stole f'om dat day to this un," concluded
the ex-slave's narrative. The interviewer comments that this "folktale"
actually is true, "except the last sentence. He still 'collects'" (Rawick
1977: vi, 1, MS: 2).

This narrative initially caught my attention because it clearly illustrates the continuity of theft as a crucial issue in defining property relationships between whites and blacks in the plantation South, even after emancipation. The laborer's sense of customary right, the refusal to surrender
this right to a more formalized exchange relation, and the planter's recourse
to both legal and extralegal coercion all are reminiscent of the dialectic
of moral economy and the law characteristic of similar struggles under
slavery. Yet it is also clear that the rules of the game of crime and punishment have been dramatically transformed by freedom: both moral
economy and the law functioned quite differently when slave and master contested property rights as juridically free individuals—the one
freed from servitude, the other from obligations.

Here, in a nutshell, is the dynamic of petty theft, as transformed by
the transition from slavery to agrarian capitalism and by the spread of
capitalist social relations across the rural South in the wake of emancipation. From this perspective, theft looks more than ever like moral
economy. Used properly, the term "moral economy" takes on historical
specificity within the context of *reconfigurations* of property rights. In
essence, new forms of appropriation and accumulation (the exploitation
of a dispossessed labor force, for example) are coupled with the en-
croachment of private forms of ownership on common right (enclosure,
for example). Consequently the scope of criminal law is expanded to
encompass economic activities that previously had been staked out beyond the reach of employers, landowners, slaveholders. In this regard
we are struck by the similarities between the eighteenth-century "social
crime" that accompanied the advent of capitalist social relations in Britain—so well documented in *Albion's Fatal Tree* (Hay et al. 1975) and

Whigs and Hunters (Thompson 1975)—and the new forms of struggle against expropriation available to the freedpeople.

While little agreement exists concerning the degree to which postbellum agricultural workers possessed labor mobility, it is clear that, as in all postemancipation societies, southern planters sought to deny former slaves access to any form of subsistence save plantation labor. The freedpeople in turn sought to accumulate enough property to achieve a modicum of independence from whites, either by renting or, preferably, by purchasing land. In their effort to create a rural proletariat, southern landowners used the criminal law to redefine the region's property relations. The work of Foner, Wiener, and Hahn demonstrates that the planters launched a "concerted legal offensive," in which "what had been 'rights' [under slavery] were now defined as crimes." Legal disputes over fence and game laws expressed class and racial conflicts over access to the means of subsistence, no longer "owed" to slaves by their masters. Freed blacks still insisted on their customary rights—often secured under slavery—to graze livestock on unfenced land, to forage for wood, and to hunt and fish where and when they pleased. After emancipation, white landowners attempted to erode these rights by using the law to redefine notions of common property in their own favor, making stock owners responsible for fencing and securing their land against the now "trespassing" hunters and fisherman. By depriving blacks of an alternative means of subsistence, such a strategy was designed to force free blacks into labor dependency on their former masters (Cohen 1991; Wiener 1978: 69–73; Foner 1983: 57–65; Hahn 1982; Reidy 1992: 222–27).

Radical Reconstruction blunted these efforts, to be sure, but, as Joseph Reidy notes, when Democrats regained control of southern legislatures, they modified "the criminal law to make plantation workers inordinately susceptible to arrest, conviction, and a prison sentence" (Reidy 1992: 222).[2] Moreover, as the definition of criminal trespass expanded considerably, the rights of sharecroppers to control and dispose of crops narrowed. The sharecropper "only has a right to go on the land to plant, work, and gather the crop. . . . The case of the cropper is rather a mode of paying wages than a tenancy," declared Georgia's Supreme Court in 1872, the year the state was "Redeemed" by Democrats; most other southern states enacted similar post-Reconstruction judicial definitions of sharecropping.[3] Presumably this meant that the customary "right" of provision grounds, developed under slavery, remained at the planter's discretion. Certainly it meant that "the cropper's share of the crop is not his until he has complied with his bargain,"[4] so that all his exchange relations were effectively tied to his landlord and he relinquished any ownership of the crop. Such interpretations stood in marked contrast to the control over shared crops that freedpeople had carved out during Reconstruction, control that, after Redemption, could be reclaimed only by criminal action (Jaynes 1986: 141–57, Woodman 1979).

Reidy remarks, however, that, if the goal of planters was to use the law to "reduce tenants into agricultural proletarians," the freedpeople were "proletarians who resisted the full implications of proletarianization" (Reidy 1992: 12–13). This resistance can be found in black workers' persistent attempts to subsist without plantation work: through casual labor, hunting, fishing, provision grounds—in short, by a retreat to peasantry. In the South Carolina Sea Islands, this largely successful withdrawal from production constituted a moral economy, one historian has argued (Strickland 1985). In the examples that follow, it appears that theft and pilfering perhaps can be understood similarly, as resistance to proletarianization through *retreat* from the market. The moral economy of crime takes on added significance, I think, when it entails an *engagement* with the market, and the economic autonomy such engagement might confer—as I argued it did under slavery as well. Sharecroppers chose to commit criminal trespass or petty larceny, in order to dispose of what they saw as their share of the crop without the landlord's interference.

Southern historians have paid a great deal of attention to transformations in the law but far too little to the persistent willingness of blacks to violate new criminal laws, even in the face of draconian penalties. Many whites insisted that this was only natural, as in 1865 and 1866 the Georgia penitentiary "was soon filled to overflowing with negro convicts, as all men of common sense saw would be the case as soon as freedom was conferred upon the slave population."[5] Yet, even at "the dawn of freedom," a Georgia planter seemed to recognize that theft was not the expression of a racial trait but rather was a rational economic calculation. "Of at least 3000 hands in Burke Cty," he complained to the Freedmen's Bureau in fall 1865, "there are not 50 who will even talk of making arrangements for the next year. . . . They are stealing every thing eatable, evidently with the view of having something to eat, so as not to be driven by necessity to labour"—starvation presumably being the only thing that could drive landless free workers to sell their labor for a wage.[6]

But petty larceny was not only an alternative means of subsistence for blacks seeking an economic life outside the bounds of plantation labor; it could also be used to help build an independent economic sphere *within* the constrained sphere of sharecropping and tenancy to which African-Americans increasingly were subjected. Even while condemning the criminal behavior of rural blacks, white commentators inadvertently disclosed the moral economy that often underlay "the improvidence as well as the thievishness of the negro." Expensive household items, difficult to sell safely or "turn to profitable account," generally were safe, Philip Bruce wrote in *The Plantation Negro as a Freeman* (1889), a classic racist tract of the 1880s. On the other hand, "the negroes are not permitted by the planter for whom they may be working to fatten more than two hogs apiece each season . . . because they are provoked to supply these animals with food from the fields of growing corn." Worse still, "the laborers are tempted . . . to rob the range of shoats to avoid incurring the expense of purchasing them." No doubt this means of acquiring bacon without acquiring debt was the reason for the "pig law" found in many southern states, making this form of larceny a felony (Reidy 1992: 225, Wharton 1847: 237, Foner 1983: 60). Bruce also noted that planters made it known that local merchants should not accept corn "in liquidation of debts," since "their laborers are stimulated to break into the cribs and barns in order to obtain the grain . . . and thus getting a new lease of credit for themselves." The South's notorious "sunset laws," prohibiting the trading of agricultural products after dark, were a response to this means of escaping the vise of the sharecropping and debt system (Foner 1983: 59, Wiener 1978: 93–96, Reidy 1992: 225). Finally, Bruce also complained that blacks would "steal the rails of the fences that are situated conveniently to his cabin" for firewood, neglecting to mention the trespass laws against foraging which made this practice necessary (Reidy 1992: 226, Bruce 1889: 86–92).

Such offenses often went unpunished, Bruce lamented, for three reasons. First, the freedpeople enforced these practices with terror: "The planter who would arrest every pilferer . . . would undoubtedly run the risk of having his buildings and crops destroyed by incendiary fires." Second, accusation and/or prosecution would drive labor away. Third, "the whole community of plantation negroes" often was united "in a conspiracy to protect the criminal." Blacks "show[ed] openly the sympathy they feel" for members of their race who stole from whites (Bruce 1889: 90–91, 248). Despite these constraints, however, planters did turn to the law as a crucial weapon in these daily struggles with their black sharecroppers over appropriation and labor. "Nearly half of the Negro prisoners [in Georgia] are confined for crimes against property," noted the 1904 Atlanta University study of Negro crime (Du Bois 1904). The same study printed a report from Crawford County, in the heart of Georgia's Black Belt, which noted that "the crime for which Negroes are most strictly held account is that of breaking contracts." This trend had begun decades before, during the first five years of restored Democratic rule in Georgia (1873–78), when the number of leased prisoners convicted of larceny increased threefold; by 1878, 270 convicts, the vast majority of them African Americans, suffered the severity of the convict lease for the crime of simple larceny.[7]

Another example drawn from Georgia nicely illustrates the ongoing tug-of-war between moral economy and the law. Despite the 1872 ruling that a cropper had no ownership rights in a crop, Georgia's Supreme Court ruled in *Padgett v. Georgia* (1888) that a cropper was *not* indictable for criminal trespass if he independently sold part of the crop, since he "had beneficial interest as part owner." Padgett had sold a bale of cotton on his own because "he wanted to pay for a wagon he had bought in Newnan," the county seat; his landlord, no doubt finding such autonomy a grave affront, then prosecuted him for criminal trespass. Indeed, the landlord in particular had objected to the fact that Padgett had gone to a neighbor to have the cotton ginned, and he had "instructed Padget[t] not to haul any more cotton to McDonald's gin but to haul it to his gin." The local court ruled that "the cropper has no right or title to the crop" and found Padgett guilty of trespass. But an appeal overturned the conviction because "the cotton was produced by [the cropper] and was in his rightful possession. . . . he was in actual possession of the premises and the landlord was not exercising over [the premises] personal superintendence," in the words of Georgia's Supreme Court. Lest we take this as a victory for sharecroppers, however, we should note that the Georgia General Assembly passed an act in its next session, mandating that "any cropper who shall sell . . . any part of the crop grown by him, without the consent of the landlord, and before the landlord has received his part of the entire crop and payment in full for all advances made to the cropper . . . shall be guilty of a misdemeanor." In the future, croppers who wanted to gin their cotton or purchase a wagon would have to come to their landlord first, or commit criminal trespass.[8]

One final example drawn from the annals of crime in postbellum Georgia illuminates the manner in which the law was brought to bear against the moral economy of theft. In Polk County in 1893, James Florence and his son were gathering fodder for David Drummond on Drummond's land. When they finished work, they took home a few ears of corn and a few bundles of fodder, perhaps ten cents' worth, to feed their own oxen. For this indiscretion they were convicted of trespass and sentenced to pay a twenty-five-dollar fine or serve twelve months on the county chain gang. Unwilling or unable to pay the fine, hard labor was their fate. The Florences petitioned Gov. J. W. Northen for a pardon (which is why we have the details on this sort of misdemeanor), claiming that "it was so late they did not have time" to get fodder from their own field and that they had intended to tell Drummond the next day in any case. But the county prosecutor informed the governor that "their conviction was proper, and their sentences not too heavy. . . . they had frequently taken corn and fodder from [Drummond's] field" and indeed could have been charged with larceny, a felony, rather than trespass, a misdemeanor. The governor concluded that, while this was a small offense, "these things become a great annoyance in a community. . . . the Solicitor and the Judge have desired to break up such petty thieving, and that this plan has been adapted to secure their aim." The Florences' pardons were refused.[9]

Obviously this handful of examples of theft as moral economy does not constitute satisfactory evidence of widespread and accepted practice, though the emancipated slaves' predilection for thievery certainly was a staple of racist rhetoric. But these examples do suggest that a careful examination of a diverse array of sources—Freedmen's Bureau records, court cases, racist lamentations, petitions for pardon, WPA narratives— may allow us to come to a fuller understanding of the dynamics of petty crime in the rural South, and that this is a necessary project. The task is complicated by the fact that rural theft of this type usually was prosecuted as a misdemeanor. This did not imply leniency, since, as James and Lit Florence knew, a misdemeanant often faced the unenviable choice of working out his fine and court costs for his landlord, who would pay them, or spending six to twelve months as a slave on a chain gang in farming, saw-milling, brick-making, turpentine farms, or working on the public roads.[10] Unfortunately, court and prison records for misdemeanants, as opposed to felony convicts, are notoriously thin before the turn of the century (at least in Georgia). I also accept Paquette's challenge to distinguish between crime as resistance and crime as predation; having looked through hundreds of pardon petitions in Georgia, it is clear to me that violent black-on-black crime was depressingly common in the postbellum South.

Nevertheless, recognizing certain crimes under certain conditions as expressions of a moral economy remains a fruitful means of linking global changes in agricultural production and labor relations with the most local social and race relations of the rural South. Clearly the freedpeople constantly sought the independence from plantation labor that access to subsistence would grant them. Land ownership, hunting, foraging, fishing, grazing stock, task work—all were means with which blacks fended off the corrosion of autonomy that accompanied the spread of capitalist labor relations, and with which they attempted to "build upon the independent economic activity in which they had engaged as Slaves" (Berlin and Morgan 1991: 23). But for those agricultural workers most constrained by their increasing proletarianization (that is, for sharecroppers), theft remained an effective "weapon of the weak," particularly when it helped to move market participation and the acquisition of property beyond the reach of the planters' control of the debt and credit system. Ironically, while theft often was attributed by blacks and whites alike to "imperfect ideas of property ownership inseparable from slavery," rural blacks often employed it to acquire or maintain their economic independence from whites, as they had when enslaved (DuBois 1904: 16, Bruce 1889: 92). Moreover, post-Redemption theft may have been in defense of a customary right rooted in Reconstruction land and labor policies, which had given sharecroppers control over the disposition of their crops (Jaynes 1986: 153–57). Always pressing on this desire for autonomy, in turn, was the effort of southern planters to control "recalcitrant laborers by nonmarket means," which bore striking similarities to the long revolution in property relations that occurred in the capitalist center as well as in its agrarian periphery. Within that vast social transformation, definitions of criminal trespass were broadened in the rural South and contested by the moral economy of agricultural laborers, who persisted in "stealing what had previously been theirs by customary right" (Reidy 1992: 240).

Notes

1. See Campbell (1991) for a similar argument.
2. For a state-by-state compendium of these laws, see Cohen (1991: 240–41).
3. *Appling v. Odom*, 46 Ga 584. For North Carolina, e.g., see *Haskins v. Royster*, 70 NC 612, in which the state supreme court declared that a cropper was "as much a servant as if his wages were fixed and payable in money."
4. *Appling v. Odom*, 46 Ga 584.
5. Howell Cobb, Mark A. Cooper, and John A. Fitten to Charles J. Jenkins, "Report of the Committee on the Location of the Penitentiary," 2 Nov. 1866, Box 53, Governor's Incoming Correspondence, Executive Dept. Papers, Georgia Dept. of Archives and History (GDAH), Atlanta, pp. 4, 7. Principal Keeper of the Georgia Penitentiary, Report, 1872–73, GDAH, p. 21.
6. A. C. Walker to Gen. D. Tilson, 24 Nov. 1865, Unregistered Letters Received, ser. 632, Ga. Asst. Cmr., RG 105, National Archives, Washington, D.C. I thank John Rodrigue of the Freedmen and Southern Society Project, Univ. of Maryland, College Park, for bringing this document to my attention.
7. DuBois (1904: 16, 46). Principal Keeper of the Georgia Penitentiary, Report, 1873, 1877–78.

8. *Padgett v. Georgia*, 81 Ga. 468; M. A. Padgett vs. State, Box 240, Georgia Supreme Court Case Files, Georgia Dept. of Archives and History. State of Georgia, General Assembly, Acts, 1889, p. 113. For lien laws as "contested terrain" in the postbellum South, see Daniel (forthcoming).
9. Petition for Pardon, James and Lit Florence, Box 41, Governor's Papers, Applications for Clemency, Georgia Dept. of Archives and History.
10. R. F. Wright to Gov. W. Y. Atkinson, in State of Georgia, General Assembly, Journal of the House, 12 Nov. 1895, p. 247. Lichtenstein (1993).

References

Berlin, Ira, and Philip Morgan
1991   Introduction. *The Slaves' Economy: Independent Production by Slaves in the Americas,* ed. Ira Berlin and Philip Morgan. *Slavery and Abolition* 12.
Bruce, Philip A.
1889   *The Plantation Negro as a Freeman.* New York: G. P. Putnam's Sons.
Campbell, John
1991   As "A Kind of Freeman"?: Slaves' Market-Related Activities in the South Carolina Upcountry, 1800–1860. *Slavery and Abolition* 12: 132–69.
Cohen, William
1991   *At Freedom's Edge: Black Mobility and the Southern White Quest for Racial Control, 1861–1915.* Baton Rouge: Louisiana State Univ. Press.
Daniel, Pete
1994   The Legal Basis of Agrarian Capitalism: The South since 1933. In *Race and Class in the South since 1840,* ed. Rick Halpern and Melvyn Stokes, 79–102. Oxford: Berg Publishers.
DuBois, William E. B., ed.
1904   *Some Notes on Negro Crime, Particularly in Georgia.* Atlanta: Atlanta Univ. Press.
Foner, Eric
1983   *Nothing but Freedom: Emancipation and Its Legacy.* Baton Rouge: Louisiana State Univ. Press.
Genovese, Eugene D.
1974   *Roll, Jordan, Roll: The World the Slaves Made.* New York: Random House.
Hahn, Steven
1982   Hunting, Fishing and Foraging: Common Rights and Class Relations in the Postbellum South. *Radical History Review* 26: 37–64.
Hay, Douglas, et. al.
1975   *Albion's Fatal Tree.* New York: Oxford Univ. Press.
Jaynes, Gerald
1986   *Branches Without Roots: Genesis of the Black Working Class in the American South, 1862–1882.* New York: Oxford Univ. Press.
Lemann, Nicholas
1991   *The Promised Land: The Great Black Migration and How It Changed America.* New York: Knopf.
Lichtenstein, Alex
1988   "That Disposition to Theft with which They Have Been Branded": Moral Economy, Slave Management, and the Law. *Journal of Social History* 21: 413–40.

1993   Good Roads and Chain Gangs in the Progressive South. *Journal of Southern History* 59: 85–110.
Naison, Mark
1992   Outlaw Culture. *Reconstruction* 1: 128–31.
Paquette, Robert
1991   Slave Resistance and Social History. *Journal of Social History* 24: 681–85.
Rawick, George
1977   *The American Slave.* Vol. 6, supp. 1. Westport, Conn.: Greenwood Press.
Reidy, Joseph P.
1992   *From Slavery to Agrarian Capitalism in the Cotton Plantation South: Central Georgia, 1800–1880.* Chapel Hill: Univ. of North Carolina Press.
Scott, James C.
1986   Everyday Forms of Peasant Resistance. *Journal of Peasant Studies* 13: 5–35.
Strickland, John Scott
1985   Traditional Culture and Moral Economy: Social and Economic Change in the South Carolina Low Country, 1865–1910. In *The Countryside in the Age of Capitalist Transformation: Essays in the Social History of Rural America,* ed. Steven Hahn and Jonathan Prude, 141–78. Chapel Hill: Univ. of North Carolina Press.
Thompson, Edward P.
1975   *Whigs and Hunters: The Origins of the Black Act.* New York: Oxford Univ. Press.
Wharton, Vernon Lane
1947   *The Negro in Mississippi, 1865–1890.* Chapel Hill: Univ. of North Carolina Press.
Wiener, Jonathan
1978   *Social Origins of the New South, Alabama 1860–1885.* Baton Rouge: Louisiana State Univ. Press.
Woodman, Harold D.
1979   Post–Civil War Southern Agriculture and the Law. *Agricultural History* 53: 319–37.

13 | The Creolization of African-American Slave Kinship in Jamaican Free Village and Maroon Communities

Jean Besson

In *The Birth of African-American Culture,* Mintz and Price contend that "in widely scattered parts of Afro-America, the 'shipmate' relationship became a major principle of social organization and continued for decades or even centuries to shape ongoing social relations" (1992 [1976]: 43). This shipmate bond, established among slaves on the Middle Passage and extended to their descendants on slave plantations, included the creation of fictive kinship ties, including the incest taboo. Such fictive kinship therefore was the very basis of the new African-American slave cultures, and the consolidation of kinship and marriage systems became a central theme in the culture-building of the slaves. This perspective on the creation of African-American slave kinship is consistent with Lévi-Strauss's (1969 [1949]) contention that the incest taboo lies at the very heart of humanity. The relevance of this assertion is even deeper in the African-American slave context, where the inhumane system of slavery included the masters' legal denial of kinship to their chattel slaves, whose children were also owned (Mintz 1974: 60).

Against this background, this essay explores the continuing creolization of slave kinship in free village and maroon communities in Jamaica, at the core of the Caribbean region and the heart of African America. More specifically, the essay examines differences and similarities in the systems of kinship and marriage that have emerged in the post-emancipation free villages of Trelawny Parish and the post-treaty maroon community of Accompong in the neighboring parish of St. Elizabeth in west-central Jamaica. Based on thorough long-term research in Trelawny and short-term preliminary fieldwork in St. Elizabeth, these case studies are of particular significance in the study of the cultures deriving from slavery.[1] For Trelawny's free villages were the vanguard of the Caribbean post-emancipation peasant movement, while the Leeward Maroon village of Accompong is the oldest surviving post-treaty corporate maroon community in African America.

These case studies have theoretical implications for understanding the creolization of African-American slave kinship. The Trelawny free village case illuminates the "mysteries" of African-American landholding kin groups referred to by Mintz and Price (Mintz and Price 1992 [1976]: 75; Mintz 1989 [1974]: 242; Price 1967: 47–48) and shows that these groups are rooted in the "proto-peasant" adaptation of plantation slaves (cf. Mintz 1989 [1974]: 151–52, 180–213). The focus on kinship in Accompong sheds light on the neglected study of Jamaican maroon kinship (cf. Palmié 1995: 298, n. 12) and reveals an ongoing process of culture-building from the slavery era to the present time. The exploration of differences and similarities in maroon and free village kinship also advances the comparative analysis of creolization in maroon and non-maroon derivations of African-American slave cultures, called for by Raymond T. Smith in his review (1975: 149) of Price, *Maroon Societies* (cf. Price 1979 [1973]: 424).

The Creation of Kinship in Jamaican Slave Culture

The Caribbean region has been described as the "core area" of African America, where "New World slavery reached a dreadful pinnacle of intensity" (Mintz 1989 [1974]: 22). The Caribbean island of Jamaica, in turn, has been identified as "the very centre of Negro slavery" (Williams 1970: 154) and the society in which "the plantation system was developed to the most extreme degree and over the longest continuous period of time" (Robotham 1977: 46).

Patterson's classic analysis of this pronounced form of African-American plantation slave society highlights the destruction of African patterns of kinship and marriage among the slaves, the presence of sexual promiscuity, and the absence of European marriage and the nuclear family (1967: 159–62, 167). However, citing Stewart (1823: 150), Lewis (1834: 350), and Kelly (1838: 45), Patterson's study also provides evidence of the significance of the "ship-mate" bond as a basis of fictive kinship and the incest taboo among the Jamaican slaves (1967: 150). Indeed, much of the evidence for Mintz and Price's discussion of the shipmate bond derives from the Jamaican case:

> In Jamaica, for example, we know that the term "shipmate" was "synonymous in their [the slaves'] view with 'brother' or 'sister'." . . . It was "the dearest word and bond of affectionate sympathy amongst the Africans," and "so strong were the bonds between shipmates that sexual intercourse between them, in the view of one observer, was considered incestuous." . . . We know also that the bond could extend beyond the original shipmates themselves and interpenetrate with biological kin ties; shipmates were said to "look upon each other's children mutually as their own," and "it was customary for children to call their parents' shipmates 'uncle' and 'aunt'" (Mintz and Price 1992 [1976]: 43).

Out of this kernel of fictive kinship and the incest taboo was created on the Jamaican slave plantations a dynamic exogamous and complex creole marriage system, as a reinterpretation of Patterson's material on the "cycle of mating" (1967: 162–67) shows.[2] This new marriage system, forged in response and resistance to the dehumanization of slavery, drew on both underlying African cultural values and a transformation of European marriage to create a Caribbean creole system of conjugality and procreation within the constraints of the slave plantations.

In the African societies from which the slaves imported to Jamaica came, marriage was not always tied to co-residence; it was also a dynamic process of increasing stability and incorporation and was not necessarily based on monogamous relations. There was also respect for age, and Patterson notes that "the well known African behaviour pattern of great respect for old age survived throughout [Jamaican] slavery" (1967: 158). These African cultural values were the seedbed of the new African-Jamaican marriage system, though the latter was not a passive African cultural survival, but a dynamic Caribbean cultural creation (Besson 1974, 1987b: 122).

This creole system was built on three conjugal forms linked within the wider parameters of serial unions and reflecting an internal status system based on age. Short-lived duolocal or extra-residential unions typified the younger slaves, entailing minimal conjugal rights and obligations but distinguished from promiscuity and casual mating. Older slaves lived in consensual cohabitation, reflecting increasing conjugal responsibilities and commitment. These two conjugal forms were linked not only sequentially within the same relationship, but also in a pattern of sequential unions; some prosperous male slaves also practiced polygyny.

In the nineteenth century, with the increasing influence of Baptist missionary activities and the planters' need to reproduce the slave population after the abolition of the slave trade, the slaves were allowed to marry legally. However, rather than adopting the European custom of early legal marriage, the slaves transformed this marital status within the contexts of their creole conjugal complex and cosmology. Legal marriage marked proven conjugal commitment among the oldest slaves, and the culmination of an internal creole status system based on increasing conjugal stability and age. Moreover, the African-Jamaican Myal and Native Baptist cosmologies did not require early "Christian" marriage as a prerequisite for conjugality and procreation (Besson 1987b: 123–25, 1995a). This status was also regarded as inappropriate for younger slaves, who were ridiculed by the slave community if they attempted to enter European legal marriage (Patterson 1967: 164).

Thus, out of the kernel of the shipmate bond was created a dynamic, exogamous, and "complex" marriage system, maximizing conjugality and affinity among the slaves. This represented an elaboration of a complex marriage system in Lévi-Straussian terms (1969 [1949]), namely, a nonprescriptive, unrestricted system of exchange (cf. Fox 1967: 221–24), a complex system created through Caribbean culture-building. This creole marriage system in turn generated extensive ego-focused bilateral kinship networks of exchange and mutual aid, elaborating biological ties on both parental sides, as evidenced in the creole kinship terms *Tata, Mama, Sister, Boda, Uncle, Aunty, Cousin,* and *Grannie,* this last designating both grandparent and grandchild (Patterson 1967: 169–70; cf. Olwig 1985).

Complementing this ego-focused bilateral kinship system, on the Jamaican slave plantations the roots of an ancestor-focused descent system emerged, articulating with customary "proto-peasant" rights to plantation backland provision grounds and slave village yards with family burial grounds (Besson 1992: 189, Mintz 1989 [1974]). Thus Stewart observed the significance among the Jamaican slaves of customary rights to yards, provision grounds, and family burial grounds:

> Adjoining to the house is usually a small spot of ground, laid out into a sort of garden, and shaded by various fruit-trees. Here the family deposit their dead, to whose memory they invariably, if they can afford it, erect a rude tomb. Each slave has, beside this spot, a piece of ground (about half an acre) allotted to him [*sic*] as a provision ground. . . . If he has a family, an additional proportion of ground is allowed him, and all

his children from five years upward assist him in his labours in some way or other. (Stewart 1823: 267, quoted in Mintz 1989 [1974]: 187)

As early as 1793, Bryan Edwards also noted a system of customary inheritance, including the transmission of land rights, among the Jamaican slaves:

> I do not believe that an instance can be produced of a master's interference with his Negroes in their peculium thus acquired. They are permitted also to dispose at their deaths of what little property they possess; and even to bequeath their grounds or gardens to such of their fellow-slaves as they think proper. These principles are so well established, that whenever it is found convenient for the owner to exchange the Negro-grounds for other lands, the Negroes must be satisfied, in money or otherwise, before the exchange takes place. It is universally the practice. (Edwards 1793: vol. 2, p. 133, quoted in Mintz 1989 [1974]: 207)

Despite Stewart's gender-specific focus on male slaves, his statement that "each slave" had customary land rights suggests full female, as well as male, participation in this customary system of land use and transmission (Stewart 1823: 267). This suggests that a Caribbean cognatic (nonunilineal) descent system was emerging, paralleling in part the African concept of landholding kin groups but departing in the New World slavery context from the African emphasis on unilineal descent.[3] This incipient cognatic descent system would burgeon fully among the Jamaican ex-slaves and their descendants after emancipation, as the case of the post-slavery free villages of Trelawny Parish shows.

The Creolization of Slave Kinship in the Free Villages of Trelawny

Trelawny Parish was the very heart of Jamaican plantation slave society, with more plantations and slaves than any other parish in the island. The parish also had a significant tradition of slave resistance and culture-building, including a pronounced proto-peasant adaptation based on the Falmouth food marketplace and customary rights to slave village yards and provision grounds. Trelawny was also the center of the Nonconformist antislavery struggle, led by the Baptist missionary William Knibb of Falmouth. After emancipation in 1838, the parish became the vanguard of the post-slavery village movement, in the wider context of the ex-slaves' flight from the estates, under Knibb's sponsorship. By 1845, there were twenty-three such peasant villages in Trelawny, hemmed in on marginal land by the persisting plantations, which continue to the present day as "properties" and consolidated corporate "centrals." It is within this context that the five free villages I studied—Alps (New Birmingham), Refuge, Kettering, Granville, and Martha Brae—were established and persist at the heart of the post-slavery Caribbean plantation-peasant interface (Besson 1984b, 1987b, 1988, 1992).

Alps (New Birmingham) was Trelawny's first free village, founded in the northern foothills of the Cockpit Country Mountains in 1838 by the Reverend Dexter, working under Knibb. Alps—along with Sligoville in the parish of St. Catherine, Jamaica's first free village—served as a model for the island's Nonconformist, church-sponsored, post-slavery village movement. Laid out around a Baptist mission house, the village was established on the former coffee plantation of Alps and was settled by ex-slaves from that estate. Refuge (Wilberforce), Kettering, and Granville, established in 1838, 1841, and 1845 respectively, were founded by Knibb himself (Besson 1984b). Like Alps and Sturge Town in the neighboring parish of St. Ann (Mintz 1989 [1974]: 157–79), these villages were established by subdividing properties purchased by the Baptist Church during intense conflict between plantations and peasants over resources. These properties were resold to members of the Baptist congregations. In this way the villages absorbed dispossessed ex-slaves from nearby plantations, such as Oxford adjoining Refuge; Braco neighboring Kettering; and Merrywood and Green Park bordering Granville. The village of Martha Brae, established on the site of a former town in the vicinity of both Green Park and the consolidated Tharpe Estates, was another variant on Trelawny's free village theme (Besson 1974, 1984a, 1984b, 1987b, 1988).[4]

Within these Baptist-founded free peasant villages, the complementary influences of Nonconformist antislavery struggle and slave resistance have contributed to the continued creolization of slave kinship. The Baptist Church upholds the model of the European nuclear family based on Christian legal marriage (cf. Mintz 1989 [1974]: 171) and baptizes so-called "illegitimate" children on special days. However, within the formal framework of the Baptist free village settlements, the ex-slaves and their descendants have continued to build an African-Caribbean kinship and marriage system upon the foundations of proto-peasant traditions and the shipmate bond. This creole system elaborates the three dimensions of this proto-peasant family system: a dynamic conjugal complex, ego-focused bilateral kinship networks, and incipient ancestor-focused cognatic descent lines.

The acquisition within free villages of property that could be used as a "marriage settlement" elaborated upon the former proto-peasant conjugal system but was not, as economic determinists claim, its essential rationale. Among the Trelawny post-slavery peasantry, a creole system still functions as the context for conjugality and procreation, and as an internal status system based on increasing conjugal stability and age (Besson 1974, 1987b, 1993). Conjugal unions progress through extra-residential relations, consensual cohabitation, and legal marriage, both in evolving unions and in a larger context of serial monogamy. In addition to generating varied and changing household structures, this dynamic "complex" marriage system, in Lévi-Straussian (1969 [1949]) terms, maximizes marital alliances and affinal ties.

This creole conjugal system continues to generate extensive ego-focused kinship ties on both parental sides, as in the proto-peasant slavery past. Such bilateral relations reflect the amity of kinship and the ethos of exchange (cf. Olwig 1985) and constitute a basis for identity among the descendants of former slaves. This bilateral kinship, stretching beyond village, parish, and island to migrant networks overseas, has no formal defining boundary but extends with interest and knowledge at least to third cousins. With no restricting boundary and no formal rights and duties, these kin categories are interlocking, unrestricted bilateral kinship networks rather than formal restricted kindreds (cf. Fox 1967: 164–73).

As well as parents, siblings, children, parents' siblings, and other ascending and descending kin, these networks include "cousins" and those known as "some family to me." The high incidence of half-siblingship, a function of serial monogamy, further elaborates these individualized kinship ties. Such bilateral kinship also reinforces proscriptions on incest and prescriptions of exogamy; for example, both sexual relations and institutionalized conjugality between first cousins are regarded as "too close," and in the Trelawny villages I have never encountered explicit cousin conjugality of any kind.

Complementing these ego-focused bilateral kinship networks are overlapping, unrestricted, ancestor-focused landholding corporations based on cognatic descent. In Trelawny's post-slavery peasant communities, the incipient proto-peasant cognatic descent lines—focused on customary rights to slave village yards and burial grounds and plantation provision grounds—have consolidated through purchases and transmission of village freehold land. Such family estates, which continue to be created in the Trelawny villages, should not be sold but should be passed on to all descendants in perpetuity, regardless of gender, birth order, and legitimacy. This system of unrestricted descent, traditionally regarded by anthropologists as unworkable, especially for landholding (Davenport 1961b: 449; Leach 1960: 117; Mintz and Price 1992 [1976]: 70; Radcliffe-Brown 1950: 43; Solien 1959), stood in direct contrast to the British colonial system of primogeniture operative in Jamaica. This unrestricted system is also more effective in the Caribbean context than African restricted unilineal descent, for the unrestricted system maximizes the transmission of freehold land rights, as a basis of both economy and identity, in the context of plantation-engendered land scarcity (Besson 1974, 1975, 1979, 1984a, 1984b, 1987a, 1987b, 1988, 1992).

In addition, unrestricted descent ensures that non-residence on family land—for example, due to migration—does not result in forfeiture of land rights, as in a restricted cognatic system (cf. Thomas-Hope 1992: 5). The unrestricted system has helped to generate ever-increasing and overlapping family lines rooted in family land, thus maximizing and integrating the descent lines of the former slaves whose masters, via the legal system, had denied them both kinship and land rights. These family lines and their associated family estates are the central mechanisms for perpetuating the identities of the culturally distinctive Trelawny post-slavery peasant communities. As I have argued elsewhere:

> [In the post-emancipation context], freehold land was not only of obvious economic importance to those ex-slaves who managed to obtain it, giving some independence from the plantations and a bargaining position for higher wages when working on them, but it also had considerable symbolic significance to a people who had not only once been landless, but property themselves. For such land symbolized their freedom, and provided property rights, prestige and personhood. Family land was also the basis for the creation of family lines and the maximization of kinship ties, in contrast to the kinlessness of the enslaved . . . The descendants of such ex-slaves perpetuate the strategy of family land today, in the face of continued plantation hegemony. (Besson 1987a: 18)

Within this context, the unrestricted cognatic descent system, which on paper poses a theoretical puzzle for anthropologists, does not present a major problem for villagers on the ground. The unrestricted system has a combination of features that draw on not only economic but also symbolic perceptions of land. This includes the view that land within the kin group is immortal and therefore can play a long-term symbolic role and can "serve generations" of ever more numerous kin. Family land generally is retained as an undivided estate, where all co-heirs may "go and come" to pick from the fruit trees, and which all may use as a family burial ground. From a short-term economic perspective, the strategy of voluntary non-use of family land by co-heirs with other options, such as migration and access to land under other forms of tenure, further sustains the functioning of the unrestricted system (Besson 1974, 1975, 1979, 1984b, 1987a, 1988).[5]

This articulation of cognatic descent with bilateral kinship and a dynamic complex conjugal system, all of which maximize dimensions of consanguinity and affinity elaborated through the process of creolization on the basis of the shipmate bond, is reflected in the kinship terminology that has evolved in the Trelawny post-slavery villages. This is a modified "Eskimo" terminology, reflecting bilateral kinship and serial monogamy (rather than the nuclear family), combined with a "Hawaiianizing tendency" highlighting a cognatic descent principle (cf. Fox 1967: 259, 256).[6] The complexity of this Jamaican free village kinship terminology has not previously been fully recognized. For example, Murdock describes the Jamaican kinship system as simply "bilateral . . . of the Eskimo type," one criterion of this type being the "absence of any functionally important descent groups, unilineal or ambilineal [cognatic]" (1960: 6). Murdock's view coincides with many analyses of African-American kinship as being simply bilateral, noncorporate, kindred organization (e.g., Davenport 1961a and 1961b; MacDonald and MacDonald 1978: 7; Marks 1976: 12–13; Mintz 1971: 39; Olwig 1985; Rubenstein 1987: 221; and R. T. Smith 1988).

The Creolization of Slave Kinship in the Leeward Maroon Community of Accompong

The Jamaican Leeward Maroon community of Accompong, in the parish of St. Elizabeth adjoining Trelawny, is the oldest surviving post-treaty corporate maroon community in African America. The community was consolidated more than two hundred and fifty years ago by the Leeward Maroon treaty of March 1739, between the great maroon leader Colonel Cudjoe and the British colonial government, after Jamaica's First Maroon War (1725–39). This treaty, which also included the larger community of Trelawny Town in the neighboring parish of St. James, subsequently disbanded through deportation to Nova Scotia after the Second Maroon War (1795–96), predates the Jamaican Windward Maroon treaty of June 1739 and the treaties of the 1760s among the Surinamese maroons, including the Saramaka, the largest surviving maroon society in African America.[7]

Like Trelawny's first free village of Alps (New Birmingham), Accompong is located in the precipitous, virtually uninhabited "karst" Cockpit Country Mountains that straddle the parishes of Trelawny, St. Elizabeth, and St. James. Accompong is situated in a heavily forested southern area of the Cockpits overlooking the Mountains of Aberdeen, the backlands of the former slave plantation of Aberdeen. On the plains below, beyond the free village of Aberdeen consolidated on the backlands of the plantation, stretches the vast corporate plantation "central" of Appleton Estates. The Leeward treaty included a grant of 1,500 acres of steep forest land and, from the colonial viewpoint, confined the maroons to a marginal reservation, much as the Windward Maroons were contained in the northeastern mountains of Jamaica (Bilby 1981, 1984a, 1984b; Kopytoff 1979). However, as Barbara Kopytoff (1979) has shown, from the maroon perspective, the treaties were sacred charters of corporate identity.

Kopytoff's ethnohistorical study (e.g., 1976a, 1976b, 1978, 1979) provides a framework tracing the origin and continuity of the historic Leeward Maroon polity; my own anthropological field research in 1979, 1989, and 1991 shows how the Accompong maroons have continued to consolidate a corporate peasant community with a strong sense of creole cultural identity (Besson 1995b and 1995c). Kopytoff also provides insight into the process of creolization among the Leeward Maroons, whereby initial African ethnic rivalries came to be transcended and redefined in a Jamaican maroon ethnicity (1976a, 1979). Within this context, Kopytoff highlights the significance of the shipmate bond:

> These processes of ethnic redefinition must have started even before the Africans reached the New World. We know that slaves who shared the middle passage considered themselves kin; and even before that, in the slave factories and baracoons of the African coast, African captives in their fear and sorrow may have found comfort in asserting kin ties with others who, if they did not come from the same village or chiefdom, at least came from a part of their known world . . . Reference groups of fellow sufferers were created and given a charter of kinship. (Kopytoff 1976a: 35)

In addition, Kopytoff indicates the importance of the process of forging new languages and cultures "on the slave plantations of the New World and in the bush where Maroons encountered one another" (1976a: 35), and she notes that the outcome of this process was "a new Afro-American creation, a new culture, and a new ethnic identity" (1976a: 46).

Despite this focus on creolization and the related significance of the shipmate bond, as Palmié rightly notes, "the evolution of the Jamaican Maroon kinship system has, unfortunately, not received sufficient attention" (1995: 298, n. 12). This is especially true in relation to the articulation of maroon kinship with community and land.[8] My anthropological research in Accompong, undertaken since Kopytoff's ethnohistorical study, sheds light on this and other neglected aspects of creolization in the Leeward Maroon kinship system.

A central focus of this creolization process are three sacred groves at the heart of the maroon commons, reputed to be the burial grounds of the "First-Time" maroons: Colonel Cudjoe and his "brothers" and "lieutenants" Johnny, Quaco, and Accompong. Here an annual post-treaty Myal ritual, handed down for more than two hundred and fifty years and hedged by sacrifice, taboos, and rules, is performed for the hero-ancestors. The ritual is held under the "Kindah Tree," which bears a sign proclaiming, "We are Family." This highlights the creole kinship base of the post-treaty maroon community; the overlapping, ancestor-focused, unrestricted cognatic descent lines are traced to the First-Time Maroons and are further consolidated by ego-focused bilateral kinship networks and cousin conjugality, themes discussed below.

There are, near the Kindah Tree, reputed early African ethnic burial grounds (Congo and Coromantee), within which contemporary maroons identify ancestral lines. These burial grounds have been superseded by a community burial ground, behind the Presbyterian Church, reflecting a transformation from African ethnic groups to a Caribbean kin-based creole community.

Most recently, during the period of my fieldwork (1979–91), there has been an emergent pattern of descent-based burial in the yards of the inner residential zone of common land. This pattern parallels not only the burial patterns of the proto-peasant slaves, but also those of the family land burial grounds in the Trelawny villages and in Accompong's neighboring free village of Aberdeen. The processual nature of this transformation is further manifested in the concern it has aroused among more conventional maroons, who see this burial pattern as undermining the tradition of common land. Nevertheless, this emergent system of cognatic landholding corporations is being reinforced by the general consolidation of descent-based rights to yards, and by the evolution of descent-based cultivation rights to provision grounds in the intermediate zone (cf. Barker and Spence 1988). These transformations, contained within the outer forest zone of common land, have occurred as external government pressure has increased to undermine the commons and maroon corporate identity.[9]

Within this emergent system of overlapping cognatic descent lines and landholding corporations,[10] Accompong maroons may practice cousin conjugality. The positive sanctioning of this practice is explicitly articulated in the maroon saying "We are Royal Family," which draws a parallel with cousin marriage among European royal families. This positive sanction (which is not prescriptive) both reflects and effects maroon endogamy, manifesting, like the outer forest zone of the maroon commons, the corporate nature of the Accompong community. Cousin conjugality articulates with multiple conjugal forms and serial monogamy, which, as in the Trelawny villages, generate a high incidence of half-siblingship and widespread bilateral kinship ties. In Accompong, however, such bilateral ties may be consolidated by further cousin conjugality. That such cousin alliance is paradoxically exogamous as well as endogamous is underlined by the sibling incest taboo, which among the Accompong maroons coincides with the prescription of exogamy, first set in place by the shipmate bond. During fieldwork, this taboo was highlighted by the negative sanction of gossip surrounding a reputed case of brother-sister incest.

Conclusion

The two case studies discussed above reveal significant similarities and differences in the creolization of African-American slave kinship in maroon and non-maroon derivations of Jamaican slave culture. Both the Trelawny post-emancipation free villagers and the post-treaty Accompong maroons have continued to prohibit incest—a prohibition established by the fictive kinship tie of the shipmate bond. Both free villagers and maroons also have established exogamous conjugality, elaborated by multiple conjugal forms and serial monogamy and rooted in the creole marriage system forged on Jamaican slave plantations. Further demonstrating continuity with the proto-peasant slaves, the Trelawny villagers have maintained a complex conjugal system that prohibits cousin conjugality and maximizes affinal ties among the free village communities that emerged, at the vanguard of the Caribbean post-slavery peasant movement, in the context of the flight from the estates (Besson 1984b, 1992). In contrast, the Accompong maroons practice both community endogamy and cousin conjugality to reinforce their corporate identity, established by the treaty of March 1739 in the oldest surviving post-treaty corporate maroon formation in African America.

Among both free villagers and maroons, bilateral kinship is important, generating widespread ego-focused kinship ties of amity, identity, and mutual aid on both parental sides, as on the Jamaican slave plantations. In both cases, these ties are elaborated through serial monogamy. In Trelawny, however, ego-focused bilateral kinship is maximized through the complex conjugal system, as on the slave plantations. In Accompong, bilateral kinship may be consolidated and contained by cousin conjugality, providing a basis of common kinship in the corporate creole maroon community.

Let us turn now to the articulation of kinship with community and land. The Trelawny villagers, at the heart of the Caribbean plantation-peasant interface, have evolved, since emancipation, unrestricted cognatic landholding corporations that are the central mechanism through which these culturally distinctive communities are perpetuated in the face of the surrounding plantations (cf. Besson 1984b: 18). Throughout the post-treaty era, the Accompong maroons, in contrast, have held land in common on their marginal reservation. However, overlapping unrestricted ancestor-focused cognatic descent lines—traced to the First-Time Maroons—have long been recognized in Accompong, within the wider context of community, where they reinforce the kinship base of creole corporate identity. Moreover, unrestricted cognatic descent landholding corporations are currently emerging in relation to yards, yard burial grounds, and provision grounds, contained within the outer forest zone of common land. These corporations are similar to the kin-based landholding corporations in Trelawny and in Accompong's neighboring free village of Aberdeen. This emergent process has coincided with increasing external government pressure to undermine the commons and erode maroon corporate identity.

These conclusions have wider relevance for understanding the creolization of African-American slave kinship, including the comparative analysis of culture-building in maroon and non-maroon derivations of African-American slave cultures (cf. Price 1979 [1973]: 424; R. T. Smith 1975: 149). This is especially so in relation to the articulation of kinship with community and landholding, including the classic thesis of Mintz and Price (1992 [1976]: 66–75).

Discussing African-American slave kinship in the Para plantation region of Suriname, Mintz and Price identify the evolution of nonexclusive overlapping nonunilineal/cognatic descent groups maximizing numbers of descendants in relation to ancestral ritual. The Saramaka maroons, however, established a restricted matrilineal system in relation to ancestral ritual, exogamy, and landholding (Mintz and Price 1992 [1976]: 68–69). Mintz and Price conclude that, after emancipation, the unrestricted ancestral ritual groups among the former Para slaves would not function effectively in the context of landholding; and since the ex-slaves could not at this late stage transform to unilineality, "the plantation communities themselves became the land-holding corporations, with individuals gaining rights to land use through their genealogical connections to ancestors who had lived there" (1992 [1976]: 70). They argue, therefore, that the principle of community became more important than the principle of unrestricted cognatic descent in the context of landholding.

Despite this observation concerning the inefficacy of unrestricted nonunilineal landholding kin groups, Mintz and Price paradoxically identify, on the basis of work by Clarke (1953) and Davenport (1961a), "late-emerging nonunilineal kinship groups . . . centered on 'family land'" in post-emancipation Jamaica, resembling "in certain ways those of the Para region of Suriname, with a ritual association between ancestors and land on which they were buried." On the basis of Bastien's work (1961), they point to somewhat similar landholding kin groups in post-revolutionary Haiti, too, but suggest these are "groups of patrikin" (Mintz and Price 1992 [1976]: 75). Consistent with their earlier contention (in the Para context) that unrestricted descent cannot function efficiently for landholding, Mintz and Price observe that "a good deal remains obscure about the precise nature of the kin groups involved in both the Haitian and Jamaican cases" (1992 [1976]: 75). Elsewhere, Price (1967: 47–48) refers to the "mysteries" of Caribbean land tenure systems; and Mintz (1989 [1974]: 242) remarks that "the problems of land tenure and the transmission of land rights among Caribbean peasantries remain largely unsolved."

Of Mintz and Price's sources on Jamaica, neither Clarke (1953) nor Davenport (1961a) identifies unrestricted nonunilineal/cognatic kin groups in the context of landholding. Clarke—writing before Goodenough (1955) had identified the nonunilineal descent group and distinguished it from the bilateral kindred—uses the concept of the "kindred" in the context of family land. Nevertheless, Clarke's rich data suggest the ancestral focus of this kin group and the unrestricted nature of descent within it. Clarke interprets this system as a survival from the Ashanti heritage, although the Ashanti hold land matrilineally with complementary non-corporate (patrilineal) filiation (Besson 1974, 1975, 1979, 1987a, 1987b). Davenport explicitly rejects an unrestricted landholding system, on the grounds that such systems must of necessity be restricted; he searches unsuccessfully for the restricting mechanism in the Jamaican case and concludes that the Jamaican landholding kin group is a residentially restricted "joint-family" system (Davenport 1961a: 449–50, 1961b: 384). In similar vein, Solien (1959), discussing Clarke's Jamaican data and the Black Carib case, argues for a necessarily restricted nonunilineal system.

The case of the Trelawny villagers, however, shows that unrestricted landholding corporations do function effectively in the context of Jamaican family land, maximizing—in a context of persisting land scarcity—kinship lines and kin-based land rights among the descendants of former plantation slaves (cf. Besson 1974, 1975, 1979, 1984b, 1987a, 1987b, 1988). Thus Mintz has noted that the Trelawny case "has begun to unravel the mystery of so-called 'family land' and kinship in Jamaica" (1989 [1974]: xxvii). In syntheses of the regional ethnographic literature, I have shown that such unrestricted kin groups function widely among Caribbean post-slavery peasantries in the contexts of the specific resource of "children's property," "generation property," and "family land" (cf. Firth 1963; Caplan 1969; Hanson 1971).[11] Such unrestricted corporations can be identified widely in the Antilles, at the heart of post-slavery plantation society, in situations of land scarcity—for example, throughout Jamaica and in Haiti, Providencia, St. John, Dominica, Montserrat, St. Vincent, Martinique, St. Lucia, Barbados, Trinidad and Tobago, and Grenada and Carriacou (Besson 1984a, 1987a, 1992).[12] Drawing their meaning from African-American slave cultures and the contemporary contexts of Caribbean post-slavery societies, these unrestricted systems reflect the dynamic process of creolization, rather than passive survivals from ancestral or colonial cultures, as others contend (Besson 1984a, 1987a).[13]

Elsewhere, at the margins (e.g., the Bahamas and Barbuda) and at the frontiers (Guyana and the Para region of Suriname) of post-slavery plantation society, an unrestricted cognatic descent system articulates with the principle of community in the context of landholding (cf. Besson 1987a, 1992, 1995c).[14] In the Jamaican Leeward Maroon community of Accompong, such a cognatic system is also emerging in the context of common land on a marginal reservation; this process has been occurring in tandem with external government pressure to undermine the commons and maroon corporate identity. In Nevis, where the stranglehold of the plantation system virtually stifled the emergence of free villages, the principles of commonage and unrestricted descent are both struggling to emerge within imposed leasehold land settlements, in a situation of constraint with strong continuities from the proto-peasant past (cf. Momsen 1987; Besson and Momsen 1987; Besson 1992).

Only in the vast forest regions of Suriname and French Guyana have African-American slaves and their descendants had the relative autonomy to retain, or forge anew, restricted African-type matrilineal descent systems for corporate landholding (Vernon 1989: 209; cf. Bilby 1989; Köbben 1979; Mintz and Price 1992 [1976]: 69; Price 1975; Thoden van Velzen and van Wetering 1988).[15] Elsewhere, in varying degrees, the unrestricted descent principle, which Mintz and Price identify in Para ritual groups but anticipate would not function effectively for land-holding (1992 [1976]: 68–70), exists widely throughout African America in the context of landholding—as a mode of adaptive resistance to the plantation system and other forms of land monopoly, maximizing rights to the precious but scarce resource of land (Besson 1974, 1975, 1979, 1987a, 1992, 1995b; cf. Mintz 1989 [1974]: 76, 132–33).[16] The creation of such unrestricted landholding systems, traditionally regarded by anthropologists as inoperable, reflects the strength of the creolization process among African-American slaves and their descendants—a process that has been described, rightly, as "the most remarkable drama of culture-building in the modern world" (Mintz 1980: 15).

Notes

1. Fieldwork was carried out in Trelawny during the period 1968–91 and in Accompong, St. Elizabeth, in 1979, 1989, and 1991. In 1991, fieldwork was also undertaken in Accompong's neighboring free village of Aberdeen. The fieldwork was funded in part by the Social Science Research Council (United Kingdom), the Carnegie Trust for the Universities of Scotland, and the University of Aberdeen Travel Fund.
2. Patterson identifies "unstable unions," "stable unions," "multiple associations," and "stable monogamous and legal marriages" among the Jamaican slaves (1967: 162–70).
3. This conclusion is further reinforced by data from the Danish West Indian island of St. John, where Olwig notes that both male and female slaves had rights, and a strong attachment, to land and a "particular preference for living and being buried on their place of birth" (1985: 41, cf. p. 49; see also Besson 1989, 1992: 190).
4. Green Park sugar plantation features significantly in Patterson's study of Jamaican slavery (1967: 60–61, 157), while the Tharpe Estates were established around 1765 and "centered around one of the most elaborate factories in Jamaica at Good Hope on the Martha Brae [River]" (Craton 1975: 254). The evidence suggests that Martha Brae village was established in the 1840s, by ex-slaves from the surrounding plantations of Holland and Irving Tower, in association with the Baptist Church, on the ruins of the former planter town of Martha Brae.
5. Migration does not result in loss of rights to family land and may involve return or circulatory migration (compare Thomas-Hope 1992: 5). Attempts are sometimes made, however, to restrict rights to family land via the legal system. Such attempts are negatively sanctioned (Besson 1988: 52–53).

6. As indicated previously, some aspects of Trelawny village kinship terminology reflect an ego-focused bilateral kinship organization and its unrestricted range. Primary kin are referred to by specific terms—*mother, father, sister, brother, daughter,* and *son*—which are not used beyond these primary contexts. Half-siblings too are referred to as *brother* and *sister,* with the added descriptors *same mother's children* or *same father's children* to denote maternal and paternal half-siblings, respectively, in contrast to full siblings, who are described as having *same mother and same father.*

In addition, parents' siblings on either side are *aunt* and *uncle,* reciprocated by *nephew* and *niece.* First cousins on both parental sides are designated in terms of the parental relationship: *two sisters' children* and *two brothers' children* for matrilateral and patrilateral parallel-cousins respectively, and *sister and brother's children* for cross-cousins. More distant cousinships may be described as *cousin* or by elaborating on the first-cousin tie if the specific relationship is known. For example, second cousins might explain that "our mothers are two sisters' chil-dren" or variations on this theme. Grandparents and ascending generations are called *grandmother, grandfather, great-grandmother, great-grandfather,* and so forth on both parental sides, with grandchildren and great-grandchildren being referred to, respectively, as *gran* and *great-gran.*

These terms reflect the principles of Eskimo kinship terminology; for, as Fox explains, while this is named after the Eskimo kinship system, "it is, in fact, quite a common scheme [of kinship classification] amongst peoples lacking unilineal descent-groups or elementary forms of [marriage] exchange" (1967: 258). Fox further notes that "what it seems to do is carve out the nuclear family for special emphasis, and then to stress the equal balance between the two kindreds united by marriage—the matrilateral and patrilateral kin of ego" (1967: 258). However, in Trelawny, the elaborations described above for distinguishing half-siblings from full siblings highlight the role of the dynamic, complex mar-riage system of serial monogamy in generating bilateral kinship ties, rather than emphasizing the nuclear family.

In addition to this modification of Eskimo kinship terminology, a "Hawaiianizing tendency" (Fox 1967: 259) of the Eskimo terminology itself may be identified. Hawaiian kinship classification "stresses . . . the separation of generations, but . . . makes no concessions to lineality or to systematic [mar-riage] exchange" (Fox 1967: 256). It is "a great respecter of generations," in con-trast to the Eskimo system, which "plays havoc with the generation principle" by applying the "rogue term 'cousin' . . . promiscuously to relatives outside a nar-rowly-defined group" (Fox 1967: 259). In Trelawny, the Hawaiianizing ten-dency is reflected, for example, in the extension of the terms *aunt* and *uncle* to refer to parents' cousins. The terms *old parents* and *older heads,* which, especially in landholding family lines, are employed to refer to ascending generations, are also variations on this Hawaiian generational theme. Fox notes that "in most societies having a Hawaiian terminology there is a tendency to some form of *extended* family or cognatic descent group" (1967: 259).

7. As Thoden van Velzen and van Wetering note, in relation to the Suriname ma-roons, "Peace treaties were concluded with the Ndjukas in 1760, the Saramakas in 1762, and with the Matawais in 1767" (1988: 9). I am grateful to Professor Thoden van Velzen for drawing my attention to these dates.

8. Among the Windward Maroons, "membership in the Maroon community is

automatically passed on (bilaterally) from parent to child, and according to traditional Maroon belief, all of the special attributes, knowledge, and powers connected with being a Maroon can only be passed on 'in the blood.' They are seen as being conferred by the original Maroon ancestors (and particularly Nanny) upon their descendants" (Bilby 1984a: 14). This indication of a cognatic descent system within the context of community could usefully be explored in relation to landholding.

9. Kopytoff (1979) documents this external pressure, from both colonial and national governments, beginning with the Maroons Allotment Act of 1842 and extending to the 1970s, despite Jamaican independence in 1962. During my fieldwork in 1991, such land disputes were still occurring. At the annual Myal ritual in 1993, a government minister "spoke of the need for the Government to aid the maroons, particularly in the matter of providing land titles to property [*sic*], as this was necessary to raise funds from financial institutions for further development" (Western Bureau, Maroons Urged to Unite, *Gleaner*, 8 Jan. 1993).

10. Kopytoff, referring to Dallas's 1803 history of the Jamaican Maroons, which indicates a line of chiefly succession among Cudjoe's maroons of largely Coromantee origin (Kopytoff 1976a: 40, Dallas 1803: vol. 1, p. 31), notes: "There is a suggestion of a lineage organisation here, but we have no real evidence of corporate lineages among the Jamaican Maroons as we have for Guiana Maroons. . . . Certainly there is nothing like that among present-day Maroons, and Katherine Dunham's [1946] report of 'clans' among the Accompong Maroons sounds like family name lines with no corporate status" (Kopytoff 1976a: 49 n 28). However, it may now be the case that the "clans" or "family name lines" noted by Dunham are indeed evolving into landholding corporations, with both similarities (landholding functions) to and differences (cognatic rather than matrilineal descent) from those of the Guiana maroons.

11. Firth (1963: 25–26) elucidates how an unrestricted system can function effectively in relation to a "specific situation" of either a "specific resource" or "specific occasion" (cf. Fox 1967: 151–52). Caribbean family land clearly fits Firth's criterion of a "specific resource" (Besson 1974: vol. 2, pp. 114–218; 1975; 1979), while the unrestricted ancestral ritual groups identified by Mintz and Price (1992 [1976]: 68) coincide with a "specific occasion." Caplan (1969) and Hanson (1971) present similar analyses for unrestricted landholding systems in Maffia Island, Tanzania, and Rapa, Polynesia, respectively.

12. For extensive reviews of ethnographic sources on this point, see Besson (1984a: 77, n. 16; 1987a; 1992: 211–12, ns. 3 and 4). These sources include Larose (1975), who shows that Haitian landholding groups (*lakous*) are unrestricted cognatic descent corporations, especially in relation to the *démembré* or family burial ground, rather than "groups of patrikin" (Mintz and Price 1992 [1976]: 75). Likewise, although Mintz and Price (1992 [1976]: 71), following Michael G. Smith (1962), note that Carriacou manifests "the most fully articulated system of unilineal descent (other than that of the Suriname Maroons) in all of Afro-America, replete with a complex ancestral cult and functioning localized patrilineages," Smith's data on family land in Carriacou clearly indicate a cognatic system of customary tenure and transmission (M. G. Smith 1962: 74, 296). My source for Tobago is my own recent fieldwork there in 1992.

13. In addition to Clarke's Ashanti survival thesis, Caribbean family land has also been attributed to English, French, and Roman-Dutch colonial survivals (Besson 1984a, 1987a, 1992).

14. Indeed, in the Para case, the evidence suggests a full-fledged, unrestricted cognatic descent landholding system. Despite their judgment that such a system will be less efficacious for landholding than for ancestral ritual, Mintz and Price state, first, that during slavery these ancestors "were buried locally" (1992 [1976]: 68), thus indicating a close articulation between ancestral ritual and the customary transmission of ancestral land. Second, after emancipation, although the plantation communities are seen by Mintz and Price as the landholding units among the former slaves, individuals in such communities gained "rights to land use through their *genealogical connections to ancestors* who had lived there" (Mintz and Price 1992 [1976]: 70; emphasis mine). Since Mintz and Price point out that this was not a unilineal system, such ancestral genealogical connections could only be cognatic. Moreover, the "principles of descent and ancestry" are still "richly particularized and anchored in the land" (Mintz and Price 1992 [1976]: 70).

15. I am grateful to Professor H. U. E. Thoden van Velzen for drawing my attention to the fact that, despite a matrilineal landholding system, the Ndjuka Maroons of Suriname also have cognatic kin groups which have not received the attention they deserve (cf. Thoden van Velzen and van Wetering 1988: xii–xiii).

16. In relation to the Jamaican Windward Maroons, Palmié hypothesizes, on the basis of Bilby's (1984a) data on the "bilateral" (i.e., cognatic) transmission of community membership, a transformation from "matrilineal tendencies" in their Akan ("Coromantee") heritage (Palmié 1995: 298, n. 12). For example, such tendencies might be reflected in their oral tradition that maroons and non-maroons are descendants of "two sister pikni" (that is, two sisters' children), thus providing evidence of matrilineal fission (Palmié 1995: 292). Palmié's hypothesis receives some support from the oral history of the Trelawny villagers. For, in the Trelawny free village of Refuge, one of the two central family lines is reputedly descended from an African slave woman from the adjoining Oxford plantation, who was one of three sisters brought on a slave ship into Jamaican slavery and subsequently dispersed on different plantations (compare Besson 1984b: 14). In addition to perhaps reflecting matrilineal tendencies, this oral tradition highlights the significance of the shipmate bond.

References

Barker, David, and Balfour Spence
1988   Afro-Caribbean Agriculture: A Jamaican Maroon Community in Transition. *Geographical Journal* 154 (2): 198–208.
Bastien, Remy
1961   Haitian Rural Family Organization. *Social and Economic Studies* 10: 478–510.
Besson, Jean
1974   *Land Tenure and Kinship in a Jamaican Village.* 2 vols. Ph.D. diss., Univ. of Edinburgh.
1975   Land Tenure and Kinship in "River Village," Jamaica, W.I. Unpublished paper, Univ. of Edinburgh.
1979   Symbolic Aspects of Land in the Caribbean: The Tenure and Transmission of Land Rights among Caribbean Peasantries. In *Peasants, Plantations and Rural Communities in the Caribbean,* ed. Malcolm Cross and Arnaud Marks, 86–116.

Guildford, England: Univ. of Surrey; and Leiden, Netherlands: Royal Institute of Linguistics and Anthropology.

1984a Family Land and Caribbean Society: Toward an Ethnography of Afro-Caribbean Peasantries. In *Perspectives on Caribbean Regional Identity*, ed. Elizabeth M. Thomas-Hope, 57–83. Liverpool: Liverpool Univ. Press.

1984b Land Tenure in the Free Villages of Trelawny, Jamaica: A Case Study in the Caribbean Peasant Response to Emancipation. *Slavery and Abolition* 5 (1): 3–23.

1987a A Paradox in Caribbean Attitudes to Land. In *Land and Development in the Caribbean*, ed. Jean Besson and Janet Momsen, 13–45. London: Macmillan.

1987b Family Land as a Model for Martha Brae's New History: Culture-Building in an Afro-Caribbean Village. In *Afro-Caribbean Villages in Historical Perspective*, ed. Charles V. Carnegie, 100–132. Kingston, Jamaica: African-Caribbean Institute of Jamaica.

1988 Agrarian Relations and Perceptions of Land in a Jamaican Peasant Village. In *Small Farming and Peasant Resources in the Caribbean*, ed. John S. Brierley and Hymie Rubenstein, 39–61. Winnipeg, Canada: Univ. of Manitoba.

1989 Review of Karen Fog Olwig, *Cultural Adaptation and Resistance on St. John*. *Plantation Society in the Americas* 2 (3): 345–48.

1992 Freedom and Community: The British West Indies. In *The Meaning of Freedom: Economics, Politics, and Culture after Slavery*, ed. Frank McGlynn and Seymour Drescher, 183–219. Pittsburgh, Pa.: Univ. of Pittsburgh Press.

1993 Reputation and Respectability Reconsidered: A New Perspective on Afro-Caribbean Peasant Women. In *Women and Change in the Caribbean*, ed. Janet H. Momsen, 15–37. London: James Currey; Bloomington: Indiana Univ. Press.

1995a Religion as Resistance in Jamaican Peasant Life: The Baptist Church, Revival Worldview and Rastafari Movement. In *Rastafari and Other African-Caribbean Worldviews*, ed. Barry Chevannes, 43–76. London: Macmillan.

1995b Free Villagers, Rastafarians and Modern Maroons: From Resistance to Identity. In *Born Out of Resistance: On Caribbean Cultural Creativity* , ed. Wim Hoogbergen. Utrecht, Netherlands: ISOR Press.

1995c Land, Kinship and Community in the Post-Emancipation Caribbean: A Regional View of the Leewards. In *Small Islands, Large Questions: Society, Culture, and Resistance in the Post-Emancipation Caribbean*, ed. Karen Fog Olwig. London: Frank Cass.

Besson, Jean, and Janet Momsen
1987 Introduction. In *Land and Development in the Caribbean*, ed. Jean Besson and Janet Momsen, 1–9. London: Macmillan.

Bilby, Kenneth M.
1981 The Kromanti Dance of the Windward Maroons of Jamaica. *Nieuwe West-Indische Gids* 55 (1–2): 52–101.

1984a "Two Sister Pikni": A Historical Tradition of Dual Ethnogenesis in Eastern Jamaica. *Caribbean Quarterly* 30 (3–4): 10–25.

1984b The Treacherous Feast: A Jamaican Maroon Historical Myth. *Bijdragen tot de Taal, Land- en Volkenkunde* 140: 1–31.

1989 Divided Loyalties: Local Politics and the Play of States among the Aluku. *Nieuwe West-Indische Gids* 63 (3–4): 143–73.

Caplan, Patricia
1969   Cognatic Descent Groups on Mafia Island, Tanzania. *Man* 4 (3): 419–31.
Clarke, Edith
1953   Land Tenure and the Family in Four Selected Communities in Jamaica. *Social and Economic Studies* 1 (4): 81–118.
Craton, Michael
1975   Jamaican Slavery. In *Race and Slavery in the Western Hemisphere: Quantitative Studies,* ed. Stanley L. Engerman and Eugene D. Genovese, 249–84. Princeton, N.J.: Princeton Univ. Press.
1978   *Searching for the Invisible Man: Slaves and Plantation Life in Jamaica.* Cambridge, Mass: Harvard Univ. Press.
Dallas, Robert C.
1803   *The History of the Maroons.* London: T. N. Longman and O. Rees.
Davenport, William
1961a   The Family System of Jamaica. *Social and Economic Studies* 10 (4): 420–54.
1961b   Introduction. *Social and Economic Studies* 10 (4): 380–85.
Dunham, Katherine
1946   *Journey to Accompong.* New York: Henry Holt.
Edwards, Bryan
1793   *The History, Civil and Commercial, of the British Colonies in the West Indies.* 2 vols. London: John Stockdale.
Firth, Raymond
1963   Bilateral Descent Groups: An Operational Viewpoint. In *Studies in Kinship and Marriage,* ed. Isaac Schapera, 22–37. London: Royal Anthropological Institute.
Fox, Robin
1967   *Kinship and Marriage.* Harmondsworth, England: Penguin Books.
Goodenough, Ward H.
1955   A Problem in Malayo-Polynesian Social Organization. *American Anthropologist* 57 (1): 71–83.
Hanson, F. Allan
1971   Nonexclusive Cognatic Descent Systems: A Polynesian Example. In *Polynesia: Readings on a Culture Area,* ed. Alan Howard, 109–32. Scranton, Pa.: Chandler.
Kelly, James
1838   *Voyage to Jamaica, and Seventeen Years Residence in that Island . . .* 2d ed. Belfast: J Wilson.
Köbben, André J. F.
1979   Unity and Disunity: Cottica Djuka Society as a Kinship System. In *Maroon Societies: Rebel Slave Communities in the Americas,* ed. Richard Price, 320–69. 2d ed. Baltimore, Md.: Johns Hopkins Univ. Press.
Kopytoff, Barbara Klamon
1976a   The Development of Jamaican Maroon Ethnicity. *Caribbean Quarterly* 22 (2–3): 33–50.
1976b   Jamaican Maroon Political Organization: The Effects of the Treaties. *Social and Economic Studies* 25 (2): 87–105.
1978   The Early Political Development of Jamaican Maroon Societies. *William and Mary Quarterly* 35: 287–307.

1979   Colonial Treaty as Sacred Charter of the Jamaican Maroons. *Ethnohistory* 26 (1): 45–64.

Larose, Serge
1975   The Haitian *Lakou;* Land, Family and Ritual. In *Family and Kinship in Middle America and the Caribbean,* ed. Arnaud F. Marks and Rene A. Romer, 482–512. Curaçao: Institute of Higher Studies in Curaçao; and Leiden, Netherlands: Royal Institute of Linguistics and Anthropology.

Leach, Edmund R.
1960   The Sinhalese of the Dry Zone of Northern Ceylon. In *Social Structure in Southeast Asia,* ed. George Peter Murdock, 116–26. Chicago: Quadrangle Books.

Lévi-Strauss, Claude
1969 [1949]   *The Elementary Structures of Kinship.* Boston: Beacon Press.

Lewis, Matthew G.
1834   *Journal of a West Indian Proprietor.* London: J. Murray.

MacDonald, John Stuart, and MacDonald, Leatrice
1978   The Black Family in the Americas: A Review of the Literature. *Sage Race Relations Abstracts* 3 (1): 1–42.

Marks, Arnaud F.
1976   *Male and Female and the Afro-Curaçaoan Household.* The Hague, Netherlands: Martinus Nijhoff.

Mintz, Sidney W.
1971   The Caribbean as a Socio-Cultural Area. In *Peoples and Cultures of the Caribbean,* ed. Michael M. Horowitz, 17–46. Garden City, N.Y.: Natural History Press.
1974   The Caribbean Region. In *Slavery, Colonialism and Racism,* ed. Sidney W. Mintz, 45–71. New York: Norton.
1980   Cultural Resistance and the Labor Force in the Caribbean Region. Paper presented at Latin America Today: Heritage of Conquest Conference, Cornell Univ., 3–5 Apr.
1989 [1974]   *Caribbean Transformations.* New York: Morningside Edition, Columbia Univ. Press.

Mintz, Sidney W., and Richard Price
1992 [1976]   *The Birth of African-American Culture: An Anthropological Perspective.* [*An Anthropological Approach to the Afro-American Past: A Caribbean Perspective.*] Boston: Beacon Press.

Momsen, Janet
1987   Land Settlement as an Imposed Solution. In *Land and Development in the Caribbean,* ed. Jean Besson and Janet Momsen, 46–69. London: Macmillan.

Murdock, George Peter
1960   Cognatic Forms of Social Organization. In *Social Structure in Southeast Asia,* ed. George Peter Murdock, 1–14. Chicago: Quadrangle Books.

Olwig, Karen Fog
1985   *Cultural Adaptation and Resistance on St. John: Three Centuries of Afro-Caribbean Life.* Gainesville: Univ. of Florida Press.

Palmié, Stephan
1995   African Frontiers in the Americas? In *Born Out of Resistance: On Caribbean Cultural Creativity,* ed. Wim Hoogbergen. Utrecht, Netherlands: ISOR Press.

Patterson, Orlando
1967   *The Sociology of Slavery: An Analysis of the Origins, Development and Structure of Negro Slave Society in Jamaica.* London: MacGibbon and Kee.
Price, Richard
1967   Studies of Caribbean Family Organization: Problems and Prospects. Manuscript, Dept. of Anthropology, Johns Hopkins Univ., Baltimore, Md.
1975   *Saramaka Social Structure: Analysis of a Maroon Society in Surinam.* Rio Piedras, Puerto Rico: Univ. of Puerto Rico.
Price, Richard, ed.
1979 [1973]   *Maroon Societies: Rebel Slave Communities in the Americas.* 2d ed. Baltimore, Md.: Johns Hopkins Univ. Press.
Radcliffe-Brown, A. R.
1950   Introduction. In *African Systems of Kinship and Marriage,* ed. A. R. Radcliffe-Brown and Daryll Forde, 1–85. London: Oxford Univ. Press.
Robotham, Don
1977   Agrarian Relations in Jamaica. In *Essays on Power and Change in Jamaica,* ed. Carl Stone and Aggrey Brown, 45–57. Kingston: Jamaica Publishing House.
Rubenstein, Hymie
1987   *Coping with Poverty: Adaptive Strategies in a Caribbean Village.* London: Westview Press.
Smith, Michael G.
1962   *Kinship and Community in Carriacou.* New Haven, Conn.: Yale Univ. Press.
Smith, Raymond T.
1975   Review of R. Price, *Maroon Societies. Man* 10: 149.
1988   *Kinship and Class in the West Indies: A Genealogical Study of Jamaica and Guyana.* Cambridge: Cambridge Univ. Press.
Solien, Nancie L.
1959   The Nonunilineal Descent Group in the Caribbean and Central America. *American Anthropologist* 61: 578–83.
Stewart, John
1823   *A View of the Past and Present State of the Island of Jamaica.* Edinburgh: Oliver and Boyd.
Thoden van Velzen, H. U. E., and W. Van Wetering
1988   *The Great Father and the Danger: Religious Cults, Material Forces, and Collective Fantasies in the World of the Surinamese Maroons.* Dordrecht, Netherlands: Foris.
Thomas-Hope, Elizabeth M.
1992   *Explanation in Caribbean Migration. Perception and the Image: Jamaica, Barbados, St. Vincent.* London: Macmillan.
Vernon, Diane
1989   Some Prominent Features of Ndjuka Maroon Medicine. *Nieuwe West-Indische Gids* 63 (3–4): 209–21.
Western Bureau
1993   Maroons Urged to Unite. *The Gleaner* (Kingston, Jamaica), 8 Jan., p. 2.
Williams, Eric
1970   *From Columbus to Castro: The History of the Caribbean, 1492–1969.* London: Andre Deutsch.

14 | The Transformation of Slave Experience

Self and Danger in the Rituals of Creole Migrant Women in the Netherlands

Ineke van Wetering

This paper deals with historical continuity, with a manifestation of "deep structure" in an African-American community's form of worship. In particular, this essay examines a complex of ritual practices established under conditions of slavery and now regarded as "traditional." I argue that this complex has been transformed in post-emancipation and neocolonial days to suit the needs of the Suriname Creoles—an increasingly mixed population segment—as they cope with the vicissitudes of existence on the periphery of a world system. This cultural complex, accepted nowadays as "genuine culture" and as a marker of Creole identity, is the result of a long historical process of cultural interpenetration in rapidly changing contexts. Migration into Europe has changed or complicated the ritual pattern to some extent, but, in general, the pattern's aim, structure, and imagery reflect the preoccupations of outsiders whose incorporation into an established world order has been at stake.

It is not the aim of this essay to trace developments over time in Suriname's African heritage or to sketch in detail the process of cultural merging. We are ill-equipped at present to accomplish these tasks. Oral history is still in its infancy, and written records are few. For the slaves' cultural activities in the era when the plantation economy was in its heyday, we have to be content with an occasional glimpse. Only in this century have scholars begun to systematize knowledge, gather reliable information, and form a coherent view of cultural practice. The work of Penard and Penard (1913), for instance, is highly valuable for our purpose, and in the 1920s Melville Herskovits and Frances Herskovits started modern fieldwork in Paramaribo, Suriname's capital. My point of departure is these researchers' early findings concerning beliefs and rituals centering on the human soul or self. As will be shown, the cultural complex discussed here had been formed by the time they began their inquiries and seems hardly to have changed until the present day. Wooding's (1981) and Schoonheym's (1980) more recent work in Para, a rural district in Suriname known as a *winti* hotbed, supports this view. Although there is some academic dispute about its precise meaning,[1] for present purposes the term *winti* may be defined as a historically grown complex of beliefs and practices derived from African and other sources, and acknowledged as "our culture (*wi kulteru*) by the population segment defining itself as "Creole."

In Suriname, all that concerned *winti* belonged to a secret domain. Actually, the practice of *winti* was officially forbidden until 1971. The coastal Creoles, a group whose members, despite highly mixed ancestry, all have an African derivation, used to convene on the plantations they came from, often on Saturday nights, to stage *winti prey*, rituals to honor the gods protecting the group. Today, collective rituals on plantations are a thing of the past (Schoonheym 1980: 81–82; Wooding 1981: 161). Rituals are a private affair of a kin group. Solidarity among kin is highly valued, and enormous efforts are made to keep kin groups and ethnic communities together. Migrants in the Netherlands and elsewhere are under constant pressure to pay return visits to the home country and to stage rituals there. Religious ties keep a sense of community alive in a group that sees its segments drifting apart. Christian churches play a part in this, as well as various associations, but *winti* religion has been no less supportive. *Winti* adherents are, as a rule, highly conscious of their ethnic identity and nationalistic in orientation.

To mobilize a kin group has become an increasingly difficult task. In addition to geographical mobility, social mobility has had an impact. After the abolition of slavery in 1863, a process of social differentiation set in. A demand for skilled labor to serve as administrative personnel, the spread of education, the government's assimilation policies, and a gradual democratization process were factors generating a peasantry, a working class, and a middle class in a population of ex-slaves that had not known of inequalities among relatives. A light-colored elite and middle class emerged, practicing, in Patterson's (1975: 316ff.) terms, a West Indian brand of metropolitan European culture. A second type of segmentary creolization involved the development of a peculiarly West Indian peasant culture, forged out of the torn shreds of surviving African culture and representing a creative response to the exigencies of small-scale tropical peasant agriculture. Like all peasant cultures, the "Afro West Indians," as Patterson calls them, were open to the influence of urban high culture. In Suriname's rural communities, the creolized peasant culture has strong religious overtones and is referred to mostly as *winti*. The term *afkodrey* (idolatry), having no negative connotations for the adherents, is also in use.

After the Second World War, massive urbanization occurred. In Paramaribo, Suriname's capital, a culture complex evolved which conforms to what Patterson (1975: 316–19) calls "synthetic Creole culture." Growing nationalism and the emancipatory strivings of a new intelligentsia stimulated revaluation of the African heritage and opposition to postcolonial imperialism (Voorhoeve and Lichtveld 1975). The ethnic organization of Suriname's social and political life (Dew 1978, Kruyer 1973) and the prevailing system of clientelism made Creole group unity particularly valuable. The Creoles have had a strong interest in nation building and were the driving force for political independence. They felt entitled to a leadership role in the postcolonial state. Outnumbered by other groups, they did much to muster a stable following. Attempts to create a unified Creole culture have drawn heavily on symbols from the "Afro West Indian segmentary Creole culture." The rituals discussed here are an integral part of this culture complex and have been transplanted to the Netherlands.

The reproduction of the complex is a fascinating subject that can only be touched upon. Nowadays, particularly in the Netherlands, new forms of synthetic Creole culture arise, supported by a new intelligentsia that reconstructs its own "Africa," relying more on travel and books than on traditions handed down in the old way. The term *winti* has gone out of fashion; young people prefer to speak of *kulturu*. The emergence of new cultural varieties creates new rivalries and new attempts to bridge widening gaps. Yet the rituals discussed here are acknowledged as basic in the new species, just as they are in the older ones, so some common ground remains.

World System and Culture in the Caribbean

A return to the cultural dimension is perhaps overdue in Caribbean studies. For a long time, this field's preoccupation with political and economic issues—in many ways laudable—has deterred students from moving in this direction. Attempts to relate the world views of the dominated and exploited to the conditions in which they live have been few indeed. The Caribbean as a cultural area, however, seems well suited to such explorations. From a very early date, capitalism was the dominant mode of production in the area; and the plantation system, modern for its time, provided the model for the organization of society (Mintz 1971: 27, 36). Yet the impact on popular beliefs made by confrontations with the modern world has hardly been traced.

As Carnegie (1992) argues, over the past several decades Caribbean ethnography gradually has fallen into neglect. In the 1960s, studies of family life and subcultural lifestyles—particularly those dealing with the notorious issue of "matrifocality"—were dismissed as ethnocentric or worse. Later, the rise of women's studies failed to redirect the focus of student interest toward life's cultural dimensions. Recently, anthropologists seem largely to have retreated into the relatively "safe" domains of history and literature, where exposure to the ethnographic present was restricted. This stance, often linked to a "postmodern" philosophical orientation, seems poorly suited to grappling with the issues at hand. Questioning the reality of life "out there," scholars risk losing contact with the discourse of, or the "definitions of the situation" given by, the people about whom they write so glowingly and whom they protect so assiduously from the dangers inherent in the anthropological gaze. Anthropologists, it is argued, tend to make people into Others (Marcus 1986, Marcus and Fisher 1986). As more is written about "othering," however, the Others are given less chance to state their own positions and be accepted on their own terms.

In anthropology, there is no consensus about a synthesis between politico-historical and symbolic anthropology, any more than about ethnography. Symbolic anthropology, in particular, has figured hardly at all in Caribbean studies. After the waning of interest in the "African heritage" as a focus for research, representations and ritual have been regarded mostly as means of resisting oppression or of creating a common ideological base for diverse groups. By now, the explanatory power of these ideas seems to have ebbed. As Mintz (this volume) reminds his fellow students, a theme like "resistance" should be historicized. The cultural strategies of a rising middle class in a new nation are different from those of former slaves, and the interests of migrants point in other directions still. Yet cultural continuities are manifest and deserve interpretation. The very continuity of the cultural code suggests its functionality on various levels—as part of a class struggle, in the maintenance of ethnic boundaries, as a survival strategy for individuals. No one simple model, however, can provide an adequate explanatory framework.

In a seminal publication, Hannerz (1987) suggests that anthropologists should pay closer attention to the cultural aspects of globalization processes. So far, he argues, the part of the profession that occupies itself with the world system has focused mostly on cultural imperialism and Western dominance, and has been more interested in bodies than in souls. Now it is time, he believes, to make up for this and to see what the periphery has done, both for itself and for the rest of the world. The periphery has not been an empty vessel receiving imperialism's exports. Neither has it lived by bread alone, however.

The subject broached here is well suited to lend force to these arguments. Creole "folk" religion—as practiced both by rural and urban populations in Suriname, and by migrants in the Netherlands—is a product of globalization and creolization. It is clear that a cultural code, now accepted as authentic, has been welded out of African, Christian, and generalized Western elements. It is relatively unimportant whether we choose *syncretism* or *creolization* as a label to characterize such processes of merging. As we shall see, a logic has been followed in structuring notions and practices.

Body Symbolism in Creole Religion

The basic model for Christian life among the Creoles has been provided by the Moravian Brethren (*Herrnhutters* or *Evangelische Broedergemeente*), who were the first allowed to proselytize among the slave population. Far from rejecting a creed first denied to them and later imposed upon them, the slaves and their descendants wove Christian elements into a pattern in which "Africa" and Christianity are inextricably intertwined. Although now the Roman Catholics and the Protestant denominations have numerous adherents among the Creole population, the Moravian church is felt to be the matrix, a focus for cultural identity and the most "ethnic" of the churches. The cultural complex, which evolved within their ranks and today is referred to as "home rituals" (*oso sani*), represents a code for dealing with the African heritage in a manner pruned of "heathenism" and therefore acceptable to the mainstream, including those who belong to other congregations. Creole Christians feel that they have successfully merged European and African religions and will take an allegation of paganism as an insult.

There remains some controversy over this matter, though. *Winti* is looked upon with ambivalence by members of the elite and middle classes that have gradually formed. A "back-to-the-roots" movement, including a rehabilitation of African cultural heritage, has inspired many of the educated; but this does not imply that they participate actively in *winti*, as the latter often is looked down upon as a lower-class affair. These matters touch deep sensibilities and can be difficult to discuss. Some will regard a few African-derived elements, such as the cult of the *winti*, the possessing spirits, as religious forms to be kept separate from Christian worship. Dissension about the issue is kept below the surface, though. The cultural code referred to allows for *winti* practices in secret, while these are denounced from the pulpit or in other formal contexts. There is a gap here between public and private life, which allows Creoles to evade overt clashes and to bridge one of the contradictions with which they have long lived. This is one reason why the politics of secrecy, so marked in more than one sector of Creole social life, have been a major force in the formation and preservation of a Creole identity. There is room for more than one definition of a cultural heritage and more than one attitude toward *winti*. There are, however, notions about which some agreement has been reached, among them those pertaining to *oso sani*.

As ritual action among Creoles centers on the reconstruction of the body—in their thought synonymous with the self or soul—body symbolism is singled out as a theme. Social codes centering on the body can be interpreted as views about society, as Mary Douglas (1966: 146–48) has argued. A preoccupation with the body's openings in ritual is held to be a symbolic counterpart of attempts to protect the political and cultural unity of a group. As Douglas (1966, 1973), Sutherland (1986 [1975]), and Okely (1983) have shown, these interpretations are no less cogent for minority groups in modern, complex societies than for tribal groups or the proverbial "primitive isolates." Thus, notions and practices regarding the body—particularly the fear of pollution and loss of vital force—should be viewed against the backdrop of the social relations within which people are enmeshed.

In applying such models to minorities or ethnic groups, attention has focused mainly on social closure, the maintenance of group boundaries. In this regard, the orientation of symbolists is no different from that of political anthropologists, who singled out boundary maintenance as a dominant theme (Barth 1969, Cohen 1981). Relevant though this theme may be (the Suriname Creoles are no exception to the rule), there is more to be said about this. The position of the Creole group in society makes multiple and often contradictory demands; openness to the outside world, as well as closure, is held to be vital. The Creoles were the first to produce middlemen between elite and mass, and entrepreneurship in obtaining favors and advantages was vital for one's position within one's group. Here we shall look into the relation between social conditions and the ideas about powers and dangers surrounding the body.[2]

In the mid-1970s, Suriname gained political independence, and many Surinamese citizens, fearing for their country's future, fled to the Netherlands and opted for Dutch nationality. Most migrants settled in the big cities, and lower-income families found lodgings in either the older, less attractive neighborhoods or in the very new ones, such as Bijlmermeer. Whereas most migrants before that period had belonged to the middle class or the elite, the large influx of the seventies brought many who were poorly equipped to make their way into mainstream society and who actively participate in *winti*. In the large apartment buildings that dominate Amsterdam's Bijlmermeer suburb, the high density of the Suriname Creole population has created conditions favorable to the preservation of subcultural lifestyles. The new residents show a marked attachment to an array of traditional institutions, including kinship, orthodox and popular religious allegiances alike, and the specific ritual complex discussed here.

Notions of Soul or Self

"Of all the supernatural forces which govern the destiny of the individual, none surpasses the role of the *akra*—the soul—in determining that destiny," Herskovits and Herskovits (1969 [1936]: 44) note when about to introduce the topic of the spirit world. The soul is looked upon mainly as immanent, present within the body. It is a link with the divine and therefore is sacred, an object of worship. There are two specific terms for the soul: *akra* (or *kra*) and *yeye*. Both are of West African origin (Herskovits and Herskovits 1969 [1936]: 44ff., Wooding 1981: 67ff.). The soul is regarded as the guiding force which may decide which type of *winti* or tutelary spirit is congenial to the person involved, the *asi* (horse) or medium. The key position of the soul in Creole religion was already clear by the time that Herskovits and Herskovits did their research in the 1920s and has not changed since. In the 1970s, Schoonheym (1980: 41) found that many Creoles make a distinction between rituals devoted to the soul, which they will refer to as *afkodrey* or *yeye wroko* (soul work), and *winti* proper, which is the cult of the deities. In the Netherlands, most ritual activity is centered on the soul, which receives more attention than the proverbial *winti*, to which Creole folk religion owes its most current name. In fact, we may say that the cult of the soul is the royal road to the *winti* in the diaspora.

The soul's discontent may become manifest in illness and misfortune. As a rule, the soul chides an afflicted person for neglect; it may expose failures and bring hidden desires to light. In any case, it will show in what way it is to be appeased. The system of divination employed to gauge the wishes of the soul has been amply recorded (Herskovits and Herskovits 1969 [1936]: 47, Schoonheym 1980: 63, Wooding 1981: 70) and will not be rehearsed here. The human vessel will have to make an offering, out of respect for the unseen forces. A standard request of souls is silver or gold jewelry, which is ritually dedicated to the spirits involved. Apart from the material value the ornaments represent, they serve to remind the wearer of the supernaturals. In addition, souls often want new clothes and a party. The continuity in the pattern of wishes is striking; there has been little change since the turn of the century (Penard and Penard 1913, Herskovits and Herskovits 1969 [1936]: 47, Stephen 1983: 36). Acquisitiveness is legitimated in *winti* religion. The rationale often adduced (Stephen 1983: 36) is that one cannot be of use to others if one neglects oneself.

Another concept mentioned by both Herskovits and Herskovits and Wooding (1981: 70) is the *djodjo*. This notion refers to two guardian spirits or *winti* who either are connected with the soul or reside in it; one is conceived as male and the other as female. Together they represent a pair of spiritual parents. Christians will compare these forces to guardian angels, but they are pictured as *winti*. Mostly, the man is diagnosed either as an Amerindian spirit, an *Ingi winti,* a headman to whom gifts of divination are attributed; or as one of the *Kromanti,* an African sky spirit, stern and strong-willed. The female tutelary spirit invariably is one of the earth or reptile deities, the *Aisa,* whose manifestations are numerous. Almost invariably now, such spirits are thought of as inherited in family lines.

In most studies, the notions *akra* and *yeye* are referred to as interchangeable, but the one most frequently mentioned is the *akra*. Probably this is not merely fortuitous. Whereas it is true that, in the abstract, no distinction is made, a difference can be noted in daily parlance. The *akra* is conceived of as a passive entity, an unconscious force that sustains life. It registers influences and guards well-being by indicating its dissatisfaction whenever the individual, by action or default, disturbs its peace. In that case, the source of the soul's discontent should be ascertained, in order to reestablish harmony. The messages of the *akra* are always indirect; displeasure is shown by misfortunes, general bad luck, signs of illness, nightmares. The term *yeye* is used when the soul suddenly erupts in action, like a divine spark, showing some clear preference or guiding the individual into some venture brought off successfully. Its open manifestation, while important, makes this aspect of the soul less elusive and so, perhaps, less significant in ritual therapy.

As in most non-Western cosmologies, in *winti* religion no distinction is made between the natural and supernatural worlds, between spirit and matter. The soul is plainly looked upon as a physical, material entity. In casual conversation it is mostly referred to as "the body," *skin* in Sranan Tongo (Stephen 1986: 16, Venema 1992: 72). Most Creoles speak Dutch, but many think in the Creole language called Sranan Tongo; concepts that are in use in their familiar vernacular they translate literally. They may say, for instance, "My body prods me," a current way of saying "I have a hunch"; or "My body tells me," meaning "This is how I really feel about the matter." "To talk with the body" is the term used for inner dialogue. A similar deviation from Western symbolism is visible in meanings attached to body parts. Ethnographic accounts state that the soul is thought to reside in the heart or the head. The evidence on this point is unclear. In ritual practice, no clear preference is shown. Neither heart nor head is singled out as the most significant part, but rather the belly, the repository and hiding place of real motives. The feet also are in higher regard than in Western thought; libations to the soul are often sprinkled on the limbs that keep the person going and in touch with the earth.

Women in Winti

The moving forces behind the ritual enterprise are the elderly heads of households who often are female. This is in line with tradition; women are the guardians of the cultural heritage, as Herskovits and Herskovits (1969 [1936]: 9) found in the 1920s in Paramaribo. Elder women also have been core figures in political party organization in the home country, as Brana Shute (1976) noted in the 1960s. In the Netherlands, Creole migrant women are similarly active today.

The cultural logic of this is fraught with contradictions. A disadvantage—lack of stable support from partners—has received considerable attention from anthropologists. In contrast, there is a clear association of femininity with power. The historical role of women in slave societies as intermediaries with the master class, noted by Mintz (1971: 28, 39) and others, to some extent explains this. Moreover, women's chances of manumission were greater than those of men (van Lier 1971 [1949]: 100), and children stood a better chance of being freed with their mothers than with anyone else. More recently, matrifocality has been a factor. Likewise, feminists who have been keen to break with "catastrophism" hoped to discover a vision of power in the position of Creole women. Yet one clear advantage has been overlooked: absence of male supervision. To a large extent, in the home and in the semiprivate women's networks, women are free to define the situation. As we shall see, these definitions are expressed in symbolic forms. Up to a point, *winti* is a woman-friendly religion. Yet the material basis fails to support claims to a more generalized form of social power. Though elder women are key figures in the home and in private life, their economic situation and public roles are far from secure. The rise of an educated middle class and political independence opened opportunities for both young and older men that dwarfed women's means of power.

Most of the women who act as sponsors of rituals belong to the lower class—a status that has put a lasting and, for the present, characteristic stamp on the Creoles' world view and ethos. These women, heads of the notorious matrifocal or female-headed households, are responsible for nuclear families and other dependent relatives. The religious impetus and orientation is geared not to the consolidation of an achieved position but rather to the realization of aspirations and the overcoming of contradictions. In addition to self-confidence, a note of despair colors these elders' activities: "It is either pump or sink," they will say. In the face of widespread individualism, elder women go to great lengths to maintain supportive networks. In staging rituals for themselves or their close kin, they try to build up collective cultural capital. Despite economic marginality and its associated lack of stability and security, the rituals create social opportunities for advancement through links to, and dependence on, more affluent relatives and patrons. This is patently felt. Though the Creole women referred to cannot be counted among the proletariat (most of them either possess or strive, with the help of kin, to acquire a house and compound in Paramaribo, making them petit bourgeois), considering the goals they set themselves, regular middle-class strategies for doing so would hardly be realistic. Although they are the recipients of social benefits in the Netherlands, a fact much appreciated, such income is viewed as a basis to be enlarged upon by other means.

As the ethnic group is not a "given" but has constantly to be rallied and mobilized, there is a "market" for ritual efforts. Elder women look upon the cultural heritage as a resource enhancing prestige and access to scarce goods. By bringing kinsmen together and making the relatively well-to-do sponsor rituals, they create an ethnic focus. The whole entourage of ethnic cuisine, costumes, and music reminds the upwardly mobile that there is a hard, tradition-oriented core ethnic group they may fall back on in times of need, but which also may make demands upon them. In providing these services, the women act as ethnic entrepreneurs, trying to tilt the balance of power in their own favor. They enhance the position of women in their relations with men, that of the lower orders vis-á-vis those more favorably placed, and that of the whole group within the wider society.

Given that there are limits to women's resources, it is not surprising that most rituals are small-scale affairs, primarily involving a matricentric family. Although migrants go to great lengths to return periodically to the home country and stage rituals there—preferably at the plantations their ancestors came from—many cannot afford this and make do with a second-best solution. Home rituals are staged in times of crisis, or on special days. New Year's Eve is an important occasion, as is the day of abolition, July 1. Ritual acts are also performed in the course of everyday life, on the feasts or emergencies that punctuate an individual's existence, such as birthdays and wakes. The tendency toward social expansion may make such occasions into large festivities involving hundreds of people. Then the sacred part of the event will concern the inner circle only, while the other guests take part in the secular activities.

This process has empowered the heads of households, who negotiate meaning between the Christian churches and their flocks. The elderly heads of households represent the rank and file of the people in contacts with the world outside the family, and they also mediate between lower- and middle-class cultures. Within a context of deep distrust toward the outside world, the church is, relatively speaking, the most positively valued institution. By making the home a focus of ritual activity, and by inviting pastors to grace ritual occasions with their presence and lead a prayer meeting, common believers achieve some control. There is a marked tendency toward sacralization; birthday parties—not necessarily endowed with other-worldly meanings in the modern Western world, and not described as part of religious life by Herskovits and Herskovits—have been turned into ritual occasions dedicated to the well-being of the soul. Schoonheym (1980: 83) was the first to note the close association of birthday party and soul cult. Particularly when it is to be a jubilee year, public sanctification is required. This is a clear instance of what Drummond and Hannerz regard as *creolization*: an institution, derived from one continent (Europe), has been taken up into, or reinterpreted as, a way of thinking that is definitely African. As such, sacralized birthday parties represent part of a larger pattern that has developed over time, probably for more than a century. The younger generation is socialized into the proper attitudes, and these, as we shall see, have been nurtured by a political economy.

Women's dominant role in popular religion has been based partly on their assets and partly on men's lack of interest. Men looking for ideological means of control have been involved in lodges and fraternities. This lack of interest has contributed to the stabilization of the complex. Under women's control, a religion of former slaves has preserved an egalitarian outlook. In the city, it remained a religion for the periphery, a labor reserve that could not be taken up into mainstream society, and has hung on by means of patronage. There are no formal organizations, no temples, priests, or congregations; neither are there written sources to rely upon. The authority structure is typical of kin-based organizations. Apart from persons recognized as ritual experts, who can be either male or female, elder kinsmen are looked upon as the fountainheads of ritual knowledge. Most *winti* lore remains secret and belongs to implicit or covert culture. If, for the moment, we overlook modern ethnographies such as Wooding's comprehensive study, which serves as a repository of sacred knowledge for a younger generation in search of its "roots," oral tradition is the only reliable source of information. Respect for older people has been very much a part of Creole culture, and this respect enabled the elder generation, active both in church and in *winti,* to mediate between middle and lower classes.

Collective Representations

The theme of resistance and rebellion is manifest in *winti* in various ways and, often indirectly, in symbolic language. At the same time, intragroup and gender relations find expression in religious notions, and the various strands are hard to disentangle. The image of the supreme being is a case in point. History and social conditions, as well as familial relations, are reflected in the symbol. In discussing qualities attributed to the deity by common believers (both men and women), it quickly becomes clear that God is regarded as having feminine virtues, as the latter are constructed in this group. Patience, forbearance, nurturance, and above all, reliability, are God's basic characteristics. One male traditional healer spontaneously exclaimed: "How could God possibly be a man? Who would ever trust a man?" God relates to mankind as a mother to her children; she will never fail them. This fits with what Powdermaker (1968 [1939]: 246–47) observed among black Christians in the Deep South of the United States: the Negro God exhibits maternal characteristics. Powdermaker sees a connection with matrifocality; the mother is the key figure in the lower-class household, and the father is a passenger. At the same time, the image can be regarded as expressing opposition to the dominant idea in Christian churches: God as a father in heaven. To the Creoles, God is a mother in the earth.

In the symbolic language of *winti*, this conviction is expressed in the image of Mother Earth, the *Aisa* figure which is regarded as first among the powers headed by the supreme being *Anana* (Sedoc 1979: 20, Stephen 1986: 43ff.). Herskovits and Herskovits (1969 [1936]: 62–63) were quick to note a difference between Maroons and Creoles in this regard. Whereas the former would readily invoke sky deities, high gods, and celestial beings, the urban population relied on earthly powers. It is enticing to try to relate this to the degree of incorporation in colonial society: the Maroons or Bush Negroes were free to build their own institutions in the public domain, so that opposition to the beliefs current in the dominant group was not immediately called for. The Creoles had to hide their beliefs and practices and were exposed directly to Christian teaching. The cult of earthly powers, though unmistakably African, may have gained ascendancy because of its potential as a focus for a counterculture. The sky deities, though equally African, may have receded into the background due to their resemblance to Christian notions. Moreover, in later periods, the earth goddess may have figured as a symbol for a world that was threatened and rapidly vanishing, but highly valued: the corporate kin group and local peasant community of the rural areas. For migrants whose positions in new places are far from secure, ties with folks back home and corresponding symbols do not rapidly lose appeal.

As Voorhoeve (1983) and Venema (1992: 131) note, the image of the deity is modeled on the mother or grandmother, the honest matron, the woman of the common people. There is more than one reason why this image is a suitable symbol. First, woman's "traditional" role as mediator between masters and slaves, church and flock, finds expression here. More than other *winti*, Aisa provides a link with Christian beliefs and institutions. Occasionally, Christian hymns have to be sung to her (Stephen 1986: 43ff.). It is not hard to see why this deity appeals to women, and why women would support and reproduce this aspect of *winti*. Mediumship of an *Aisa winti* is hotly contested; there are many aspirants, but not all have the required characteristics that grant authority (Stephen 1986: 44, Venema 1992: 112). Finally, she may be looked upon as one of the few models of universalism in a deeply particularistic society and so may have an umbrella function, bridging contradictions (Stephen 1986: 43ff.). *Aisa* will not look after her own children only, but will take pity on any child. In Suriname, it is repeatedly stressed, it used to be easy to find elder women ready to look after children. Women could rely on each other to share responsibilities and to uphold a generalized maternal authority.

The earthiness of the main divinity corresponds to the conception of the self noted above and to other traits in the cult of all *winti*. This earthiness also is found in the attitudes of the believers, whose strong preference for the concrete over the abstract can be linked to economic reasoning and behavior. Lower-class Creoles have little confidence in words, in the designs and promises of the privileged. They rather put their trust in material tokens of involvement, such as food, money, and services. Moreover, they value the present over the future. The spiritual, if real, is manifest in material forms. This predilection often has been observed as a marked trait in any peasant society, but the striking fact in this case is the degree to which the element of resistance to hegemonic thinking and control has been enmeshed in a coherent system.

Another notion by which lower-class Creoles distinguish themselves from the socially secure is the concept of knowledge. Again, there is no trust in abstractions, whether derived from schools or books; it is experience (*ondrofeni*) which counts, the hard-won knowledge that only life itself can bring. Numerous songs and proverbs attest to this. This attitude underpins the authority of elder people. Little attempt is made consciously to enculturate the younger generation, and discussions about world views are actively discouraged. The young are made familiar with religion by ritual practice and are expected gradually to gain an understanding of its meanings.

Like *ondrofeni,* all that matters is acquired willy-nilly, or at least passively. Whenever a *winti* manifests itself in a new medium, it almost invariably turns out to be a spirit that has been in the family before. This has been true in the home country (Schoonheym 1980: 58), and in the Netherlands it is no different (Stephen 1983: 12–13). Apart from *Aisa* mediumship, as a rule possession by spirits is not actively sought. Ancestors are thought to lay claim to their descendants by manifesting themselves or by sending their tutelary spirits. Acquiescence is the proper response. Mediumship is an outstanding example of a passive way of making contact with the supernatural. As Lewis (1971) has stressed, possession is a means by which the powerless in society are assured of the presence of divine forces among them. There also is an element of immanence: the powers descend into the human vessels. Spirits often are honored by observance of taboos—i.e., not by action but by refraining from action.

Trance and dissociation have been noted as forms of religious experience that are far more common among African Americans than in Africa, where they were rather exceptional (Pollak-Eltz 1970: 199).

In all the traits mentioned, a connection with the conditions of slavery is obvious. Yet more is involved than conscious resistance to oppression. Slaves, to a significant degree, must have been concerned with the vicissitudes of material existence and with the preservation of the body and the self. As Genovese noted, "For slaves, . . . faith in God meant faith in oneself—in one's own soul and worth." Frailties in human beings were not regarded as fatal but instead were accepted as part of the human condition (Genovese 1976 [1972]: 262). These observations about slave life in the United States have a parallel in Suriname: *sakafasi* (humility and a passive suffering of the inevitable) was propagated, as was a self-image of weakness (Jones 1981: 48). The slaves' personalities were defined as *potiwan, zwakawan,* and *mofinawan* (poor, weak, and deprived). Nowadays this tendency is much deplored (Jones 1981: 48), but the compensating attention paid to the strength of the soul has gone almost unnoticed in modern studies. Where an active pursuit of interests was hardly feasible and always full of risks, values based in passivity would spread and be capitalized upon. At least this is a good guess. Status as a minority group in a colonial society may have been conducive to the conservation of this part of sacred culture; for some segments, this status has remained largely unchanged after migration.

The great faith in the wisdom accumulated in tradition makes *winti* adepts unreceptive to new and fashionable movements, whether presented in the form of Rastafarianism, "Soul," or any other manifestation of black consciousness. In keeping with this, they prefer to call themselves *Nengre* (i.e., Negroes) rather than "blacks," the label favored by politically-minded individuals. To *winti* adepts, these terms and preoccupations smack of forms of ethnic organizing benefiting the new middle class, or else they are regarded as proper for the young to dabble in. Traditionalists feel sure that real life, later, will impress upon these young people what really matters.

Individualism and World View

The prevalent Creole tendency toward individualism corresponds to a condensation process in the world of ideas. This process presumably got under way in Suriname, as all the "classic" sources indirectly attest. Now it continues in the diaspora. In an urban context, and after migration, the head of a family should be able to deal with all sorts of situations that demand ritual action, and in Creole belief these are many. In the home country, kinsmen to be consulted were never far off. Ideally, any kin group would encompass, or could muster, a number of mediums of different *winti*. In Suriname, a sufficient number of specialists would be available to treat any afflictions that might turn up. In the Netherlands, an individual head of a household often has to cope alone, being sustained, however, by the belief that the whole cosmos, the complex world of gods and spirits, is represented in the human soul.

This form of condensation has facilitated the incorporation of African-derived notions into a Christian world view. In the Christian creed, the relation between the supreme deity and the individual soul is basic to religious experience. Conceivably, there has been a two-way process; the Christian outlook may have fostered the condensation process in *winti*. Speculation on an actual historic process is hazardous, but syncretism may have been stimulated by urbanization and increasing fragmentation of corporate kin groups. In this packaged form, ready for transportation to new surroundings, *winti* was carried to the Netherlands.

In broad outline, there is a consensus among believers about the pantheon of forces residing in the soul. In one significant respect, though, a divergence in outlook is notable. Believers who aspire to middle-class status stress the unambiguously positive elements in their religion. In an understandable eagerness to erase the social stigma clinging to *winti*, and in order to facilitate an open acknowledgment of African heritage as part of Creole identity in the wider world, there is a tendency to gloss over the ambivalent character of the gods. This, however, will not persuade an older elite group which entertains modern, Western views and leaves to elder women some dabbling in home rituals, as an alternative tradition of the sort the West is rich in. Nor will this satisfy the adepts of old. Rank-and-file adherents have no scruples concerning morally ambiguous traits of the deities. In fact, the lower orders insist on the presence in the self of a third power, in addition to the benevolent but strict parental deities: the inner demon. Middle-class people tend to deny this third power as unorthodox, but the lower orders insist on the little imp's presence. Within the category of demons, a host of spiritual forces is classified together which, theologically speaking, belong to different pantheons—such as the sky, bush, or Amerindian spirits. The cosmology of the Creoles is complex—in fact, almost too complex for the rather simple type of social organization within which it evolved. What we observe is, again, a process of condensation: classifying together different types of spirits that bring similar messages.

The demonic third force is invariably male, aggressive, and rebel-
lious, tending to thwart the purposes of the high *winti*. Various terms
for the imps are in use, among which the term *bakru* stands out. These
beings are pictured as the "little people," well known in the whole of
West Africa: small, about three feet high, and pitch-black. Though not
evil by nature, they easily may turn to badness. They love to play pranks
on people and will readily steal or lie. Lacking good sense and moral
discrimination, they can be bribed with relatively small gifts to perform
heinous crimes. Among the "little people" are various spirits associated
with specific dangers. There are *Ampuku* or forest spirits who may act
as succubi or incubi and may disrupt sexual functioning. Their aggres-
siveness is matched by that of the *Bus' Ingi*, the Amerindians of the forest. *Obia* is classified at times as a specific *winti* and at other times as a
generalized spiritual force.

Creole women are aware of different shades of meaning and tend
to have different associations with the various beings, but these do not
always coincide. In possession dances, the different characters are displayed and so are retained in the collective memory, but the shades of
meaning generally do not function in the interpretation of concrete cases.
Often these are shrugged off as something typical of the ancestors, which
need not detain the descendants overmuch. For all practical purposes,
many Creoles stick to a threefold classification and regard the bewildering variety of beings as subtypes.

Women look upon the demons with ambivalence. On the one
hand, they are dangerous forces, and undue involvement with them will
not go unpunished. On the other hand, they are powers indispensable
in the struggle for survival. The Creoles of the lower class accept the
higher deities as models for behavior, and much ritual is dedicated to
affirming allegiance to these beneficial forces. But the inner demons
need to be cultivated as well, for it is consciously realized that one has
to fall back on less respectable strategies in times of need. The demons
are represented as naughty children, and they have to be "pampered."
Demons are powerful symbols for assertiveness—an indispensable quality—but fear is always rife that the *bakru* will bring one to grief or cause
one to slide down the social scale. Mostly, however, women discuss the
demons gleefully; the pranks of the "little ones" are an inexhaustible
source of fun.

As adherents so persuasively state, the two religious systems—the
Christian and the African-American—are not at odds. Neither are they
interchangeable, however. Nor is either superfluous. An alliance to both
systems allows the mediator, household head, or ritual expert to bridge

a gap between the life experiences of the lower class and the values of wider society. The defiance common in the lower strata—among women and, in particular, among men—is legitimated in *afkodrey*; the lesser spirits are acknowledged and served. At the same time, though, they are placed in a hierarchical order; they have to respect the higher powers. Mediums of lower deities who would be most unwilling to submit to a Christian God—more like a stepfather than a father—accept the authority of the higher *winti*. The higher powers are expected to achieve a reconciliation to the inevitable demands for a certain degree of conformity with mainstream society.

Rituals

The herbal ablution is a key rite within the complex of rituals concerning the soul. Although performed alone, it also forms part of larger ritual contexts. Its aim is to counteract two ills that may befall the soul: weakness and defilement. People voice complaints about both spontaneously, and reactions to these are direct: the soul has to be purified and fortified. This is not a discourse of ritual experts; it is discussed in the course of daily life, by common people. The soul is described as a host in the body, which is compared to a house. The soul should be watchful for any evil force or spirit entering and warn the inhabitant of danger. Signs betraying the soul's discontent may range from illness, accidents, and bad luck to despondent moods. The evil may be due to the afflicted one's own carelessness, or it may be caused by others. Jealousy, gossip, and the "tying" of the soul by ill-intentioned magicians may produce the negative effects mentioned.

Emergencies that might imperil the soul include a visit to the hospital or—worse but not uncommon—prison; contact with official persons, administrators, or policemen; or, for the young, school examinations. These require a herbal ablution or *wasi*. Immediately upon return from such an unpleasant situation, one discards all clothing worn and other reminiscences of the event and prepares a bath. If "modern" parents or other responsible persons who should know better neglect to do this, it causes amazement bordering on indignation, since it betrays an astounding indifference to the fate of persons near and dear. As a rule, there is hardly a trace of suspicion that such ablutions would be "idolatry"; on the contrary, their performance is viewed as a truly Christian concern, a home ritual befitting respectable families. It is important that the afflicted person should "speak"—that is, give utterance to all fears and worries. As long as these latter are inside the body—or, more pre-cisely, the belly—the emotions might cause harm. Once brought into the open, they become innocuous. As has been recorded over and over again (Herskovits 1934; Fortes and Horton 1983 [1959]: 71ff.; Marwick 1965: 95; Turner 1980: 569, 580), this "speaking," an element basic in African systems of therapy, is strongly reminiscent of Freudian therapeutic technique.

In case the affliction is of longer duration, the bath is taken up into a cycle of rituals, which may turn into a virtual retreat. For a period of three days or a week, one lights a candle, takes a Bible and a glass of water, and prays. A glass of rum is required in case one wants to call upon the ancestors (cf. Schoonheym 1980: 61). Each night and each morning, one should lay the problem before all beneficial powers—God, the high *winti* residing in the soul, and, if one wishes to do so, the ancestors—and ask for support. They will respond by sending dreams that show their presence, and in this way they demonstrate that they stand by their "child." The bath is a purification ritual; all linger-ing evil should be washed away. Once rid of pollution, the soul experi-ences new strength. As indicated above, the two recurrent complaints and dangers of the soul are *doti skin*, being saddled by impurities, and loss of vital force. Seclusion from active social life is recommended, as it is clearly realized that a period of meditative sensory deprivation is conducive to contact with spiritual forces.

A *kra tafra*, a dinner party dedicated to the soul, may crown the cycle. Although the invited special guests are not told what the purpose is, usually they deduce this from the many details: the types of food and drinks served, the colors chosen for clothes and the decoration of the table, the type of music played. This perpetuates a tradition of not openly discussing *winti*, but of honoring it in an implicit way. As this type of communal ritual is easier to realize than a large-scale ritual, a *winti prey*, at present it is one of the most frequently practiced rites.

In recent publications popularizing *winti*, recipes are given for the proper preparation of ablutions (see, for instance, Stephen 1983). Such texts cater mainly to a clientele of middle-class Creoles in search of "roots." Members of the lower class prefer to stick to family traditions and look disdainfully upon such unhallowed writings, which in any case they will not read. Invariably, some traditional ingredients are recom-mended which are imported from Suriname and are for sale in special shops and ethnic markets. Any big city has such distribution centers. Such needs stimulate ethnic enterprise and, to some extent, boost the economy of a peripheral area strongly dependent on money orders.

Recipes are not strictly adhered to, however. There is ample scope for improvisation. In this regard, an ambiguity is inherent in *afkodrey*. It is regarded as essential that the ties to the home country be reinforced, and it can hardly be doubted that the aromatic qualities of herbs activate memories of childhood and life back home which affect the soul. Yet adaptation to new circumstances is equally legitimized. Although the magical efficacy of herbs is stressed in *winti* theology, the authority of the invading spirits who guide the mediums' choice of ritual ingredients is equally orthodox. Thus, in the Netherlands, a debate has arisen whether it is allowable to use, for instance, endive in a herbal concoction. Some defend the practice on the grounds of having rebaptized the plant as a substitute for a proper weed which cannot be obtained in the Netherlands. Others abhor such innovation. Schoonheym (1980: 57) has recorded a conception of ritual purity which excludes the use of flowers in herbal concoctions. Most migrant women, however, highly value and even insist upon their favored flowers in ablutions. A way out is provided by the conviction that souls have different tastes. Nevertheless, this shows that creolization is full of ambiguities and may have the effect of undermining ethnicization by deepening differences of opinion.

Soul worship mainly acts as an underpinning for ethnic identity, though. It comes very naturally to most Creoles, yet it remains shot through with ambivalence for persons of uncertain class allegiance. The following case study will demonstrate this. Syncretism is obvious here, and the element of bricolage is equally striking. Cornelli—a name current among Creole women—belongs to a respected family that boasts a number of Moravian pastors. She relates her experiences on the brink of *afkodrey*.

When I fell ill lately, my aunt in Rotterdam wanted to come and prepare a herbal bath, but I hesitated. We have been staunch supporters of the church all along, and you never know what powers are evoked. But I did not want to offend her; her intentions were doubtlessly beyond reproach. But a cousin who is a Rosicrucian warned me: "These powers are very real, but once you have contacted the higher ones you should leave the lower. Do not tamper with such a *law wasi*" [nonsense bath]. My aunt arrived and made the ablution, with all proper ingredients. But the thing misfired completely. All of a sudden I started to cry profusely and I did not know why. I woke up at five in the morning with a terrible pain in the stomach; for three days I have vomited and had a diarrhoea. The doctor came and thought the antibiotics were to blame, but that was not the real cause, I felt: it was the ablution. My cousin phoned to ask how I

was, and told me he would offer a dedication for me in his sanctum. He
asked my aunt what had happened and when he was told about the bath,
he replied: "I had thought so." I was completely weak and miserable, but
all of a sudden I had the hunch to rise and go out. My aunt wanted to
stop me; "You will drop dead in the street," she warned. But I ran
straight to the chemist's and bought all sorts of perfumes I like, a box of
candles, roses, and freesias. I prepared a bath, in the copper vessel you see
over there, which is dedicated to my *yeye*. I felt sound again. I called my
aunt, we prayed and prayed, till sweat was running all over. "You are like
my mother," I said to her, "You have raised me, pray for me, say anything you wish." We recited Psalm 23 and 51, and the Lord's Prayer. I
felt completely relieved, healed and strong.

Many Creoles practicing *afkodrey* have a sacred place in the house, some
corner in the bedroom. Others dedicate a whole room to the soul and
the inherent spirits. The copper vessel Cornelli pointed to is one of
Aisa's paraphernalia. As a rule, it contains a doll in national Creole
women's costume, a bottle of champagne, and other objects belonging
to the cult, such as candles, beads, and shells. The male spirits have their
own cult objects, drinks, and often a white costume a medium can wear.
The demon is often represented as a boy doll in a navy suit and cap. The
powers should take a material form and remind the adepts of their presence. For some Protestants, a Bible is an essential attribute in a shrine.
Once I observed one at the base of a prayer pole erected in an earthen
vessel. The pole is a most traditional element in a sanctuary, the earth-
enware pot an in-between solution, as there is no earth in an apartment
building. But without a Bible, the sacred unit would lack persuasive
force, it was felt. For anyone raised in church the objects that have
meaning there should be represented in one's private chapel as well.
People are advised to add and improvise according to their own conviction; dreams often provide inspiration for such bricolage. The whole
point is that the believer externalizes notions of the sacred and valuable;
whatever the soul wishes is beneficial. The objects, chosen out of a sincere
predilection, will answer and support one when in need. The basic argument is: *Efu yu teli den, den e teli yu baka* (If you take them into account,
they will consider you as well).

So far, beliefs and practices have been described, but no connection
has been made to social structures that constrain and foster them. In
order to get an inkling of such connections, and to gauge to what extent believers are aware of them, we shall turn to another case. Here a
traditional healer explains to a Dutch woman who is unacquainted with

afkodrey what is the purpose of home rituals and how to go about them.[3] It is clear that the adepts, though not to be viewed as the sociologists of their own life experiences, nevertheless come very close to being exactly this; the wearer of the shoe knows where it pinches.

Muriel is a ritual expert, a Creole mother of a big family. She has a job as a cook in a center for problem children from Suriname, but fears that others want to oust her. Annemarie is Dutch, is in the same age group, and also feels that her job is in jeopardy because of imminent funding cutbacks. Annemarie says she often feels depressed and unable to cope. She likes her colleagues and is on good terms with them; nevertheless, she often holds back from going to the office. And this, precisely, will not do her reputation any good. Muriel shakes her head: "You Dutch are so foolish, you are so completely open. One cannot simply assume that others are well disposed towards you. We Surinamese, we are more careful. First of all, we do not enter into all places and situations without ado. We do not accept food anywhere. Whenever I enter someplace, I feel my way. If something seems wrong, I do not say much and leave quickly. My 'ego' warns me that something is amiss, and, even though I cannot explain it, I respond."

"But what should I do if I do like the people involved?" Annemarie asks.

"They may be quite friendly," Muriel replies, "but you can not look into their hearts. And also, you think you appreciate them, but your 'ego' may assess the situation differently. What you think is not all. If one's ego is distrustful, one ought to be guided by it."

Annemarie again: "Often, I do not feel like going to my working-place, but what can I do? I do not want to lose the job."

Muriel: "You will have to fortify the 'ego' and seek power."

"But how should I go about that?"

And then, to Annemarie, who has not seen the inside of either church or Bible for a long time and would prefer more straightforward "shamanistic" advice, Castañeda-style, for instance: "Before you turn in, take your Bible and light a candle. Then, you start to speak. Everything that weighs down on you, you should mention, it does not matter what it is. You should do this for a week. Then *Aisa* will send you fine, clear dreams that provide an answer. But, be careful, in that week you should not leave the house before you have talked to yourself: 'As I have left, so I want to return.' Whatever people will say to you in the course of the day, in what way they treat you, it will not affect you. It is for them, not for you. This is what I teach my children. They should know how to protect themselves. On no account, they may be 'open.' Wherever you go, you should 'talk to yourself,' you have to call your 'ego,' because you will most certainly need it."

Often, Creole women refer to the soul as the "I" or "ego," which they emphatically distinguish from the conscious self-image: "You may think that you like or want to do this or that, but your ego is different," they will say. Not a conscious force, its strivings should be ascertained or divined and, when known, appeased, honored, fortified. Dreams are considered to be important messages of the soul.

Another healer disclosed that, whenever she arrived at an unknown place, she would start by saluting the spirits that have their abode there. When on good terms with them, then one need not be so fearful of the people there. Traditional songs convey the same lesson:

> Mi nene leri mi, pikin te yu go waka pe,
> yu mu bari a doti wan odi, bifo yu bari frenti odi-e.
> (My grandmother taught me, child, wherever you go,
> first salute the earth, before you greet friends.)

These lessons stress personal independence, which is regarded as highly valuable, particularly for those in dependent or servile positions, as many Creoles have been. Also, the autonomy instilled by the spirit world is important in a group that endorses interdependence and trust in networks. Observers have been struck by the self-reliance of lower-class Creoles; their religion has made a vital contribution in this regard. Many small details of ritual practice affirm efforts to take a stand against a prejudiced world and not be overwhelmed by it. Likewise, the values of a spirit-supported personal autonomy counteract the effects of dependency relations fostered by kinship norms.

Ablutions are performed by members of the lower and the new middle classes alike. Shelley, a woman who had found a job in a welfare organization for migrants from Suriname, felt threatened at her office. Everybody who had a job there was most circumspect. One colleague would never touch a doorknob without a handkerchief and also daily swept her seat, fearing *hebi* ("heaviness" or "trouble") or even witchcraft. One day Shelley found her desk covered by some unknown dust or powder, and in the evening she had not felt well. For security's sake, she immediately prepared an ablution to take away any evil influence. To fight it, she prepared a bad-smelling concoction. The traditional laundry bleaching blue was mixed with garlic and herrings' guts. It had to smell awful. While having her bath from top to bottom, she talked to herself and the evil in the shower cell and pictured all the bad things lurking there: "There you are, but what are you after? I do not know you, so what are you bent on? If you do not like this body, get lost, but if you have a positive feeling for it, show it. Remember, I am here, not to be duped by you." Next she took a sweet-smelling bath to please her soul and affirm the good; she sealed herself. The concoction had been prepared in a new plastic tub that had not been used before, most certainly not for washing hands or cloths, but in fact not even for cups or glasses. For that would have spoiled the bath's effect, because of "all the mouths that had gone into it"—that is, all envious or angry words spoken by these mouths. When applying the "sweet" bath, she had asked *Aisa* for support: "All evil that I meet on my path, wave it aside for me, and the evil that is behind me, let it not come near me." It is clear that other people are pictured as evildoers, and the threatened person as a paragon of innocence. The afflicted person is like a child, to be protected by mother *Aisa*.

Also, it is patently clear that the evil is imagined as something concrete, a material object, visible and tangible. This conviction occasionally creates problems for Bijlmermeer's citizens. Housing agencies complain of the demandingness of Creole tenants; they refuse newly painted apartments on the grounds that other Creole families have lived there before. The idea is that they have used the shower cells for baths, where many evil things, once washed off, are still lurking, waiting for new inhabitants and victims. Neither soap nor bleach can wash them off; evil is thought of as highly clinging and contagious.

Discussion

As Turner (1980: 577) observes, religious ideas and ritual may be looked upon as metasocial commentary. More than a mere "reflection" of structures, they also manifest a program of action. This is fully true of Creole beliefs and rituals. The fears most often mentioned are of defilement and loss of vital force. These feelings can be assumed to relate to the unstable position most *afkodrey* adepts occupy with regard to scarce material and immaterial resources. Most of the time, access to such goods is precarious for the lower orders. As indicated above, a major pitfall is a state of "openness" to the outside world, since it carries risks of pollution and weakening. Yet few groups are as "open" as Creoles: always keen on keeping old networks intact and always on the lookout for new contacts and opportunities. Obviously, people have "second thoughts" about these favored and indispensable strategies. The soul is constantly in jeopardy and has to be "sealed" by ritual. Muriel's well-meant advice, in particular, relates to perilous situations which are common anywhere but are most prevalent in societies where individuals have to be socially expansive and where, moreover, clientelism is a main feature of the social organization.

Despite its different colonial background, Suriname's social structure is much like that of a Latin American society. A small elite, national and international, controls the means of power, and the lower classes are dependent. Patron-client relations are channels of distribution for valuables, and demand inevitably exceeds supply. In the Dutch welfare state, the situation is different to some extent; there is a support system that makes the struggle for survival less desperate. Yet kinship ties to people back home who are less fortunate entail demands and make migrants constantly alert for additional income and potential windfalls. Economic recession enhances these effects.

The basis of patron-client relations is the social expectation that a patron will further the interests of followers in order to advance her or his own. Such a promise will secure a following. In reality, however, private gain repeatedly takes precedence over the common interest. Sometimes it is simply impossible to satisfy the rank and file, but often the temptations of expediency and short-term gain are too great. Deliberate deceit need not be involved, but followers lack the means to hold a patron to his word. A standard complaint and warning among Creoles concerns being "used," putting one's energy into some enterprise and being deprived of one's proper reward.

Doubt about the outcomes of transactions are expressed in distrust of the spoken word and in a preoccupation with difference between appearance and reality—the outside and the inside of the body, the personality and the soul. There is a constant danger of weakening the body-soul by an output of energy, and the inside has to be protected continuously from evil things that might be taken in. As a rule, if things misfire, the patron is nowhere to be found and cannot be made to account for his dealings, and the followers often are saddled with unforeseen but unpleasant consequences. By opening relations that seem promising, the symbols say, one often takes in evil and hence experiences loss and a lack of resilience.

In the foregoing, Creole notions about the soul have been interpreted as symbolizing the perils in clientelism, but ideas about pollution and power loss might apply equally to notoriously exploitive intraclass relations. The symbols specify dangers not in terms that relate to Western social theories, but rather in terms pertinent to the experiences of individuals. Two arguments might explain this focus. In groups where people strongly rely on individual strategies, collective representations may be expected to express this and to specify social dangers in terms of risks to the individual self. Moreover, at the level of day-to-day experience, class relations will, as a rule, be mediated by patron-client relations, so there is, perhaps, no need to make a distinction.

One of the research questions posed earlier was what the periphery has done for itself and for the world. It seems that one of the outcomes of globalization has been an intensification of ritual activity. Suriname's Creole migrants are not exceptional in this regard. A heightened preoccupation with beliefs and activities that formerly were labeled "superstitious" and were expected to disappear has been reported in diverse forms in many parts of the world. The Creole migrants who practice their form of syncretism see this as a most "natural" and sensible thing to do. When discussing beliefs and practices with outsiders, they define and defend these as parts of a coping strategy, with effects on both a personal and a collective, ethnic level. When decoding the ritual language, students may discover a hidden logic and clues concerning the contradictions within which people live.

Notes

1. An often-cited definition of *winti* is given by Wooding (1981: 137): "an Afroamerican religion which centers round the belief in personified supernatural beings, who take possession of a human being, eliminate his consciousness, after which they unfold the past, the present and the future, and are able to cause and cure illnesses of a supernatural origin." Schoonheym (1980: 41), however, prefers the term *afkodrey* to denote the religious complex peculiar to the creoles. He argues that the soul cult is the core, rather than the winti proper, as the former is acknowledged by a greater number of adherents. Schoonheym's view is corroborated by the material presented here.
2. Fieldwork data upon which this paper is based were collected mainly in Bijlmermeer, one of Amsterdam's new suburbs, mainly between 1982 and 1987.
3. The following account is not a literal rendering; it is a compilation of various conversations on the matter. The two main characters are not two specific persons, but were constituted from fieldwork materials of several ritual experts and inquisitive outsiders.

References

Barth, Fredrik
1969   Introduction. In *Ethnic Groups and Boundaries,* ed Fredrik Barth, 9–38. Bergen: Universitetsforlaget and London: Allen and Unwin.
Bastide, Roger
1978 [1960]   *The African Religions of Brazil: Toward a Sociology of the Interpenetration of Civilizations.* Baltimore, Md.: Johns Hopkins Univ. Press.
Brana Shute, Rosemary
1976   Women, Clubs and Politics. *Urban Anthropology* 5 (2): 157–85.
Carnegie, Charles V.
1992   The Fate of Ethnography: Native Social Science in the English-Speaking Caribbean. *New West Indian Guide* 66 (1–2): 5–25.
Cohen, Abner
1981   *The Politics of Elite Culture: Explorations in the Dramaturgy of Power in a Modern African Society.* Berkeley: Univ. of California Press.
Cross, Malcolm, and Han Entzinger
1988   *Lost Illusions: Caribbean Minorities in Britain and the Netherlands.* London: Routledge.
Dew, Edward M.
1978   *The Difficult Flowering of Suriname: Ethnicity and Politics in a Plural Society.* The Hague, Netherlands: Martinus Nijhoff.
Douglas, Mary
1966   *Purity and Danger.* Harmondsworth, England: Penguin.
1973   *Natural Symbols.* Harmondsworth, England: Penguin.
Drummond, Lee
1980   The Cultural Continuum: A Theory of Intersystems. *Man* (N.S.) 15 (2): 352–74.
Fortes, Meyer, and Robin Horton
1983 [1959]   *Oedipus and Job in West African Religion.* Cambridge: Cambridge Univ. Press.
Genovese, Eugene D.
1976 [1972]   *Roll, Jordan, Roll.* New York: Vintage Books.
Hannerz, Ulf
1987   The World in Creolization. *Africa* 57 (4): 546–59.
Herskovits, Melville J.
1934   Freudian Mechanisms in Primitive Negro Psychology. In *Essays Presented to C. G. Seligman,* ed. E. E. Evans-Pritchard et al., 75–84. London: Kegan Paul.
Herskovits, Melville J., and Frances S. Herskovits
1969 [1936]   *Suriname Folklore.* New York: AMS Press.
Jones, J. F.
1981   Kwakoe en Christus. Ph.D. thesis, Free Univ., Brussels.
Kruyer, G. J.
1973   *Suriname, neo-kolonie in rijksverband.* Meppel, Netherlands: Boom.
Lewis, Joan M.
1971   *Ecstatic Religion.* Harmondsworth, England: Penguin.
Marcus, George E.
1986   Contemporary Problems of Ethnography in the Modern World System. In

Writing Culture, ed. James Clifford and George E. Marcus, 165–93. Berkeley: Univ. of California Press.

Marcus, George E., and Michael M. J. Fisher
1986   *Anthropology as Cultural Critique.* Chicago: Univ. of Chicago Press.

Marwick, M. G.
1965   *Sorcery in Its Social Setting.* Manchester, England: Manchester Univ. Press.

Mintz, Sidney W.
1971   The Caribbean as a Socio-cultural Area. In *Peoples and Cultures of the Caribbean,* ed. Michael M. Horowitz. Garden City, N.Y.: Natural History Press.

Mintz, Sidney W., and Richard Price
1976   *An Anthropological Approach to the Afro-American Past: A Caribbean Perspective.* ISHI Occasional Papers 2. Philadelphia: ISHI.

Norton, R.
1983   Ethnicity, "Ethnicity" and Culture Theory. *Man* 18 (1): 190–91.

Okely, Judith
1983   *The Traveller Gypsies.* Cambridge: Cambridge Univ. Press.

Patterson, Orlando
1975   Context and Choice in Ethnic Allegiance: A Theoretical Framework and Caribbean Case-study. In *Ethnicity: Theory and Experience,* ed. Nathan Glazer and Daniel P. Moynihan, 305–49. Cambridge, Mass.: Harvard Univ. Press.

Penard, F. P., and A. P. Penard
1913   Surinaamsch bijgeloof. *Bijdragen tot de Taal-, Land- en Volkenkunde van Nederlandsch Indië* 67: 157–83.

Pollak-Eltz, Angelina
1970   *Afro-Amerikaanse godsdiensten en culten.* Roermond, Netherlands: J. J. Romen and Zonen.

Powdermaker, Hortense
1968 [1939]   *After Freedom.* New York: Russell and Russell.

Schoonheym, Peter
1980   *Je geld of. . . je leven.* ICAU Mededelingen 14. Utrecht, Netherlands: Instituut voor Culturele Antropologie.

Sedoc, N. O.
1979   *Aisa Winti.* Paramaribo: n.p.

Stephen, Henri M. J.
1983   *Winti: Afro-Surinaamse religie en magische rituelen in Suriname en Nederland.* Amsterdam: Karnak.

1986   *De macht van de Fodoe Winti. Fodoe rituelen in de winti-kultus in Suriname en in Nederland.* Amsterdam: Karnak.

Sutherland, Anne
1986 [1975]   *Gypsies: The Hidden Americans.* Prospect Heights, Ill.: Waveland Press.

Turner, Victor W.
1980   Encounter with Freud: The Making of a Comparative Symbologist. In *The Making of Psychological Anthropology,* ed. George D. Spindler, 558–83. Berkeley: Univ. of California Press.

Van Lier, R. A. J.
1971 [1949]   *Frontier Society.* The Hague, Netherlands: Martinus Nijhoff.

van Wetering, Wilhelmina
1987   Informal Supportive Networks: Quasi-Kin Groups, Religion and Social Order

among Suriname Creoles in the Netherlands. *Netherlands Journal of Sociology* 23 (2): 92–101.

In press   A Demon in a Garbage Chute. In *Afro-Caribbean Worldviews*, ed. Barry Chevannes. The Hague, Netherlands: Institute of Social Studies.

Venema, Tijno
1992   *Famiri nanga Kulturu: Creoolse sociale verhoudingen en Winti in Amsterdam.* Amsterdam: Het Spinhuis.

Voorhoeve, Jan
1983   The Obiaman and His Influence in the Moravian Parish. *Bijdragen tot de Taal-, Land-en Volkenkunde* 139 (4): 411–20.

Voorhoeve, Jan, and Ursy M. Lichtveld
1975   *Creole Drum.* New Haven, Conn.: Yale Univ. Press.

Wooding, Charles J.
1981   *Evolving Culture: A Cross-Cultural Study of Suriname, West Africa and the Caribbean.* Washington, D.C.: Univ. Press of America.

Bibliography

Abel, Annie Heloise
1915–25   *Slaveholding Indians.* 3 vols. Cleveland: Arthur H. Clark.
1992a [1915] *The American Indian as Slaveholder and Secessionist.* Rpt. of *Slaveholding Indians.* Vol. 1. Lincoln: Univ. of Nebraska Press.
1992b [1919] *The American Indian as Slaveholder and Secessionist.* Rpt. of *Slaveholding Indians.* Vol. 2. Lincoln: Univ. of Nebraska Press.
Agiri, Babatunde
1981   Slavery in Yoruba Society in the Nineteenth Century. In *The Ideology of Slavery in Africa,* ed. Paul E. Lovejoy, 123–48. Beverly Hills, Calif.: Sage.
Ailenroc, M. R.
1903   *The White Castle of Louisiana.* Louisville, Ky.: John P. Morton.
Aitken, Hugh G. J., ed.
1971   *Did Slavery Pay? Readings in the Economics of Black Slavery in the United States.* Boston: Houghton Mifflin.
Ajax [A. J. Axwijk]
1961   De vlucht van Boni en Aloekoe. *De West,* 10 and 11 Nov. 1961.
Ajayi, Jacob F. A., and John D. Y. Peel, eds.
1992   *Peoples and Empires in African History.* London: Longman.
Andrews, George R.
1980   *The Afro-Argentines of Buenos Aires, 1800–1900.* Madison: Univ. of Wisconsin Press.
Andrews, Thomas F.
1965   Freedmen in Indian Territory: A Post–Civil War Dilemma. *Journal of the West* 4 (3): 367–76.
Andrews, William L.
1986   *To Tell a Free Story: The First Century of Afro-American Autobiography.* Urbana: Univ. of Illinois Press.

Aptheker, Herbert
1939 Maroons within the Present Limits of the United States. *Journal of Negro History* 24 (2): 167–84. Rpt. in *Maroon Societies,* ed. Richard Price, 151–67. Baltimore, Md.: Johns Hopkins Univ. Press, 1979 [1973].
1969 [1943] *American Negro Slave Revolts.* New York: International Publishers [New York: Columbia Univ. Press].
Arhin, Kwame
1979 *West African Traders in the Nineteenth and Twentieth Centuries.* London: Longman.
Asad, Talal
1987 Are There Histories of Peoples Without Europe? A Review Article. *Comparative Studies in Society and History* 29: 594–607.
Bailyn, Bernard
1986 *The Peopling of British North America.* New York: Vintage Books.
Barker, David, and Balfour Spence
1988 Afro-Caribbean Agriculture: A Jamaican Maroon Community in Transition. *Geographical Journal* 154 (2): 198–208.
Barth, Fredrik
1969 Introduction. In *Ethnic Groups and Boundaries,* ed. Fredrik Barth, 9–38. Bergen: Universitetsforlaget and London: Allen and Unwin.
Bartl, Renate
1986 Die Beziehungen zwischen Schwarzen und Indianern in Nordamerika. Master's thesis, Dept. of American Cultural History, Univ. of Munich, Germany.
Bastide, Roger
1978 [1960] *The African Religions of Brazil: Toward a Sociology of the Interpenetration of Civilizations.* Baltimore, Md.: Johns Hopkins Univ. Press.
Bastien, Remy
1961 Haitian Rural Family Organization. *Social and Economic Studies* 10: 478–510.
Bauer, Raymond, and Alice Bauer
1942 Day-to-Day Resistance to Slavery. *Journal of Negro History* 28: 388–419.
Beck, Hartmut
1981 *Brüder in vielen Völkern.* Berlin: Evangelische Verlagsanstalt.
Beckles, Hilary M.
1989 *Natural Rebels: A Social History of Enslaved Women in Barbados.* London: Zed Books.
Berlin, Ira D.
1980 Time, Space and the Evolution of Afro-American Society on British Mainland North America. *American Historical Review* 85 (1): 44–78.
Berlin, Ira D., and Philip D. Morgan
1991 Introduction. In *The Slaves' Economy: Independent Production by Slaves in the Americas,* ed. Ira D. Berlin and Philip Morgan, 1–30. London: Frank Cass. (= *Slavery and Abolition* 12 [1].)
———, eds.
1991 *The Slaves' Economy: Independent Production by Slaves in the Americas.* London: Frank Cass. Special issue of *Slavery and Abolition* 12 (1).
Besson, Jean
1974 *Land Tenure and Kinship in a Jamaican Village.* 2 vols. Ph.D. diss., Univ. of Edinburgh.

1975   Land Tenure and Kinship in "River Village," Jamaica, W.I. Unpublished paper, Univ. of Edinburgh.

1979   Symbolic Aspects of Land in the Caribbean: The Tenure and Transmission of Land Rights among Caribbean Peasantries. In *Peasants, Plantations and Rural Communities in the Caribbean,* ed. Malcolm Cross and Arnaud Marks, 86–116. Guildford, England: Univ. of Surrey; Leiden, Netherlands: Royal Institute of Linguistics and Anthropology.

1984a   Family Land and Caribbean Society: Toward an Ethnography of Afro-Caribbean Peasantries. In *Perspectives on Caribbean Regional Identity,* ed. Elizabeth M. Thomas-Hope, 57–83. Liverpool: Liverpool Univ. Press.

1984b   Land Tenure in the Free Villages of Trelawny, Jamaica: A Case Study in the Caribbean Peasant Response to Emancipation. *Slavery and Abolition* 5 (1): 3–23.

1985   Land Tenure in the Free Villages of Trelawny: A Case Study in the Caribbean Peasant Response to Emancipation. *Slavery and Abolition* 5: 3–23.

1987a   Family Land as a Model for Martha Brae's New History: Culture Building in an Afro-Caribbean Village. In *Afro-Caribbean Villages in Historical Perspective,* ed. Charles V. Carnegie, 100–132. Kingston, Jamaica: African-Caribbean Institute of Jamaica.

1987b   A Paradox in Caribbean Attitudes to Land. In *Land and Development in the Caribbean,* ed. Jean Besson and Janet Momsen, 13–45. London: Macmillan.

1988   Agrarian Relations and Perceptions of Land in a Jamaican Peasant Village. In *Small Farming and Peasant Resources in the Caribbean,* ed. John S. Brierley and Hymie Rubenstein, 39–61. Winnipeg, Canada: Univ. of Manitoba.

1989   Review of Karen Fog Olwig, *Cultural Adaptation and Resistance on St. John. Plantation Society in the Americas* 2 (3): 345–48.

1992   Freedom and Community: The British West Indies. In *The Meaning of Freedom: Economics, Politics, and Culture after Slavery,* ed. Frank McGlynn and Seymour Drescher, 183–219. Pittsburgh, Pa.: Univ. of Pittsburgh Press.

1993   Reputation and Respectability Reconsidered: A New Perspective on Afro-Caribbean Peasant Women. In *Women and Change in the Caribbean,* ed. Janet H. Momsen, 15–37. London: James Currey; Bloomington: Indiana Univ. Press.

1995a   Religion as Resistance in Jamaican Peasant Life: The Baptist Church, Revival Worldview and Rastafari Movement. In *Rastafari and Other African-Caribbean Worldviews,* ed. Barry Chevannes, 43–76. London: Macmillan.

1995b   Free Villagers, Rastafarians and Modern Maroons: From Resistance to Identity. In *Born Out of Resistance: On Caribbean Cultural Creativity,* ed. Wim Hoogbergen. Utrecht, Netherlands: ISOR Press.

1995c   Land, Kinship and Community in the Post-Emancipation Caribbean: A Regional View of the Leewards. In *Small Islands, Large Questions: Society, Culture, and Resistance in the Post-Emancipation Caribbean,* ed. Karen Fog Olwig. London: Frank Cass.

Besson, Jean, and Janet Momsen

1987   Introduction. In *Land and Development in the Caribbean,* ed. Jean Besson and Janet Momsen, 1–9. London: Macmillan.

Bethell, Tom

1977   *George Lewis: A Jazzman from New Orleans.* Berkeley: Univ. of California Press.

Bilby, Kenneth M.
1981   The Kromanti Dance of the Windward Maroons of Jamaica. *Nieuwe West-Indische Gids* 55 (1–2): 52–101.
1984a The Treacherous Feast: A Jamaican Maroon Historical Myth. *Bijdragen tot de Taal-, Land- en Volkenkunde* 140: 1–31.
1984b "Two Sister Pikni": A Historical Tradition of Dual Ethnogenesis in Eastern Jamaica. *Caribbean Quarterly* 30 (3–4): 10–25.
1989   Divided Loyalties: Local Politics and the Play of States among the Aluku. *Nieuwe West-Indische Gids* 63 (3–4): 143–73.
Blassingame, John W.
1973   *Black New Orleans, 1860–1880.* Chicago: Univ. of Chicago Press.
1977   *Slave Testimony: Two Centuries of Letters, Speeches, Interviews, and Autobiographies.* Baton Rouge: Louisiana Southern Univ. Press.
Blight, David W.
1991   The World the Slave Traders Made: Is There a Postrevisionism in Slavery Historiography? *Reviews in American History* 19: 37–42.
1993   Introduction. In Frederick Douglass, *Narrative of the Life of Frederick Douglass, An American Slave, Written by Himself,* ed. David W. Blight, 1–20. Boston: Bedford Books.
Blom, Anthony
1787   *Verhandeling van den landbouw in de Colonie Suriname.* Amsterdam: Smit.
Boles, John B., ed.
1988   *Masters and Slaves in the House of the Lord: Race and Religion in the American South, 1740–1870.* Lexington: Univ. of Kentucky Press.
Bowser, Frederick P.
1974   *The African Slave in Colonial Peru, 1524–1650.* Stanford, Calif.: Stanford Univ. Press.
Brain, Robert
1980   *Art and Society in Africa.* New York: Longman.
Brana Shute, Rosemary
1976   Women, Clubs and Politics. *Urban Anthropology* 5 (2): 157–85.
Brathwaite, Edward
1971   *The Development of Creole Society in Jamaica, 1770–1820.* New York: Oxford Univ. Press.
Braund, Kathryn E. Holland
1991   The Creek Indians, Blacks, and Slavery. *Journal of Southern History* 57 (4): 601–36.
Breen, Timothy H.
1973   A Changing Labor Force and Race Relations in Virginia, 1660–1710. *Journal of Social History* 7: 3–25
1984   Creative Adaptations: Peoples and Cultures. In *Colonial British America,* ed. Jack P. Greene and J. R. Pole, 195–232. Baltimore, Md.: Johns Hopkins Univ. Press.
Breen, Timothy H., and Steven Innes
1980   *Myne Owne Ground: Race and Freedom on Virginia's Eastern Shore, 1640–1675.* New York: Oxford Univ. Press.
Brown, Soi-Daniel W.
1983   From the Tongues of Africa: A Partial Translation of Oldendorp's Interviews. *Plantation Society* 2 (1): 37–61

Bruce, Philip A.
1889   *The Plantation Negro as a Freeman.* New York: G. P. Putnam's Sons.
Bush, Barbara
1990 [1985]   *Slave Women in Caribbean Society, 1650–1838.* Bloomington: Indiana
       Univ. Press. Originally published Kingston, Jamaica: Heinemann.
Buxton, Thomas F.
1840   *The African Slave Trade and Its Remedy.* London: John Murray.
C. [pseudonym]
1859   Slavery among the Indians. *Southern Literary Messenger* 28: 333–35.
Campbell, John
1991   As "A Kind of Freeman"?: Slaves' Market-Related Activities in the South
       Carolina Upcountry, 1800–1860. *Slavery and Abolition* 12: 132–69.
Campbell, Mavis C.
1988   *The Maroons of Jamaica, 1655–1796.* Granby, Conn.: Bergin and Garvey.
Campbell, Randolph B.
1987   Planters and Plain Folks: The Social Structure of the Antebellum South. In
       Interpreting Southern History, ed. John B. Boles and Evelyn Thomas Nolen,
       48–77. Baton Rouge: Louisiana State Univ. Press.
Caplan, Patricia
1969   Cognatic Descent Groups on Mafia Island, Tanzania. *Man* 4 (3): 419–31.
Carnegie, Charles V.
1992   The Fate of Ethnography: Native Social Science in the English-Speaking Car-
       ibbean. *New West Indian Guide* 66 (1–2): 5–25.
Carstens, J. L.
1981 [c. 1740]   *En Almindelig beskrivelse om alle de Danske, Americanske eller West-
       Jndiske Ey-lande.* Copenhagen: Dansk Vestindisk Forlag.
Casanelli, Lee V.
1987   Social Construction on the Somali Frontier: Bantu Former Slave Communi-
       ties in the Nineteenth Century. In *The African Frontier,* ed. Igor Kopytoff,
       216–38. Bloomington: Indiana Univ. Press.
Casely Hayford, Augustus
1992   A Genealogical Study of Cape Coast Families. Ph.D. diss. Univ. of London.
Casely Hayford, Augustus, and Richard Rathbone
1992   Politics, Families and Freemasonry in the Colonial Gold Coast. In *Peoples and
       Empires in African History,* ed. Jacob F. A. Ajayi and John D. Y. Peel, 143–60.
       London: Longman.
Clarke, Edith
1953   Land Tenure and the Family in Four Selected Communities in Jamaica. *Social
       and Economic Studies* 1 (4): 81–118.
Cohen, Abner
1981   *The Politics of Elite Culture: Explorations in the Dramaturgy of Power in a Mod-
       ern African Society.* Berkeley: Univ. of California Press.
Cohen, David W., and Jack P. Greene, eds.
1972   *Neither Slave nor Free: The Freedmen of African Descent in the Slave Societies of
       the New World.* Baltimore, Md.: Johns Hopkins Univ. Press.
Cohen, William
1991   *At Freedom's Edge: Black Mobility and the Southern White Quest for Racial Con-
       trol, 1861–1915.* Baton Rouge: Louisiana State Univ. Press.

Cohen Rodríguez, P., and D. C. Hesseling
1935   Papiamentse en Negerengelse spreekwoorden. *West-Indische Gids* 18: 161–73.
Cooper, Frederick
1977   *Plantation Slavery on the East African Coast.* New Haven, Conn.: Yale Univ.
        Press.
1979   The Problem of Slavery in African Studies. *Journal of African History* 20: 103–
        25.
1981   Islam and Cultural Hegemony: The Ideology of Slaveowners on the East Afri-
        can Coast. In *The Ideology of Slavery in Africa,* ed. Paul E. Lovejoy, 271–307.
        Beverly Hills: Sage.
Cortinovis, Irene E.
1974   Jazz on the Riverboats: The Way a Piano Player Tells It. *Journal of Jazz Studies*
        1 (2): 72–78.
Costa Lima, Vivaldo da
1976   O conceito de "nação" nos Candomblés da Bahia. *Afro-Asia* 12: 65–91.
Craton, Michael
1975   Jamaican Slavery. In *Race and Slavery in the Western Hemisphere: Quantitative
        Studies,* ed. Stanley L. Engerman and Eugene D. Genovese, 249–84.
        Princeton, N.J.: Princeton Univ. Press.
1978   *Searching for the Invisible Man: Slaves and Plantation Life in Jamaica.* Cam-
        bridge, Mass: Harvard Univ. Press.
1979   Changing Patterns of Slave Families in the British West Indies. *Journal of In-
        terdisciplinary History* 10: 1–35.
1982   *Testing the Chains: Resistance to Slavery in the British West Indies.* Ithaca, N.Y.:
        Cornell Univ. Press.
1984   The Historical Roots of the Plantation Model. *Slavery and Abolition* 5: 189–
        221
Creel, Margaret W.
1988   *"A Peculiar People": Slave Religion and Community-Culture Among the Gullahs.*
        New York: New York Univ. Press.
Cross, Malcolm, and Han Entzinger
1988   *Lost Illusions: Caribbean Minorities in Britain and the Netherlands.* London:
        Routledge.
Curtin, Philip D.
1970   *The Atlantic Slave Trade: A Census.* Madison: Univ. of Wisconsin Press.
1984   *Cross-Cultural Trade in World History.* New York: Cambridge Univ. Press.
Dallas, Robert C.
1803   *The History of the Maroons.* London: T. N. Longman and O. Rees.
Daniel, Pete
1994   The Legal Basis of Agrarian Capitalism: The South since 1933. In *Race and
        Class in the South since 1840,* ed. Rick Halpern and Melvyn Stokes, 79–102.
        Oxford: Berg Publishers.
Davenport, William
1961a   The Family System of Jamaica. *Social and Economic Studies* 10 (4): 420–54.
1961b   Introduction. *Social and Economic Studies* 10 (4): 380–85.
David, Paul A., Herbert G Gutman, Richard Sutch, Peter Temin, and Gavin Wright
1976   *Reckoning with Slavery.* New York: Oxford Univ. Press.
Davis, Charles T., and Henry Louis Gates, Jr., eds.
1985   *The Slave's Narrative.* New York: Oxford Univ. Press.

Davis, David Brion
1984   *Slavery and Human Progress.* New York: Oxford Univ. Press.
1986 [1974] Slavery and the Post–World War II Historians. In *From Homicide to Slavery: Studies in American Culture,* by David Brion Davis. New York: Oxford Univ. Press. (Originally published in *Daedalus* 103: 1–16.)
de Beet, Chris
1984   *De eerste Boni-oorlog, 1765–1778.* Utrecht, Netherlands: Centrum voor Caraïbische Studies, Rijksuniversiteit Utrecht.
de Goeje, C. H.
1908   *Verslag der Toemoekhoemak-expeditie (Tumuc-Humac-expeditie).* Leiden, Netherlands: Brill.
de Groot, Silvia W.
1975   The Boni-Maroon War, 1765–1793: Surinam and French Guiana. *Boletín de Estudios Latinoamericanos y del Caribe* 18: 30–48.
1977   *From Isolation towards Integration* Verhandelingen van het Koninklijk Instituut voor Taal-, Land- en Volkenkunde 80. The Hague, Netherlands: Martinus Nijhoff.
1988   Het Korps Zwarte Jagers in Suriname: Collaboratie en opstand 1. *OSO: Tijdschrift voor Surinaamse Taalkunde, letterkunde, Cultuur en Geschiedenis* 7 (2): 147–60.
1989   Het Korps Zwarte Jagers in Suriname: Collaboratie en opstand 2. *OSO: Tijdschrift voor Surinaamse Taalkunde, letterkunde, Cultuur en Geschiedenis* 8 (1): 7–21.
de Kom, Anton
1971 [1934] *Wij slaven van Suriname* Amsterdam: Contact.
De Marees, Pieter
1602   *Beschryvinge ende historische verhael vant Gout Koninckrijck van Gunea.* Amsterdam: Cornelis Claesz. English version is *Description and Historical Account of the Gold Kingdom of Guinea,* ed. Albert van Dantzig and Adam Jones. Oxford: Oxford Univ. Press for the British Academy, 1987 [1602].
De Marrée, J. A.
1817–18   *Reizen op en Beschrijving van de Goudkust van Guinea.* 2 vols. 's Gravenhage, Netherlands: Gebroeders van Cleef.
De slaventijd in odo's
1960   *De slaventijd in odo's: Een boekje over Suriname's heden en verleden.* Paramaribo: Radhakishun.
Debrunner, Hans
1967   *A History of Christianity in Ghana.* Accra: Waterville Publishing House.
Degn, Christian
1974   *Die Schimmelmanns im atlantischen Dreieckshandel.* Neumünster, Germany: Wachholtz.
Deive, Carlos Esteban
1989   *Los guerrilleros negros: Esclavos fugitivos y cimarrones en Santo Domingo.* Santo Domingo, Dominican Republic: Fundación Cultural Dominicana.
Deschamps Chapeaux, Pedro
1971   *El negro en la economía habanera del siglo XIX.* Havana, Cuba: UNEAC.
Dew, Charles B.
1987   The Slavery Experience. In *Interpreting Southern History,* ed. John B. Boles and Evelyn Thomas Nolen, 120–61. Baton Rouge: Louisiana State Univ. Press.

Dew, Edward M.
1978   *The Difficult Flowering of Suriname: Ethnicity and Politics in a Plural Society.*
         The Hague, Netherlands: Martinus Nijhoff.
Dillard, J. D.
1990   Review of Highfield and Barac, *C. G. A. Oldendorp's History of the Missions . . .*
         Journal of Pidgin and Creole Languages 5: 309–15.
Dillard, Joey Lee
1972   *Black English.* New York: Random House.
Dirks, Robert
1987   *The Black Saturnalia: Conflict and Its Ritual Expression on British West Indian
         Slave Plantations.* Gainesville: Univ. of Florida Press.
Dominguez, Virginia R.
1986   *White by Definition: Social Classification in Creole Louisiana.* New Brunswick,
         N.J.: Rutgers Univ. Press.
Donnan, Elizabeth
1930–35   *Documents Illustrative of the Slave Trade to America.* Washington, D.C.:
         Carnegie Institute.
Douchez, F.
1839   *Causeries sur la côte de Guinée, à propos de l'expédition du général Verveer pendant
         l'été de 1838.* La Haye and Amsterdam.
Douglas, Mary
1966   *Purity and Danger.* Harmondsworth, England: Penguin.
1973   *Natural Symbols.* Harmondsworth, England: Penguin.
Douglas, Mary, and Baron Isherwood
1979   *The World of Goods.* New York: Basic Books.
Douglass, Frederick
1993 [1845]   *Narrative of the Life of Frederick Douglass, An American Slave, Written by
         Himself,* ed. David W. Blight. Boston: Bedford Books.
Drummond, Lee
1980   The Cultural Continuum: A Theory of Intersystems. *Man* (N.S.) 15 (2): 352–
         74.
Du Bois, William E. B., ed.
1904   *Some Notes on Negro Crime, Particularly in Georgia.* Atlanta: Atlanta Univ.
         Press.
Dumett, Raymond, and Marion Johnson
1988   Britain and the Suppression of Slavery in the Gold Coast Colony, Ashanti,
         and the Northern Territories. In *The End of Slavery in Africa,* ed. Suzanne
         Miers and Richard Roberts, 71–116. Madison: Univ. of Wisconsin Press.
Dumont de Montigny, Jean François Benjamin
1853 [1753]   Historical Memoirs of M. Dumont. *Historical Collections of Louisiana.*
         Vol. 5. New York: Lamport, Blakeman and Law.
Dunham, Katherine
1946   *Journey to Accompong.* New York: Henry Holt.
Dunn, Richard S.
1977   A Tale of Two Plantations: Slave Life at Mesopotamia in Jamaica and Mount
         Airy in Virginia, 1799 to 1828. *William and Mary Quarterly* 34: 32–65.
Edwards, Bryan
1972 [1793]   *The History Civil and Commercial of the British Colonies in the West Indies.*
         New York: Arno Press. Originally published London: John Stockdale. 2 vols.

Edwards, Paul
1990   "Master" and "Father" in Equiano's *Interesting Narrative*. *Slavery and Abolition*
        11: 216–26.
Edwards, Paul, and Rosalind Shaw
1989   Equiano's Invisible *Chi*: Igbo Belief and Tradition in the *Interesting Narrative*.
        Journal of Religion in Africa 19: 146–56.
Elkins, Stanley M.
1959   *Slavery: A Problem in American Institutional and Intellectual Life*. Chicago:
        Univ. of Chicago Press.
1975   The Slavery Debate. *Commentary* 60 (6): 40–55.
Ellis, Alfred B.
1885   *A History of the First West India Regiment*. London: Chapman and Hall.
Ellison, Ralph
1964   *Shadow and Act*. New York: Random House.
Eltis, David
1987   *Economic Growth and the Ending of the Transatlantic Slave Trade*. New York:
        Oxford Univ. Press.
1993   Labour and Coercion in the English Atlantic World from the Seventeenth to
        the Early Twentieth Century. In *The Wages of Slavery. From Chattel Slavery to
        Wage Labour in Africa, the Caribbean and England,* ed. Michael Twaddle, 207–
        26. London: Frank Cass.
Eltis, David, and Lawrence C. Jennings
1988   Trade Between Western Africa and the Atlantic World in the Pre-Colonial
        Era. *American Historical Review* 93: 936–59.
Equiano, Olaudah
1987 [1814]   *The Interesting Life of Olaudah Equiano*. Rpt. in *The Classic Slave Narra-
        tives,* ed. Henry Louis Gates, 1–181. New York: Mentor.
Fage, John D.
1969   Slavery and the Slave Trade in the Context of West African History. *Journal of
        African History* 10: 393–404.
Faust, Drew Gilpin
1987   The Peculiar South Revisited: White Society, Culture, and Politics in the Ante-
        bellum Period, 1800–1860. In *Interpreting Southern History,* ed. John B. Boles
        and Evelyn Thomas Nolen, 78–119. Baton Rouge: Louisiana State Univ. Press.
Feest, Christian
1976   *Das rote Amerika: Nordamerikas Indianer,* 275–98. Vienna: Europaverlag.
Feinberg, Harvey M.
1969   Elmina, Ghana: A History of Its Development and Its Relationship with the
        Dutch in the Eighteenth Century. Ph.D. diss., Boston Univ.
1989   Africans and Europeans in West Africa: Elminans and Dutchmen on the
        Gold Coast during the Eighteenth Century. Philadelphia: *Transactions of the
        American Philosophical Society* 79, part 7: 1–186.
Finley, Moses I.
1968   Slavery. In *International Encyclopedia of the Social Sciences,* ed. David Sills, 14:
        307–13. New York: Macmillan.
1980   *Ancient Slavery and Modern Ideology*. New York: Viking Press.
Firth, Raymond
1963   Bilateral Descent Groups: An Operational Viewpoint. In *Studies in Kinship and
        Marriage,* ed. Isaac Schapera, 22–37. London: Royal Anthropological Institute.

Focke, H. C.
1855   *Neger-Engelsch woordenboek*. Leiden, Netherlands: Van den Heuvel.
1858   De Surinaamsche Negermuzyk. *West Indië* 2: 93–110.
Fodor, István
1975   *Pallas und andere afrikanische Vokabularien vor dem 19. Jahrhundert*. Hamburg: Helmut Buske.
1977   Zur Geschichte des Gã (Accran): Protten (1764) und Oldendorp (1777). In *Zur Sprachgeschichte und Ethnohistorie in Afrika*, ed. Wilhem Möhling et al., 47–56. Berlin: Reimer.
Fogel, Robert W.
1989   *Without Consent or Contract*. New York: Norton.
Fogel, Robert W., and Stanley L. Engerman
1974   *Time on the Cross: The Economics of American Negro Slavery*. New York: Little, Brown.
Foner, Eric
1983   *Nothing but Freedom: Emancipation and Its Legacy*. Baton Rouge: Louisiana State Univ. Press.
Forde, Daryll
1956   *Efik Traders of Old Calabar*. London: Oxford Univ. Press.
Fortes, Meyer, and Robin Horton
1983 [1959]   *Oedipus and Job in West African Religion*. Cambridge: Cambridge Univ. Press.
Fox, Robin
1967   *Kinship and Marriage*. Harmondsworth, England: Penguin Books.
Fox-Genovese, Elizabeth
1988   *Within the Plantation Household: Black and White Women of the Old South*. Chapel Hill: Univ. of North Carolina Press.
Frazier, E. Franklin
1966 [1939]   *The Negro Family in the United States*. Chicago: Univ. of Chicago Press.
Frederickson, George M.
1981   *White Supremacy: A Comparative Study in American and South African History*. New York: Oxford Univ. Press
Freyre, Gilberto
1947 [1934]   *The Masters and the Slaves*. New York: Knopf.
Friederici, Georg
1925–36   *Der Charakter der Entdeckung und Eroberung Amerikas durch die Europäer*. Stuttgart-Gotha, Germany: Andreas Perthes.
Gaspar, David Barry
1985   *Bondmen and Rebels: A Study of Master-Slave Relationships in Antigua*. Baltimore, Md.: Johns Hopkins Univ. Press.
1988   Slavery, Amelioration and Sunday Markets in Antigua, 1823–1831. *Slavery and Abolition* 9: 1–28.
1991   Antigua Slaves and Their Struggle to Survive. In *Seeds of Change*, ed. Herman J. Viola and Carolyn Margolis, 130–37. Washington, D.C.: Smithsonian Institution Press.
Gautier, Arlette
1985   *Les soeurs de Solitude: La condition féminine dans l'esclavage aux Antilles du XVIIe au XIXe siècle*. Paris: Editions Caribéennes.

Geertz, Clifford.
1973   *The Interpretation of Cultures.* New York: Basic Books.
Geggus, David
1987   The Enigma of Jamaica in the 1790s: New Light on the Causes of Slave Rebellions. *William and Mary Quarterly* 49: 274–99.
1991   Haitian Voodoo in the Eighteenth Century: Language, Culture, Resistance. *Jahrbuch für Geschichte von Staat, Wirtschaft und Gesellschaft Lateinamerikas* 28: 21–51.
Genovese, Eugene D.
1971 [1969]   *The World the Slaveholders Made.* New York: Vintage Books.
1974   *Roll, Jordan Roll: The World the Slaves Made.* New York: Pantheon.
1976 [1974]   *Roll, Jordan, Roll.* New York: Vintage Books.
1979   *From Rebellion to Revolution: Afro-American Slave Revolts in the Making of the Modern World.* Baton Rouge: Louisiana State Univ. Press.
Gilbert, Glen G.
1986   Oldendorp's History and Other Early Creole Materials in the Moravian Archives in Herrnhut, East Germany. *Carrier Pigeon* (Apr.): 5–7.
Gocking, Roger
1984   Creole Society and the Revival of Traditional Culture in Cape Coast during the Colonial Period. *International Journal of African Historical Studies* 17: 601–22.
Gois Dantas, Beatriz
1988   *Vovó Nago e Papai Branco: Usos e abusos da África no Brasil.* Rio de Janeiro, Brazil: Graal.
Goodenough, Ward H.
1955   A Problem in Malayo-Polynesian Social Organization. *American Anthropologist* 57 (1): 71–83.
Goody, Jack
1980   Slavery in Space and Time. In *African and Asian Systems of Slavery,* ed. James L. Watson, 16–42. Berkeley: Univ. of California Press.
Gordon, C. A.
1874   *Life on the Gold Coast.* London: Baillière, Tindall, and Cox.
Gramberg, J. S. G.
1861   *Schetsen van Afrika's Westkust.* Amsterdam: Weijtingh and Brave
Greenfield, Sidney M.
1977   Madeira and the Beginnings of New World Sugar Cane Cultivation and Plantation Slavery: A Study in Institution Building. In *Comparative Perspectives on Slavery in New World Plantation Societies,* ed. Vera Rubin and Arthur Tuden, 536–52. New York: New York Academy of Sciences.
Griffin, Larry D.
n.d.   Black Slaves in the Cherokee Nation. Manuscript in Cherokee Nation Collection, John Vaughn Library, Northeastern State College, Tahlequah, Okla.
Guda, Trudy, ed.
1984   *Aleks de Drie: Wan tori fu mi eygi srefi.* Paramaribo: Ministerie van Onderwijs, Wetenschappen en Cultuur.
1985   *Aleks de Drie: Sye! Arki tori!* Paramaribo: Ministerie van Onderwijs, Wetenschappen en Cultuur.
Guerra y Sánchez, Ramiro
1964 [1927]   *Sugar and Society in the Caribbean.* New Haven, Conn.: Yale Univ. Press.

Gutman, Herbert G.
1975   *Slavery and the Numbers Game.* Urbana: Univ. of Illinois Press.
1976   *The Black Family in Slavery and Freedom, 1750–1925.* New York: Random House.
Hahn, Steven
1982   Hunting, Fishing and Foraging: Common Rights and Class Relations in the Postbellum South. *Radical History Review* 26: 37–64.
Hair, Paul E. H.
1963   The Languages of Western Africa, c. 1700: A Note and a Query. *Bulletin of the Society for African Church History* 1: 17–20
1966   Collections of Vocabularies of Western Africa before the Polyglotta: A Key. *Journal of African Languages* 5: 208–17
1989   A Further Note on Oldendorp's Interviews. *Plantation Society* 2: 343.
Hair, Paul E. H., Adam Jones, and Robin Law, eds.
1992   *Barbot on Guinea.* London: Hakluyt Society.
Hall, Catherine
1992   Missionary Stories: Gender and Ethnicity in England in the 1830s and 1840s. In *Cultural Studies,* ed. Lawrence Grossberg, Cary Nelson, and Paula Treichler, 240–70. New York: Routledge.
Hall, Gwendolyn Midlo
1992   *Africans in Colonial Louisiana: The Development of Afro-Creole Culture in the Eighteenth Century.* Baton Rouge: Louisiana State Univ. Press.
Hall, Neville T.
1992   *Slave Society in the Danish West Indies.* Mona: Univ. of the West Indies Press.
Halliburton, Richard, Jr.
1974/75   Origins of Black Slavery among the Cherokees. *Chronicles of Oklahoma* 52: 483–96.
1975   Black Slave Control in the Cherokee Nation. *Journal of Ethnic Studies* 3 (2): 23–35.
1977   *Red Over Black: Black Slavery Among the Cherokee Indians.* Westport, Conn.: Greenwood.
Hamilton, J. C.
1889/90   Slavery in Canada. *Transactions of the Royal Canadian Institute* 1: 102–8.
Hamilton, J. Taylor
1900   *A History of the Church Known as the Moravian Church.* Bethlehem, Pa.: Times Publishing.
Hanley, Eric
1987   Review of Fog Olwig, *Cultural Adaptation and Resistance on St. John. Man* 22: 210.
Hannerz, Ulf
1987   The World in Creolization. *Africa* 57 (4): 546–59.
Hanson, F. Allan
1971   Nonexclusive Cognatic Descent Systems: A Polynesian Example. In *Polynesia: Readings on a Culture Area,* ed. Alan Howard, 109–32. Scranton, Pa.: Chandler.
Hartley, L. P.
1968   The Go-Between. In *The Collected Stories of L. P. Hartley,* ed. David Cecil. London: Hamish Hamilton.

Hay, Douglas, et. al.
1975   *Albion's Fatal Tree.* New York: Oxford Univ. Press.
Heintze, Beatrix, and Adam Jones, eds.
1987   *European Sources for Sub-Saharan Africa before 1900: Use and Abuse.*
(= *Paideuma* 33.)
Helman, Albert, et al.
1978   *Cultureel mozaïek van Suriname.* Zutphen, Netherlands: Walburg Pers.
Henty, G. A.
1874   *The March to Coomassie.* London: Tinsley.
Herskovits, Melville J.
1934   Freudian Mechanisms in Primitive Negro Psychology. In *Essays Presented to
C. G. Seligman,* ed. E. E. Evans-Pritchard et al., 75–84. London: Kegan Paul.
1966   A Footnote to the History of Negro Slaving. In *The New World Negro,* ed.
Frances S. Herskovits, 83–89. Bloomington: Indiana Univ. Press.
1973 [1945]   Problem, Method and Theory in Afroamerican Studies. In *Work and
Family Life: West Indian Perspectives,* ed. L. Comitas and D. Lowenthal, 287–
93. Garden City, N.Y.: Anchor Books.
1989 [1941]   *The Myth of the Negro Past.* Boston: Beacon Press. Originally published
New York: Harper and Bros.
Herskovits, Melville J., and Frances S. Herskovits
1969 [1936]   *Surinam Folklore.* New York: AMS Press. Originally published in Colombia University Contributions to Anthropology. New York: Colombia Univ.
Hesseling, D. C.
1905   *Het negerhollands der deense Antillen. Biyydrage tot de Geschiedenis der Nederlandse
taal in Amerika.* Leiden, Netherlands: A. W. Sijthoff.
Heuman, Gad, ed.
1985   *Out of the House of Bondage.* London: Frank Cass. (= *Slavery and Abolition* 5
[3].)
Higginbotham, A. Leon, Jr.
1978   *In the Matter of Color: Race and the American Legal Process: The Colonial Period.*
New York: Oxford Univ. Press.
Higginbotham, Jay
1977   *Old Mobile: Fort Louis de la Louisiane, 1702–1711.* Mobile, Ala.: Museum of
the City of Mobile.
Higman, Barry
1979   African and Creole Slave Family Patterns in Trinidad. In *Africa and the Caribbean,* ed. Margaret E. Crahan and Franklin W. Knight, 41–64. Baltimore,
Md.: Johns Hopkins Univ. Press.
1984   *Slave Populations of the British Caribbean, 1807–1834.* Baltimore, Md.: Johns
Hopkins Univ. Press.
Hodge, Frederick Webb
1975 [1907–10]   *Handbook of American Indians North of Mexico.* 2 vols. Washington, D.C.: U.S. Govt. Printing Office.
Hoffmann, Léon-François
1990   Histoire, mythe et idéologie: La cérémonie du Bois-Caiman. *Études Créoles* 13:
9–34.
Holloway, Joseph E.
1990   *Africanisms in American Culture.* Bloomington: Indiana Univ. Press.

Holt, Thomas C.
1992   *The Problem of Freedom: Race, Labor, and Politics in Jamaica and Britain, 1832–1838.* Baltimore, Md.: Johns Hopkins Univ. Press.
Hoogbergen, Wim S. M.
1978   *De Surinaamse "Weglopers" van de 19e eeuw.* Bronnen voor de Studie van Bosnegersamenlevingen, no. 1. Utrecht, Netherlands: Center for Caribbean Studies.
1983   Marronage en Marrons, 1760–1863: De niet-gepacificeerde Marrons van Suriname. In *Suriname: De schele onafhankelijkheid,* ed. Glenn Willemsen, 75–110. Amsterdam: De Arbeiderspers.
1984   *De Boni's in Frans Guyana en de Tweede Boni-oorlog, 1776–1793.* Bronnen voor de Studie van Bosnegersamenlevingen, no. 10. Utrecht, Netherlands: Center for Caribbean Studies.
1988   Boni, Aluku en Kormantin Kodjo: Over de vroegste Boni-geschiedenis. *SWI-Forum* 5 (1): 59–86. Paramaribo: Stichting Wetenschappelijke Informatie.
1989   Aluku. *New West Indian Guide* 63 (3 and 4): 175–98.
1990   *The Boni Maroon Wars in Suriname.* Leiden, Netherlands: E. J. Brill.
1993a De verdwenen Marrons van Krabbeholle. *OSO: Tijdschrift voor Surinaamse Taalkunde, letterkunde, Cultuuren Geschiedenis* 12 (1): 6–27.
1993b Marronage and Slave Rebellions in Suriname. In *Slavery in the Americas,* ed. Wolfgang Binder, 165–95. Würzburg, Germany: Königshausen and Neumann.
Horton, Robin
1971   Stateless Societies in the History of West Africa. In *History of West Africa.* Vol. 1, ed. A. Ajayi and M. Crowder, 72–113. London: Longmans.
Hostmann, F. W.
1850   *Over de beschaving van negers in Amerika door kolonisatie met Europeanen.* Amsterdam: J. C. A. Sulpke.
Huggins, Nathan I.
1990 [1977]   *Black Odyssey: The African American Ordeal in Slavery.* New York: Vintage.
Hull, Gloria T.
1988   Shaping Contradictions: Alice Dunbar-Nelson and the Black Creole Experience. *New Orleans Review* 15 (1): 34–37.
Hutton, J. E.
1922   *A History of the Moravian Missions.* London: Moravian Publishing Office.
Iets over Suriname
1854   Iets over Suriname. *Globe* 12: 151–61.
IJzermans, Jan
1987   Ontstaan en ontwikkeling van de creoolse populaire muziek in Suriname: 1800–1940. *OSO: Tijdschrift voor Surinaamse Taalkunde, letterkunde, Cultuur en Geschiedenis* 6: 49–66.
Inikori, Joseph E.
1982   Introduction. In *Forced Migration,* ed. Joseph E. Inikori, 13–60. New York: Africana Publishing Company.
Inikori, Joseph E., and Stanley L. Engerman, eds.
1992   *The Atlantic Slave Trade.* Durham, N.C.: Duke Univ. Press.
Jackson, Walter
1986   Melville Herskovits and the Search for Afro-American Culture. In *Malinowski, Rivers, Benedict, and Others: Essays on Culture and Personality,* ed. George W. Stocking, 95–126. Madison: Univ. of Wisconsin Press.

James, C. L. R.
1938   *The Black Jacobins*. London: Becker and Warburg.
James, Parthena Louise
1967   Reconstruction in the Chickasaw Nation: The Freedman Problem. *Chronicles of Oklahoma* 45 (1): 44–57.
Jaynes, Gerald
1986   *Branches Without Roots: Genesis of the Black Working Class in the American South, 1862–1882*. New York: Oxford Univ. Press.
Jeekel, C. A.
1869   *Onze bezittingen op de kust van Guinea*. Amsterdam: C. F. Stemler.
Jenkins, Ray
1985   Gold Coast Historians and the Pursuit of the Gold Coast Past, 1882–1917. Ph.D. thesis, Univ. of Birmingham, England.
1988   West Indian and Brazilian Influences in the Gold Coast—Ghana, c. 1807–1914: A Review and Reappraisal of Continuities in the Post-Abolition Links between West Africa and the Caribbean and Brazil. Paper presented at the 12th Annual Conference of the Society for Caribbean Studies, London.
1990   Intellectuals, Publication Outlets and "Past Relationships": Some Observations on the Emergence of Early Gold Coast–Ghanaian Historiography in the Cape Coast–Accra–Akropong Triangle, c. 1880–1917. In *Self Assertion and Brokerage: Early Cultural Nationalism in West Africa*, ed. Paulo F. de Moraes Farias and Karen Barber, 68–77. Birmingham, England: Center for West African Studies.
Johnson, James, and Michael Roark
1984   *Black Masters*. New York: Norton.
Jones, Adam
1989   Schwarze Frauen, weisse Beobachter: Die Frauen der Goldküste in den Augen der europäischen Männer, 1600–1900. In *Der europäische Beobachter aussereuropäischer Kulturen: Zur Problematik der Wirklichkeitswahrnehmung*. (= *Zeitschrift für Historische Forschung*, Beiheft 7, 153–68).
1990a   Prostitution, Polyandrie oder Vergewaltigung? Zur Mehrdeutigkeit europäischer Quellen über die Küste Westafrikas zwischen 1660 und 1860. In *Aussereuropäische Frauengeschichte: Probleme der Forschung*, ed. Adam Jones, 123–58. Pfaffenweiler, Germany: Centaurus.
1990b   *Zur Quellenproblematik der Geschichte Westafrikas, 1450–1900*. Stuttgart, Germany: Franz Steiner.
Jones, J. F.
1981   Kwakoe en Christus. Ph.D. thesis, Free Univ., Brussels.
Joyner, Charles
1984   *Down by the Riverside: A South Carolina Slave Community*. Urbana: Univ. of Illinois Press.
Kaplow, Susan B.
1971   African Merchants of the Nineteenth-Century Gold Coast. Ph. D. diss., Columbia Univ.
1978   Primitive Accumulation and Traditional Social Relations on the Nineteenth-Century Gold Coast. *Canadian Journal of African Studies* 12: 19–36.
Kappler, A.
1881   *Holländisch-Guiana: Erlebnisse und Erfahrungen während eines 43 jährigen Aufenthalts in der Kolonie Surinam*. Stuttgart, Germany: Kohlhammer.

Karasch, Mary
1979   Commentary on "Afro-American Slave Culture" by Monica Schuler. *Historical Reflections* 6 (2): 138–41.
1987   *Slave Life and Culture in Rio de Janeiro, 1808–1850.* Princeton, N.J.: Princeton Univ. Press.
Katz, William Loren
1985   *Black Indians: A Hidden Heritage.* New York: Atheneum.
Kawashima, Yasuhide
1986   *Puritan Justice and the Indian: White Man's Law in Massachusetts, 1630–1763.* Middletown, Conn.: Wesleyan Univ. Press.
Kay, Marvin L. Michael, and Lorin Lee Cary
1985   "They Are Indeed the Constant Plague of Their Tyrants": Slave Defense of a Moral Economy in Colonial North Carolina, 1748–1772. In *Out of the House of Bondage,* ed. Gad Heuman, 37–56. London: Frank Cass.
Kea, Ray A.
1982   *Settlement, Trade and Politics in the Seventeenth-Century Gold Coast.* Baltimore, Md.: Johns Hopkins Univ. Press.
Keller, Albert Galloway
1908   *Colonization.* Boston: Ginn and Company.
Kelly, James
1838   *Voyage to Jamaica, and Seventeen Years Residence in that Island . . .* 2d ed. Belfast: J Wilson.
Kennedy, William
1974 [1841]   *Texas: The Rise, Progress and Prospects of the Republic of Texas.* Book 2. Clifton, N.J.: Kelley
Kerdijk, Lodewijk
1978   *Reisjournaal van Lodewijk Kerdijk: West-Afrika 1857–1858,* ed. A. F. Schepel. Schiedam, Netherlands: Interbook International.
Kerr, Derek Noel
1983   Petty Felony, Slave Defiance, and Frontier Villainy: Crime and Criminal Justice in Spanish Louisiana, 1770–1803. Ph.D. diss., Tulane Univ..
Kinnaird, Lawrence, ed. and trans.
1946–49   *Spain in the Mississippi Valley, 1765–1794.* 3 vols. Materials from the Spanish Archives. Washington, D.C.: United States Government Printing Office.
Kiple, Kenneth F.
1984   *The Caribbean Slave: A Biological History.* Cambridge: Cambridge Univ. Press.
Klein, Martin, and Paul E. Lovejoy
1979   Slavery in West Africa. In *The Uncommon Market,* ed. Henry A. Gemery and Jan S. Hogendorn, 181–212. New York: Academic Press.
Kloosterboer, W.
1960   *Involuntary Labour Since the Abolition of Slavery.* Leiden, Netherlands: E. J. Brill.
Knight, Franklin W.
1970   *Slave Society in Cuba during the Nineteenth Century.* Madison: Univ. of Wisconsin Press.
Köbben, André J. F.
1979a   *In vrijheid en gebondenheid: Samenleving en cultuur van de Djoeka aan de Cottica.* Bronnen voor de Studie van Bosnegersamenlevingen, no. 4. Utrecht, Netherlands: Center for Caribbean Studies.

1979b   Unity and Disunity: Cottica Djuka Society as a Kinship System. In *Maroon Societies: Rebel Slave Communities in the Americas,* ed. Richard Price, 320–69. 2d ed. Baltimore, Md.: Johns Hopkins Univ. Press.

Kolchin, Peter
1983   Reevaluating the Antebellum Slave Community: A Comparative Perspective. *Journal of American History* 88: 581–603.

Kopytoff, Barbara Klamon
1976a   The Development of Jamaican Maroon Ethnicity. *Caribbean Quarterly* 22 (2–3): 33–50.
1976b   Jamaican Maroon Political Organization: The Effects of the Treaties. *Social and Economic Studies* 25 (2): 87–105.
1978   The Early Political Development of Jamaican Maroon Societies. *William and Mary Quarterly* 35: 287–307.
1979   Colonial Treaty as Sacred Charter of the Jamaican Maroons. *Ethnohistory* 26 (1): 45–64.
1987   Religious Change among the Jamaican Maroons: The Ascendance of the Christian God within a Traditional Cosmology. *Journal of Social History* 20: 463–84.

Kopytoff, Igor
1986   The Cultural Biography of Things: Commoditization as a Process. In *The Social Life of Things,* ed. Arjun Appadurai, 64–91. Cambridge: Cambridge UP.

Kopytoff, Igor, and Suzanne Miers
1977   Introduction: African "Slavery" as an Institution of Marginality. In *Slavery in Africa: Historical and Anthropological Perspectives,* ed. Suzanne Miers and Igor Kopytoff, 3–81. Madison: Univ. of Wisconsin Press.

Kruyer, G. J.
1973   *Suriname, neo-kolonie in rijksverband.* Meppel, Netherlands: Boom.

Kulikoff, Alan
1986   *Tobacco and Slaves: The Development of Southern Cultures in the Chesapeake, 1600–1800.* Chapel Hill: Univ. of North Carolina Press.

Laman, Karl
1962   *The Kongo III.* Studia Ethnographica Upsaliensia No. 12. Lund, Sweden: Hakan Ohlssons Boktryckeri.

Lange, Jacob [Jacobus Langius]
1658   *Daemonomanie ofte der Moore wonderheden.* Amsterdam: B. Schouwers.

Larose, Serge
1975   The Haitian *Lakou*; Land, Family and Ritual. In *Family and Kinship in Middle America and the Caribbean,* ed. Arnaud F. Marks and Rene A. Romer, 482–512. Curaçao: Institute of Higher Studies in Curaçao; and Leiden, Netherlands: Royal Institute of Linguistics and Anthropology.
1977   The Meaning of Africa in Haitian Vodu. In *Symbols and Sentiments,* ed. Ioan M. Lewis, 85–116. London: Tavistock.

Latham, A. J. H.
1973   *Old Calabar, 1600–1800.* Oxford: Clarendon Press.

Law, Robin
1977   *The Oyo Empire, c. 1600–c. 1800.* Oxford, England: Clarendon Press.

Le Page du Pratz, Antoine
1975 [1774]   *The History of Louisiana,* ed. Joseph G. Tregle, Jr. Facsimile reproduction of 1774 edition. Baton Rouge: Louisiana State Univ. Press.

Leach, Edmund R.
1960   The Sinhalese of the Dry Zone of Northern Ceylon. In *Social Structure in South-east Asia,* ed. George Peter Murdock, 116–26. Chicago: Quadrangle Books.
Lemann, Nicholas
1991   *The Promised Land: The Great Black Migration and How It Changed America.* New York: Knopf.
Lenoir, J. D.
1973   The Paramacca Maroons. Ph.D. diss. New York: New School for Social Research.
Lévi-Strauss, Claude
1969 [1949]   *The Elementary Structures of Kinship.* Boston: Beacon Press.
Levine, Lawrence W.
1977   *Black Culture and Black Consciousness: Afro-American Folk Thought from Slavery to Freedom.* New York: Oxford Univ. Press.
Lewis, Gordon K.
1983   *Main Currents in Caribbean Thought.* Baltimore, Md.: Johns Hopkins Univ. Press.
Lewis, Joan M.
1971   *Ecstatic Religion.* Harmondsworth, England: Penguin.
Lewis, Matthew Gregory
1834   *Journal of a West India Proprietor.* London: John Murray.
Lichtenstein, Alex
1988   "That Disposition to Theft with which They Have Been Branded": Moral Economy, Slave Management, and the Law. *Journal of Social History* 21: 413–40.
1993   Good Roads and Chain Gangs in the Progressive South. *Journal of Southern History* 59: 85–110.
Linebaugh, Peter, and Marcus Redicker
1990   The Many-Headed Hydra: Sailors, Slaves, and the Atlantic Working Class in the Eighteenth Century. *Journal of Historical Sociology* 3: 225–52.
Littlefield, Daniel C.
1981   *Rice and Slaves: Ethnicity and the Slave Trade in Colonial South Carolina.* Baton Rouge: Louisiana State Univ. Press.
Littlefield, Daniel F., Jr.
1977   *Africans and Seminoles: From Removal to Emancipation.* Westport, Conn.: Greenwood.
1978   *The Cherokee Freedmen.* Westport, Conn.: Greenwood.
1979   *Africans and Creeks: From the Colonial Period to the Civil War.* Westport, Conn.: Greenwood.
1980   *The Chickasaw Freedmen.* Westport, Conn.: Greenwood.
Littlefield, Daniel F., Jr., and Lonnie E. Underhill
1977   Slave "Revolt" in the Cherokee Nation, 1842. *American Indian Quarterly* 3: 121–31.
Lombardi, John V.
1974   Comparative Slave Systems in the Americas: A Critical Review. In *New Approaches to Latin American History,* ed. Richard Graham and Peter H. Smith, 156–74. Austin: Univ. of Texas Press.
Long, Edward
1970 [1774]   *The History of Jamaica.* London: Frank Cass.

Look Lai, Walton
1993 *Indentured Labor, Caribbean Sugar.* Baltimore, Md.: Johns Hopkins Univ. Press.
Loth, W. L.
1880 Verslag van eene expeditie tot het traceereu van een weg van de Tempatiekreek naar de rivier Suriname. Rapport aan Z. E. den Gouverneur van Suriname. *Tijdschrift van het Aardrijkskundig Genoofschap* 4: 250–55.
1904–5   Rapport over de exploratie van het Lawa-gebied. Handelingen der Staten Generaal [Minutes of Parliament.] *Koloniaal Verslag,* 1905, appendix no. 5: *Suriname.* s'Gravenhage: Staatsuitgeverij.
Louisiana General Correspondence. 54 vols. Louisiana Division, New Orleans Public Library, New Orleans, La.
Lovejoy, Paul E., ed.
1981 *The Ideology of Slavery in Africa.* Beverly Hills, Calif.: Sage.
Lowenthal, Ira P.
1987 "Marriage Is 20, Children Are 21:" The Cultural Construction of Conjugality and the Family in Rural Haiti. Ph.D. diss., Johns Hopkins Univ.
MacDonald, John Stuart, and MacDonald, Leatrice
1978 The Black Family in the Americas: A Review of the Literature. *Sage Race Relations Abstracts* 3 (1): 1–42.
MacGaffey, Wyatt
1968 Kongo and the King of the Americans. *Journal of Modern African Studies* 6: 171–81.
1972 The West in Congolese Experience. In *Africa and the West,* ed. Philip Curtin, 49–74. Madison: Univ. of Wisconsin Press.
1978 African History, Anthropology, and the Rationality of Natives. *History in Africa* 5: 101–20.
Maduell, Charles R., ed.
1972 *The Census Tables for the French Colony of Louisiana from 1699 through 1732.* Baltimore, Md.: Genealogical Publishing Company.
Manning, Patrick
1990 *Slavery and African Life: Occidental, Oriental and African Slave Trades.* Cambridge: Cambridge Univ. Press.
Marcus, George E.
1986 Contemporary Problems of Ethnography in the Modern World System. In *Writing Culture,* ed. James Clifford and George E. Marcus, 165–93. Berkeley: Univ. of California Press.
Marcus, George E., and Michael M. J. Fisher
1986 *Anthropology as Cultural Critique.* Chicago: Univ. of Chicago Press.
Marks, Arnaud F.
1976 *Male and Female and the Afro-Curaçaoan Household.* The Hague, Netherlands: Martinus Nijhoff.
Martin, François-Xavier, ed.
1816 *A General Digest of the Acts of the Legislatures of the Late Territory of Orleans and the State of Louisiana.* 3 vols. New Orleans: Peter K. Wagner.
Martin, Joel W.
1991 *Sacred Revolt: The Muskogees' Struggle for a New World.* Boston: Beacon Press.
Marwick, M. G.
1965 *Sorcery in Its Social Setting.* Manchester, England: Manchester Univ. Press.

McCain, William D., ed.
1948   *Laws of the Mississippi Territory, May 27, 1800.* Beauvoir Community, Miss.: Book Farm.

McCarthy, Mary
1983   *Social Change and the Growth of British Power in the Gold Coast.* Lanham, N.Y.: Univ. Press of America.

McCracken, Grant
1988   *Culture and Consumption.* Bloomington: Indiana Univ. Press.

McDermott, John Francis, ed.
1940   *Tixier's Travels on the Osage Prairies.* Norman: Univ. of Oklahoma Press.

McFarlane, Alan
1987   Evil. In Alan McFarlane, *The Culture of Capitalism,* 98–122. London: Blackwell.

McGlynn, Frank, and Seymour Drescher, eds.
1992   *The Meaning of Freedom: Economics, Politics and Culture after Slavery.* Pittsburgh, Pa.: Univ. of Pittsburgh Press.

McGowan, James Thomas
1976   Creation of a Slave Society: Louisiana Plantations in the Eighteenth Century. Ph.D. diss., Univ. of Rochester.

McLoughlin, William G.
1974   Red Indians, Black Slavery and White Racism: America's Slaveholding Indians. *American Quarterly* 26: 367–85.

McMurtrie, Douglas C., ed.
1942   *Regulations to be Observed by the Syndic and Alcads of the Jurisdiction of Baton Rouge.* Evanston, Ill.: Printed privately .

McSheffrey, Gerald M.
1983   Slavery, Indentured Servitude, Legitimate Trade and the Impact of Abolition in the Gold Coast, 1874–1901: A Reappraisal. *Journal of African History* 24: 349–68.

Meillassoux, Claude
1982   The Role of Slavery in the Economic and Social History of Sahelo-Sudanic Africa. In *Forced Migration,* ed. Joseph E. Inikori, 74–99. New York: Africana Publishing Company.
1986   *Anthropologie de l'esclavage.* Paris: Presses Universitaires de France.

Menard, Russell, and Stuart B. Schwartz
1993   Why African Slavery? Labor Force Transitions in Brazil, Mexico, and the Carolina Lowcountry. In *Slavery in the Americas,* ed. Wolfgang Binder, 89–114. Würzburg, Germany: Königshausen and Neumann.

Merrell, James H.
1984   The Racial Education of the Catawba Indians. *Journal of Southern History* 50 (3): 363–84.
1989   Some Thoughts on Colonial Historians and American Indians. *William and Mary Quarterly* 46 (1): 94–119.

Miers, Suzanne, and Igor Kopytoff, eds.
1977   *Slavery in Africa: Historical and Anthropological Perspectives.* Madison: Univ. of Wisconsin Press.

Miers, Suzanne, and Richard Roberts, eds.
1988   *The End of Slavery in Africa.* Madison: Univ. of Wisconsin Press.

Mill, John Stuart
1849   *Principles of Political Economy.* London: Routledge.

Miller, Joseph E.
1988   *Way of Death: Merchant Capitalism and the Angolan Slave Trade, 1730–1830.*
        Madison: Univ. of Wisconsin Press.
Mintz, Sidney W.
1955   The Jamaican Internal Marketing Pattern: Some Notes and Hypotheses. *Social
        and Economic Studies* 4 (1): 95–103.
1959   Labor and Sugar in Puerto Rico and in Jamaica, 1800–1850. *Comparative
        Studies in Society and History* 1: 273–83.
1961   The Question of Caribbean Peasantries: A Comment. *Caribbean Studies* 1:
        31–34.
1969a   Review of H. Orlando Patterson, *The Sociology of Slavery. Caribbean Studies* 8
        (4): 65–70.
1969b   [1961] Slavery and Emergent Capitalism. In *Slavery in the New World*, ed.
        Laura Foner and Eugene D. Genovese, 27–37. Englewood Cliffs, N.J.:
        Prentice-Hall.
1970   Creating Culture in the Americas. *Columbia University Forum* 13: 4–11.
1971a   The Caribbean as a Socio-Cultural Area. In *Peoples and Cultures of the Carib-
        bean*, ed. Michael M. Horowitz, 17–46. Garden City, N.Y.: Natural History
        Press.
1971b   Toward an Afro-American History. *Cahiers d'Histoire Mondiale* 13 (2): 317–
        32.
1974   The Caribbean Region. In *Slavery, Colonialism and Racism*, ed. Sidney W.
        Mintz, 45–71. New York: Norton.
1977   The So-Called World System: Local Initiative and Local Response. *Dialectical
        Anthropology* 2: 253–70.
1978a   Was the Plantation Slave a Proletarian? *Review* 2 (1): 81–98.
1978b   Caribbean Marketplaces and Caribbean History. *Nova Americana* 1: 333–44.
1979a   The Dignity of Honest Toil. *Comparative Studies in Society and History* 21 (4):
        558–66.
1979b   The Role of Water in Steward's Cultural Ecology. *Journal of the Steward An-
        thropological Society* 11: 17–32.
1981a   Cultural Resistance and the Labor Force in the Caribbean Region. In *Latin
        America Today: Heritage of Conquest*, ed. D. Hazen, T. Holloway, and D. Jones,
        28–42. Ithaca, N.Y.: Cornell Univ., Latin American Studies Program.
1981b   Economic Role and Cultural Tradition. In *The Black Woman Cross-Culturally*,
        ed. Filomena Chioma Seatdy, 515–34. Cambridge, Mass.: Schenkman.
1985a   From Plantations to Peasantries in the Caribbean. In *Caribbean Contours*, ed.
        S. W. Mintz and S. Price, 127–53. Baltimore: Johns Hopkins Univ. Press.
1985b   *Sweetness and Power: The Place of Sugar in Modern History.* New York: Pen-
        guin.
1989   [1974] *Caribbean Transformations.* New York: Columbia Univ. Press.
1992   Panglosses and Pollyannas; or, Whose Reality Are We Talking About? In *The
        Meaning of Freedom*, ed. Frank McGlynn and Seymour Drescher, 245–56.
        Pittsburgh, Pa.: Univ. of Pittsburgh Press.
1993   Tasting Food, Tasting Freedom. In *Slavery in the Americas*, ed. Wolfgang
        Binder, 257–75. Würzburg, Germany: Königshausen und Neumann.
Mintz, Sidney W., and Douglas Hall
1960   *The Origins of the Jamaican Internal Market System.* Yale University Publica-
        tions in Anthropology (New Haven: Dept. of Anthropology), vol. 57: 1–26.

Mintz, Sidney W., and Richard Price
1992 [1976]   *The Birth of African-American Culture: An Anthropological Perspective.*
   Boston: Beacon Press. [Originally published as *An Anthropological Approach to
   the Afro-American Past: A Caribbean Perspective.* ISHI Occasional Papers 2.
   Philadelphia: Institute for the Study of Human Issues.]

Mississippi Provincial Archives
1927–32   *Mississippi Provincial Archives: French Dominion.* Vols. 1–3, ed. Dunbar
   Rowland and Albert Godfrey Sanders. Jackson: Mississippi Dept. of Archives
   and History.
1984   *Mississippi Provincial Archives: French Dominion.* Vols. 4–5, ed. Patricia Day
   Galloway. Baton Rouge: Louisiana State Univ. Press.

Momsen, Janet
1987   Land Settlement as an Imposed Solution. In *Land and Development in the Caribbean,* ed. Jean Besson and Janet Momsen, 46–69. London: Macmillan.

Moreno Fraginals, Manuel
1976   *The Sugarmill: The Socioeconomic Complex of Sugar in Cuba.* New York:
   Monthly Review Press.
1978   *El ingenio: Complejo económico social cubano del azúcar.* Havana, Cuba: Editorial
   de Ciencias Sociales.
1984   Cultural Contributions and Deculturation. In *African in Latin America,* ed.
   Manuel Moreno Fraginals, 5–22. Paris: UNESCO.

Moreno Fraginals, Manuel, Frank Moya Pons, and Stanley L. Engerman, eds.
1985   *Between Slavery and Freedom: The Spanish-Speaking Caribbean in the Nineteenth
   Century.* Baltimore, Md.: Johns Hopkins Univ. Press.

Morgan, Edmund S.
1972   Slavery and Freedom: The American Paradox. *Journal of American History* 59:
   5–29.
1975   *American Slavery—American Freedom: The Ordeal of Colonial Virginia.* New
   York: Norton.

Morgan, Philip D.
1982   Work and Culture: The Task System and the World of Lowcountry Blacks,
   1700–1880. *William and Mary Quarterly* 39: 563–99.
1983   The Ownership of Property by Slaves in the Mid-Nineteenth-Century Low
   Country. *Journal of Southern Studies* 49: 399–420.
1984   Black Life in Eighteenth-Century Charleston. *Perspectives in American History*
   1: 187–232.
1988   Task and Gang Systems: The Organization of Labor on New World Plantations. In *Work and Labor in Early America,* ed. Stephen Innes, 189–220.
   Chapel Hill: Univ. of North Carolina Press.

Morrissey, Marietta
1989   *Slave Women in the New World: Gender Stratification in the Caribbean.*
   Lawrence: Univ. of Kansas Press.

Mullin, Michael
1985   Women and the Comparative Study of American Negro Slavery. *Slavery and
   Abolition* 6: 25–40.

Mullin, Michael
1992   *Africa in America: Slave Acculturation and Resistance in the American South and
   the British Caribbean, 1736–1831.* Urbana: Univ. of Illinois Press.

Murdock, George Peter
1960   Cognatic Forms of Social Organization. In *Social Structure in Southeast Asia*,
        ed. George Peter Murdock, 1–14. Chicago: Quadrangle Books.
Naison, Mark
1992   Outlaw Culture. *Reconstruction* 1: 128–31.
Nash, Gary B.
1988   *Forging Freedom: The Formation of Philadelphia's Black Community, 1720–1840.*
        Cambridge, Mass.: Harvard Univ. Press.
Nash, June
1981   Ethnographic Aspects of the World Capitalist System. *Annual Review of An-
        thropology* 10: 393–423.
Nepveu, Jean
1775   "Annotaties op het boek van J. D. Herlein 'Beschryvinge van de volkplantinge
        Zuriname.'" Manuscript, Amsterdam Municipal Archives, collection
        Marquette 230.
Nieboer, Herman J.
1900   *Slavery as an Industrial System.* The Hague, Netherlands: Martinus Nijhoff.
Nishida, Mieko
1993   Manumission and Ethnicity in Urban Slavery: Salvador, Bahia, 1808–1888.
        Hispanic American Historical Review 73: 361–91.
Northrup, Solomon
1968 [1853]   *Twelve Years a Slave*, ed. Sue Eakin and Joseph Logsdon. Baton Rouge:
        Louisiana State Univ. Press, 1968.
Northup, David
1978   *Trade Without Rulers: Pre-Colonial Economic Development in South-Eastern Ni-
        geria.* Oxford, England: Clarendon Press.
Norton, R.
1983   Ethnicity, "Ethnicity" and Culture Theory. *Man* 18 (1): 190–91.
Oakes, James
1982   *The Ruling Race: A History of American Slaveholders.* New York: Knopf.
Okely, Judith
1983   *The Traveller Gypsies.* Cambridge: Cambridge Univ. Press.
Okihiro, Gary Y., ed.
1986   *In Resistance: Studies in African, Caribbean, and Afro-American History.*
        Amherst: Univ. of Massachusetts Press.
Oldendorp, Christian G. A.
1777   *Geschichte der Mission der evangelischen Brüder auf den caraibischen Inseln S. Tho-
        mas, S. Croix und S. Jan*, ed. Johann Jakob Bossart. Barby, [Saxony]: Christian
        Friedrich Laux.
1784   *Fuldstændigt Udtog af C. G. A. Oldendorps Geschichte . . . .* Trans. Niels Prahl.
        Copenhagen: J. R. Thiele.
1784   *Tillförlätlig underrättelse om Negrene på Gvinea kusten. . . .* Uppsala: J. Edman.
1786   *Historiska Beskrifning öfwer Ewangeliske Brödernas Mißions-Arbete på Caraibiske
        Öarne St. Thomas, St. Croix och St. Jan.* Stockholm: P. A. Brodin.
1987   *A Caribbean Mission: C. G. A. Oldendorp's History of the Mission of the Evangeli-
        cal Brethren on the Caribbean Islands of St. Thomas, St. Croix, and St. John.* En-
        glish ed. Trans. Arnold R. Highfield and Vladimir Barac. Ann Arbor: Karoma
        Publishers.

Olivier, Lord [Sidney Haldane]
1936   *Jamaica: The Blessed Isle.* London: Faber and Faber.
Olmsted, Frederick Law
1862   *The Cotton Kingdom.* 2 vols. New York: Mason Brothers.
Olwig, Karen Fog
1985   *Cultural Adaptation and Resistance on St. John: Three Centuries of Afro-Caribbean Life.* Gainesville: Univ. of Florida Press.
1987   Village, Culture and Identity on St. John, Virgin Islands. In *Afro-Caribbean Villages in Historical Perspective,* ed. C. V. Carnegie, 20–44. *African-Caribbean Institute of Jamaica Research Review* 2.
1989   An Eighteenth-Century Ethnographer of the Danish West Indies. *Plantation Society* 2: 337–42.
1993   *Global Culture, Island Identity: Continuity and Change in the Afro-Caribbean Community of Nevis.* Reading, Pa.: Harwood Academic Publisher.
Ontwerp
[1744] *Ontwerp tot een beschryving van Surinaamen.* N.p.
Oostindie, Gert
1989   *Roosenburg en Mon Bijou: Twee Surinaamse Plantages, 1720–1870.* Dordrecht, Netherlands: Foris.
1993a The Economics of Suriname Slavery. *Economic and Social History in the Netherlands* 5: 1–24.
1993b Voltaire, Stedman, and Suriname Slavery. *Slavery and Abolition* 14 (2): 1–34.
Ortiz, Fernando
1940   *Contrapunteo cubano del tabaco y el azúcar.* Havana, Cuba: Montero.
1947 [1940]   *Cuban Counterpoint.* Trans. Harriet de Onís. New York: Knopf.
1975 [1916]   *Los negros esclavos.* Havana, Cuba: Editorial Ciencias Sociales.
1986   *Los negros curros,* ed. Diana Iznaga. Havana, Cuba: Editorial Ciencias Sociales.
Palmer, Colin A.
1976   *Slaves of the White God: Blacks in Mexico, 1570–1650.* Cambridge: Cambridge Univ. Press.
Palmié, Stephan
1991   *Das Exil der Götter: Geschichte und Vorstellungswelt einer afrokubanischen Religion.* Frankfurt, Germany: Peter Lang.
1993   Ethnogenetic Processes and Cultural Transfer in Afro-American Slave Populations. In *Slavery in the Americas,* ed. Wolfgang Binder, 337–63. Würzburg, Germany: Königshausen and Neumann.
1995   African Frontiers in the Americas? In *Born Out of Resistance: On Caribbean Cultural Creativity,* ed. Wim Hoogbergen. Utrecht, Netherlands: ISOR Press.
Paquette, Robert
1991   Social History Update: Slave Resistance and Social History. *Journal of Social History* 24 (3): 681–85.
Parish, Peter J.
1989   *Slavery: History and the Historians.* New York: Harper and Row.
Park, Mungo
1983 [1799]   *Travels into the Interior of Africa.* London: Eland Books.
Patterson, Orlando
1967   *The Sociology of Slavery: An Analysis of the Origins, Development and Structure of Negro Slave Society in Jamaica.* London: MacGibbon and Kee.

1975 Context and Choice in Ethnic Allegiance: A Theoretical Framework and Caribbean Case-study. In *Ethnicity: Theory and Experience,* ed. Nathan Glazer and Daniel P. Moynihan, 305–49. Cambridge, Mass.: Harvard Univ. Press.
1982 *Slavery and Social Death.* Cambridge, Mass.: Harvard Univ. Press.
Peel, John D. Y.
1990 The Pastor and the Babalawo: The Interaction of Religions in Nineteenth-Century Yorubaland. *Africa* 60: 338–69.
Penard, F. P., and A. P. Penard
1913 Surinaamsch bijgeloof. *Bijdragen tot de Taal-, Land- en Volkenkunde van Nederlandsch Indië* 67: 157–83.
Perdue, Theda
1979a *Slavery and the Evolution of Cherokee Society, 1540–1866.* Knoxville: Univ. of Tennessee Press.
1979b Cherokee Planters: The Development of Plantation Slavery Before Removal. In *The Cherokee Indian Nation: A Troubled History,* ed. Duane King, 110–28. Knoxville: Univ. of Tennessee Press.
1982 Cherokee Planters, Black Slaves, and African Colonization. *Chronicles of Oklahoma* 60 (3): 322–31.
1988 *The Cherokee.* New York: Chelsea House.
Philips, Ulrich B.
1963 [1929] *Life and Labor in the Old South.* New York: Little, Brown.
Phillips, William D., Jr.
1985 *Slavery from Roman Times to the Early Transatlantic Trade.* Minneapolis: Univ. of Minnesota Press.
1991 The Old World Background of Slavery in the Americas. In *Slavery and the Rise of the Atlantic System,* ed. Barbara L. Solow, 43–61. Cambridge: Cambridge Univ. Press.
Pike, Ruth
1972 *Aristocrats and Traders: Sevillian Society in the Sixteenth Century.* Ithaca, N.Y.: Cornell Univ. Press.
Polimé, T. S., and H. U. E. Thoden van Velzen
1988 *Vluchtelingen, opstandelingen en andere Bosnegers van Ooost-Suriname, 1986–1988.* Bronnen voor de Studie van Afro-Surinaamse Samenlevingen, no. 13. Utrecht, Netherlands: Instituut voor Culturele Antropologie.
Pollak-Eltz, Angelina
1970 *Afro-Amerikaanse godsdiensten en culten.* Roermond, Netherlands: J. J. Romen and Zonen.
Pope, Polly
1972 A Maroon Settlement on St. Croix. *Negro History Bulletin* 35: 153–54.
1975 Danish Colonialism in the West Indies: A Case of Transculturation Failure. In *War: Its Causes and Correlates,* ed. Martin A. Nettleship, R. Dale Givens, and Anderson Nettleship, 573–82. The Hague, Netherlands: Mouton.
Porter, Kenneth W.
1932 Relations between Negroes and Indians within the Present Limits of the United States. *Journal of Negro History* 17 (3): 287–367.
1933 Notes Supplementary to Relations between the Negro and Indian Within the Present Limits of the United States. *Journal of Negro History* 18: 282–321.
1941 Abraham. *Phylon* 2 (2): 105–16.
1943a Three Fighters for Freedom. *Journal of Negro History* 28: 51–72.

1943b Florida Slaves and Free Negroes in the Seminole War, 1835–1842. *Journal of Negro History* 28: 390–421.

1945   Negroes and the East Florida Annexation Plot. *Journal of Negro History* 30: 9–29.

1946a John Caesar: Seminole Negro Partisan. *Journal of Negro History* 31: 190–207.

1946b Negroes on the Southern Frontier, 1670–1763. *Journal of Negro History* 33: 53–78.

1951a Negroes and the Seminole War, 1817–1818. *Journal of Negro History* 36: 249–80.

1951b The Seminole in Mexico, 1850–1861. *Hispanic American Historical Review* 31: 1–36.

1956   Negroes and Indians on the Texas Frontier. *Journal of Negro History* 41 (3): 185–214; and (4): 285–310.

1964   Negroes and the Seminole War, 1835–1842. *Journal of the Southern History* 30 (4): 427–50.

Posey, Darrell A.

1979   Origin, Development and Maintenance of a Louisiana Mixed-Blood Community: The Ethnohistory of the Freejacks of the First Ward Settlement. *Ethnohistory* 26 (2): 177–92.

Postma, Johannes Menne

1990   *The Dutch in the Atlantic Slave Trade, 1600–1815.* Cambridge: Cambridge Univ. Press.

Powdermaker, Hortense

1968 [1939] *After Freedom.* New York: Russell and Russell.

Price, Richard

1967   Studies of Caribbean Family Organization: Problems and Prospects. Manuscript, Dept. of Anthropology, Johns Hopkins Univ.

1975   *Saramaka Social Structure: Analysis of a Maroon Society in Surinam.* Rio Piedras, Puerto Rico: Univ. of Puerto Rico.

1979 [1973] *Maroon Societies: Rebel Slave Communities in the Americas.* 2d ed. Baltimore, Md.: Johns Hopkins Univ. Press.

1983   *First Time: The Historical Vision of an Afro-American People.* Baltimore, Md.: Johns Hopkins Univ. Press.

1987   A Caribbean Mission: Blood, Sweat, and Tears—and More Blood. *Nieuwe West-Indische Gids* 61: 175–81.

1990   *Alabi's World.* Baltimore, Md.: Johns Hopkins Univ. Press.

Price, Sally, and Richard Price

1980   *Afro-American Arts of the Suriname Rain Forest.* Los Angeles: Museum of Cultural History, Univ. of California at Los Angeles.

Priestley, Margaret

1969   *West African Trade and Coast Society: A Family Study.* London: Oxford Univ. Press.

Prude, Jonathan

1991   To Look upon the "Lower Sort": Runaway Ads and the Appearance of Unfree Laborers in America, 1750–1800. *Journal of American History* 78: 124–59.

Radcliffe-Brown, A. R.

1950   Introduction. In *African Systems of Kinship and Marriage,* ed. A. R. Radcliffe-Brown and Daryll Forde. London: Oxford Univ. Press.

Ranger, Terrence

1983   The Invention of Tradition in Colonial Africa. In *The Invention of Tradition,* ed. E. Hobsbawm and T. Ranger, 211–62. Cambridge: Cambridge Univ. Press.

Ratekin, Mervyn
1954   The Early Sugar Industry in Española. *Hispanic American Historical Review* 34: 1–19.
Rathbone, Richard
1985   Some Thoughts on Resistance to Enslavement in West Africa. In *Out of the House of Bondage*, ed. Gad Heuman, 11–22. London: Frank Cass.
1993   *Murder and Politics in Colonial Ghana.* New Haven, Conn.: Yale Univ. Press.
Raunkiær, Ingeborg
1917   *Iserts Breve fra Dansk Guinea, 1783–87.* Copenhagen: G. E. C. Gad.
Rawick, George
1977   *The American Slave.* Vol. 6, supp. 1. Westport, Conn.: Greenwood.
Raynal, G. F.
1774   *Histoire philosophique et politique des établissements et du commerce des Européens dans les deux Indes.* Amsterdam: n.p.
Records of the Superior Council of Louisiana.
1918–39   French judicial records published intermittently in *Louisiana Historical Quarterly* 1: 109, 3: 414, 3: 443–44, 5: 466–77, 6: 283, 10: 258, 13: 309, 16: 334–35, 19: 768–71. Trans. Heloise H. Cruzat.
Reidy, Joseph P.
1992   *From Slavery to Agrarian Capitalism in the Cotton Plantation South: Central Georgia, 1800–1880.* Chapel Hill: Univ. of North Carolina Press.
Reinders, Marileen
1993   De Watermama. *CAhier* 2 (4): 43–51.
Reis, João José
1982   Slave Rebellion in Brazil: The African Muslim Uprising in Bahia, 1835. Ph.D. diss., Univ. of Minnesota.
Reynolds, Edward
1974   *Trade and Economic Change on the Gold Coast, 1807–1874.* London: Longman.
Robertson, Claire C.
1983   Post-Proclamation Slavery in Accra: A Female Affair? In *Women and Slavery in Africa*, ed. Claire C. Robertson and Martin A. Klein, 220–42. Madison: Univ. of Wisconsin Press.
Robertson, Claire C., and Martin A. Klein, eds.
1983   *Women and Slavery in Africa.* Madison: Univ. of Wisconsin Press.
Robertson, Rev. [Robert]
1730   *A Letter to the Right Reverend of the Lord Bishop of London.* London: J. Wilford.
Robotham, Don
1977   Agrarian Relations in Jamaica. In *Essays on Power and Change in Jamaica*, ed. Carl Stone and Aggrey Brown, 45–57. Kingston: Jamaica Publishing House.
Rodney, Walter
1966   African Slavery and Other Forms of Social Oppression on the Upper Guinea Coast in the Context of the Atlantic Slave Trade. *Journal of African History* 7: 431–43
1972   *How Europe Underdeveloped Africa.* London: Bogle-L'Ouverture Publications.
Roethler, Michael
1964   Negro Slavery among the Cherokee Indians, 1540–1866. Ph.D. diss., Fordham Univ., New York.

Rose, Willie Lee
1982   The New Slavery Studies: An Old Reaction or a New Maturity? In *Slavery and Freedom*, ed. William W. Freehling. Baltimore, Md.: Johns Hopkins Univ. Press.

Rowlands, Michael
1985   Exclusionary Tactics in the Logic of Collective Dynamics. *Critique of Anthropology* 5 (2): 47–69.

Rubenstein, Hymie
1987   *Coping with Poverty: Adaptive Strategies in a Caribbean Village.* London: Westview Press.

Rubin, Vera, ed.
1971 [1957]   *Caribbean Studies: A Symposium.* Seattle: Univ. of Washington Press.

Rupp-Eisenreich, Britta
1985   Les Frères Moraves, ethnologues de la condition esclave? (Iles Vierges, Petit Antilles, 1731–1768). In *Naissance de l'ethnologie? Anthropologies et missions en Amérique XVIe-XVIIIe siècles*, ed. Claude Blanckaert, 125–73. Paris: Les èditions du Cerf.

1987   Les "informateurs" africains des missionaires pietistes et moraves. In *Images de l'Africain de l'antiquité au XXe siècle*, ed. Daniel Droixhe and Klaus H. Kiefer, 45–61. Frankfurt: Peter Lang Verlag.

1989   L'ethnicité, critère descriptif au XVIIIᵉ siècle: Le cas de la traite danoise. In *Les ethnies ont une histoire*, ed. Jean-Pierre Chrétien and Gérard Prunier, 49–60. Paris: Karthala.

Ryder, A. F. C.
1969   *Benin and the Europeans, 1485–1897.* London: Longmans.

Salmons, Bill
1979   Mammy Wata: Wassergötter in Nigeria. In *Moderne Kunst aus Afrika*, ed. Sabine Hollburg, 125–34. Berlin: Berliner Festspiele GmbH.

Saucier, Corinne
1943   *The History of Avoyelles Parish, Louisiana.* New Orleans: Pelican Publishing Company.

Schmidt, Johan Christian
1788   Blandede Anmærkninger, samlede paa og over Ejlandet St. Croix i Amerika. *Samleven* 41: 225–40.

Schoonheym, Peter
1980   *Je geld of . . . je leven.* ICAU Mededelingen 14. Utrecht, Netherlands: Instituut voor Culturele Antropologie.

Schuler, Monica
1979   Afro-American Slave Culture. *Historical Reflections* 6 (2): 121–37.

1980   *Alas, Alas, Kongo: A Social History of Indentured African Immigration into Jamaica, 1841–1865.* Baltimore, Md.: Johns Hopkins Univ. Press.

Schwartz, Stuart B.
1977   Resistance and Accommodation in Eighteenth-Century Brazil: The Slaves' View of Slavery. *Hispanic American Historical Review* 57: 69–81.

1982   Patterns of Slaveholding in the Americas: New Evidence from Brazil. *American Historical Review* 87: 55–86.

1985   *Sugar Plantations in the Formation of Brazilian Society: Bahia, 1550–1835.* Cambridge: Cambridge Univ. Press.

Scott, James C.
1986   Everyday Forms of Peasant Resistance. *Journal of Peasant Studies* 13: 5–35.
Scott, Rebecca J.
1985   *Slave Emancipation in Cuba: The Transition to Free Labor.* Princeton, N.J.: Princeton Univ. Press.
Scott, Rebecca J., Seymour Drescher, Hebe Maria Mattos de Castro, George Reid Andrews, and Robert M. Levine
1988   *The Abolition of Slavery and the Aftermath of Emancipation in Brazil.* Durham, N.C.: Duke Univ. Press.
Sedoc, N. O.
1979   *Aisa Winti.* Paramaribo: n.p.
Sharpe, Barrie
1986   Ethnography and a Regional System. *Critique of Anthropology* 7 (3): 33–65.
Sheridan, Richard
1986   The Maroons of Jamaica, 1730–1830: Livelihood, Demography, and Health. In *Out of the House of Bondage,* ed. Gad Heuman, 152–72. London: Frank Cass.
Silva, Eduardo
1993   *Prince of the People: The Life and Times of a Brazilian Free Man of Colour.* London: Verso.
Siwpersad, J. P.
1979   *De Nederlandse regering en de afschaffing van de Surinaamseslavernij (1833–1863).* Groningen, Netherlands: Bouma's Boekhuis.
Smith, Adam
1952   *An Inquiry into the Nature and Causes of the Wealth of Nations.* Chicago: Encyclopedia Britannica.
Smith, Michael G.
1962   *Kinship and Community in Carriacou.* New Haven, Conn.: Yale Univ. Press.
1965   *The Plural Society in the British West Indies.* Berkeley: Univ. of California Press.
Smith, Raymond T.
1975   Review of R. Price, *Maroon Societies. Man* 10: 149.
1988   *Kinship and Class in the West Indies: A Genealogical Study of Jamaica and Guyana.* Cambridge: Cambridge Univ. Press.
Sobel, Mechal
1979   *Trabelin' On: The Slave Journey to an Afro-Baptist Faith.* Westport, Conn.: Greenwood.
1987   *The World They Made Together: Black and White Values in Eighteenth-Century Virginia.* Princeton, N.J.: Princeton Univ. Press.
Solien, Nancie L.
1959   The Nonunilineal Descent Group in the Caribbean and Central America. *American Anthropologist* 61: 578–83.
Solow, Barbara L., ed.
1991   *Slavery and the Rise of the Atlantic System.* Cambridge: Cambridge Univ. Press.
Solow, Barbara L., and Stanley L. Engerman, eds.
1987   *British Capitalism and Caribbean Slavery: The Legacy of Eric Williams.* Cambridge: Cambridge Univ. Press.
Sordam, Max, and Hein Eersel
1985   *Sranantongo/Surinaamse taal: Een korte inleiding tot het Sranantongo, met uitgebreide woordenlijst.* Baarn, Netherlands: Bosch and Keuning.

Sosa Rodríguez, Enrique
1982   *Los ñáñigos.* Havana, Cuba: Casa de las Américas.
Stampp, Kenneth M.
1971   Rebels and Sambos: The Search for the Negro's Personality in Slavery. *Journal of Southern History* 37: 367–92.
Starling, Marion Wilson
1988 [1981]   *The Slave Narrative: Its Place in American History.* Boston: G. K. Hall.
Stedman, John Gabriel
1988 [1790]   *Narrative of a Five Years Expedition against the Revolted Negroes of Surinam* Edited, with introduction and notes, by Richard Price and Sally Price. Baltimore, Md.: Johns Hopkins Univ. Press.
Stein, Peter
1984   Die ersten "Kreolisten": Die Herrnhuter Missionare im 19. Jahrhundert auf St. Thomas. *Unitas Fratrum* 15: 53–63.
1985a Die Anfänge der Verschriftung einer Kreolsprache: Das Negerhollands im 18 Jahrhundert. In *Entstehung von Sprachen und Völkern,* ed. P. Sture Ureland, 437–57. Tübingen, Germany: Niemeyer.
1985b Bemerkungen zur Edition der "Sklavenbriefe" aus St. Thomas, 1737–1769 (Kurzfassung). In *Akten des 1. Essener Kolloquiums über 'Kreolsprachen und Sprachkontakte' vom 26.1.1985 an der Essener Universität,* ed. Norbert Boretzky, Werner Enninger, and Thomas Stolz, 135–42. Bochum, Germany: Brockmeyer.
1989   When Creole Speakers Write the Standard Language: An Analysis of Some of the Earliest Slave Letters from St. Thomas. In *Wheels Within Wheels: Papers of the Duisburg Symposium on Pidgin and Creole Languages,* ed. Martin Pütz and René Dirven, 153–78. Frankfurt: Peter Lang.
Stephen, Henri M. J.
1983   *Winti: Afro-Surinaamse religie en magische rituelen in Suriname en Nederland.* Amsterdam: Karnak.
1986   *De macht van de Fodoe Winti. Fodoe rituelen in de winti-kultus in Suriname en in Nederland.* Amsterdam: Karnak.
Stern, Steve J.
1988   Feudalism, Capitalism, and the World System in the Perspective of Latin America and the Caribbean. *American Historical Review* 93: 829–72.
Stewart, John
1823   *A View of the Past and Present State of the Island of Jamaica.* Edinburgh: Oliver and Boyd.
Stolz, Thomas
1986   *Gibt es das kreolische Sprachmodell? Vergleichende Grammatik des Negerholländischen.* Frankfurt: Peter Lang
Stolz, Thomas, and Peter Stein
1986   Language History in the Former Danish Antilles: Non-Linguistic Evidence for a Diachronic Description of the Negro-Dutch Language. *Amsterdam Creole Studies* 9: 103–22
Strickland, John Scott
1985   Traditional Culture and Moral Economy: Social and Economic Change in the South Carolina Low Country, 1865–1910. In *The Countryside in the Age of Capitalist Transformation: Essays in the Social History of Rural America,* ed. Steven Hahn and Jonathan Prude, 141–78. Chapel Hill: Univ. of North Carolina Press.

Stuckey, Sterling
1987   *Slave Culture: Nationalist Theory and the Foundation of Black America.* New York: Oxford Univ. Press.
1990   "Ironic Tenacity": Frederick Douglass's Seizure of the Dialectic. In *Frederick Douglass: New Literary and Historical Essays,* ed. Eric J. Sundquist, 32–35. New York: Cambridge Univ. Press.
Sutherland, Anne
1986 [1975]   *Gypsies: The Hidden Americans.* Prospect Heights, Ill.: Waveland Press.
Swanzy, Henry
1956   A Trading Family in the Nineteenth-Century Gold Coast. *Transactions of the Gold Coast and Togoland Historical Society* 2: 87–120.
Szwed, John F.
1974 [1969]   An American Anthropological Dilemma: The Politics of Afro-American Culture. In *Reinventing Anthropology,* ed. Dell Hymes, 153–81. New York: Vintage Books.
Tadman, Michael
1989   *Speculators and Slaves: Masters, Traders, and Slaves in the Old South.* Madison: Univ. of Wisconsin Press.
Tannenbaum, Frank
1946   *Slave and Citizen: The Negro in the Americas.* New York: Random House.
Teenstra, M. D.
1835   *De landbouw in de kolonie Suriname voorafgegaan door eene geschied- en natuurkundige beschouwing dier kolonie.* 2 vols. Groningen, Netherlands: Eekhoorn.
Terray, Emmanuel
1974   Long-Distance Exchange and the Formation of the State: The Case of the Abron Kingdom of Gyaman. *Economy and Society* 3: 315–45.
1983   Gold Production, Slave Labor, and State Intervention in Precolonial Akan Societies. *Research in Economic Anthropology* 5: 885–914.
Thoden van Velzen, H. U. E.
1984   The Djuka Civilisation. *Sociologia Neerlandica* 20 (2): 85–97.
1994   Priests, Spirit Mediums, and Guerrillas in Suriname. In *Transactions: Essays in honor of Jeremy F. Boissevain,* ed. Jojada Verrips, 209–28. Amsterdam: Het Spinhuis.
Thoden van Velzen, H. U. E, and W. van Wetering
1988   *The Great Father and the Danger: Religious Cults, Material Forces, and Collective Fantasies in the World of the Surinamese Maroons.* Caribbean Series 9, Koninklijk Instituut voor Taal-, Land- en Volkenkunde. Dordrecht, Netherlands: Foris.
Thomas-Hope, Elizabeth M.
1992   *Explanation in Caribbean Migration: Perception and the Image: Jamaica, Barbados, St. Vincent.* London: Macmillan.
Thompson, Edgar T.
1932   The Plantation. Ph.D. diss., Univ. of Chicago.
Thompson, Edward P.
1975   *Whigs and Hunters: The Origins of the Black Act.* New York: Oxford Univ. Press.
Thompson, Robert Faris
1983   *Flash of the Spirit: African and Afro-American Art and Philosophy.* New York: Random House.

Thornton, John K.
1992   *Africa and Africans in the Making of the Atlantic World, 1400–1680.* New York: Cambridge Univ. Press.
Thwaites, Reuben Gold, ed.
1896–1901   *The Jesuit Relations and Allied Documents.* 73 vols. Cleveland, Ohio: Burrows.
Tomich, Dale W.
1990   *Slavery in the Circuit of Sugar: Martinique and the World Economy, 1830–1848.* Baltimore, Md.: Johns Hopkins Univ. Press.
Tonkin, Elizabeth
1990   West African Ethnographic Traditions. In *Localizing Strategies: Regional Traditions of Ethnographic Writing,* ed. R. Fardon, 137–51. Edinburgh: Scottish Academic Press.
Trevor, J. C.
1950   Aspects of Folk Culture in the Virgin Islands. Ph.D. diss., Cambridge Univ.
Trigger, Bruce G., ed.
1978–   *Handbook of North American Indians.* 20 vols. Washington, DC: Smithsonian Institution.
Trouillot, Michel-Rolph
1982   Motion in the System: Coffee, Color, and Slavery in Eighteenth-Century Saint-Domingue. *Review* (Binghamton, N.Y.), vol. 3: 331–88.
1992   Banana Wars: The Sweetness of Commodities. Paper presented at the Annual Meeting of the American Anthropological Association, San Francisco, Calif., 2–6 Dec. 1992.
1995   In the Shadow of the West: Power, Resistance and Creolization in the Making of the Caribbean Region. In *Born Out of Resistance: On Caribbean Cultural Creativity,* ed. Wim Hoogbergen. Utrecht: ISOR Press.
Turner, Mary
1982   *Slaves and Missionaries: The Disintegration of Jamaican Society, 1787–1834.* Urbana: Univ. of Illinois Press.
1991   Slave Workers, Subsistence and Labour Bargaining: Amity Hall, Jamaica, 1805–1832. In *The Slaves' Economy,* ed. Ira Berlin and Philip D. Morgan, 92–106. London: Frank Cass.
Turner, Victor W.
1980   Encounter with Freud: The Making of a Comparative Symbologist. In *The Making of Psychological Anthropology,* ed. George D. Spindler, 558–83. Berkeley: Univ. of California Press.
Unsworth, Barry
1992   *Sacred Hunger.* New York: Doubleday.
Usner, Daniel H., Jr.
1985   American Indians on the Cotton Frontier: Changing Economic Relations with Citizens and Slaves in the Mississippi Territory. *Journal of American History* 72 (2): 297–317.
1986   Food Marketing and Interethnic Exchange in the Eighteenth-Century Lower Mississippi Valley. *Food and Foodways* 1 (3): 279–310.
1989   American Indians in Colonial New Orleans. In *Powhatan's Mantle: Indians in the Colonial Southeast,* ed. Peter H. Wood, Gregory A. Waselkov, and M. Thomas Hatley, 104–27. Lincoln: Univ. of Nebraska Press.

1992   *Indians, Settlers, and Slaves in a Frontier Exchange Economy: The Lower Missis-sippi Valley before 1783.* Chapel Hill: Univ. of North Carolina Press, for the Institute of Early American History and Culture.

1984   "Fragment of This Erratic Race": American Indians in Nineteenth-Century New Orleans. Paper read at American Society for Ethnohistory meeting in New Orleans.

van Breugel, G. P. C.

1842   *Dagverhaal van eene reis naar Paramaribo en verdere omstreken in de kolonie Suriname.* Amsterdam: Sulpke.

Van Deburg, William L.

1979   *The Slave Drivers.* New York: Oxford Univ. Press.

Van den Berghe, Pierre L.

1967   *Race and Racism: A Comparative Perspective.* New York: John Wiley.

van Kempen, Michiel

1989   *Surinaamse schrijvers en dichters* Amsterdam: De Arbeiderspers.

Van Lier, Rudolph A. J.

1971 [1949]   *Frontier Society: A Social Analysis of the History of Suriname.* The Hague, Netherlands: Martinus Nijhof.

Van Stipriaan, Alex

1992   Het dilemma van plantageslaven: Weglopen of blijven. *OSO: Tijdschrift voor Surinaamse Taalkunde, letterkunde, Cultuur en Geschiedenis* 11: 122–41.

1993a   *Surinaams contrast: Roofbouw en overleven in een Caraïbische plantagekolonie, 1750–1863.* Leiden, Netherlands: KITLV Uitgeverij.

1993b   "Een verre verwijderd trommelen . . . ": Ontwikkeling van Afro-Surinaamse muziek en dans in de slavernij. In *De kunstwereld produktie, distributie en receptie in de wereld van kunst en cultuur,* ed. A. Bevers et al., 143–73. Rotterdam, Netherlands: Faculteit der Historische en Kunstwetenschappen, Erasmus Universiteit Rotterdam, Uitgeverij Verloren.

Van Wetering, Wilhelmina

1987   Informal Supportive Networks: Quasi-Kin Groups, Religion and Social Order among Suriname Creoles in the Netherlands. *Netherlands Journal of Sociology* 23 (2): 92–101.

In press   A Demon in a Garbage Chute. In *Afro-Caribbean Worldviews,* ed. Barry Chevannes. The Hague, Netherlands: Institute of Social Studies.

Venema, Tijno

1992   *Famiri nanga Kulturu: Creoolse sociale verhoudingen en Winti in Amsterdam.* Amsterdam: Het Spinhuis.

Verger, Pierre

1953   Influence du Brésil au Golfe du Bénin. In *Les Afro-Américains,* 11–101. Mémoires de l'Institut Français d'Afrique Noire, no. 27. Dakar, Senegal: IFAN.

1976   *Trade Relations Between the Bight of Benin and Bahia from the Seventeenth to the Nineteenth Century.* Ibadan, Nigeria: Ibadan Univ. Press.

Vernon, Diane

1989   Some Prominent Features of Ndjuka Maroon Medicine. *Nieuwe West-Indische Gids* 63 (3–4): 209–21.

von Dewitz, August Karl Ludwig

1882   *In Dänisch-Westindien: Hundert- und Fünfzig Jahre der Brüdermission in St. Thomas, St. Croix und St. Jan.* Niesky, Germany: Direction der Brüdergemeine.

Voorhoeve, Jan
1983   The Obiaman and His Influence in the Moravian Parish. *Bijdragen tot de Taal-, Land-en Volkenkunde* 139 (4): 411–20.
Voorhoeve, Jan, and Ursy M. Lichtveld, eds.
1975   *Creole Drum: An Anthology of Creole Literature in Surinam.* New Haven, Conn.: Yale Univ. Press.
Wade, Richard C.
1964   *Slavery in the Cities: The South, 1820–1860.* New York: Oxford Univ. Press.
Wallerstein, Immanuel
1974–89   *The Modern World System.* New York: Academic Press.
Ward, J. R.
1988   *British West Indian Slavery, 1750–1834.* Oxford, England: Clarendon Press.
Warner-Lewis, Maureen
1991   *Guinea's Other Suns: The African Dynamic in Trinidad Culture.* Dover, England: Majority Press.
Watson, James L.
1980   Slavery as an Institution: Open and Closed Systems. In *African and Asian Systems of Slavery,* ed. James L. Watson, 1–15. Berkeley: Univ. of California Press.
————, ed.
1980   *African and Asian Systems of Slavery.* Berkeley: Univ. of California Press.
Watts, David
1987   *The West Indies: Patterns of Development, Culture and Environmental Change Since 1492.* Cambridge: Cambridge Univ. Press.
Weatherly, U. G.
1923   The West Indies as a Sociological Laboratory. *American Journal of Sociology* 29: 290–304.
Webber, Thomas L.
1978   *Deep Like the Rivers: Education in the Slave Quarter Community.* New York: Norton.
West, Hans
1793   *Bidrag til beskrivelse over Ste Croix med en kort Udsigt over St. Thomas, St. Jean, Tortola, Spanishtown og Crabeneiland.* Copenhagen: Friderik Wilhelm Thiele.
West Indisch Plakaatboek
1973   *West Indisch Plakaatboek: I Suriname: Plakaten, ordonnantiën en andere wetten, uitgevaardigd in Suriname, 1667–1816,* ed. J. A. Schiltkamp and Th. de Smit. Amsterdam: Emmering.
Westergaard, Waldemar
1917   *The Danish West Indies under Company Rule.* New York: Macmillan.
Western Bureau
1993   Maroons Urged to Unite. *The Gleaner* (Kingston, Jamaica), 8 Jan., p. 2.
Wharton, Vernon Lane
1947   *The Negro in Mississippi, 1865–1890.* Chapel Hill: Univ. of North Carolina Press.
White, Deborah Grey
1985   *Ar'n't I a Woman? Female Slaves in the Plantation South.* New York: Norton.
Wiener, Jonathan
1978   *Social Origins of the New South, Alabama 1860–1885.* Baton Rouge: Louisiana State Univ. Press.

Williams, Eric
1970   *From Columbus to Castro: The History of the Caribbean, 1492–1969.* London: Andre Deutsch.
Willis, William S.
1963   Divide and Rule: Red, White, and Black in the Southeast. *Journal of Negro History* 48 (3): 157–76.
Winsnes, Selena A., ed. and trans.
1992   *Letters on West Africa and the Slave Trade: Paul Erdmann Isert's Journey to Guinea and the Caribbean Islands in Columbia (1788).* Oxford: Oxford Univ. Press.
Wittfogel, Karl A.
1957   *Oriental Despotism: A Comparative Study of Total Power.* New York: Yale Univ. Press.
Wolf, Eric
1971 [1959]   Specific Aspects of Plantation Systems in the New World: Community Sub-Cultures and Social Classes. In *Peoples and Cultures of the Caribbean,* ed. Michael M. Horowitz, 163–78. Garden City, N.Y.: Natural History Press.
1982   *Europe and the People Without History.* Berkeley: Univ. of California Press.
Wood, Peter H.
1974   *Black Majority: Negroes in Colonial South Carolina, From 1670 Through the Stono Rebellion.* New York: Knopf.
1978   "I Did the Best I Could for My Day": The Study of Early Black History during the Second Reconstruction, 1960 to 1976. *William and Mary Quarterly* 35: 185–225.
Wooding, Charles J.
1972   *Winti: Een Afroamerikaanse godsdienst in Suriname: Een cultureel-historische analyse van de religieuze verschijnselen in de Para.* Meppel, Netherlands: Krips Repro.
1981   *Evolving Culture: A Cross-Cultural Study of Suriname, West Africa and the Caribbean.* Washington, D.C.: Univ. Press of America.
Woodman, Harold D.
1979   Post–Civil War Southern Agriculture and the Law. *Agricultural History* 53: 319–37.
Woodson, Carter G.
1920   The Relations of Negroes and Indians in Massachusetts. *Journal of Negro History* 5 (1): 45–57.
Woodward, C. Vann
1968 [1960]   The Irony of Southern History. In C. Vann Woodward, *The Burden of Southern History,* 121–45. Baton Rouge: Louisiana State Univ. Press.
Wright, J. Leitch, Jr.
1981   *The Only Land They Knew: The Tragic Story of the American Indians in the Old South.* New York: Free Press.
Yarak, Larry W.
1986   Murder and Theft in Early-Nineteenth-Century Elmina. In *Banditry, Rebellion and Social Protest in Africa,* ed. Donald Crummey, 33–47. London: James Currey.
1989   West African Coastal Slavery in the Nineteenth Century: The Case of the Afro-European Slaveowners of Elmina. *Ethnohistory* 36: 44–60.

Contributors

RENATE BARTL is a Ph.D. candidate in American cultural history, ethnology, and political science at the University of Munich. She is director of the Hallertauer Museum of Bavarian Ethnology and Folk Art in Mainburg, Germany. Co-author of a publication on Sahagún's writings about Aztec calendrical systems, she currently is preparing her doctoral dissertation on ethnic groups of partly Native American descent in the eastern United States.

JEAN BESSON, Ph.D. (University of Edinburgh, 1974), is senior lecturer in anthropology at Goldsmiths College, University of London, England, where she teaches the social anthropology and cultural history of the Caribbean region. She has conducted extensive fieldwork in rural Jamaica and comparative research in the eastern Caribbean. Dr. Besson has published several articles on Caribbean postslavery peasantries. She is coeditor of *Land and Development in the Caribbean* (Macmillan, 1987) and editor of *Caribbean Reflections* (Karia Press, 1989).

DAVID W. BLIGHT is associate professor of history and black studies at Amherst College, Massachusetts. He is author of *Frederick Douglass's Civil War: Keeping Faith in Jubilee* (LSU Press, 1989), and editor of *Narrative of the Life of Frederick Douglass, An American Slave* (Bedford Books, 1993). He is currently writing a book on W. E. B. Du Bois and American historical memory.

ADAM JONES teaches African history and culture history at the Institut für Afrikanistik, University of Leipzig, Germany. His research has focused on coastal West Africa in the seventeenth, eighteenth, and nineteenth centuries. He has published a number of critical editions of European sources covering this region, as well as studies of the methodological problems raised by such sources.

ALEX LICHTENSTEIN received his Ph.D. in American civilization from the University of Pennsylvania in 1990. He is currently an assistant professor of history at Florida International University in Miami. His articles and essays on labor and race relations in the American South have appeared in the *Journal of Social History,* the *Journal of Southern History, Radical History,* and *Reviews in American History.*

GUDRUN MEIER received her degree in anthropology from the Lips-Institut in Leipzig, Germany, and has been director of the Herrnhut branch of the Staatliches Völkerkundemuseum Dresden (Dresden Ethnographic Museum) since 1966. Currently she is curator at the Staatliches Museum für Völkerkunde Dresden and head of the exhibition and public relations department. Her regional area of specialization is Central Asia. Her publications deal with this region, issues in museum anthropology, and Moravian missionary endeavors in Asia and the Americas. She is head staff coordinator of the Oldendorp editorial project.

SIDNEY W. MINTZ is William L. Straus, Jr., Professor of Anthropology at Johns Hopkins University, Baltimore, Maryland, and a specialist in the anthropology and social history of the Caribbean region. He has done fieldwork in Puerto Rico, Jamaica, and Haiti. He co-authored *The People of Puerto Rico* (1956) and *The Birth of African-American Culture* (1992); and he was sole author of *Worker in the Cane* (1960), *Caribbean Transformations* (1974), and *Sweetness and Power* (1985). Currently he is working on a collection of essays on the anthropology of food.

KAREN FOG OLWIG is associate professor at the Institute of Anthropology, University of Copenhagen, Denmark. She has carried out archival research and anthropological fieldwork on St. John, U.S. Virgin Islands, and on Nevis in the Leeward Islands. She is author of *Cultural Adaptations and Resistance on St. John: Three Centuries of Afro-Caribbean Life* (1985) and *Global Culture, Island Identity: Continuity and Change in the Afro-Caribbean Community of Nevis* (1993).

GERT OOSTINDIE directs the department of Caribbean Studies at the Royal Institute of Linguistics and Anthropology in Leiden, Netherlands, and is professor of Caribbean studies at Utrecht University. He has published on Caribbean history, decolonization, and migration, including *Roosenburg en Mon Bijou: Twee Surinaamse plantages, 1720–1870* (1989).

STEPHAN PALMIÉ teaches American and Caribbean culture history at the Amerika-Institut of the University of Munich. He has done fieldwork among Cuban migrants in Miami, Florida, as well as archival research in Jamaica and Cuba. His publications include a monograph on Afro-Cuban religion, *Das Exil der Götter: Geschichte und Vorstellungswelt einer afrokubanischen Religion* (Frankfurt, 1991), and various articles on the ethnography and ethnohistory of Caribbean cultures.

RICHARD RATHBONE teaches history at the School of Oriental and African Studies, University of London, where he is also dean of the Graduate School. His most recent work includes the two-volume *Ghana: British Documents on the End of Empire* (1992) and *Murder and Politics in Colonial Ghana* (1993).

H. U. E. THODEN VAN VELZEN teaches anthropology at the Amsterdam School of Social Science Research. His long-standing interest in Suriname's Ndyuka Maroon society and culture dates back to an initial two years of anthropological fieldwork in Suriname during the early 1960s. In the later part of that decade, Thoden van Velzen conducted fieldwork in southwestern Tanzania, focusing on the Ujamaa program. In the 1970s and 1980s, he returned to Suriname's interior for several periods of study. His main work is *The Great Father and the Danger: Religious Cults, Material Forces and Collective Fantasies in the World of the Surinamese Maroons* (1988), co-authored with Ineke van Wetering. His main theoretical interest is the relationship between psychoanalysis and anthropology. Thoden van Velzen held the Chair of Cultural Anthropology at Utrecht University from 1971 until 1991.

DANIEL H. USNER, JR., is associate professor of history at Cornell University, where he teaches courses on Native American history. His publications include *Indians, Settlers, and Slaves in a Frontier Exchange Economy* (University of North Carolina Press, 1992), co-winner of the American Historical Association's John H. Dunning Prize.

ALEX VAN STIPRIAAN teaches history and culture of the Caribbean at Erasmus University, Rotterdam, Netherlands. In addition to his major study, Surinaams contrast: Roofbouw en overleven in een Caraïbische plantagekolonie 1750-1863 (1993), he has published various articles dealing with Suriname slavery and the emergence of Afro-Suriname culture.

INEKE VAN WETERING is senior lecturer at the Free University, Amsterdam. She obtained her Ph.D. in anthropology from the University of Amsterdam in 1973, with a dissertation on witchcraft among Ndyuka Maroons in Suriname. She co-authored *The Great Father and the Danger: Religious Cults, Material, and Collective Fantasies in the World of the Surinamese Maroons* (1988). Since the 1980s, she has been researching the religious culture of creole migrants in the Netherlands, particularly a women's group in Amsterdam's Bijlmermeer.

Index

abolition, ix, xxiii, 44, 45, 56, 58, 86,
101, 102, 171, 190, 211
abolitionism and antislavery, 3, 4, 43, 192
accommodation, xviii, 8, 15–20
Accompong maroons (Leeward ma-
roons), 187, 195–98, 201
Accra, 57, 58, 64, 103, 104, 105
adoption, xv, 134, 162, 173
African cultural models, 24, 26–29, 36, 189
African-Brazilians, xxiii, 57, 59, 61
Afro-Europeans, 59–60, 65, 100, 102, 104
agency, historical, xvi–xvii, xxi, xxviii
Akan, 58, 62, 63, 103, 104, 108, 205
Aluku, 114, 116–22, 126, 137
Amerindians. *See* Native Americans
ancestral cults, 122
ancestry. *See* descent, kinship
Asante, 41, 58, 100, 204
Asian contract labor, xxx, 86
assimilation. *See* incorporation
Atlantic economy, xxiv–xxvi, xxix, 42, 44,
46, 55, 61, 63, 101
Atlantic World, xvi, xx, xxiii–xxvi, xxix,
xxxii, 43, 44

beliefs, 123, 211, 216, 221–22, 225, 232,
235; *see also* cosmology, deities and
spirits, religious knowledge
Big Men, 105, 123, 125–26, 135
Bight of Biafra, xxv, 55
body symbolism, 215
Boni (maroon leader), 112, 114, 116–21,
126, 137–38, 121

Brazil, xxi, xxxv, 56, 57
bridewealth, x–xi, 105, 106–7, 109

Cape Coast, 57, 100
Cherokee, 163–67, 169–71, 172, 173
Cherokee slave laws, 166–67
Chickasaw, 149, 152, 155, 163–65, 167,
169–71, 172
Choctaw, 149–52, 155, 156, 164, 167,
169–71, 172
Christianity, xxiii, xxvii, 29, 33, 57, 61,
62, 214–15, 220; *see also* missions
and missionaries, Moravians
Civil War (US), xii, 2, 162, 169–70
clients. *See* patronage and clientelism
coercion, x, xxx, 178
commonage, 197, 199, 201
Confederate States, 162, 169–70
conjugality. *See* marriage and conjugality,
slave marriage
conspiracies, 35, 150
consumption, xxii, 45–52, 103
conversion, xxiii, xxvii, xxxv, 33, 57
cosmology, 62, 190, 213, 225
Creek, 164–69, 171, 172, 173
creole languages, 63, 69, 70, 71, 75, 89,
218
creoles, 69, 94, 141; *see also* Suriname
Creoles
creolization, xxiv, xxv, xxxiv, 88, 187–
88, 191–92, 195–99, 201–2, 211,
214, 220; cultural, xxiv, 91; linguistic, 196

crime, 176, 180–81, 183
criminal justice, xxix, 176, 178–85
Cuba, xiii, xxiv–xxv, xxxi, 41, 82
cult groups, 28, 202, 204
cultural continuities, xix, xxvii, 25, 213
cultural exchange, xx–xxi, xxxvi, 62, 145, 155–56, 165
cultural similarities, xix, 188, 198–99, 201
culture, expressive, 2–4, 34, 89–90
culture-building, xviii, xix–xxi, xxvi, 25, 187–90, 199, 202
customary rights, xxii, 178, 184, 190, 193

Dahomey, 25, 50
Danish West Indies, xxvii, 23–37, 67–75
deities and spirits, xxii, 28, 30, 92–95, 115, 130, 131, 215–16, 221–25; ambivalent character of, 131, 225; Amerindian, 92, 217, 225–26; ancestors, 122, 223; demons (*bakru*), 225–27; earth deity (*aisa*), 93, 217, 222, 230–31, 233; forest (*ampuku*), 127, 131, 225–26; *kromanti*, 93, 126, 217
demography, xxi, xxiv, 78, 80, 83–85, 95, 96, 146–47, 154, 166–67
dependency and dependent labor, x–xi, 23, 123, 125, 177, 179; *see also* incorporation, kinship, labor relations, patronage and clientelism, sharecropping
descent, ideologies of, 28, 59–60, 134–35, 141, 191–92, 194–95, 197, 200, 202, 205
descent groups
—cognatic, 191–95, 197, 199–201, 204–5
—unilineal 62, 122, 123, 125–26, 129, 191, 194, 199, 201–2, 204–5
diaspora, Caribbean in the Netherlands, 210–35
disciplinary measures and punishment, 7, 13, 16, 106, 166, 176, 178–79, 181–83
discrimination. *See* racial discrimination and exclusion
divination, 125, 136, 217
Douglass, Frederick, xxviii, 1–4

ecology, xxi, xxviii, 67, 70, 78–96
elites, xiv, 59–65, 70, 105–6, 211, 214–15, 234
Elkins, Stanley, xii–xiii, xvii, 5, 8, 43
Elmina, 57, 64, 101–7
emancipation, xxii, xxiii, xxviii–xxix, 2, 15, 26, 43, 56, 125, 156, 170–71, 178–79, 187–88, 191, 199
enslavement, xxx, 29–30, 40, 103
escape. *See* flight and maronage
ethnic groups, 27, 71, 211, 215, 219–20
ethnicity, xxiii, 60, 71, 72, 196
ethnography, 70, 213
Euro-American societies, xx, 154
exchange relations, 145–46, 152–56, 178

family land, xxii, 26, 37, 194–95, 197, 200–201, 202
female slave ownership, xxviii, xxxv, 100–109
female slaves, xxiii, xxxv, 32, 100, 101, 103, 147, 151, 156, 218; productive vs. reproductive value of, 100–106
"Five Civilized Tribes," 163–66, 168, 170
flight and maronage, xxii, xxxiv, 5, 87, 109, 118–19, 124, 129, 140, 148, 156, 166, 167
food production, xxii, 18, 80, 85, 101, 130, 153, 179, 191
Frazier, E. Franklin, xix, xxxiii, 25
free African-Americans, xii, 151, 155, 170
free village communities (Jamaica), 187, 191–92, 198, 201
freedom, x, xv, 33, 36, 116–17, 148, 177, 178
freedpeople, xxxiv, 12, 55–65, 171, 172, 177–79, 181, 183
frontiers, xxi, xxviii, 126, 127–30, 154, 173

Gã, 58, 60, 62, 104
gender, xxiii, 108, 191, 193, 218–21
Genovese, Eugene, 5–9, 17, 51, 176–77, 224

Ghana, 55–65, 101
Gold Coast, xxvii, 55–65, 100–109

Haiti, xxii, xxxv, 17, 49, 200, 204
Herrnhuter Brüdergemeine. *See*
    Moravians
Herskovits, Melville J., xviii–xix, xxxiii,
    14, 25, 50, 211, 216, 218, 220, 222,
    228
historiography, comparative, xxiii, xxxi,
    23, 78–79
historiography, revisionist, 1–9

identity, xxvi, 24, 34, 194, 197, 199, 201,
    210; cultural, 24, 63, 196, 214; eth-
    nic, xxvi, 59–65, 196
incorporation, xv, xxvii, xxxiv, 23–24,
    27–29, 31–33, 36, 48–49, 104, 125,
    134, 156, 189
indentured labor, x–xi, 86
Indian Removal, 157, 166–68
individualism, 219, 224, 235
infanticide, 115, 120
intentionality, 14, 23
Islam, xxxi, 29, 40, 51, 57, 61

Jamaica, xxix, 18, 19, 58, 187–205

kin groups, 27–28, 34, 95, 104, 122, 188,
    191, 194, 200, 211, 219, 225; corpo-
    rate, xv, 122, 191, 193, 199, 201,
    204, 222
kinship, xv, xxi, xxiv, xxix, 27–28, 30,
    31–32, 37, 42, 59–61, 62, 67, 122,
    142, 187–205, 216, 219, 221; fictive
    or ritual, 32, 187–89, 196, 198; net-
    works, xxi–xxii, 37, 102, 190, 192–
    93, 197–98, 219, 234; terminology,
    88, 190, 195, 203; *see also* descent
    groups, descent ideology, shipmate
    relationship
knowledge, cultural, xix–xx, 219, 223;
    religious, 126, 132, 134, 221

labor regimes and labor relations, xi, xxi,
    43, 80–82, 85, 95, 96, 140, 177,
    179; *see also* plantation economy,
    sharecropping, wage labor

Lagos, 57
land, symbolic significance of, 194
land rights, transmission of, 191, 193–
    94, 197, 200–201, 205
land tenure, xxii, xxix, 166, 177, 179,
    182, 188, 193–95, 199–202, 204
law, xii–xiii, 71, 146, 151, 155–57, 168,
    177–81
Leeward Maroons. *See* Accompong
legitimate trade, 56
linguistic communities, 29
literacy, 35, 61, 62
Louisiana, 145–58
Lower Mississippi Valley, xxvi, 145–58

manumission, xxi, 103, 218
markets and marketing, xxii, 15, 18, 19,
    104, 146, 153, 155–57, 176, 180–82,
    184, 191
maronage. *See* flight and maronage
maroons, xxii, xxxiii, xxxiv–xxxv, 15, 50,
    95, 96, 112–44, 152, 173, 187–88,
    195–98, 201, 222; indigenous histo-
    riography, xxviii, 114–17, 139–40,
    141; Jamaica, xxix, 50, 187–88, 195–
    98; Louisiana, xxvi, 148; post-treaty
    or "pacified," 113, 116, 123–24, 195–
    98; relation to colonial states, xxviii,
    50, 113, 125, 127, 128, 195–96, 204;
    Suriname, xxviii, 50, 87, 112–44,
    203, 222; *see also* Accompong, Aluku
    Boni, Leeward Maroons, Matawai,
    Ndyuka, Paramaka, Saramaka,
    Windward Maroons
marriage and conjugality, 30, 59, 62, 63,
    67, 69, 102, 105, 107, 108, 129, 147,
    157, 169, 187–88, 192–93, 195,
    198–99, 202
master-slave relationships, xvi, xvii, 6, 7,
    16, 32, 33, 100–108, 176
Matawai, 113, 203
methodology, xxiii, xxvi
Middle Passage, 86, 116, 187, 196
migration and migrants, xxix, 195, 202,
    210, 213, 216, 222, 224, 229, 235
Mintz, Sidney W. and Richard Price,
    xix–xx, xxxiv, 25, 26, 187–89, 199–
    200, 202, 205

missions and missionaries, xxxv, 35, 36, 58, 67–75, 101, 103, 141, 168, 190, 191–92, 214; *see also* Moravians
moral economy, xxii, xxix, 176–84
Moravians, xxviii, 24, 33, 35, 37, 50, 58, 67–75, 141, 214, 229
motivation. *See* intentionality
murder, 119, 121, 129
music, 2–4, 34, 90

Natchez, 147, 148–51
Native Americans, xxvi, 67, 71, 113, 130, 145–58, 162–73; allegiance to Confederacy, 162, 169–70; enslavement of, 146–48, 150, 165; indigenous slavery among, 163, 165, 173; relations with African-Americans, 145–58; as slavecatchers, 148, 155, 167, 173; as slaveholders, xxvi, 145, 162–73
Ndyuka, xxviii, 87, 96, 112–44, 203; exploitation of runaways by, 125–26, 132–33; political ideology of, 122, 139–40; relationship to "new maroons," 124–28, 131, 133, 141, 142; social organization, 122–23
Nevis, 26–27, 35, 201
New Orleans, 147, 149–55

obias (obeahs), 115–16, 118, 119, 120, 121, 126, 128, 132, 134–36
Oldendorp, C. G. A., 24, 29–35, 37, 67–74
ordeals, 130, 132, 142

Para region (Suriname), 86, 94, 199–202, 205, 211
Paramaka, 114, 125, 128–29, 137, 142
Paramaribo, 94, 112, 117, 123, 125, 127, 128, 140, 211–12, 218
paternalism, xxiv, xxx, 5, 8, 51
patronage and clientelism, 23, 27–28, 100, 123–27, 212, 221, 234–35
pawnship, x, 103, 104, 105
peasantry, 15, 26, 86, 94, 180, 188–205, 196, 201, 211, 222–23
Phillips, U. B., xiv, xvii
plantation economy, xi, xiii, xxx, 45–46, 57, 67, 69, 79–89, 154, 164, 176,
179, 188, 191, 202, 210, 213; *see also* labor regimes and labor relations, sharecropping
plantations as social units, 31–33, 91, 94–95, 189, 199–200
polder technology, 80–82
Porto Novo, 57
power, 2, 45, 138–40, 234
prestige, 104–5, 166, 173, 219
priests. *See* religious specialists
production, relations of, 101–4
proletarianization, xxviii–xxix, 179–80, 183
property relations, 176–77, 184
property rights, x–xi, xv, xxix, 166, 177, 182, 194
proto-peasantry, xxii, 15, 34, 94, 188, 190–93, 197–98, 201
provision grounds, xxii, 18, 26, 34, 37, 85, 179, 190–91, 193, 197, 199
Puerto Rico, 43

race, conceptions and ideologies of, 61, 63, 166
racial classification, 151, 154, 156–58, 171
racial discrimination and exclusion, 63
rebellion, xvii, xxii, 87
relations of exchange, 152–53
relations of production, capitalist, 42, 178, 184, 213
religion, African, 29–30, 33, 214
religious specialists, xxiii, 30, 103, 115, 116, 123, 126, 129, 131–37, 138, 139, 142, 220–21, 224, 227, 232, 235
repatriates. *See* returnees
resistance, xvi–xviii, xxviii, 4–5, 12–20, 26–27, 72, 152, 176, 177, 179, 189, 202, 213, 221, 223; cultural, xxviii, 15, 17, 26; day-to-day, xxviii, 13, 16; individual, 5, 17; violent, 13
returnees, xxvii, 55–65
ritual, xviii, xxii, 28, 29–30, 32, 35, 90, 91, 123–24, 197, 199–200, 204–5, 210–16, 219, 223, 225–33, 235
Rodney, Walter, xiv–xv, 51

Saramaka, 87, 96, 113, 115, 135, 139, 140, 195, 199, 203
Seminoles, 164–65, 167–69, 171, 172

sexual relations, 32, 88, 104, 131, 147, 188–89, 193

sharecropping, 177–84

shipmate relationship, 32, 88, 187–88, 192, 195, 197–98, 205

Sierra Leone, 62

Slave Coast, 55

slave communities, xxiv, 5–6, 36

slave cultures, xvi, xxix, 2, 89–96, 188

slave drivers, xi, xxx, 31

slave experience, xviii, 23, 210

slave family, xviii, xxi, xxii, 34, 69, 71

slave importation, 36, 45, 91–92, 146–47

slave law, xii–xiii, xxxi, 71, 147

slave marriage, 7, 69, 189–90

slave narratives, 1–4, 101

slave origins, 24, 29, 67, 71, 91–92

slave rebellions and revolts, xvii, xxxiii, 16, 18, 87, 95, 150

slave religion, xxiii, 6, 26, 34, 91–94, 96, 224

slave songs, 2–4, 90, 96, 101

slave suicide, 14, 16, 48, 149

slave trade, ix, xiv–xv, xxiv–xxv, xxxi, xxxii, 6–9, 51, 55–56, 71, 108, 173, 190

slavery, African forms of, xiii–xv, xxx, xxxii, 24, 26–29, 31, 41, 51, 56

slavery, ancient, ix–x

slavery, as social system, xii, xvi, 17

slavery, conceptions of, xv, 27–29

slavery, definitions of, x, xv, 108

slavery, domestic, xii, xxx, 31, 32, 102

slavery, "hydraulic" qualities in Suriname, 79–96

slavery, in Europe, xii, 42–43, 51

slavery, urban, xi–xii, xxx–xxxi

Smith, Adam, 51

social death, xx, 23, 31, 33

social divisions and social differentiation, 166, 170, 211

South (US), xxiv, xxix, 1–9, 43, 154, 162–73, 221

spirits. See deities and spirits

St. Croix, 24, 68, 69, 72

St. Domingue, 18, 48, 82

St. John, 24, 26–27, 68, 72

St. Thomas, 24, 68, 69, 71, 73, 74

subsistence agriculture, 15, 18, 19, 31, 34, 88, 103

subsistence, means of, xxix, 179–80, 183

Suriname, xxviii, xxix, 49, 79–98, 112–44, 199–201, 211–12, 223–24, 232; Creoles, xxix, 210–35

Tannenbaum, Frank, xii–xiii

theft, 16, 153, 176–84

trade languages, 61, 154

traders, 6–9, 57, 60, 101–3, 108, 168, 181

tradition, oral, 90, 96, 205

Twi, 60–61

victimization, xvii, xxviii, 1–9

violence, xvi, xxx, xxxiii, 14, 18, 115, 118, 119, 120, 121, 167

Virginia, xi, 42

Volta River, 55–56

wage labor, xxviii, 15, 45, 130, 157, 179–80

Watramama, 92–94, 96

West India Regiments, 57, 58

Whydah, 50, 57, 92

Williams, Eric, xxxii

Windward Maroons, 195–96, 203–5

winti, 92, 93, 211–12, 214–18, 221–22, 224–26, 228–29, 235

witchcraft and sorcery, 28, 33, 34, 49, 51, 115, 123, 130, 137, 138, 142, 232

women, xxiii, xxviii, xxxv, 32, 100–109, 147, 151, 156, 218–35; as heads of households, 218–20; as political figures, 218; as ritual experts, 134–36, 219–21

working conditions. See labor regimes

world system and world systems theory, xxiv–xxvi, 44, 45, 51, 210, 212, 214

Yoruba, xxiii, xxv, xxxv, 41

Slave cultures and the
cultures of slavery